# IRISH CANADIAN CONFLICT AND THE STRUGGLE FOR IRISH INDEPENDENCE, 1912–1925

Between 1912 and 1925, Ireland convulsed with political and revolutionary upheaval in pursuit of self-government. Canadians of Irish descent, both Catholic and Protestant, diligently followed these conflicts, and many became actively involved in the dramatic events overseas.

*Irish Canadian Conflict and the Struggle for Irish Independence* tells the unique story of how Irish Canadians identified with their ancestral homeland during this revolutionary era. Drawing on ethnic weekly newspapers and fraternal society records, Robert McLaughlin finds new interpretations of how Orange Canadian unionists and Irish Canadian nationalists viewed their heritage, their membership in the British Empire, and even Canadian citizenship itself.

McLaughlin also provides strong evidence that neither time nor distance diminished Irish Canadians' attachment to their familial homeland or their identification with their respective ethnic communities in Ireland. *Irish Canadian Conflict and the Struggle for Irish Independence* reconsiders existing contextual frameworks and confronts the challenging questions inherent in understanding this period.

ROBERT MCLAUGHLIN teaches World History at the University of Hartford.

# Irish Canadian Conflict and the Struggle for Irish Independence, 1912–1925

ROBERT McLAUGHLIN

UNIVERSITY OF TORONTO PRESS
Toronto Buffalo London

© Robert McLaughlin 2013
Toronto Buffalo London
www.utorontopress.com

ISBN 978-1-4426-4186-0 (cloth)
ISBN 978-1-4426-1097-2 (paper)

---

Library and Archives Canada Cataloguing in Publication

McLaughlin, Robert, 1964–
　Irish Canadian conflict and the struggle for Irish independence,
1912–1925 / Robert McLaughlin.

　Includes bibliographical references and index.
　ISBN 978-1-4426-4186-0 (bound)　　ISBN 978-1-4426-1097-2 (pbk.)

　1. Irish Canadians – Politics and government – 20th century.　2. Irish
Canadians – History – 20th century.　3. Orangemen – Canada – History –
20th century.　4. Ireland – Politics and government – 1910–1921.
5. Ireland – Politics and government – 1922–1949.　I. Title.

FC106.I6M34 2012　　　971.004'9162　　　C2011-908280-2

---

University of Toronto Press acknowledges the financial assistance to its publishing program of the Canada Council for the Arts and the Ontario Arts Council.

University of Toronto Press acknowledges the financial support of the Government of Canada through the Canada Book Fund for its publishing activities.

# Contents

*Acknowledgments*  vii

Introduction  3

1 Orange-Canadian Unionists and the Irish Home Rule Crisis, 1912–1914  25

2 Irish-Canadian Nationalists: Home Rulers Once Again, 1912–1914  52

3 The War Years: Unity and Disintegration, 1914–1918  80

4 From Home Rulers to Sinn Féiners: The Rise of the Self-Determination for Ireland League of Canada, 1919–1921  109

5 'No Surrender': Orange-Canadian Unionists and Northern Ireland, 1919–1925  151

6 Irish-Canadian Nationalists: Free Staters and Republicans, 1922–1925  176

Conclusion  194

*Notes*  199
*Bibliography*  253
*Index*  265

Illustrations follow page 24.

# Acknowledgments

Although researching and writing historical subjects is largely a solitary endeavor, no project such as this can be accomplished without generous assistance from others. I am eternally indebted, both personally and academically, to numerous people and institutions. I owe a debt of gratitude to the Canadian-American Center at the University of Maine for the numerous fellowships I received. Ray Pellitier and Stephen Hornsby were particularly supportive of my ideas and allowed me the opportunity to implement those ideas. Thank you to Richard Judd, Janet Tebrake, Beth McKillen, and Howard Cody for reading through such a tedious work on such short notice. The staff at Fogler Library at the University of Maine is wonderful and is deserving of great thanks to say the least, particularly Bonnie. Thank you to the staffs at the Provincial Archives of New Brunswick, the National Archives of Canada, and the Archives of Ontario. A special thanks is extended to the staff at the National Library of Ireland, and especially Noel Brady.

On a more personal level, thank you to my good friend John Potter, who not only gave me free rein of his house in Montreal, he also loaned me his car for research jaunts to Ottawa. Thank you to Will Katerberg, and Tammy Windsor, who each allowed me to stay with them on separate research forays to Fredericton. Thank you to Micheline Sheehy Skeffington for translating all of the Gaelic passages I uncovered. Thank you to Ellen King, Betsy Hedler, Micah Pawling, and most especially Brian Payne. Your excellent work made me strive harder to excel. Thank you to Betsy Beattie, whose enthusiasm and kind comments spurred this project at its earliest, and toughest stages. I wish, most especially, to thank my advisor Scott See. I could not have accomplished this project without him.

I would also like to thank my editor at the University of Toronto Press, Len Husband. Len's enthusiasm for this project was infectious and has been much appreciated. I consider myself to have been extremely fortunate to have an editor like Len working on my behalf.

Lastly, mere words cannot convey the debt of gratitude I owe to my family. My father accompanied me on two glorious research trips to Toronto. His support, both personal and financial, allowed this project to develop, which I will never forget. My wife Lia, and my daughters Kiera and Ellie have been my greatest supporters. They have witnessed the peaks and the valleys, the joys and the misery. Without their love and encouragement this project may never have been completed. I thank them from the bottom of my heart.

IRISH CANADIAN CONFLICT AND THE STRUGGLE
FOR IRISH INDEPENDENCE, 1912–1925

# Introduction

On Sunday evening, 5 April 1998, just four days before the 9 April deadline of the ongoing Northern Ireland peace process, the independent chairman of the peace talks (and former United States senator from Maine) George Mitchell, and his colleagues faced yet another dilemma regarding the proposed agreement. British and Irish officials had just delivered the first draft of the crucially important but highly controversial Strand Two portion of the negotiations dealing with North/South joint governing councils. Mitchell and his colleagues – the former Finnish prime minister Harri Holkeri and General John de Chastelain of Canada – quickly examined the document and realized immediately that the extensive number of proposed North/South governing bodies would be utterly unacceptable to the Ulster Unionist Party, the largest Protestant political party in Northern Ireland.[1] Exacerbating this immediate problem, the British and Irish governments insisted that this Strand Two draft be included without change in the overall agreement document as if it were the product of Mitchell and his colleagues, not that of British and Irish negotiators.

According to Mitchell, General de Chastelain quickly assessed 'the circumstances and suggested we had essentially three options: we could accede to their demand; we could include their Strand Two within our comprehensive draft but identify it as theirs, not ours; or we could rewrite it and then include it as ours, as it would then be.'[2] Option three was quickly ruled out, and Mitchell and his colleagues eventually decided to accede to the wishes of the two governments and include the Strand Two document without changes. Not surprisingly, the Ulster Unionists rejected it outright. After furious negotiations and the acquiescence of the Irish government on the number and scope of the North/South governing councils, the Northern Ireland Peace Agreement was accepted on Good Friday, 10 April 1998. It brought peace and, for the first time, an equitable power-sharing form of self-government to that troubled statelet. Although numerous roadblocks have since been placed in the path of this exercise in self-government, history was made on that Good Friday, and it continues to be made in Northern Ireland.

The acceptance of the Good Friday Peace Agreement brought about a political settlement to issues and demands that had previously been contested with violence. Although the peace settlement obligated participants to completely decommission weapons, the Provisional Irish Republican Army (IRA) disarmed at a slower pace than anticipated. Nevertheless, the settlement fostered a political climate that enabled the IRA to decommission large stocks of weapons in October 2001, in April 2002, and again in November 2003. Prior to the commencement of the Good Friday negotiations, General de Chastelain had been appointed Chairman of the Independent International Commission on Decommissioning (IICD), and in that role, he verified each of these instances of IRA weapons destruction. Most recently, following the IRA stand-down and announced cessation of all military operations in July 2005, Jean de Chastelain verified that IRA weapons had been put beyond use. He and his colleagues on the IICD, along with witnesses Harold Good, the former president of the Methodist Church of Ireland, and the Redemptorist priest Father Alec Reid, spent a week examining the weapons that had been rendered inoperative. At the press conference to announce the IRA's weapons destruction, General de Chastelain stated: 'We are satisfied that the arms decommissioning represents the totality of the IRA's arsenal.'[3] Although his role in the Northern Ireland peace process was less prominent than that of George Mitchell, it was – and it continues to be – no less significant. General de Chatelain has played a pivotal role in the Northern Ireland peace process; and though most North Americans do not realize it, he has not been the lone Canadian involved in Northern Ireland's political affairs.

In late 1999, Tony Blair's Labour government announced a new investigation into the events surrounding the shootings of thirteen unarmed civilians by British elite paratroopers on 30 January 1972 during a civil rights protest in Derry. A three-person legal commission was appointed to investigate whether the British Army was culpable in those deaths, commonly referred to in the years since as Bloody Sunday. The Saville Commission, chaired by English Law Lord Mark Saville, included Sir

Edward Somers of New Zealand as well as William Hoyt, retired Chief Justice of the Supreme Court of New Brunswick.[4] The commission expected to interview witnesses for only two years; instead it took four, taking testimony from its 919th and final witness in February 2004.[5] The commission's final report has still not been published; the point here is that yet another Canadian judge has been tasked with investigating the possibility of political murder in Northern Ireland.

Similarly, retired Canadian Supreme Court Justice Peter Cory was appointed by the Irish and British governments 'to examine six of Northern Ireland's most controversial murders and make a recommendation as to whether or not a full judicial inquiry should be held into the cases.'[6] In late 2003, Justice Cory submitted his report to the British government, recommending that full judicial inquiries be held in the four most controversial murders. The report has yet to be released to the public. While this recent succession of Canadian involvement in Irish political affairs is significant, it is no sudden phenomenon, and in fact continues a tradition dating back to the late nineteenth century.

In 1892, the leader of Canada's Liberal Party, Edward Blake, gave up his position to represent South Longford for the Irish Parliamentary Party at Westminster, a seat he retained until he retired in 1907. Blake's membership in the IPP proved fortuitous for that party in the years following the scandal over Charles Stewart Parnell's adulterous behaviour. Blake raised thousands of dollars in Canada for the IPP, almost single-handedly saving it from financial ruin during two particularly critical years: 1893–4 and 1897–8.[7] Blake also had the political foresight – seemingly when no British politician did – to realize that if 'home rule were not granted Ireland's discontent would increase perhaps to the point where nothing short of complete separation would satisfy her.'[8]

Likewise, in November 1911, Irish politics, more specifically, Ulster Unionism, gained a tremendous sponsor when Andrew Bonar Law replaced Arthur Balfour as leader of Britain's Conservative Party. Andrew Bonar Law was born in New Brunswick, but his father, a Presbyterian minister, moved the family back to Ulster when Bonar Law was a young boy. The family eventually settled in Scotland, where years later the son made his mark as a Glasgow ironmaster and metal broker. Although he lived in Scotland, he always nurtured a deeply felt sense of fealty to his Ulster roots. Historian Patrick Buckland once described him as a 'Scots-Canadian Presbyterian of Ulster descent who claimed to care about only two things in politics – tariff reform and Ulster.'[9] As Conservative leader, Bonar Law dedicated himself to Ulster and to the

Unionists' efforts to prevent Irish Home Rule, even if that meant armed revolt.

There is also Sir Hamar Greenwood, a Canadian, who served as a British Liberal MP beginning in 1906 and who was named Chief Secretary of Ireland in April 1920.[10] Conservative MP and media mogul Maxwell Aiken, Lord Beaverbrook, a New Brunswicker, was a close personal friend of Andrew Bonar Law as well as a supporter of the Unionist cause. And in 1924, when the British government formed a Boundary Commission to examine possible alterations to the boundary between Northern Ireland and the Irish Free State, as was specified in the 1921 Anglo-Irish Treaty, former Canadian prime minister Robert Borden was asked to chair the commission.[11]

Given the number of prominent Canadians involved in Irish political affairs at the beginning of the twentieth century, and given – more important – that political autonomy seemed so close at hand for Ireland, questions arise: To what extent were Canadians of Irish descent interested in political events in Ireland? Was there an Irish nationalist movement in Canada in the 1910s and 1920s, as there had been the late 1880s and to a lesser extent in the early 1890s? Did Irish Canadians retain an interest in seeing their ancestral homeland attain political independence? Did they maintain a distinct ethnic awareness in the New World? To what extent did this ethnic awareness and identity inform their perceptions of the homeland? And if Irish Canadians were interested in events in Ireland, was there a divergence of opinion along religious lines with respect to independence for Ireland?

Contrary to the assertions of Canadian historians devoted to the subject, this work argues the Irish in Canada most definitely maintained an interest in events in Ireland between 1912 and 1925. Indeed, many participated actively in those events, testifying to their intense interest in and dedication to the issue. There was, as well, a sharp divergence of opinion along religious lines regarding Ireland's future political status: those of Irish-Catholic descent supported Ireland's demands for self-government, while those of Irish-Protestant descent believed that Ireland should remain united with Britain. These conflicting visions of Ireland, which mirrored the ongoing struggle between Catholics and Protestants in Ireland, represented yet another flare-up between Irish Catholics and Irish Protestants in Canada, which had been ongoing since the early nineteenth century.

The Irish first arrived in what is now Canada in the late sixteenth century, establishing seasonal camps on the Avalon Peninsula of Newfoundland to facilitate fishing on the Grand Banks. More permanent Irish settlements developed in eastern Nova Scotia in the 1760s, but consistent Irish immigration began in earnest only after the Napoleonic Wars in 1815, when Irish emigrants found favourable rates on empty timber ships returning to Canada. Historical geographers Cecil Houston and William Smyth note that 'Irish settlement occurred first in parts of the Maritime colonies in the 1760s, but after 1815, when the mass movements began, it took place on several fronts – eastern Nova Scotia, the Gulf of St Lawrence region and Saint John Valley of New Brunswick, the St Lawrence and Ottawa valleys of Lower Canada, and the southern peninsular Upper Canada [Ontario].'[12] Houston and Smyth found that in the heaviest wave of Irish immigration after 1815, Irish Protestants predominated: 'Protestants were more prominent and Ulster ports combined with Cork as the main source of emigrants.'[13] Tragically, in 1845, and most especially in 1847, much of Ireland faced starvation as a result of the potato blight. The Great Famine that resulted set off a near tidal wave of emigration, with well over one million Irish emigrating. Most of them were Catholics from the south and west of Ireland, and many of them made landfall at Canadian ports like Quebec City and Saint John – more specifically, at those ports' respective quarantine stations at Grosse Isle and Partridge Island.

By 1871, the year of Canada's first census, roughly 850,000 people of Irish heritage lived in Canada, with over 60 per cent of them being Irish Protestants.[14] Over 80 per cent of those of Irish heritage lived in Ontario or New Brunswick. Ontario was 'home to two-thirds of the Irish in Canada, and three-quarters of Canadian Irish Protestants.'[15] By the dawn of the twentieth century, the Irish and those of Irish descent had settled in every province and in every major city; most of them, however, were in Ontario and New Brunswick, and most were of Irish-Protestant background. Murray Nicolson's examination of the 1901 Canadian census found that of the 988,721 who declared themselves to be of Irish heritage, those of Irish-Catholic descent made up only '37.9 per cent of the Irish national group.'[16] Well into the twentieth century, those of Irish-Protestant descent outnumbered those of Irish-Catholic descent by a ratio of almost two to one.

As evidenced in the work of Bruce Elliott, whose amazingly detailed research traced the migration of 775 Irish Protestant families from North Tipperary to London, Ontario, and the Ottawa Valley between 1818 to 1855, much of the Canadian scholarship tends to differentiate between research on Irish Protestants and that on Irish Catholics.[17] Donald Akenson, for example, asserts that the Irish Protestants of Leeds County, Ontario, developed a sense of ethnic awareness in the 1830s and 1840s. As Irish Protestants came to Canada in large numbers after 1815, they acquired the vacant upland spaces not already occupied by Yankee Loyalist families in eastern and central Upper Canada (present-day Ontario). During the 1834 provincial parliamentary election, Akenson continues, the Irish Protestants of Leeds County developed a collective ethnic consciousness, which coalesced around an effort to elect one of their own to the vacant provincial seat. Ogle R. Gowan, the father of the Canadian Orange Order, won the election with the support of his Irish-Protestant shillelagh-wielding poll workers in what Akenson describes as a 'violent exercise in representative government.'[18] Akenson maintains that this election episode helped these Irish-Protestant immigrants develop an ethnic consciousness.

This electoral expression of Irish-Protestant ethnic solidarity contrasts dramatically with historian Donald Mackay's assertion that 'the majority who settled in Canada took up farming[. T]here were, for example, few Irish ghettoes and the raw Irish politics of cities like Boston and New York were foreign to the Canadian experience.'[19] Through their collective assertiveness, the Irish Protestants of Leeds County had been able to rest local control from the Yankee family elites in a traditional demonstration of Irish power politics. Even so, by the late nineteenth century an exclusively Irish-Protestant identity was no longer discernible; most probably, it had merged with a broader British-Protestant identity that concerned itself with parochial matters but also with imperial matters. The institution most obviously associated with and emblematic of this transformation was the Protestant fraternal society known as the Loyal Orange Order.

Founded in 1795 in Loughall, County Armagh, Ireland, the Orange Order came of age in the late eighteenth century when intense agrarian violence cut across much of Ireland. Various secret oath-bound societies such as the Whiteboys, the Ribbonmen, Thrashers, the Defenders, and the Peep o' Day Boys exacted revenge against landlords, tax collectors, and anyone careless enough to harass one of their members.[20] Although most of these secret societies 'were motivated by agrarian grievances, some, especially from the north of Ireland, had a distinct sectarian tinge.'[21] The Orange Order sprang from the Peep o' Day Boys and evolved into a more formal fraternal organization by adopting many Masonic rituals and traditions, notably the hierarchical series of degrees through which a member passed to remain in good standing.

The Orange Order lodges that were established across Ulster and Ireland served as a network of defensive garrisons to protect Protestant ascendancy and interests. The Orange Order served a similar role once it arrived in Canada.

In 1799, four years after the Order was founded in Ireland, Orange Order members serving as British soldiers met in Halifax in the first known meeting in British North America.[22] The following year, in 1800, Orange members of the British regulars convened in Montreal. Within a few years – and especially after 1815, when hundreds of thousands of Irish Protestants began arriving in Canada – the Orange Order had gained a tenacious hold in Canada. The ritual regalia and Masonic traditions were transferred to North America, where they replicated themselves easily in the devoutly Protestant areas 'along the north shore of Lake Ontario and the Fundy coast of New Brunswick.'[23] The most obvious Orange tradition that made its way to North America was unquestionably the celebration of King William of Orange's victory over Catholic King James II at the Battle of the Boyne in Ireland on 12 July 1690. According to the Orangemen, this victory had preserved the Protestant faith for Britain. The annual 12 July marches throughout the British Empire served as yearly reminders of Catholic defeat and as an annual source of contention in areas where Orange Protestants lived in proximity to Irish Catholics.

Most scholars point to the Orange Order's transformation and adaptation to the British North American setting as an indication of its evolution into a uniquely Canadian institution. They view the ethnically varied membership of the Canadian Orange Order as an indication of its adaptation and transformation to he North American setting. Beginning in the 1830s, and certainly by the 1840s with the massive influx of Famine Irish, the original Irish-Protestant institution had begun accepting members of various ethnicities – Scots, English, Welsh, Germans, and descendants of the American Congregationalist Loyalists. The only criterion for membership was being a dedicated Protestant.[24] It is interesting that as an institution demanding unquestioning devotion to the Crown, the Orange Order did not declare itself to be the sole proprietors of loyalty, as their own official rule book stated: 'The Orange Society, lays no claim to exclusive loyalty or exclusive Protestantism, but it admits no man within its pale whose principles are not loyal, and whose creed is not Protestant.'[25] This does not suggest that the Irish influence in the Canadian Orange Order was completely jettisoned after the mid-nineteenth century ethnic expansion. Scott See insists that while 'Canadian Orangeism created a style of its own, it kept the two most important Irish values intact,' those of loyalty to the Crown and a near fanatical anti-Catholicism.[26] Houston and Smyth also argue that those of Irish descent were not too far removed from Orange membership, stating that the 'ethnic backgrounds of the Orangemen were more representative of the wider protestant community than an Irish immigrant minority. But the wide dispersal of the Irish meant that they would be found in most lodges to one degree or another.'[27] The greatest demonstration of the Orange Order's shift toward an indigenously Canadian identity came in the form of its political and social orientation.

Scott See contends that the Orange Order made itself uniquely Canadian by engaging in local political issues and by altering its social orientation:'Canadian Orangemen charted a course that addressed local issues and attempted to correct indigenous problems.' After noting a number of those issues, See adds that 'Orangemen supported the government in the abortive Rebellions of 1837, and they zealously opposed the Rebellions Loses Act which they believed favoured Catholics. They campaigned against the separate schools issue and the Jesuit Estates Act, and played an active role in crushing the Northwest Rebellions and the Fenian threats. Although they were motivated by the ubiquitous Orange tenets of loyalty and anti-Catholicism, British North American Orangemen steered a political course that was uniquely Canadian.'[28]

Hereward Senior, who primarily examined Canadian Orangeism from the perspective of its political adroitness and proclivities, observed that Canadian Orange lodges were more than mere political conduits and often provided 'a religious service with the reading of scripture, and acted as a guardian of morality as well as a means of organizing social life in frontier communities.'[29] In this vein, See notes that without the imminent threat of harassment at the hands of militant Catholic agrarian groups, as had been so pervasive in Ireland – Canadian Orangemen developed social justifications for their organization's existence. As the siege mentality waned among Irish Protestants, many lodges declared themselves temperance and benefit lodges, offering rudimentary insurance and death benefits for widows.[30]

Houston and Smyth also examine the Canadian Orange Order from the grassroots level. In so doing, Houston and Smyth maintain that the Orange Order's brand of 'ultra-loyalism and ultra-protestantism' was a 'philosophy differing in degree, not in kind, from that of the mass of

Canadian protestants.'[31] Houston and Smyth expressly state; 'it is our intent to broaden the interpretation of Canadian Orangeism through a study of its geography and its role as a bond for protestant communities in a developing nation.'[32] Moreover, they suggest that 'the primary function of the order in Canada was expressed at the local level through the social activities and ritual glamour of individual lodges. Anything from convivial forum for local affairs to service as a surrogate church could be provided within a lodge.'[33] Houston and Smyth emphasize that the Orange Order was not merely a source of social division and an instigator of violent clashes in Canadian society, but was a well-accepted fraternal society with a mainstream membership: 'It was not, as is often portrayed today, an anachronism, an unwanted extreme, solely a source of anti-catholicism and social divisiveness. It was rather a bulwark of colonial protestantism.'[34] There must have been some degree of acceptance of its principles, they argue, because by the end of the nineteenth century perhaps one adult Protestant male in three was a member.[35] In this regard, the Orange Order, through its contacts with wives, brothers, friends, and relatives, had tremendous influence on Canadian political culture.

Houston and Smyth argue compellingly that the Orange Order was no more discriminatory than much of mainstream English-Protestant Canadian society and that it did have broad appeal. But simply acknowledging that the Orange Order may not have been an anachronism and was far more accepted than many may wish to admit today does not erase the fact that the Orange Order was a profoundly divisive and racist institution. Houston and Smyth's approach seems to indicate a reluctance to address the overtly sectarian nature of the Orange Order; moreover, none of the scholars mentioned earlier address the extent to which the Canadian Orange Order maintained an interest in and connections with events in the north of Ireland. More recent research, though, has addressed many of these issues head-on.

A recent compilation of impressive scholarship edited by David A. Wilson, *The Orange Order in Canada*, presents a more thorough picture of the Orange Order.[36] In examining the associationalism of the Order diaspora, Donald MacRaild acknowledges that although 'there is no denying the centrality of prejudice to explanations of Orangeism ... Canadian scholars are almost alone in noting the importance of Orangeism in the making of modern civic society, regularly acknowledging the different layers of meaning and action which shaped a more complicated Orangeism than is usually recognized.'[37] In examining the Order in other countries, MacRaild notes that in

> the northeast of England members sincerely debated the efficacy of public processions because of the risk of embarrassing drunkenness or violence. The need to obscure the mark of sectarian violence with the stamp of mutualism shaped the thinking of men who recognized the value of making Orangeism more respectable.
>
> Even then the paradox emerged as leading Orangemen tried to offset the movment's reputation for intolerance by highlighting its improving ethos while still maintaining its essentialist defence of Protestantism.[38]

Included in Wilson's volume is a fascinating piece by one of the foremost researchers on the Orange Order, Eric Kaufmann.[39] With regard to the Orange Order in Ontario in the early twentieth century, Kaufmann found that ethnicity more than any other factor played an role in Orange lodge development, stating, 'what stands out is not class but ethnicity: while 29% of Ontario's Protestant population was of Irish ancestry, 61% of Ontario's Orangemen were of Irish ethnicity.'[40] Kaufmann explains that the proliferation of Orange lodges in nineteenth-century proliferation of Orange lodges in Ontario resulted from the increased presence of Catholics: 'We explain much of the geographical membership variation in terms of three key cultural factors (in descending order of importance): Irish-Protestant ethnicity, the proportion of local Catholics and the Protestant denomination.'[41] Not surprisingly, during the nineteenth century, as Irish-Catholic immigration increased, and as Orange membership roles increased in response, ethno-religious collective violence increased in direct proportion. In New Brunswick, riots flared throughout the mid-nineteenth century: in Woodstock in 1837, in Fredericton in 1842 and 1845, and most brutally in Saint John and Portland in 1847 and 1849.[42] Similar violent eruptions occurred in Toronto and throughout the Ottawa Valley.[43] In Toronto alone, Gregory Kealey found evidence of no fewer than twenty-two riots between Orangemen and Irish Catholics between 1867 and 1892.[44]

Brian Clarke examined religious riots in Victorian Toronto and rightly acknowledges that it was 'from the standpoint of ultra-loyalist and ultra-Protestant colonials of British origin that [Canadian] Orangemen viewed their country, their empire and the world around them.'[45] In Toronto, though, Orangemen were a unique cohort and far from an ordinary fraternal organization. In describing the Orange Order in Toronto, Clarke states:

> In Toronto, the Orange Order was no ordinary voluntary association or male fraternity organization, such as the Ancient Order of Foresters, and the like. It occupied a privileged place in the civic order. Its members regularly occupied the mayoralty and frequently sat on city council. Many Orangemen served on the city police force and in its fire department. The Order's major celebration, the Twelfth of July, was a public holiday in all but name. Businesses closed. Public buildings, businesses and homes were decorated with flags and bunting, as was the custom for civil celebrations.[46]

Partly echoing Kealey, Clarke writes that between '1870 and 1889, there were some twenty-two significant outbreaks of religiously motivated collective violence in the city, sixteen of which occurred during the 1870s.'[47] The two largest and most deadly of these riots occurred during the Papal Jubilee of 1875 and the visit from Ireland of Jeremiah O'Donovan Rossa in 1878. Clarke found that religious riots typically started with young men gathering to confront members of the other community: as many violent exchanges started with Catholic assaults on Protestant neighbourhoods as with Protestant attacks on Catholics. Yet Clarke asserts that 'religious riot became less common in the 1880s and eventually disappeared altogether.'[48] Brian Clarke's research is undoubtedly excellent, but this is not entirely accurate. Well into the twentieth century, one issue continued to raise Orange Protestant ire and brought them onto the streets; that being the issue of Irish independence. This issue arose in 1886, in 1893, and again in 1912–14 (continuing to 1922). Few scholars, though, have examined this issue, which was of crucial importance to Orange Canadians.

William Jenkins is one of the few scholars to examine in any meaningful way how Canadian Orangemen reacted to the Irish Home Rule crisis of 1912–14 (another is Phillip Currie, who will be discussed in the next chapter; yet another is the present author).[49] Jenkins skilfully constructs an argument that:

> the ideology of a globalizing British 'civilization' required not only continued geographical expansion and the conversion of the 'non-civilized,' but also vigilant defenders who would spread and uphold the principles. The

Orange sentinels in the watchtower saw themselves to be in the vanguard of such initiatives, with manifestations of popery as their prime target. Discourses and imaginations of 'disloyalty' were extended from local antagonisms (as expressed in the street disturbances of the 1870s and 1880s, for example) onto wider horizons.[50]

In fact, Canadian Orangemen relied on their own newspaper, the *Sentinel and Orange and Protestant Advocate,* to sharpen 'Orange awareness of the geopolitical manoeuvrings of the Roman church worldwide, highlighting the existence of wider Protestant unity.'[51] With reference to Irish Home Rule and Catholicism, Jenkins states:

> In view of Toronto's Orangemen, the Irish home rule issue was part of a wider struggle against Catholicism. Within Toronto itself, Irish Catholicism no longer appeared dangerous. The city's Irish-Catholic population had become largely Canadianized, middle class, politically unthreatening and 'loyal' by the early twentieth century. They rarely paraded the streets on St. Patrick's Day, and while the rhetoric of Irish republicanism found space to express itself in eastern American cities, such language no longer resonated among the majority of Toronto's English-speaking Catholics.[52]

While William Jenkins may be one of the few historians to address the contentious nature of the Orange reaction to the Home Rule issue, his assimilationist analysis of Orange attitudes toward Irish Catholics may be somewhat too simple. Canadian Orangemen unquestionably viewed the Irish Home Rule question as being emblematic of the looming threat of assertive and self-confident Catholicism, and they hardly viewed Irish Catholics voicing approval of Irish self-government as non-threatening. Orange Canadians espoused a virulent anti-Catholicism that at times, and as late as 1920, engendered ethno-religious violence. At least one other researcher has found similar instances of virulent anti-Catholicism.

In examining Canadian anti-Catholicism, J.R. Miller concluded that 'this nationalistic phase was at its most intense in the generations between 1880–1920.'[53] Orange Canadians espoused a British imperial nationalism, one that was fraught with ethnic overtones and whose front-line of defence was the maintenance of the union between Ireland and Britain. This shifted, when convenience dictated, to maintaining union between Ulster and Britain, in order to preserve the empire from Catholic/Papal encroachment, which threatened Protestant ascendancy and power. Those Canadians who advocated the maintenance of the union between Ireland and Britain were not confined to, but certainly included those in, the Orange Order. By 1914 a Canadian Unionists League had emerged, particularly around Toronto, in support of the union between Ireland and Britain. Thus, 'Orange-Canadian unionists' incorporating both Orangemen and unionists developed a community of like-minded individuals within Canada designed to provide Ireland's unionists with moral, financial, and material support. While Orange-Canadian unionists protested combustible Canadian issues such as the perpetuation of separate schools, and of marriage laws that permitted interfaith marriage, and while they advocated that immigrants be prohibited from voting until having been resident for five years, they most furiously fought the implementation of Irish Home Rule.

All of these issues, of compelling importance to Canadian Orangemen, were clearly articulated in the Grand Master's address at the 1912 annual meeting of the Provincial Grand Orange Lodge of Ontario West in London, Ontario. Grand Master Harry Lovelock asserted that 'the past year has been one of much unrest throughout our Province [Ontario], and indeed the whole Dominion, and our Order has been actively engaged combating such questions as the marriage question, the bi-lingual school situation, and the Home Rule problem in the Old Land, in which so many of our brethren in Canada are so deeply interested.'[54] He characterized the Home Rule problem 'in the Old Land' as an issue that carried as much weight as any other for Canadian Orangemen.

During the Irish Home Rule crisis of 1912 to 1914, Canadian Orangemen, who firmly believed they were just in voicing their concerns in imperial matters that threatened to weaken the imperial connection, fully supported Irish Protestant opposition to Home Rule for Ireland. Under the 1912 bill, which was far more tepid than the previous two bills, Ireland would remain a constituent part of Great Britain, with the British government retaining authority over important aspects of financial and security matters. Among other things, these included naval and military affairs, treaties and foreign affairs, navigation, trade marks, copyrights, lighthouses, old age pensions, national insurance, and post office savings banks.[55] Although this bill conferred less authority on a Dublin parliament than either of the previous Home Rule bills, it received more vehement opposition from the overwhelmingly Protestant Irish unionists.

Orange-Canadian unionists entirely supported their Irish Protestant 'brethren' in opposing Home Rule for Ireland. They maintained connections in the 'old land' and funded an armed resistance to the democratic will of the British Parliament, which was contrary to everything they espoused. Orange-Canadian unionists were far from the only source of funding for such extralegal activities in Ulster during the Home Rule crisis of 1912–14, but they were the largest contributors. In this context, Orange-Canadian unionists' identity can be determined only by examining their words, deeds, and actions. As recent research indicates, other ethnicities in Canada engaged in similar activities by maintaining connections with and funding political movements the 'old land.' Therefore, the activities of Orange-Canadian unionists were quite similar to the activities of many ethnicities in Canada at that time.

With the advent of 'new social history' and advances in the field of ethnic history, particularly since the 1970s, researchers have found that numerous ethnicities in Canada exhibited strong nationalist proclivities.[56] Most notable among these were the Poles and the Ukrainians during and after the First World War. Zofia Shahrodi found that Polish Canadians in Toronto were actively engaged in political events aimed at achieving nationhood for Poland.[57] Zoriana Yaworsky Sokolsky found that Ukrainians in Toronto actively supported their Ukrainian countrymen following the First World War. During 1919 and again in 1922, the Taras Shevchenko Society organized 'public protest meetings in the Star Theatre and Massey Hall against the Polish and Russian oppression in Ukraine[,] and in 1921 and 1922 sent telegrams to the Supreme Council of the Peace Conference in Paris when the later discussed the fate of Eastern Galicia (Western Ukraine).'[58] Clearly, these Ukrainian and Polish immigrants were very politically active, and maintained connections with communities in the 'old land' enabling them to contribute to and participate in political events in the homeland. Through their words, actions, and deeds, these Polish and Ukrainian immigrants demonstrated considerable ethnic retention and identification with their ancestral homeland. Considering this is the case, the question arises: Has recent scholarship indicated any nationalist tendencies among Canadians of Irish-Catholic descent, especially during the most tumultuous revolutionary period in Ireland, 1912 to 1922?

Much of the scholarly discourse concerning the Irish-Catholic experience in Canada has focused on settlement patterns, kinship ties, cultural transference, religious background, and employment. Rarely does it address questions relating to nationalism.[59] Without question, a great deal has been learned regarding the socio-economic, geographic, and demographic structures of the Irish in Canada during the nineteenth and early twentieth centuries, yet one crucial component of the Irish tradition has been almost entirely overlooked by Canadian scholars. As historian Gerald Stortz commented: 'One aspect of the immigrant experience, that of Irish nationalism, has received scant attention.'[60] Donald Akenson, in his pioneering 1984 study of the Irish in rural Ontario, claimed that Irish Catholics in Canada could not have been bothered with nationalism. Akenson remarked that Irish Catholics adapted so well to Canadian society that they lost interest in events in Ireland, and have therefore been overlooked by historians: 'As far as Irish nationalism was concerned, few Irish Canadian Catholics could be bothered. And thus, few historians of Ireland have bothered about them. The historians of the nineteenth century can well argue the near invisibility of the Irish Catholics is itself a prime indication of their success in adapting to life in this part of the New World.'[61] Akenson's assertion begs us to ask: Was this really the case? Were Irish Catholics in Canada so exceptional as to possess no interest in political developments in their ancestral homeland, particularly during the politically volatile and turbulent years 1912 to 1922?

In reviewing the historical literature concerning Irish Catholics in Canada, few works if any convey the impression the Irish in any way cared about or participated in events in Ireland. Of course the Poles and Ukrainians were more recent immigrants to Canada and therefore, it is assumed, more likely to identify with and show interest in events in the 'homeland.' The Irish were second, third, or even fourth generation Canadians, and most scholars assume that they had lost all interest in events in Ireland. Scholarly research on Irish Catholics in Canada generally examines either hierarchical endeavours to establish distinctly Catholic institutions to blunt further assimilation into Protestant society, or it examines lay people's attachment to those institutions. Murray Nicolson's examination of Catholic institutions between 1850 and 1900 highlights the efforts of a Catholic minority to fend off the growing pressure to assimilate into a mainly Protestant society. Nicolson concludes that 'successive bishops in Toronto fought to acquire a separate system of education and other social institutions and agencies so as to retain and protect the religious rights of their flock.'[62]

Terrence Murphy's 'Trusteeism in Atlantic Canada' describes the conflicting interpretations of ownership that resulted from the laity-financed construction of churches in the early nineteenth century, prior to ecclesiastical instalment in Halifax and Saint John. Murphy contends that the importance of trusteeism 'lies largely in the insight it gives us into the experience of the first few generations of Catholic immigrants as they laid the foundations of ecclesiastical life.'[63]

Brian Clarke's earlier work asserts that Irish nationalism in Toronto was really only expressed through the establishment of Irish-Catholic voluntary benevolent institutions and through devotion to the Church. The St Vincent de Paul Society (founded 1850), the Young Mens Saint Patrick's Association (1855), and the Hibernian Benevolent Society (1858) are but a few examples of the former. Clarke contends that Toronto's lay Irish Catholics played an active part in the late nineteenth century's devotional revolution in Toronto, so as to place the city on playing field spiritually equivalent with those of Rome, Dublin, New York, and Quebec.[64]

As noted earlier, Gerald Stortz bemoans the fact that Canadian historians have overlooked an entire aspect of the Irish immigrant experience: that of nationalism. In attempting to fill this gap with a study on Irish nationalist activities in Toronto, Stortz asserts, 'for urban Irish in general, however, the political question was not at the forefront of their concerns: their identification was with the church rather than the Home Rule movement and with Canada rather than Ireland.'[65] This assessment of course was to be expected from Stortz, whose study openly admits that 'groups which could fall under a definition of nationalism, but were by definition antagonistic to the Roman Catholic Church, have been ignored.'[66] Stortz did not even examine the political orientation of those lay organizations most likely to identify with the Home Rule movement. Instead, his work examines the efforts by successive Toronto bishops to distance themselves – and by implication the Church – from more radical Irish nationalist movements, such as the Land League, which had branches in Toronto in the late nineteenth century. Stortz concludes that 'the links between church and Irish nationalism, which had been so apparent [at mid-century], were tenuous at best by the end of the century.'[67]

Likewise, Terrence J. Fay's work on Canadian Catholicism, of which the Irish are a significant portion, identifies Irish nationalism only as a fading and fleeting sentiment, as a relic of the Old World with no place in the New. Fay asserts that with the outbreak of the First World War in 1914, the Irish enlisted in large numbers to defend the British Empire. In so doing they were finally accepted by the Protestant majority and fully inculcated into Canadian society. Fay insists: 'Many Old World

Introduction 19

nationalisms of the Irish, Scots, Germans, and Italians disappeared as Catholics became deeply involved in the preservation of English civilization and identified themselves with Canada. English-speaking Catholics supported national registration and conscription and pursued the British vision of democracy, Christianity, and Canadian autonomy within the British Commonwealth.'[68] Ultimately, though, Fay's work is a synthesis of other historical works, and for the above section relies almost exclusively on the work of historian Mark McGowan.

McGowan is a productive historian of the Irish-Catholic experience in Toronto (and by implication Ontario) during the late nineteenth and early twentieth centuries.[69] McGowan's work articulates a theme similar to that of all the historians previously mentioned: an Irish-Catholic laity casting aside its affinity for Ireland, and the Irish pursuit of independence, for a new Canadian nationalism based on a moderate form of British imperialism coupled with continued devotion to the Catholic Church. The title of McGowan's most important monograph conveys precisely this image: *The Waning of the Green*.[70] Central to McGowan's argument is that 'from 1887 to 1922, English-speaking Catholics in Toronto submerged their overt ties to Ireland, embraced many of the values of Canadian society, and allowed their faith life to make some needed adjustments to the North American environment.' McGowan's work is an attempt to create a broader portrait of 'Catholic social and religious life' and to move beyond the image of Toronto as the Belfast of North America.[71] Also central to his argument is the idea that a generation of Canadian-born priests and nuns fostered this shifting allegiance. McGowan notes: 'This change in attitude was completed by the rise of a home-grown clergy and male and female religious communities. From 1887 to 1922 the dominance of Irish-born and Irish-educated priests and religious in the Archdiocese of Toronto was overturned by a new generation of Canadian-born and Canadian-educated men and women.'[72]

In addition, McGowan exhaustively examines the history of the Catholic press in Toronto and London, Ontario. He argues that for a time in the mid-nineteenth century, the news in Toronto's Catholic press centred on Irish news and politics, Celtic culture, and updates from the Irish counties. He then adds that in the decades after the 1887 William O'Brien visit, the 'passion of Catholics of Irish birth and descent had once shown for the "homeland" was replaced by all things Canadian.'[73] McGowan accurately argues that the 'pages of the local Catholic newspaper and the observations of their editors open an important window on the life of the English-speaking Catholic community.'[74] Because these papers relied on a small ethnic population to sustain them, editors and columnists 'who ventured too far away from the accepted views of Catholic readers did so at their own peril.' In this context, there can be no doubt that Mark McGowan's argument is convincing: 'In their role as religious and political tribunes and as advocates of loyal and patriotic citizenship, it is most reasonable to regard catholic weeklies as "the most direct and influential monitor of public sentiment."'[75] McGowan then notes that from 1893 to 1922 the number of articles and editorials concerning Ireland dramatically decreased, while those 'preoccupied with issues germane to Canadian society, politics, and culture' proliferated.

McGowan's work is incredibly detailed and well researched, but there are glaring flaws and weaknesses. His circumscribed approach to identifying Irish-Canadian expressions of fealty to Ireland is problematic. Instead of simply asking, and researching, the question which most directly gets to the crux of the matter – to what extent did the Irish in Canada concern themselves with the political affairs of Ireland?–McGowan instead examined to which suburbs the Irish moved, and which jobs they attained. Instead of examining what the *Catholic Register* said about Ireland, he focuses on what the *Register* said about Canada and the Empire. Instead of looking at what the members of the Ancient Order of Hibernians did or said about events in Ireland, he simply looked at declining membership roles in Irish fraternal societies and concluded that there was a loss of interest in Ireland. McGowan's research approach fostered and culled the conclusion that there was a weakened Irish nationalist identity in Canada after 1887, simply because he did not look for such an identity.

Unlike most historical scholarship on the subject, the present work argues that those of Irish descent in Canada followed political events in Ireland between 1912 and 1925 with unmatched intensity. Moreover, the evidence clearly indicates that interest in Irish political events was not confined to one Canadian community or the other – Irish Catholic or Irish Protestant. The extent to which Canadians of Irish descent supported a particular community in Ireland rested almost entirely with one's religious affiliation. Like Irish Catholics in Ireland, those of Irish-Catholic descent in Canada overwhelmingly favoured a self-governing Ireland, whether this meant Home Rule or independence. Conversely, Orange-Canadian unionists favoured maintenance of the union between Great Britain and Ireland as the only means of preserving the British Empire and protecting Protestant privilege. These opposing factions residing in Canada viewed political developments in Ireland not merely as descendants of a cherished homeland, but as citizens of the British Empire who foresaw grave consequences for the empire if political promises were (or were not) kept in good faith. Ultimately, these competing factions in Canada gave whatever support they could to the corresponding community in Ireland. Irish Catholics in Canada principally supported Irish nationalists in the 'homeland' with resolutions and rallies calling for Irish independence. Orange-Canadian unionists held rallies and offered resolutions of support, but they also provided Ulster unionists with hundreds of thousands of dollars in financial support. A few, indeed, actually went to the north of Ireland as volunteers and trained Protestant Ulstermen on the latest weaponry.

The level of support emanating from Canada for the two communities in Ireland, be it unionist or nationalist – arose not only from religious affiliation but also from a sense of ethnic identification. Contrary to McGowan's assertions that there were few maudlin references to, or sentiments about, the 'old sod,' the language used in fraternal society resolutions and in the ethnic press made repeated references to the 'homeland,' or 'our people in [the] old land,' or 'our brethren in the old land.' Irish nationalists in Canada saw themselves as being part of the diaspora, as part of a greater Ireland beyond the sea. This becomes readily apparent when one reads Saint John's Irish-Catholic weekly, the *New Freeman* – a name adopted from Dublin's nationalist newspaper *Freeman's Journal*. Similar sentiments are apparent in the record books of the St Patrick's Society of Montreal, a fairly moderate Irish-Catholic fraternal society,[76] and in the speeches and resolutions of the Ancient Order of Hibernians of Ontario. These sources have not been used previously, and they provide a far more nuanced image of lay Irish Catholics in early twentieth-century Canada.

Although there was strong Irish nationalist, and even republican, sentiment in Canada following the First World War, one should not assume outright that every Irish-Catholic Canadian held such sentiments. It is possible, even probable, that only 30 to 50 per cent of those of Irish Catholic descent possessed such sentiments, depending on which estimate one chooses to trust. No detailed rolls have survived for the Self-Determination for Ireland League of Canada – only press accounts. In October 1920, after only three months of existence, the Self-Determination League had 20,000 members. At that time it was estimated by Katherine Hughes, the National Organizer, that in another three months the league would have 100,000 members.[77] In January 1921, the league claimed in a press statement that it had attracted 300,000 members. This figure seems wildly exaggerated, especially when one considers that there were only around 450,000 Canadians of Irish Catholic descent.[78] Even the 100,000 figure seems high, when one considers that most members of the league were male heads of households. The influence of the patriarchs likely extended to their wives and children, meaning one could easily multiply by a factor of four the number of members of the league to arrive at the number of Irish nationalists in Canada.[79] But that in turn would mean that 400,000 Irish Catholics in Canada were Irish nationalists. This seems unlikely, as that would account for almost every Irish Catholic in the country. The figure that *is* certain is 20,000. So it seems more likely that the league's membership peaked at between 30,000 and 50,000. This would likely mean that roughly 160,000 Irish Catholics in Canada were Irish nationalists; that figure translates into roughly 35 per cent of the Irish-Catholic population of Canada in 1911.

Of course, these figures are estimates and are not overly significant. The true significance of an Irish nationalist presence in Canada between 1912 and 1925 lay not in its numerical strength but in the fact of its existence. That these Irish-Canadian nationalists organized a national movement to protest against an overtly oppressive British policy in Ireland is significant. This public protest seemed even more significant that it occurred in the face of intense criticism and intimidation on the part of Orange-Canadian unionists. The significance of a dedicated Irish nationalist movement in Canada in the early twentieth century is also heightened by misleading assertions by other historians, who have overlooked numerous sources to draw erroneous conclusions.

There is also considerable evidence that Irish Catholics in Canada were far more likely to support French-Canadian aspirations than most historians have intoned. In one example, Robert Choquette asserts the 'most noisy and troublesome controversies centered on the schools, where French-Canadian and Irish-Canadian clerics contended for control ... In other words, the French and Irish Catholics, well used to locking horns in the ecclesiastical arena, now had to learn to coexist within school boards. Harmony did not come easily.'[80] Like most historians who make this claim, Choquette cites diocesan sources. But some lay Irish-Catholic Canadians, principally in the Ancient Order of Hibernians, expressed a desire to see a more friendly and fraternal feeling extended to the French Canadians (see chapters 2, 4, and 6). This sentiment carried through to the 1920s, most notably among ardent

Irish nationalists. Whether this was mere political expediency is open to debate, but it is an area of research crying out for further investigation than the cursory examination delivered here, particularly on the French side.

Much of Canadian historical scholarship presents the first three decades of the twentieth century as an era of competing nationalisms, essentially shaped by English-Canadian imperialism and French-Canadian Catholicism.[81] These competing nationalisms exhibited contrasting visions of the clearest path forward for Canadian national cultural development. This study argues that a few other competing nationalisms also defined the period, two of these being Irish-Canadian nationalism and Orange-Canadian unionism. Irish-Canadian nationalists argued that the only sensible and fair settlement to the Irish Question was to allow Ireland to experience the same prosperity that Canada had experienced as an independent dominion. For their part, Orange-Canadian unionists insisted that any attempt to give Ireland even limited self-government would be the first step in the dismemberment of the empire; worse still, it would place the most loyal portion of the empire, the Irish Protestants, under the heel of their traditional enemy – the Catholics. As the two sides honed their arguments, staunchly supporting their Irish coreligionists back in the 'old sod,' a separate debate emerged in Canada regarding what it meant to be a loyal Canadian. Orange-Canadian unionists, in true imperialist fashion, argued that only those who publicly declared their loyalty to the Crown were truly loyal Canadians. It followed that anyone who advocated Irish independence was disloyal, for that person supported a weakened empire. Irish-Canadian nationalists argued back that *they* were the truly loyal Canadians, for they were exercising their right to free speech as Canadian citizens in demanding that Britain keep its wartime promises to allow small nations the right of self-determination. And these arguments over Canadian identity were not confined to the editorial pages; they made their way into the streets in 1920. Although Toronto's Protestants contributed to the Catholic Army Hut fundraising campaign during the First World War, ethno-religious violence in Canada continued well into the twentieth century and was only exacerbated by the issue of Irish independence.

With regard to writing history, and writing on the Orange Order in particular, Donald MacRaild acknowledges what most historians have found: 'Sources remain a problem.'[82] MacRaild almost jokingly emphasizes: 'In general, though, historians have not been able to gain access to the manuscript records of the Order, and many writers have sorry stories to tell of records [supposedly] destroyed.'[83] This was most certainly the case when the current author inquired about access to Canadian Orange Order documents. MacRaild notes that most historians resort to using newspaper accounts of the Order, or government Select Committee reports, or the scarcely available aggregate statistics of the Order. The sources used here are the official organ of the Canadian Order, the *Orange Sentinel*; the published annual reports of the Grand Orange Lodge of British America, Ontario West, and New Brunswick; and a bit of limited correspondence between the Grand Orange Lodge of British America and the Provincial Orange Lodge of New Brunswick.

What follows is simply an effort to chronicle side by side the reactions of Irish Canadians to events in Ireland during the tumultuous years 1912 to 1925. That the corresponding responses in Canada essentially mirrored events and debates in Ireland was a result of the unique ethnic make-up of those of Irish descent in Canada. Donald Akenson wrote that the Irish Protestants in Ontario were 'a beautiful, almost laboratory case' study of Irish ethnic solidarity.[84] It seems unlikely that one could find a more fitting place than Canada to study the responses of those of Irish descent to the tumultuous political events in Ireland between 1912 and 1925.

An Orange Order parade in rural small-town Ontario in the early 1900s. Notice the banner of King William of Orange on horseback. (Archives of Ontario 10041587)

Another photograph of the parade in the early 1900s. Again, notice the prominent place occupied by a different banner of King William of Orange, this one commemorating the defeat of Catholic James II at the Battle of the Boyne 12 July 1690. (Archives of Ontario 10041588)

An Orange Order parade down Adelaide Street in Toronto in the 1910s. There were literally ten of thousands of people in attendance. (Archives of Ontario S9571)

Samuel Hughes, MP on Parliament Hill. Hughes, an ardent Orangeman, served as Minister for Munitions in the Robert Borden Conservative government during the First World War. Samuel Hughes was a perfect example of the prominent place held by Orangemen in Canadian society in the early twentieth century. (Archives of Ontario S9055)

Horatio C. Hocken served as Mayor of Toronto in 1912 and in 1913–1914. Hocken was also one of the most publicly outspoken Orangemen opposed to the notion of Irish independence. (City of Toronto Archives)

Ancient Order of Hibernians pamphlet announcing that U.S. Hibernians President Matthew Cummings would be speaking at Massey Hall on 17 March 1908. Notice the pamphlet's shamrock borders, and at the bottom: GOD SAVE IRELAND. (Toronto Metropolitan Library Archives 725338671)

First World War recruitment poster of the Irish Canadian Rangers, who were headquartered in Montreal. Notice the thatched roof cottage in the background, and clusters of shamrocks in the soldiers hands, in his rifle barrel, and on his hat. (Toronto Metropolitan Library Archives 725341238)

First World War recruitment poster of the Irish Canadian Rangers. Notice the ships ostensibly leaving Halifax harbour and turning toward Britain and Europe. (Toronto Metropolitan Library Archives 725344715)

*Chapter One*

# Orange-Canadian Unionists and the Irish Home Rule Crisis, 1912–1914

In 1911, more than one million Canadians identified themselves as being of Irish heritage.[1] Across eastern Canada, the place names of Irish towns and counties testify to the influence of Irish settlement during the nineteenth century. Throughout Ontario and New Brunswick in particular, townships with names like Cork, Carlow, Dublin, Dundalk, Dunboyne, Duntroon, Dungannon, Donegal, Erin, Fingal, Killarney, New Dundee, Newry, Maynooth, Enniskillen, Tyrone, Tyrconnell, and Shannon dot the provincial countryside. Those nineteenth-century Irish immigrants brought with them not only the names of the places they left but also the culture, traditions, and institutions of those places. One such institution that made its way across the Atlantic was the Protestant fraternal society known as the Orange Order. Although Orange lodges were established in every Canadian province, and the Order was successfully inculcated into the country's social fabric, it was nevertheless a fraternal institution replete with paradoxes and contradictions. For some, the Orange Order's adaptation to a North American setting and successful growth reflected Canadian national development.[2] For others, the Order represented an organized sectarianism, fostering division, discrimination, and bigotry on an unparalleled scale.[3]

Originally founded in Loughall, County Armagh, in 1795, in an atmosphere of intense, even violent, competition between Catholics and Protestants for scarce land and meagre employment opportunities, the Orange Order has often been identified as a stalwart defender of Protestantism and Britishness.[4] As a result of steady Irish-Protestant immigration after the Napoleonic Wars, the Orange Order was able to establish a firm foothold in Canada. The siege mentality pervasive among Irish Protestants was transferred and even intensified on the colonial frontiers of British North America, where perceived threats from French-Canadian Catholicism and American republicanism were all encompassing.[5] The establishment of Orange lodges served as a defensive garrison to preserve the privileged position of Protestant subjects of the Crown. Irish-Protestant fears of Catholic encroachment were only heightened after the massive influx of Irish-Catholic immigrants during the Potato Famine years 1845 to 1852. The subsequent clashes and riots between Irish Catholics and members of the Orange Order during the nineteenth century astounded most colonial Canadian settlers, if not for their ferocity then certainly for the consistency with which the riots arose.[6] In Toronto alone, no less than twenty-two riots broke out between Orangemen and Irish Catholics between 1867 and 1892.[7] Eventually, after legislative recognition and incorporation in the 1870s and 1880s, the Orange Order attained a degree of political influence enjoyed by few organizations in Canadian public life.

Although numerous historical works concentrate on the nineteenth-century origins and activities of the Canadian Orange Order, few address the activities of the Order during the early twentieth century, a critical period in Canadian history. Moreover, many questions about one of Canada's most powerful fraternal institutions remain unexamined. How did Canadian Orangemen view themselves, their role in national affairs, and their role in the British Empire? Was the Orange Order in Canada a nativist institution concerned solely with local issues, as many historians have portrayed it, or did it concern itself with matters relating to the empire? To what extent did Canadian Orangemen oppose home rule for Ireland, and why? Was there any cooperation between Canadian Orangemen and Orangemen back in Ireland, and if so, how did this cooperation manifest itself? These and other questions can be at least partly answered by examining the responses of Canadian Orangemen – and Protestant Canadians more generally – to the crisis that developed over the 1912 proposal for Irish Home Rule.[8]

As an institution demanding of its members near fanatical devotion to the British Crown, the Orange Order expressed the view that Canada, as a nation, needed to embrace its Britishness with more devout vigour. The Loyal Orange Association of British America, as it was officially known well into the 1920s, was an ethno-religious institution founded on the principle of loyalty to the British Crown and sustained by virulent anti-Catholic activism.[9] Like the institution itself, the symbols and ritual regalia of the Order was transferred from Ireland to

North America. The secret codes and initiation oaths, along with the Masonic tradition of a hierarchical series of degrees through which members passed in order to progress as members in good standing, were all maintained in the Canadian Order.[10] But the most inspirational and lasting symbol of the Orange Order has always been King William of Orange, who preserved the Protestant faith in England by defeating Catholic James II at the Battle of the Boyne in Ireland on 12 July 1690. The annual Orange parades and marches on 12 July commemorate this battle and served as a yearly reminder of Catholic defeat. During the 1910s and 1920s, thousands of people habitually lined the streets of Toronto to view the Orange parades.[11] In fact, Toronto was so intensely Orange in its makeup and sentiment that it was commonly referred to as 'the Belfast of Canada.'[12] As these names and nicknames suggest, by the early twentieth century the Canadian Orange Order was firmly rooted as a British Protestant institution.

Recent scholarship points out, quite rightly, that the term 'British' involves more than a narrow English identity. Citing the many regional and ethnic distinctions in the United Kingdom, James Loughlin notes that the term British can 'imply diversity no less than uniformity.'[13] In this context of diverse British identity, one should also include the empire's dominions. Canadian Orangemen, for example, saw themselves as thoroughly British, whether they were of Irish Protestant, American Loyalist, or English heritage.

The social stratification of the Orange Order reflected a cross section of Protestant Canadian society. Men from all walks of life and every profession joined the organization. In rural areas, farmers, clergy, and local merchants all engaged in the social and ritual activities offered by the local lodge. In urban areas, labourers, businessmen, physicians, lawyers, and politicians mingled as members of a social institution that sent down roots in every province.[14] By the early twentieth century, the Loyal Orange Association in Canada claimed well over 200,000 members, with Ontario West alone boasting 150,000.[15]

The Canadian Orange Order enabled members of the various Protestant denominations to band together to impede Catholic advancements in settlement and/or employment. This tradition, which harkened back to Ireland, was easily replicated in North America, where French and Irish Catholics were widely viewed as disloyal to the Crown by virtue of their faith. As one historian notes: 'The belief that Roman Catholicism was incompatible with British nationality was one that would find expression well into the twentieth century.'[16]

Although the Order may have adapted to a new setting in North America with a more varied ethnic membership and a number of lodges declaring themselves 'benefit' or temperance lodges, the actions and proclamations of the Orange Order in Canada largely mirrored the intolerance and bigotry of its Irish counterpart. One of the main goals of the Orange Association in Canada 'was to maintain Protestant domination in North America, and keep the colonies [Canadian provinces] firmly rooted in the British Empire.'[17] To achieve these goals, a garrison network of lodges was established across Canada, most heavily in New Brunswick and Ontario, in order to halt the spread of French Catholicism and Irish-Catholic immigration. In this way the Order put in place a 'Protestant barrier against the dissemination of a Catholic culture.'[18] One of the Order's rallying cries in Canada was 'One School, One Flag, and One Language.'[19] The Order looked to British institutions, and *only* British institutions, as the appropriate models for Canadian development, be these cultural, commercial, or political. In this context, the Canadian Orange Order undermined any sense that French Canadians, or Catholics generally, could contribute to society. The Order was even to a large extent xenophobic.[20] For the Orange Order, issues such a separate schools, immigration policy, and the marriage laws became matters of the utmost importance. In this respect the Orange Order in Canada was a nativist institution primarily concerned with issues germane to Canada. Nonetheless, Canadian Orangemen were also ardent imperialists, keenly aware of issues relating to the empire.

The term *imperialism*, in the context of Canadian history, does not convey an image of advanced industrialized countries plundering and subjugating less-developed nations, all under the guise of missionary benevolence. Rather, Canadian imperialists favoured a 'closer union of the British Empire through economic and military co-operation and through political changes which would give the dominions influence over imperial policy.'[21] Noted historian Carl Berger adds that imperialism was a form of English-Canadian nationalism.[22] Most English – or more accurately British – Canadians expressed their nationalism through an almost devout reverence for British institutions and the British tradition in Canadian society. Along with members of the British Empire League and the Imperial Federation League, Canadian Orangemen were among the most enthusiastic promoters of stronger ties with the empire. Berger asserts that 'the Orange Order ... provided some of the most vociferous advocates of imperial unity,' and in true Orange fashion, 'it often appeared that to the motto of one race, one flag, one throne, they wanted to add, one religion.'[23] Not surprisingly, Canadian Orangemen were intensely opposed to any alteration to the British imperial structure which tended to loosen rather than strengthen those imperial ties. The third Irish Home Rule Bill proposed just that – to loosen the imperial structure by conferring on Ireland a limited form of self-government.

One of the few works that examines the Orange-Canadian reaction to the proposed Irish Home Rule legislation of 1912 is Philip Currie's article on Toronto Orangemen. Unfortunately, Currie's approach and analysis are limited to placing the Order's opposition to Home Rule in the proper historical context. Currie writes that the nature of Orange-Canadian opposition to Home Rule 'can only be understood in the context of Canadian politics, and the emergence of a new consciousness in English Canada in the years between the South African conflict [Boer War] and the First World War.'[24] Currie correctly argues that Irish nationalists were not the only North Americans who 'expressed an interest in the political affairs of Ireland': 'Toronto Orangemen disapproved of Irish Home Rule. It would have been an odd thing if they had not. What is notable is the extent and nature of that opposition after 1911, and what this suggests about the Order, Toronto, and many English Canadians generally in the years immediately preceding the Great War. In these years there was an intensity to the anti-Home Rule campaign that was not evident a generation before.'[25]

Currie asserts that Canadian Orangemen had been opposed to the two Irish Home Rule Bills of 1886 and 1893. Why, though, was there more intense opposition to the 1912 legislation? His work never answers this question, nor does it examine the 'extent and nature of that opposition.'

Although Currie does concede that the 'nature of the Order's concern was *influenced* by the ethnic origins of Canadian Orangeism,' he gives no real explanation for Orange-Canadian opposition to Irish Home Rule.[26] In striving to put Orange-Canadian opposition to Home Rule in the proper historical context, Currie leads the reader to believe that opposition to Home Rule arose simply as a result of general resentment over the way Canadian national interests were constantly being overlooked by British statesmen in various negotiations with the United States. Yet was this the reason for Orange-Canadian resistance to Irish Home Rule? Resentment of British statesmen was merely an additional factor, not the primary one, in Orange-Canadian opposition to Home Rule. Canadian Orangemen opposed Irish Home Rule for more personal, even visceral, reasons. Canadian Orangemen, by and large, felt an ethnic/familial connection to, and empathy with, Irish Protestants in their struggle to resist the perceived Irish-Catholic onslaught that threatened their place in British society. Orange-Canadian opposition to Home Rule echoed the same ethno-religious arguments offered by their Irish Protestant brethren in the old country.

Simply put, Irish unionists were those who wished to maintain the union between Ireland and Britain that had been established in 1801. In the early nineteenth century, Unionism had attracted many adherents. Unionism brought together not only northern and southern Protestants but also people of various denominations and socio-economic backgrounds. Under the Unionist political banner one might find southern landed gentry, northern Presbyterian bourgeoisie, commercial magnates, and Orange labourers.[27] As historian Alvin Jackson notes, Unionist history was one of 'retreat and retrenchment.'[28] Irish Unionism gradually lost its support and receded back to its stronghold in northeastern Ulster. By the time of the Third Home Rule Bill (1912), the most loyal adherents to the Unionist cause were the Ulster Unionists in the northeastern corner of Ulster.

The idea of Irish self-government was anathema to Ulster unionists, whose 'infuriated reaction to the threat of home rule unleashed violence into twentieth-century Irish politics.'[29] Irish Protestants constituted only 25 per cent of Ireland's population and were clustered largely in the northeast. Irish and Ulster unionists were adamantly opposed to the 1912 bill for numerous reasons, not the least of which was the strong likelihood that it would pass.

Unlike the two previous Home Rule Bills, which had been vetoed in the House of Lords (1886) or voted down in the House of Commons (1893), this Home Rule Bill was likely to become law. The 1911 British parliamentary election had been fought largely over the issue of the House of Lords' veto power. The Liberals, who needed the support of the Irish Parliamentary Party (IPP) to form a majority, passed the Parliament Act of 1911, which ended the Lords' power to veto the will of the majority as represented in the House of Commons. From that point on, the Lords could only suspend a bill for two years. Furthermore, any bill that passed in three successive sessions of the House of Commons would become law. So when the Irish Home Rule Bill was introduced in 1912, assuming it passed twice, it would become law in 1914. The end to this long-standing impediment to Irish nationalist ambitions was not lost on Irish Unionists, nor on their Canadian supporters, who anticipated that in return for providing Herbert Asquith's Liberal government with a parliamentary majority, the Irish Parliamentary Party (IPP) would demand home rule for Ireland. The prospect of being ruled by a parliament in Dublin strongly dominated by Catholics was, to say the least, highly objectionable to Irish Unionists, particularly the Ulster Unionists, who were the political voice of the Ulster Protestants. Ulster Unionists immediately prepared to thwart any movement toward establishing a Home Rule parliament in Ireland.

Ulster unionist opposition to Home Rule was organized and led by the wealthiest and most elite Protestants in Ulster society. The two most prominent figures in that opposition were Sir Edward Carson and Captain Sir James Craig. Edward Carson, an Orangeman and an Anglican Dubliner, was educated at Trinity College Dublin, was a successful barrister, a former Solicitor General for Ireland, and a Westminster MP. Carson was possibly best known for his devastating prosecution of playwright Oscar Wilde.[30] Captain Sir James Craig was a millionaire whiskey distiller, an MP, and an Orange Grand Master for County Down and had served with distinction as a British officer in the Boer War.[31] In 1911, Carson and Craig resurrected the Ulster Unionist Council, which was essentially an executive coordinating committee comprised of 200 members: 100 nominated from Unionist political clubs, 50 from the Grand Orange Lodges, and 50 from among MPs and peers. The council tasked itself with drafting a constitution in order to establish a provisional government to defend Protestant interests in the event that a parliament was founded in Dublin.[32]

In their endeavour to thwart Home Rule, the Ulster Unionists were wholeheartedly supported by the British Conservative Party.[33] The Conservatives were led by Andrew Bonar Law, a Canadian of Ulster descent, whose father – a Presbyterian minister – moved the family back to Ulster when Bonar Law was a young boy. Bonar Law nurtured a profound personal commitment to Ulster.[34] He made no secret of being an ultra-Unionist, and through his caustic and inflammatory rhetoric, particularly in the House of Commons, the Conservatives brought to that body a 'new style' of invective exchange seldom seen in the past.[35] Conservatives and Unionists alike railed against the supposed conspiracy between the Liberals and the IPP, repeatedly declaring that the British Empire would crumble if Ireland were set free, though it was not to be endowed with complete independence, for that was not the Liberals' goal. The Conservative–Unionist alliance stood as a formidable obstacle to the implementation of Home Rule.

On a more fundamental and indeed visceral level, Irish Protestants opposed Home Rule as a matter of racial (ethnic) distinction. The vast majority of Ulster Protestants were descendants of the seventeenth-century English and Scottish settlers who confiscated the best lands in Ireland and who had secured better employment opportunities by virtue of their connections to the English Crown. In the eighteenth century, in part by virtue of a penal code inflicted on Catholics, Protestants consolidated their ascendant privilege, which remained intact until threatened by Home Rule. Notwithstanding occasional differences among the Protestant denominations – Anglican, Presbyterian, Methodist, Baptist – when confronted with the prospect of organized Catholic encroachment on their established rights, the Protestants would band together, usually under the banner of the Orange Order. In the early twentieth century, Ulster Protestants believed themselves to be both racially distinct from and superior to Irish Catholics. As in Canada, religion was an integral part of everyday life and served as a constant reminder of distinctiveness. Historian Joseph Lee brilliantly captures these sentiments:

> Their own peculiar institution, the Orange Order, which included two thirds of adult Protestant males [in Ulster], fostered a sense of community among Protestants and institutionalized the instinct of racial superiority over the conquered Catholics ... Race and religion were inextricably intertwined in Ulster unionist consciousness. Unionists could not rely on the criterion of colour, for Catholics lacked the imagination to go off-white, nor on the criterion of language, for Catholics had unsportingly abandoned their own. It was therefore imperative to sustain Protestantism as the symbol of racial superiority.[36]

Ulster Protestants believed they were correct in feeling superior to Catholics – that it was only 'natural that they should dominate Catholics ... To be dominated by them [in a home rule parliament] would be a perversion of nature.'[37] Belief in the superiority of certain races and the inferiority of others held considerable sway not only in Ireland but in Britain, Canada, the United States, and Europe as well.[38] Thomas Kennedy asserts that 'ideas about the importance of race and its effect on character as well as history retained considerable power at the beginning of the twentieth century.'[39]

Although Sir Edward Carson seldom resorted to arguments of racial inferiority in his public statements against Home Rule, he seems to have fully believed 'that the Celtic race in Ireland was an inferior element in the population.'[40] Writing to Sir John Marriott, he asserted: 'The Celts have done nothing in Ireland but create trouble and disorder. Irishmen who have turned out successful are not in any case that I know of true Celtic origin.'[41] This staunch belief in Catholic inferiority was perpetuated by Canadian Orangemen, as were images of Irish Catholics as dirty and lazy.

Coupled with the self-image of superiority held by Irish Protestants was the image of native Catholics as a feckless and inferior lot. Irish Catholics were seen as dirty, lazy, drunken, and untrustworthy 'bog trotters,' incapable of self-improvement, and without question incapable of governing themselves.[42] In Irish-Protestant eyes, any Irish-Catholic parliament was doomed to fail. By 1912, attitudes had changed little if at all since 1886, when the *Belfast Newsletter* declared that an Irish parliament 'would be the laughing stock of the civilized world.'[43] Significantly, though, Ulster Unionist and Orange-Canadian opposition to Irish Home Rule was not solely confined to matters of religious differences and racial distinctions.

Ulster Unionists also opposed Irish Home Rule for fear it would jeopardize their material prosperity. For them, Ulster unionist concerns over the future economic viability of their province under a Home Rule parliament were equally as critical as issues of racial distinctions. During the nineteenth century, the development of vast shipyards, linen mills, rope factories, tobacco manufacturers, and distilleries made Ulster, and specifically Belfast, one of the most important industrial centres in Britain.[44] Wealthy unionists feared losing everything they built under a Home Rule Irish parliament, which inevitably would be controlled by men whom they believed lacked sufficient business acumen to manage a country. Political historian Paul Bew writes that the 'religious-ideological gulf between the two communities had its counterpart in a material-economic one ... There is no question, for example, that economic factors played a key role in the generation of unionist opposition to home rule.'[45] Ulster unionists continually declared that economic ruin would befall Ulster if Westminster established a Home Rule parliament in Dublin. For this argument they found a sympathetic ear not only among British Conservatives, but also in Canada.

The 1912 *Canadian Annual Review of Public Affairs* noted that Canadians were well apprised of the proposed Irish Home Rule legislation: 'The Home Rule controversy of this year evoked many Parliamentary and political references in Great Britain to Canada's constitution and condition while it aroused some discussion also in Canada.'[46] In 1912 the Home Rule issue indeed 'aroused some discussion' in Canada, but many undoubtedly felt that the issue would somehow find a political solution. During 1913 and 1914, Canadian Orangemen became active participants in the escalating crisis. Meanwhile, Canadian Orangemen adopted and disseminated many of the same arguments against Home Rule as were being put forward by their Irish coreligionists: Irish independence threatened to weaken the Empire; Protestants would be deprived of their civil and religious liberties as a minority in a Catholic country dominated by Rome; business in Belfast would suffer if controlled by inept Catholic parliamentarians; the Irish were incapable of governing themselves; and a political conspiracy between the Liberals and the IPP brought about this corrupt Home Rule bargain. In this respect, Canadian Orangemen served as a North American sounding board for the vitriol of Ulster Unionist leaders and as a counterweight to Irish nationalism in the United States.

Those issues of greatest importance to Canadian Orangemen were expressed clearly in the Grand Master's address to the 1912 annual meeting of the Provincial Grand Orange Lodge of Ontario West, held in London, Ontario. This meeting was held a month before the Irish Home Rule legislation was to be introduced in the British House of Commons, and the issue had already assumed a prominent place in Orange-Canadian consciousness. Grand Master Harry Lovelock stated:

> The past year has been one of much unrest throughout our Province [Ontario], and indeed the whole Dominion, and our Order has been actively engaged combating such questions as the marriage question, the bi-lingual school situation, and the Home Rule problem in the Old Land, in which so many of our brethren in Canada are so deeply interested.

Lovelock included the Home Rule problem 'in the Old Land' as a prominent issue for Canadian Orangemen. Specifically addressing the Home Rule question, he continued:

> As your Grand Master I feel that I voice the sentiments of this Grand Lodge when I say that our brethren in the Old Land have our undying sympathy in their efforts to prevent the passage of a Home Rule bill for Ireland, and that our hopes and prayers are being exercised on their behalf, and if need be, our personal and financial assistance. The very soil of Ireland is sacred to us because of the traditions of the past. Not only is it consistent for Irish Orangemen and Protestants to oppose Home Rule,

but it is consistent for Orangemen and Protestants of every nationality, because the passage of that bill means ultimately being ruled from the Tiber instead of the Thames.[47]

At the 1912 annual meeting of the Grand Orange Lodge of New Brunswick, Grand Master the Reverend Byron H. Thomas expressed similar sentiments when referring to Irish Home Rule. He emphasized that if Home Rule were granted to Ireland, the country would eventually be dominated by the Catholic Church:

> Your Grand Master puts himself on record as being in every sense of the word opposed to the proposal to give home rule to Ireland. Home Rule means Rome rule. Too much of that thing is in evidence in the British Empire already ... Home Rule is the battle cry of the Jesuits, who are determined in every conceivable way to strengthen the hands of the hierarchial system, and make the church of Rome supreme.[48]

Through these expressions of sympathy with Irish Unionists, made by their elected leaders, Canadian Orangemen demonstrated the importance they placed on the Home Rule issue. In so doing, they also emphasized that Canadian Orangemen believed the Home Rule issue to be most significantly, for them, a religious issue. These statements also exemplify the extent to which Orangemen kep themselves well versed on events in Ireland. They did so by reading not only the commercial daily newspapers but also their own official organ, the *Sentinel and Orange and Protestant Advocate*, a weekly published in Toronto.

On 11 April 1912 the *Orange Sentinel* reported that two days previously the Ulster Unionists held a rally at Balmoral, an estate outside Belfast, to denounce Home Rule. As the Conservative leader Andrew Bonar Law arrived, 80,000 Ulster Orangemen greeted him with raucous cheers, waving Union Jacks. Ascending the podium, Bonar Law railed that he had 'come here to give you the assurance that we Unionists regard your cause as the cause of the Empire. We will do all that men can do to defeat a conspiracy as treacherous as any that has ever been formed against the life of a great nation ... If we defeat Home Rule now it will be defeated forever.'[49] On 27 July another monster rally gathered outside Belfast, at Blenheim Place, where Bonar Law declared that he knew of 'no length to which the Ulster Unionists would go' in which he would relinquish his support.[50] In essence, Bonar Law, the leader of His Majesty's loyal opposition in the House of Commons, gave the Ulster Orangemen sanction to resist the will of the British Parliament – by force of arms if necessary.

On 29 September 1912, Carson and his colleagues orchestrated an even larger event, one of astonishing proportions, and Canadian Orangemen were kept well abreast of every development. Invoking the memory of the sixteenth-century Scottish Covenanters, Edward Carson and Sir James Craig gathered with other MPs, peers, Protestant church leaders, and average unionist citizens at City Hall in Belfast to sign the Solemn League and Covenant. Additional signing ceremonies took place simultaneously across Ulster, after which Protestant religious services were held. The Covenant was a pledge by Ulster men and women to resist the establishment of an Irish parliament. Many, including Lord Londonderry, signed their names in their own blood. Throughout Ulster, more than 447,000 men and women signed the Covenant, which repudiated Parliament's authority to place them under the control of a Dublin Parliament.[51] The language of the Covenant starkly expressed the religious and material concerns of the Unionists, and also provides a fine example of the inherent contradictions of Ulster Unionism: proclaiming loyalty to the Crown while resisting the lawfully introduced legislation of the King's Parliament. The Covenant read:

> Being convinced in our conscience that Home Rule would be disastrous to the material well-being of Ulster as well as the whole of Ireland, subversive of our civil and religious freedom, destructive of our citizenship and perilous to the unity of the Empire, we, whose names are underwritten, men of Ulster, loyal subjects of His Gracious Majesty King George V, humbly relying on the God whom our fathers in days of stress and trial confidently trusted, do hereby pledge ourselves in solemn covenant throughout this time of threatened calamity to stand by one another in defending for ourselves and our children our cherished position of equal citizenship in the United Kingdom, and in using all means which may be found necessary to defeat the present conspiracy to set up a Home Rule Parliament in Ireland. And in the event of such a parliament being forced upon us we further solemnly and mutually pledge ourselves to refuse to recognize its authority ... God save the king.[52]

The *Orange Sentinel* reported in depth on the Covenant signing, noting that in every industrial and farming centre of Unionist Ulster 'a miniature replica of Belfast' was in place, complete with signing ceremonies. The *Orange Sentinel* referred to the official signing ceremony in Belfast as 'the patriotic meeting' and described it as taking place in an atmosphere of jubilation, which lasted long after midnight.[53]

Within days of the signing of the Solemn League and Covenant in Belfast, an anti-Home Rule rally was held in Toronto to honour the visiting Walter Long, MP. The *Orange Sentinel* pointed out that although Toronto Orangemen fully opposed Home Rule, the gathering was not held under their auspices, but was rather 'an assemblage of Protestants opposed to Home Rule.'[54] Nevertheless, the Orange presence was quite evident. Shortly before the rally began, '1,000 Orangemen from the Western District' arrived, complete with fife and drum corps, having marched from their lodges. The turnout for this rally at Massey Hall was so overwhelming that an overflow rally assembled at Victoria Hall. At the Massey Hall rally, many prominent Canadian citizens were seated on the platform with Walter Long. They included the staunch Canadian imperialists Col. George Taylor Denison, a founder of the Canada First movement; Col. George Sterling Ryerson (neither Denison nor Sterling was an Orangeman); the Toronto City Controller, H.C. Hocken; Canadian MP T.G. Wallace; Member of the Ontario Provincial Parliament, T.R. Whiteside; three Toronto aldermen; and 'numerous other clergymen and leading citizens.'[55] As in Ulster, the leaders of the Canadian opposition to Irish Home Rule were prominent citizens.[56] The rally, which unfolded without incident, indicated the public opposition to Irish Home Rule that existed in Canada, particularly in Ontario.

At their annual meetings, both provincial and national, Canadian Orangemen repeatedly referred to Irish Home Rule as an issue of the utmost importance, emphasizing the commonality of the ethno-religious struggles in Canada and Ulster. On 12 March 1913, in Windsor, Ontario, at the annual meeting of the Grand Orange Lodge of Ontario West, Grand Master Fred Dane spoke eloquently on numerous issues of great importance to Ontario Orangemen: French separate schools in Ontario; the Borden government's Canadian naval bill, which was intended to help support the British fleet by providing Canada with its own navy to protect its own coasts; and the need to maintain the unity and integrity of the British Empire. But he also spoke about the situation in Ireland in such a way as to leave little doubt of the intense emotional connection many Canadians felt toward Ireland. He spoke of his visit to the north of Ireland the previous year, noting that thirty years had elapsed since he 'last had the pleasure of celebrating the 12th of July in the city of my birth [Belfast].'.[57] He then spoke in stirring terms about the political developments in Ireland:

This Right Worshipful Grand Lodge has gone on record before, and I feel convinced it has not in the least changed its view, and still dreads the handing over of a loyal minority to the tender mercy of a disloyal majority ...

I am convinced that the Government of Ireland by a Home Rule Parliament would certainly lead to bitter racial and sectarian strife, be a lasting injury to its commerce and industries, would involve ruin to civil and religious liberties, and would be the first step in the disintegration of the great Empire to the building up of which Irishmen, and in no small degree the descendants of the Ulster plantation, have contributed their full share.

He closed his address with an Ulster poem:

> They live in peace when left alone,
>   And honest toil pursue,
> They earn their money, and pay their debts,
>   As honest men still do.
> They don't believe in dynamite,
>   Or with assassins join;
> The right they claim their fathers won
>   At Derry, and the Boyne.[58]

Fred Dane no doubt felt a deep sense of ethnic and familial connection to Ireland, and as such was elected by the members of Ontario West to represent them as their Grand Master. For Fred Dane, an Ulster Canadian, supporting the Ulster Unionist cause was an integral part of being a Canadian Orangeman, viewing as he did the fight in Ulster and in Canada as a single unified struggle against Catholic encroachment.

The Grand Orange Lodge of British America, the most exalted lodge in the Dominion, expressed the same sentiments on these issues when it met in annual session at the British Hall in St John's, Newfoundland. Grand Master Col. James H. Scott voiced his strong approval of a Canadian contribution to the British navy; his dissatisfaction with Papal edicts on marriage, which proclaimed that the children of mixed marriages – between a Protestant and a Catholic – were automatically to be raised Catholic; and his desire for a single school system. As well, he commented on the escalating Home Rule crisis in Ireland, recommending 'that a suitable expression of the sentiments of the brethren present be spread upon our records and forwarded to the Provincial Grand Lodge of Ulster and to the Right Hon. Sir Edward Carson, the valiant leader of the Irish Unionists party, and defender of the rights of the loyalists of Ireland.'[59] The committee brought forth its *Report of the Special Committee re Home Rule*, which stated:

> We, the Orangemen of Canada and Newfoundland, assembled in the 84th annual assembly, representing every city, town and village throughout British North America, desire to place on record and assure our Orange brethren and Protestant people of Ireland that we view with alarm the proposal to grant Home Rule to Ireland, believing that the foundations of the Empire will be weakened, if not entirely undermined, if this obnoxious measure is put into effect.
>
> We believe that this is not just a measure affecting Ireland, but the whole British Empire throughout the world, and that the Battle of the Boyne is being fought over again by the Protestants of Ireland ...
>
> Resolved – That this Most Worshipful Grand Orange Lodge of British America places itself upon record as being unalterably opposed to the coercion of our brethren in Ulster to submit to a Parliament in College Green [Dublin], and we hereby pledge active support to our brethren in their struggle for civil and religious liberty. Their battle will be our battle to maintain the integrity of the British Empire and in withstanding the onslaught of the Papacy upon Protestant Ulster.[60]

Copies of the resolution were sent to the British cabinet, the Leader of the Opposition, the Right Honouable Sir Edward Carson, and the Grand Masters of Ireland and Belfast. Canadian Orange leaders made certain that the British political establishment understood that they 'actively' and wholeheartedly supported their Irish brethren in opposing Home Rule for Ireland.

In a similar vein, the *Orange Sentinel* editorial of 12 June encapsulated the situation in Ulster and expressed the sentiments of Orange Canadians:

> There is every reason to believe that the Protestants of Ulster are preparing to forcibly resist the authority of the proposed Irish parliament. They are determined people who know how to fight and how to die, and may yet show that there is just as much to be feared by British governments as that of the Fenians and disloyalists who have imposed their will on the Asquith ministry ... We have too much admiration for our own race, to believe that Britishers will cowardly insure their own security by throwing their sturdiest champions to Redmond's wolves ...
>
> It is difficult for persons who have never lived in Ireland to appreciate

the bitterness of racial and religious differences in that country, a bitterness so intense after centuries of clashing as to make it unwise to give either side complete control over the other. Yet we believe we do not exaggerate when we say that even in Canada the people of Ontario would shed blood rather than submit to any new arrangement of the provinces that would put them under the control of the people of Quebec. If that is true here, with comparative good-will between all races and creeds, can any wonder be felt that Ulstermen who have been persecuted for centuries in spite of British protection, should resist a proposal to leave them absolutely at the mercy of their traditional enemies.[61]

In stating that they had too much 'admiration for *our own race* [my emphasis]' to envision Britishers sacrificing Ulster Protestants to the disloyal Irish Catholics, the official organ of Canadian Orangemen spoke for the vast majority of Orangemen, who possessed similar beliefs as the Ulster Unionists. As British Canadians, the Orangemen identified themselves as being ethnically distinct from the purportedly disloyal and untrustworthy Irish Catholics, or even French Canadians. The same editorial intimated that most Ontarians would rather fight and die than be placed in a subservient position to French Canadians. These were telling statements of the fractious nature of Canadian society in the early twentieth century. Moreover, these themes of ethnic and religious distinctiveness, loyalty and disloyalty, and subjugation would constantly be revisited by Orange Canadians throughout the Irish revolutionary period. As the editorial indicated, the Protestants of Ulster were indeed moving toward forcible resistance to a Home Rule parliament.

For two years, Carson, Craig, and the leading men of Ulster had seen to it that Protestant interests would, if necessary, be forcibly defended.[62] In January 1913, word spread that the Ulster Unionists had established and were training their own paramilitary organization. The Ulster Volunteer Force (UVF) was manned almost exclusively by Ulster Orangemen and was commanded – at least nominally – by retired General Sir George Richardson, who achieved fame in Africa at Wazari and in the Zhol Valley and who had led a cavalry brigade against the Boxer Rebellion. Although Richardson's command was bestowed largely for propaganda purposes, the UVF drilled in deadly earnest. Initially, the men were ill equipped, some practising with wooden rifles, but preparations were under way to remedy those inadequacies. By late 1913 the UVF was able to boast 100,00 members, and they would soon be a well-armed, well-equipped force ready to resist the lawful will of the British Parliament.[63] The emergence of the UVF at first seemed farcical, and the Asquith government simply dismissed these demonstrations of bluff and bluster as further examples of Ulster bravado. Yet the Belfast Police Commissioner acknowledged that while the leaders might be bluffing, it was 'impossible to doubt the fanaticism and determination of the rank and file.'[64] Orange Canadians supported the creation of the UVF and viewed their stance as the latest incarnation of the Battle of the Boyne.

In early March 1914 the Asquith government announced a compromise position to break the Ulster deadlock. Asquith proposed that any county that wanted to could vote itself out of the Irish parliament for a period of six years. This would be long enough to ensure that at least one if not two elections would be held, thereby giving the people of Britain a chance to voice their opinion on Home Rule. The *Orange Sentinel* was indignant that such an offer was even proposed, and asked, 'How could Ulster Protestants accept such an offer and be true to their comrades on other parts of the island?'[65] The *Sentinel* believed there were 'two irreconcilable forces in Ireland' and that only a 'madman persist that one of these irreconcilable forces should accept the domination of the other.' According to the *Sentinel*, the best system was the one already in place, with a third party – namely, Britain – in charge of the administration of Ireland.[66] In the event, these protests were rendered moot: Sir Edward Carson rejected the proposal, stating that 'we do not want a sentence of death with a stay of execution of six years.'[67] Significantly, the notion of county exclusion from Home Rule had been put forward by a standing government. Later that month the Irish question was further complicated when British officers in Ireland seemingly refused orders to move against Ulster. The events surrounding the Curragh Mutiny, as it became known, were as confusing as they were intriguing. After Carson rejected the six-year county exclusion option, the Asquith government felt compelled to secure its position in Ulster, especially in light of the growing strength of the UVF. Fearing that the UVF might take steps to acquire weapons, on 14 March the Secretary of War, Col. J.E.B. Seely, ordered British troops in Ireland north to secure the weapons depots at Armagh, Omagh, Carrickfergus, and Enniskillen, four strategic points in Ulster.[68] Unbeknownst to the Asquith government, Ulster Unionist leaders were already aware of this intended action: Major General Henry Wilson, Director of Military Operations at the War Office and a staunch Unionist from a well-to-do Protestant family from County Longford, had told Bonar Law and Sir Edward Carson the entire plan days before over dinner.[69]

Keenly aware of how provocative these moves might seem to the Ulster Unionists, and equally aware of how many British officers serving in Ireland were of Ulster heritage, the government decided that any officer who resided in Ulster would be permitted to 'disappear' while the northward movement of troops was under way.[70] Unfortunately for the Asquith government, the Commander-in-Chief of Ireland was the rather inept General Sir Arthur Paget, who confused his instructions and misinformed his subordinates of the intended course of action. Paget informed his officers they had been ordered to attack and secure Ulster or resign their commissions and go home. As a result, fifty-five officers of the Third Calvary Brigade at the Curragh camp in County Kildare, led by General Sir Herbert Gough and his three colonels, resigned their commissions rather than move against loyalist Ulster. Then Secretary Seely, in an equally inept manoeuvre, assured the officers that they would not lose their commissions and that they would not have to 'enforce the present Home Rule Bill in Ulster.'[71] The Asquith government retracted the pledge made by Seely, but by then it was too late: the Asquith government appeared as if it were not even in control of its own military.

In Canada, the *Orange Sentinel* reported these events with near glee, announcing that 'Seventy out of Seventy-six Officers at One Camp Sent in Their Resignations.'[72] Extreme exaggeration characterized the article filed from Belfast on 24 March, which read: 'Troops from the Curragh and a number of other centres were ordered north, and officers elsewhere were required to give an assurance that they would fight against Irish Protestants.' The *Orange Sentinel* portrayed the Asquith government as humiliated having to back down in the face of a mutiny 'in the military and naval forces.' The *Orange Sentinel* also reported that the Ulster Provisional Government was prepared to take over the region if the British government made 'any movements toward coercion.' Sir Edward Carson declared: 'The Government is attempting to cow Ulster by intimidation and provocation, but both will fail.'[73] As far as Canadian Orangemen knew, Carson and his cohorts were fully prepared to establish their own government in Ulster and defy the rule of law rather than submit to Irish Home Rule.

Shortly thereafter, the *Orange Sentinel* announced with near hysteria that the empire was on the verge of civil war. To Canadian readers, it must have appeared as if war would break out in Ireland at any moment:

> The empire is on the brink. Any moment it may be plunged into the abyss of civil strife, and Briton be found shedding the blood of brother Briton ...
>
> When the Irish situation is considered on its merits, no valid argument against the exclusion of Ulster is found. To say that it does not require the Irish Protestants to concede anything is absurd: they are required to abandon their fellows in other provinces to the mercy of an intolerant people, a sacrifice for the good of the empire for which the British ministers must accept responsibility ...
>
> Men do not risk their lives and neglect their business as Ulstermen are doing for the sake of a [political] party, but because they believe their rights and liberties, their faith and their social environment will be disastrously affected. And when a million people feel as intensely as the Ulstermen do, it is a criminal act to attempt coercion.[74]

The *Orange Sentinel*, the voice of Canadian Orangemen, was now demanding 'the exclusion of Ulster.' Carson had originally rejected the six-year 'stay of execution'; now he was demanding the permanent exclusion from Home Rule of all nine Ulster counties, while leaking word that he would settle for the permanent exclusion of the six easternmost counties. This plan of a six-county exclusion had been agreed to by Carson and his colleagues and the British cabinet late in 1913.[75] Apparently, Orange Canadians were beginning to accept that Ulster's exclusion from Home Rule was the only way to resolve the impasse. News then arrived in Canada indicating that the Ulster unionists dramatically altered the Irish crisis.

On April 25, 1914, an explosive news dispatch arrived from Belfast. It indicated that a 'sensation was caused by the landing of 40,000 rifles and 500,000 rifles [rounds] at Ulster ports tonight.'[76] Over the previous two years, arms had been smuggled cautiously into Ulster, but rarely more than 100 at a time. Now, in an act of bluster and bravado aided by sheer luck, the UVF landed 35,000 rifles and 3,000,000 rounds of ammunition from Germany at three Ulster ports – Larne, Bangor, and Donaghadee.[77] Nearly two-thirds of all the cars in Ulster were used in a well-executed operation to disperse the weapons throughout the province. Some may argue that this episode of gun running might have transpired quite differently had local police chosen to leave their barracks that night. Ulster Protestant unwillingness to live cooperatively with their Catholic neighbours now took on a militaristic intransigence.[78]

The funds to purchase these weapons came from numerous sources. In Ireland, Edward Carson and numerous members of Belfast's business community established the Carson Fund, which included a £1,000,000 indemnity for UVF members.[79] In Britain, Lord Milner, former High Commissioner of South Africa, joined forces with Walter Long's Union Defence League and solicited his wealthy friends for contributions. Among those who contributed money in support of the UVF were Lord Rothschild, Lord Iveagh, and the Duke Of Bedford, each of whom donated £10,000; as well as Waldorf Astor (son of the American millionaire) and Rudyard Kipling, each of whom donated £30,000.[80] Additionally, financial support for the Ulster Unionist cause also came from the dominions. As historian A.T.Q. Stewart notes: 'The [Ulster] expatriates' most valuable contribution was probably their financial aid, which was considerable.'[81] And the greatest contributor among the overseas dominions was unquestionably Canada.

As early as October 1913, an *Orange Sentinel* editorial revealed that Canadian supporters of the Ulster unionist cause were in fact contributing funds to help arm the UVF. The editorial recalled the 'Ulster Will Fight' slogan made famous by Lord Randolph Churchill during the battle over the first Home Rule Bill in 1886, and once again expressed the close emotional connection between Canadian Orangemen and events in the 'Old Land':

> There are thousands of men and women in Canada who believe that 'Ulster will fight' and that 'Ulster will be right' in her resistance to the authority of an Irish parliament. We have ample evidence that men and money from Canada will be available for that struggle. While this is true, we would like to emphasize the desirability of the most careful consideration of every step taken on this side to give encouragement to the Protestants of Ireland. This is no time for bluff or bluster ... They are looking eagerly ... to this Dominion for signs that they will not be left to battle alone for their faith and liberties and the good of the Empire. It would be cruel to delude them with false hopes. For every soldier and nurse Canada offers in case of emergency, two should be forthcoming, and the volunteers should be so seized with the justice of the cause for which they are enrolled that they would be glad to help it at the sacrifice of their property, liberty and lives.[82]

Contributing to an armed resistance against the British Parliament was a fairly dramatic step to take for avowedly loyal British subjects, whether they lived in Ireland or in Canada. Evidently, thousands of people in Canada were willing to contribute to just such a cause, and Canadian Orangemen were prominent among them.

At the 1914 annual meeting of the Grand Orange Lodge of British America, Grand Master Col. James H. Scott indicated that Walter Long had contacted him in the hope of obtaining funds.[83] On Scott's recommendation, that lodge sent $1,000 to what it termed the 'Ulster Fund.' Although this might sound like a modest sum, it should be noted that the Newfoundland Disaster Fund received only $500 and the True Blue Orphanage of Ontario, the Orange Orphanage of Prince Edward Island, and the Orange Orphanage of Nova Scotia received only $100 each.[84] Thus the Ulster Fund, on very short notice, received considerably more money than did some well-established Orange institutions. Throughout 1913 and 1914, Ulster Unionists solicited money from Canadian Orangemen and any other Canadians who supported the Unionists' stance.

Any member of the Canadian Orange Order who regularly read the *Orange Sentinel* was well aware of Walter Long's appeal for funds. The *Sentinel* printed Long's call for funds on its front page of 30 April 1914. In that call, Long stated: 'I have authority from Grand Master of Ireland to appeal to you [Col. Scott, of Walkerton, ON] as Grand Master of Canada for financial help, which he believes you will be good enough to give to the cause of Ulster.'[85] Below the appeal for financial support appeared the following; 'We are sure our readers will gladly do all they can to help in the preservation of the rights and liberties of the Irish Protestants.' Only seven days after this appeal had been written in London, it appeared on the front page of the *Orange Sentinel* in Canada.

Canadian Orangemen immediately responded. Orange lodges contributed to the Ulster unionist cause in whatever amounts they could. The Grand Orange Lodge of British America sent $1,000 for Ulster's defence, and the Grand Orange Lodge of Ontario West sent $500.[86] Local lodges also contributed what they could: '£423 from Toronto loyalists, £100 from Ulster and Loyal Irishman's Society of Victoria ... £100 from Montreal County loyal Orange lodge.'[87] The local Hazeldean Orange Lodge No. 246 diligently sent the following notice to the *Sentinel*: 'At our last regular meeting ... although few members were out, we subscribed about $25 to the Ulster Fund.' The *Sentinel* responded in bold print: WELL DONE, HAZELDEAN![88]

Then in June 1914 an appeal for the Ulster Equipment Fund also appeared in the pages of the *Sentinel*. The Grand Secretary of Ontario East, Bro. F.M. Clarke, sent circulars to every primary county lodge master in the jurisdiction requesting that donations be made by any wishing to contribute to Ulster's cause. The notice stated that it was not intended that 'these subscriptions should be confined to members of the Order, but the lists should be used so as to give any who may be a sympathizer with the Ulster movement a chance to contribute ... as it is not purely an Orange matter but one in which Protestantism is generally interested.' The original letter from Ireland's Imperial Grand Master read in part:

> The manhood of Ulster have displayed a magnificent example to all the world. For two years they have given their time, leisure, and their money preparing themselves for the coming struggle ... We appeal for subscriptions to the Equipment Fund, to enable these men to defend their homes and their rights as citizens of the United Kingdom ...
>
> The rich men of Ulster have already contributed largely to the general funds of the party; the rank and file are prepared to lay down their lives if necessary in the cause of the Union. Each person should carefully consider how much of this world's goods he is prepared to sacrifice to oppose Home Rule, and give it at once.[89]

There can be little doubt what types of 'equipment' these funds were to purchase. There were also indications that additional Canadian fundraising networks had been established. When the *Orange Sentinel* reported in bold letters that the **Grand Black Chapter Voted $2,000 to Ulster**, it also noted that the money would be forwarded to the Canadian Unionist League (CUL) office in Belfast. The statement read: 'Regina, May 26 – Expressing approval of the course pursued by the Protestants in Ulster, the Grand Black Chapter of British North America, in session here to-day, passed a vote of $2,000, which will be forwarded to the Canadian Unionist League in Belfast.'[90]

On 18 May the Toronto Unionist League forwarded $1,500 as an 'expression of their sympathy with the Unionists of Ireland.'[91] The *Orange Sentinel* also received individual contributions directly, and notified readers that such remittances should be sent to the CUL's treasurer in Toronto.[92] Supplementing the numerous Orange lodges, Canadian Unionist League branches became conduits of Ulster Unionist fund raising. Although the CUL undoubtedly cooperated with the Orange

Order, those Protestant Canadians not affiliated with the Orange Order who wished to demonstrate their support for the Irish Protestants' struggle could do so by joining or contributing to this indigenous unionist organization. The Canadian Unionist League even maintained an office in Belfast, creating a direct monetary pipeline from Toronto to Belfast. By late summer 1914, Orange-Canadian unionists had contributed more than $100,000 to the UVF's arms-purchasing power of the UVF.[93] In all likelihood, Canadian unionists contributed a sum much larger than this, but as a result of the numerous options for contributing funds directly to the Ulster unionists, an exact figure will never be known.

In a similar vein, the total CUL membership cannot be ascertained, nor can the level of CUL support outside Toronto. Nonetheless, the level of support in and around Toronto was impressive. For example, membership in the CUL was sufficient to include a Ladies Division, with the *Orange Sentinel* continually running announcements of its upcoming meetings.[94] It is possible that CUL branches extended to New Brunswick. At the 1914 annual meeting of the Grand Orange Lodge of New Brunswick, Grand Master William B. Wallace alluded to the CUL in his opening address: 'Unionist leagues have been formed and many established in Canada to assist the Irish Patriots.'[95] Even if CUL branches did not extend beyond Toronto, New Brunswick Orangemen were familiar with that league's existence and purpose. The mere existence of this organization, moreover, indicates that a larger Orange-Canadian unionist community supported the Ulster unionists' cause.

This was made clear in early May 1914 at an anti–Home Rule rally at Queen's Park in Toronto. The *Orange Sentinel* reported that 6,000 men and women from all walks of life, 'including prominent professionals and business men, and men who are leaders in public life,' turned out to protest Home Rule for Ireland.[96] Held under the auspices of the CUL, the rally confirmed the existence of a Canadian unionist community in and around Toronto. Men who arrived wearing Orange Order regalia were asked to remove such items to ensure that the rally was not mistakenly perceived as a purely Orange Order event. The tone of the rally was extremely serious, quite unlike that of the high-spirited Twelfth of July parades. The *Sentinel* reported that many of those attending the rally 'had relatives or friends in the Province [Ulster] that they believed to be threatened with war or persecution.'[97] In an obvious demonstration of Orange solidarity, nearly every man in attendance wore a badge on which a picture of Sir Edward Carson was printed.

Toronto Mayor Horatio Clarence Hocken, a devout Orangeman and fanatical anti-Catholic, led the rally, which included prominent speakers such as W.D. McPherson, an Ontario MPP and future Orange Grand Master of Canada.[98] McPherson asserted: 'Ordinarily, the people of Canada would have no right to interfere in the domestic affairs of the United Kingdom, but there is no part of the Empire which will not be vitally affected by civil war in the Motherland, and that is ample justification for our meeting to-day.'[99] With respect to the Irish Home Rule bill, Orange-Canadian unionists clearly believed they were justified in voicing their opinions in imperial matters.

During the rally, Mayor Hocken read a cable from Sir Edward Carson, which asked: 'We fight against betrayal and for civil and religious liberty. Will Canada help us?' The crowd responded with 'a wild burst of cheering, shouting: "We will; we will," as they waved their hats and countless small flags and banners.'[100] The cheering carried on for several minutes before Mayor Hocken could resume speaking.

At the conclusion of the rally the attendees unanimously endorsed a resolution condemning Home Rule for Ireland. The resolution fully expressed the sentiments of Orange-Canadian unionists and reiterated the Ulster Unionists' arguments against Home Rule:

> That this mass meeting of the citizens of Toronto, [sic] publically assembled and presided over by his worship the Mayor of Toronto, recognize that the peace of Ireland, and indeed the Empire, is in great and imminent peril by reason of the anticipated passage by the Imperial House of Commons of the third reading of the Government of Ireland Bill, and believing that the final enactment of such bill will inevitably lead to extreme dissension in Ireland and disaster to the Empire, the degradation of the citizenship of those citizens of Ulster and the other Provinces opposed to the said bill, and do irreparable injury to their material prosperity and harass them in the exercise of their civil and religious liberty, hereby ENTER OUR MOST EMPHATIC PROTEST AGAINST THE ESTABLISHMENT IN IRELAND OF ANY FORM OF GOVERNMENT DIFFERENT FROM THAT POSSESSED BY THE OTHER COMPONENT PARTS OF THE UNITED KINGDOM, and particularly any institution, legislative or executive, which would mark Ireland as a nationality distinct from Great Britain ...
>
> WE ASSURE OUR LOYAL FELLOW SUBJECTS IN IRELAND OF OUR UNITED AND DETERMINED SUPPORT, BOTH MORAL AND FINANCIAL, in their struggle to maintain their rights of full citizenship under the

flag of the great and glorious British Empire, of which we, as Canadians, are justly proud to form a part.[101]

The resolution exemplified the inconsistency with which Ulster unionists and their Orange-Canadian allies argued their case against Home Rule. Though Canadian unionists repeatedly asserted that they were ethnically distinct from Irish Catholics, they protested the creation of a legislature or executive 'which would mark Ireland as a nationality distinct from Great Britain.' Unionists, be they in Canada or Ulster, argued this incongruous position for one reason: they feared endangering the Irish Protestants' ascendant position of dominance in Ireland. If Ireland were accorded its own legislature, Irish Protestants would find themselves a minority in a state controlled by Catholics. To unionists in Ulster or Canada, this was anathema.

Orange-Canadian unionists, many of whom were Irish Protestant by heritage, felt a deep personal connection to the men and women of Ulster. They shared a common ethnic and religious heritage that was diminished neither by generational nor by oceanic separation. Many Orange-Canadian unionists still had relatives in Ireland, particularly in Ulster. Many of them would have known members of the UVF. Indeed, Canadian unionists were encouraged, through the *Sentinel*, to learn in which regiments of the UVF their relatives served. In May 1914 the *Orange Sentinel* ran an article from Belfast with this caption: 'Special to The Sentinel by "Craigavon."' That article covered the UVF's training exercises and encouraged Ulster Canadians to ask into the activities of this force in their old country.[102] Craigavon in his article declared: 'Protestant Donegal men and women in Canada interested – and who is not? – in the Ulster Volunteer movement in their old country ... The North of Ireland looks with confidence to sons and daughters afar.'[103]

An article the following week, also penned in Belfast by 'Craigavon,' mentioned specific regions in which volunteer operations occurred, and how 'people in Canada now, hailing from the resident districts in Ulster mentioned, will, I know, read with pride and pleasure of the action of their kit and kin.' The article added that some Canadians had actually become volunteers:

> Your readers will be interested to know that Mr. A. Allen, late of the Northwest Mounted Police of Canada, is the company commander [B Company, 2nd Battalion, Armagh Volunteers], and takes a keen interest in this branch of Volunteer work [instruction in the use of a new type of rifle].

Ulster people read with deep pleasure of the great meeting held at Queen's Park, Toronto, presided over by Mayor Hocken, in support of their cause. It has been recorded in all the papers here.[104]

The article further acknowledged that news reports in Belfast of the Queen's Park rally in Toronto aroused 'deep pleasure' among Ulster's Protestants. Craigavon assured Canadian readers that Ulster unionists believed that 'Sir Edward Carson's stirring message to the gathering – "We fight against betrayal and for civil and religious liberty. Will Canada help us?" – will find, we know, a warm response in the Land of the Maple Leaf. May God Defend the Right.'[105] In this passage, James Craig, through the pseudonym 'Craigavon,' implicitly expressed the shared sense of connection and identity, and – most important – a shared sense of struggle among Ulster Unionists and their Orange-Canadian compatriots. If words like these were being penned to evoke a sense of shared ethnic heritage between Ulster Canadians and the old country, they succeeded well. Orange-Canadian unionists in the end contributed hundreds of thousands of dollars to the arming of the UVF, and provided a North American counterweight to Irish nationalist support in the United States.

While the stalemate in Ireland held through the summer of 1914, civil war seemed inevitable. In July, King George V called the parties to Buckingham Palace for a conference to try one final time to hammer out a compromise. A reaffirmation of previous positions was the only result, with Sir Edward Carson and James Craig demanding six-county permanent exclusion from Home Rule, while Herbert Asquith and John Redmond would concede only a six-year exclusion for those counties voting out of Home Rule.[106] As the delegates left London on 24 July, the darkening clouds of war began to engulf Europe in a most horrific struggle, which ultimately served to postpone the Irish Home Rule crisis.

In August 1914, when Britain became ensnared in the widening European conflagration, Ulster unionists and most Irish nationalists pledged to support the British war effort. At last, having stumbled through the Home Rule crisis, and having been outmaneuvered by the Ulster Unionists at every turn, Prime Minister Asquith found an opening. An amending bill was attached to the Home Rule Bill, which, on enactment, would suspend Home Rule for the duration of the war. The amending bill included the provision that Ulster had to be reconciled before the law could be put into effect.[107] Even though the King signed the Home Rule Bill and it was placed on the statute books in late September, it was not implemented, and any attempt at implementation would require the entire subject to be revisited.[108]

Inasmuch as historians such as Paul Bew try to portray Edward Carson as a moderate Unionist, dragged by the militant extremists in the Unionist camp to the brink of armed rebellion against Britain, he, Edward Carson was the recognized leader of Ulster Unionism, and he wilfully beat the Orange drum. Through their speeches, Carson and Bonar Law sanctioned armed rebellion against British institutions and nearly brought the empire to its knees. Carson and his cohorts clearly demonstrated that armed resistance to British legislative initiatives was a legitimate means of attaining political objectives, a tradition continued with great regularity in twentieth-century Irish politics.

Orange-Canadian unionists readily recognized and supported Carson as the leader of the Ulster Unionists and the nominal leader of the Ulster Volunteer Force. In Canada, Carson was hailed as the valiant leader and saviour of Ireland's Protestants, who were threatened with minority status in an Irish Home Rule state.[109] Carson and his colleagues were lauded as the greatest example 'in the world's history ... of patience and self-restraint.' The *Sentinel* opined that over the previous two years 'the Empire owes a debt of gratitude' to Carson and Craig, who 'have so controlled events in Ulster, that a civil war has been averted.'[110] Instead of viewing Carson and his colleagues as intransigent zealots, as did others, Orange-Canadian unionists chose to see them as the saviours of the Empire.

Canadian Orangemen were more than interested spectators during the Home Rule crisis: they were active participants. Through moral and financial support, Orange Canadian unionists wholeheartedly endorsed Ulster Orangemen in their armed resistance to British institutions – a resistance that contradicted all they professed. Orange Canadians' fidelity to their Irish brethren was based not only on a distrust of British politicians, but also on ethnic identification with their Ulster Protestant coreligionists, whom they saw as intrinsically British and Protestant and therefore as superior to Catholics. Orange-Canadian unionists repeatedly declared their unquestioned loyalty to the British Crown, yet their active support of the armed resistance by their Orange brethren in Ireland denoted a loyalty that could be described more accurately as conditional. In the ensuing years, while violence in Ireland escalated dramatically, Orange-Canadian unionists continued to demonstrate greater fidelity to intransigent self-serving Ulster Unionists than to the British institutions to which they professed such devout loyalty.

*Chapter Two*

# Irish-Canadian Nationalists: Home Rulers Once Again, 1912–1914

Having fallen relatively dormant for almost two decades after the fractious split among Irish nationalist politicians over the Charles Stewart Parnell affair, and the subsequent defeat of the second Home Rule Bill in 1893, Irish nationalist impulses in Canada slowly began to resuscitate after the third Irish Home Rule Bill was introduced in the British House of Commons on 11 April 1912. Irish-Canadian nationalists, who were overwhelmingly Catholic, began to enliven themselves at the prospect of their ancestral homeland becoming 'a nation once again.'[1] With the introduction of the bill, the *Catholic Register*, a Catholic weekly in Toronto, proudly but bitterly noted:

> The intense interest aroused all over the English-speaking world by the introduction of a third Home Rule Bill into the British House of Commons, goes to show the large place occupied by Ireland and her sons today, despite all of the disadvantages under which they have been for so long a period struggling towards the light ...
>
> If she [Ireland] succeeds in getting Home Rule all her efforts and her sufferings, down the ages, will be crowned with peace and prosperity.[2]

In a more critical appraisal of the bill's deficiencies, the *New Freeman*, an Irish-Catholic weekly in Saint John, New Brunswick, stated in an unflinching nationalist critique:

> Again, no Home Rule bill will make peace between the two countries [Ireland and England] which does not allow the Irish people to attain their rightful share of the world's wealth through the development of their own natural resources, including among these the natural aptitudes of the peo-

ple for other industries than farming. Nothing short of this will put a stop to the emigration of the young and energetic to the fields where there are no such restrictions upon their energies. However heartily the Irish nation may accept the bill, and hope for great things from it, they will, sooner or later, rebel against its restriction ... It is not a question of opinion here, but of hard fact; and every sort of Irishman, not excepting the Unionists, feels this more or less. A poverty-stricken Ireland, suffering all the miseries which attend uniformity of occupation, is not a spectacle to satisfy either Irishmen at home, or Irishmen of the greater Ireland beyond [the] seas ...

The new Parliament in Dublin, however the English Parliament may try to tie its hands, will make Ireland's discontent more audible to the world and perilous to the British Empire, until it becomes the national legislature of a free and self-governed people.[3]

Though the *New Freeman* criticized the latest Home Rule Bill, which offered Ireland less autonomy than the two previous versions, the paper endorsed the bill, maintaining that John Redmond, leader of the Irish Parliamentary Party (IPP), and 'his associates are right in accepting this half a loaf ... a bill which goes so far toward restoring to Ireland her self-government.'[4]

These editorials, which read as if they were written in Dublin or Galway rather than cities in Canada, were indicative not only of a rejuvenation of Irish-Canadian nationalist spirit, but also of the extent to which many Irish Canadians identified with their ancestral homeland.[5] The vast majority of Irish-Catholic Canadians were descendants of those who fled Ireland during the Potato Famine in the late 1840s, and were thus a number of generations removed from Ireland; yet many of them continued to view British rule in Ireland as an occupation and as the perennial cause of Irish poverty. Additionally, an Irishman (and presumably Irishwoman) remained an Irishman whether living in Ireland or in 'the greater Ireland beyond the seas.' This powerful ethnic identification with Ireland on the part of Irish-Catholic Canadians is obvious in their writings, speeches, and editorials during the Home Rule crisis of 1912–14 and become even more pronounced after 1916.[6] Irish-Catholic Canadians argued that the Irish were not British but rather a distinct ethnicity deserving of national recognition. They also repeatedly countered the arguments put forward by those opposing Irish Home Rule – namely, the Orange Order – that Irish Protestants would be persecuted and denied religious freedom under an Irish parliament. Unlike those in Canada who opposed Irish Home Rule, Irish-Canadian nationalists held few if any large-scale rallies supporting Home Rule between 1912 and 1914. Instead, expressions of support for Irish Home Rule were largely confined to the speeches and resolutions of Irish-Catholic fraternal societies and to the editorial pages of Irish-Catholic Canadian weeklies. Even so, Irish-Canadian nationalists were intensely dedicated to Home Rule for Ireland, just as they had been two decades earlier.

During the debates over the first two Home Rule Bills in the late 1880s and early 1890s, Irish-Canadian nationalists wholeheartedly supported the movement for Irish Home Rule through parliamentary methods. This, had it succeeded, would have bestowed on Ireland a measure of local autonomy similar to that enjoyed by Canadians. Throughout the Irish Home Rule crisis of 1912–14, Irish-Canadian nationalists continued to support the efforts of the IPP and its leader, John Redmond, to achieve self-government for Ireland through appeals to the British sense of justice and fair play. Prior to 1916, unlike many of their Irish-American neighbours and cousins, Irish-Canadian nationalists did not support revolutionary republicanism. But over time, with British Conservatives and Ulster Unionists constantly thwarting Ireland's efforts to achieve Home Rule through constitutional methods, even Irish-Canadian nationalists turned more radical.

Contrary to the assertions of some Canadian historians, who have stated that 'Irish Canadians were totally concerned with Canadian affairs' and that 'Irish nationalism [in Canada] and ethnic separatism gave way to a new appreciation and identification with English Canada and its values,' Irish-Canadian nationalism intensified greatly in Canada during the first quarter of the twentieth century.[7] With each passing year, as efforts to achieve Irish Home Rule through legal means were repeatedly thwarted by Orange obstructionists, Irish-Canadian nationalist verve edged closer toward republicanism.[8] This is not to suggest that Irish-Catholic Canadians had no interest in Canadian issues – quite the contrary – they had dedicated themselves to improving the daily lives of Catholics in Canadian society. Moreover, those leading the Irish nationalist movement in Canada during the first three decades of the twentieth century were far from revolutionaries. Rather, they were typical hard-working Canadians engaged in all manner of employment – insurance managers, solicitors, hardware merchants, newspaper editors, secretaries, archivists, railway managers, timber brokers, and so on. These were Canadians of Irish descent – some Protestant, most Catholic – who truly loved their country and who merely wished to see their ancestral homeland bestowed with the same freedoms as Canada. But as a result of events in Ireland and the intense anti-Catholic bigotry expressed by Canadian organizations such as the Orange Order and the Protestant Protective Association, Irish-Catholic Canadians were continually forced to re-examine their place in Canadian and imperial society. During the early twentieth century, many Irish-Catholic Canadians forged a new identity: that of loyal Canadians who retained an ethnic identification with, and support for, the national aspirations of their ancestral homeland. At times this new Irish-Catholic Canadian identity found expression in efforts to form closer ties with their French-Canadian coreligionists. While there can be no question that most Irish-Catholic Canadians achieved greater social and economical success in these years, they never relinquished the hope that someday Ireland would achieve some form of independence. In maintaining this hope, early twentieth-century Irish-Canadian nationalists mirrored the hopes and dreams of their grandparents and great-grandparents.

Throughout the 1880s and early 1890s, many Irish Canadians strongly supported Irish nationalist movements for self-government and self-reliance. When the agrarian agitation of the 1879–80 Land War caused so much distress in Ireland, support from Canada was quickly forthcoming. The Irish Land League made an effort to reform the antiquated system of landownership by encouraging small farmers to withhold rents. After Charles Stewart Parnell, one of the Land League's founders, visited Toronto and Montreal in March 1880, local branches of the league formed in the Canadian Maritimes and central Canada.[9] Irish-Canadian Land Leaguers raised $80,000 to relieve distress in Ireland. In addition, through their perceived strength at the polls, Irish Canadians and their representatives were able to persuade the Canadian government to vote in favour of sending $100,000 to Ireland.[10]

When the original Irish Home Rule Bill was introduced in the British House of Commons in 1886, Irish-Canadian support for this measure soon became evident. Inspired by a large meeting held by the Montreal branch, on 15 April the Toronto branch of the Irish National League held a rally in support of Home Rule. John Cameron, editor of the prominent Liberal newspaper *The Globe*, addressed the rally. Cameron described the Irish question as a Canadian issue as well, one 'whose settlement would bring peace and prosperity to the Empire.'[11] The influence of the supposedly unified Irish vote was also soon evident. Resolutions in support of the Irish Home Rule Bill were passed in the Canadian House of Commons, the Quebec legislature, the Ontario legislature, and the

Nova Scotia legislature.[12] All of these resolutions expressed roughly the same sentiment: a desire to see Ireland receive some form of limited self-government while remaining within the empire. It is likely, though, that these resolutions were passed in the hope of securing the Irish vote in Canada, rather than as the result of a deep-seated concern that Ireland achieve Home Rule.[13] The resolutions presumably had little impact, as the British government never moved to secure Home Rule for Ireland.

In 1900 the fractious split in Irish politics over the Charles Stewart Parnell affair resolved itself, and the IPP united under the leadership of John Redmond, who immediately set out to re-establish the Party as the standard bearer for all Irish nationalists. As neither British politicians nor political parties were funded until 1911, raising money became a top priority. Toward that end, in 1901 John Redmond formed the United Irish League of America, 'which became an enormously successful auxiliary of the Irish Party.'[14] In 1902–3, Redmond, with John Dillon and Joseph Devlin, made numerous fund-raising tours of the United States, Canada, and Australia, using the United Irish League primarily as a fund-raising apparatus. In the fall of 1902, Joseph Devlin spoke throughout New England before moving on to Toronto, Montreal, and Ottawa. By February 1903, Devlin had raised $30,000.[15] Although few if any records exist, it is known that the United Irish League did have branches in Canada and that it was active in fund-raising. In September 1912, Charles Doherty, Canadian Member of Parliament for St Anne's in Montreal as well as Minister of Justice in Robert Borden's Conservative government, was appointed 'Vice-President of the United Irish League of Canada at the Associations convention, where the members subscribed $135,000 to finance the efforts of Irish nationalists in the homeland.'[16] In the years preceding the third Home Rule Bill, the United Irish League was far from the only Irish nationalist fraternal society active in Canada.

During the early twentieth century, many Irish fraternal associations remained active in Canada. Among them were the Emerald Benevolent Association, the Irish Catholic Benevolent Union, the St Patrick's Society, and the Ancient Order of Hibernians. None of these fraternal organizations was overtly republican, nor did they advocate the complete separation of Ireland from Britain through revolutionary methods. Rather, these nationalist fraternal societies put forward the same constitutional nationalist arguments as the IPP: that Ireland should receive limited self-government over local issues while remaining a constituent part of Great Britain. The most active of these Irish fraternal societies was the Ancient Order of Hibernians.

The Ancient Order of Hibernians (AOH) was, and is, an ethno-religious fraternal benevolent society whose membership is restricted by faith, age, and ethnicity. Founded in Ulster in the 1790s, during a time of agrarian violence and sectarian strife, the AOH stood as a defender of Roman Catholics and more generally the Roman Catholic faith.[17] The founding of the AOH in Ireland coincided with the emergence of the increasingly violent Protestant fraternal organization known as the Orange Order. In the late 1820s the AOH made its way to the United States; it did not emerge in Canada until 1887, when the first Canadian branch was formed in Woodstock, New Brunswick.[18] The AOH has always been a strictly Irish-Catholic fraternal society, one whose membership was restricted to men 'Irish or of Irish descent through either parent, a practical [practising] Catholic, not less than sixteen nor over forty-five years of age, and in good bodily health.'[19] In the early 1900s there were roughly 1,500 Hibernians in Ontario; by 1913 there were 4,737 Hibernians in Canada.[20] These figures may seem insignificant, but it must be remembered that this was an organization made up exclusively of Irish-Catholic adult males. The AOH had a Ladies Auxiliary, and men over forty-five were allowed to join as honorary members, but neither group was allowed to participate in benefits programs, which became an increasingly important part of AOH membership. During the era of rapid industrialization in North America, providing even rudimentary insurance and death benefit programs became a critical component of fraternal society membership.

Canadian historian Mark McGowan notes that at a time of rapid industrialization and a general increase in Canadian fraternal society membership, Irish nationalist fraternal societies experienced dramatic declines in membership. McGowan in part cites this as an indication of decreased interest in Irish affairs among Irish-Catholic Canadians. While it is true that by 1915 membership in both the Emerald Benevolent Association and the Irish Catholic Benevolent Union had declined to less than half of their respective memberships two decades earlier, McGowan admits that the AOH was 'the only such organization to weather the sharp declines of the 1890s and actually increase its membership.'[21] He asserts that 'the AOH was more of an ethno-cultural insurance society than a vociferous exponent of Irish nationalism' and that 'Canadian Hibernians had less to do with lobbying the British Parliament for Irish Home Rule than they did with instilling an appreciation of Irish culture in Canada.'[22] While it may be true that the AOH in Canada did little lobbying of the British Parliament, there is evidence that the AOH was far more resolute in its nationalism than McGowan has recognized.

In examining Irish nationalism in Manitoba, Australian historian Richard Davis imparts a far different view of the role of the Ancient Order of Hibernians. For Davis, the establishment of an AOH branch in Winnipeg in 1908 marked the turning point in the development of an Irish nationalist movement in Manitoba. Davis notes that during the 1880s and 1890s, the 'distraction of Irish-French hostility [over control of the Church] is one reason for the slow development of Irish self-consciousness in Manitoba,' noting that in the first years of the twentieth century 'there was little nationalist activity in Manitoba.'[23] He argues that the 'turning point was the establishment in 1908 of a Winnipeg branch of the Ancient Order of Hibernians ... The AOH was an excellent example of institutionalized Irish-Catholic nationalism.'[24] From 1908 to 1913 the Winnipeg AOH made 'reasonable progress,' with the addition of a Ladies Auxiliary and the establishment of a Hibernian football club. Lectures were held in Winnipeg in support of the Irish nationalist cause, such as that delivered by the IPP's T.P. O'Connor in 1910. A year later, Father Michael O'Flanagan spoke in Winnipeg on the Gaelic Revival, which emerged in Ireland during the early 1890s, as a means to preserve the Irish language.[25] All of this activity fostered a greater sense of Irish consciousness in Manitoba and generated support for Home Rule. Hibernians in Ontario engaged in similar activities and expressions of Irish nationalist sentiment.

In August 1904 the Ontario provincial convention of the Ancient Order of Hibernians, held in St Thomas, expressed sentiments which readily conveyed a sense of ethnic identification with Ireland. The convention's proceedings were dominated by questions relating to insurance and finances, but there were also clear expressions of Irish nationalism. M.J. O'Farrell, the Provincial President, instructed the convention on the importance of adopting the nine resolutions presented to the convention. Most of those resolutions either thanked local officials for their support or made reference to financial matters; three of the resolutions, however, made specific reference to ethnic and political issues of significance to this body of Irish-Catholic Ontarians. Resolutions four through six read:

    4. That the Ancient Order of Hibernians of the Province of Ontario place

on record their confidence in the Irish Parliamentary Party, and pray that Mr. John Redmond, M.P., may be long spared to the Irish people in their noble struggle for political freedom.

5. That we, the members of the Ancient Order of Hibernians of the Province of Ontario are of the opinion that Irish history and the Irish language should be introduced into our Separate Schools, and that books relating thereto should be placed on the shelves of the free libraries of this Province, and recommend that the officers and members of all Divisions of the Order in the Province endeavor to carry this opinion into operation.

6. That we, the member of the A.O.H. in convention assembled, believe in a closer, more friendly, more fraternal feeling being extended to our French co-religionists of the Province, a better understanding would be reached in the onward march of progress. We realize and must feel that their aspirations are singularly in touch with ours and worthy of our hearty appreciation.[26]

Clearly, some Irish Catholics in Ontario wished to see their ancestral homeland achieve political freedom and maintained a distinct ethnic identity that was even sympathetic to French-Canadian aspirations.

Resolutions five and six unambiguously expressed the sentiments of a body of Irish-Catholic Canadians who wished to maintain a distinct ethnic identity into the twentieth century. Resolution five stated that Ontario Hibernians wanted Irish history and the Irish language to be introduced into 'our Separate Schools.' McGowan's work casts the Hibernians as the custodians of Irish culture in Canada in that they promoted 'the study of Irish history in Catholic schools and the preparation of a history of the Irish people in Canada.'[27] However, he McGowan makes no reference of the wish to introduce the Irish language into Ontario's separate schools. These resolutions indicate that there were Irish-Catholic Canadians who viewed themselves as a distinct ethnic group in Canadian society and who wished to preserve its ethnic identity through education.

The mere fact that resolution six called on Ontario's Hibernians to extend friendlier relations toward their French coreligionists is significant. The last sentence of this resolution states: 'We realize and must feel that their aspirations are singularly in touch with ours and worthy of our hearty appreciation.' French Canadians in Ontario aspired to a distinct ethnic, linguistic, and religious identity in a sea of English Protestantism. That their aspirations in this regard might be in line with those of Irish-Catholic Canadians was remarkable, and in stark contrast to the often cited image of conflict between Irish Catholics and French Canadians.

Examples abound in Canadian historical writing of conflicts between Irish Catholics and French Canadians. Yet one does not often read about pitched street battles between French and Irish Canadians (as one does when it comes to rioting between Orange and Irish Catholics).[28] More often than not, the conflicts cited between Irish and French focused on which side's bishop would control a diocese and its schools.[29] As Chad Gaffield has shown, many Irish and French Canadians did not follow ecclesiastical orders like sheep; instead, they considered their own particular circumstances and made decisions that best addressed their needs.[30] Resolutions five and six suggest that while Irish bishops and clergymen might have opposed French separate schools because they feared losing power to French-Canadian bishops, most lay Irish Catholics in Ontario supported separate schools as a means of retaining their own cultural identity. It is also possible that Irish Catholics in Ontario called for Gaelic to be taught in Ontario's separate schools as a response to events in Ireland.

The desire to have the Irish language taught in Ontario's separate schools might well have been a response to the Gaelic Revival in Ireland. Although efforts to preserve Ireland's Gaelic traditions dated back to 1806 with the founding of the Gaelic Society of Dublin, and 1818 with the founding of the Iberno-Celtic Society, the Gaelic Revival did not begin in earnest until the late 1880s and early 1890s. It began largely as an effort by scholars and intellectuals to stem the tide of Anglicization and to preserve the Gaelic language and traditions, which were quickly disappearing. In November 1884 the Gaelic Athletic Association (GAA) was founded by Michael Cusack in Thurles, County Tipperary. Societies dedicated to the preservation of the Gaelic language arose in 1876 with the founding of the Society for the Preservation of the Irish Language. In 1880 a breakaway group formed the Gaelic Union; then in 1893 the Gaelic League was formed. The two most influential founders of the Gaelic League were Eion MacNeill, a Professor of Gaelic at University College Dublin and a Roman Catholic from County Antrim; and Douglas Hyde, the son of a Church of Ireland rector from County Sligo who grew up in Roscommon, where he learned Irish. Along with William Butler Yeats, Hyde helped found the Irish Literary Society of London and the National Literary Society in Dublin. Although these literary societies fostered the development of great Irish playwrights such as J.M. Synge, as far as Hyde was concerned these literary organizations did not go far enough. For Hyde, the Gaelic League rightly advocated the 'preservation and advancement of a national identity based solely on the Gaelic cultural and linguistic heritage.'[31] Well into the twentieth century, the societies that spearheaded the Gaelic Revival resurrected an Irish literary and linguistic tradition that in turn fostered a sense of cultural nationalism the likes of which the IPP could never have provided.

One Canadian historian, David Shanahan, contends that as a result of the Gaelic Revival, Ireland was so dramatically transformed that Irish Canadians no longer identified with their ancestral homeland. As a result, they turned their backs on Ireland, thereby hastening the process of Canadian assimilation:

> At this time [1890–1910] in Canada there was nothing to parallel what was happening in Ireland. The Irish Canadians were totally concerned with Canadian affairs. Their main object as Irish people in Canada was to ensure their fair share of the patronage and bounty flowing from Ottawa and the Provinces. Unlike Ireland, there was nothing in Canada to encourage the self-examination taking place there, the re-evaluation of what exactly it meant to be Irish (or Gaelic) ... The Irish in Canada did not need to ask themselves what it meant to be Irish – they knew already. Ireland was the past, the homeland, unchanging and distant. It was Canada which challenged them to rethink their identities in the context of its demands and environment. As the Irish in Ireland were becoming preoccupied with making their present live up to their past, their co-patriots in Canada were busy trying to escape the past and look to the future in the new land.[32]

These conclusions about the impact of the Gaelic Revival in Canada seem contradictory and raise many questions. Shanahan states that Ireland was altered by the Gaelic Revival to such an extent that Irish Canadians were unable to identify with their homeland. But then Shanahan states that Ireland was the homeland and was 'unchanging.' He also states that 'there was nothing in Canada to encourage the self-examination' going on in Ireland. But then he states that 'it was Canada which challenged them to rethink their identities.' Moreover, in stating that 'their main object as Irish people in Canada was to ensure their fair share of the patronage and bounty flowing from Ottawa and the Provinces,' Shanahan merely falls back on old, worn-out stereotypes of the Irish as only being proficient as builders and exploiters of political machinery.

Shanahan also errs in describing Ireland as 'distant' to Irish Canadians. By the early twentieth century, Ireland was anything but distant. Improvements in communication networks with transatlantic cables, and the advent of steamliner service between Britain and Canada, made Ireland closer than ever. By the early twentieth century, news travelled faster than it ever had previously. Moreover, as Canada and Ireland were integral parts of the British Empire, significant news events in either country were published in the other within a day. Any proposed alteration to the Imperial political structure necessarily implied potential changes for *all* dominions, including Australia, Canada, New Zealand, and South Africa. Events in Ireland, especially developments in the Home Rule debate, were constantly being reported in Canada's major newspapers, such as *The Globe* in Toronto and *The Gazette* in Montreal. But news from Ireland was covered most thoroughly by Canada's Irish-Catholic press. In these ethno-religious weekly newspapers, events in Ireland were scrutinized, analysed, and editorialized. Just as the *Orange Sentinel* provides insight today into the opinions and beliefs of Orange-Canadian unionists; in the same way, the Catholic weekly newspapers provide a glimpse into the views, beliefs, and expectations of the Irish-Canadian nationalist community.[33]

In 1912, the first year of the third Irish Home Rule crisis, Toronto's *Catholic Register* was careful not to denounce British rule in Ireland. Perhaps this reflected the Church's influence over the newspaper. In January 1893, at the insistence of Archbishop John Walsh, the rival papers *Irish Canadian* and *Catholic Weekly Review* were combined to form the *Catholic Register*.[34] Both papers had experienced financial trouble, exacerbated by constant feuding between their editorial staffs. The *Catholic Register* barely survived a series of changes in ownership and editors until 1908, when it was bought by the Catholic Church Extension Society. The Extension Society was an immigrant and frontier aid society that expanded not only the editorial focus of the *Register* but also its readership. In 1905 the number of subscriptions had been 3,000; within three years this figure doubled. By 1919 the number of paid subscriptions had risen to 13,000, and editors such as Father Alfred E. Burke and later J.A. Wall gave 'the *Register* a national voice, thereby converting it from a mirror of the local church into one of the most influential Catholic weeklies in Canada.'[35] The *Catholic Register* focused mainly on issues of great importance to Catholic Canadians, such as separate schools. With respect to Ireland, the *Register* expressed a moderate nationalism that focused largely on Ireland's devotion to Catholicism. One editorial that examined Home Rule stated:

> Practically all the trials and persecutions through which Ireland has passed have been caused by the mere fact that she was a Catholic nation and her dominant partner a Protestant one. In this regard, too, it is worthy of remark that if Ireland loses the present opportunity for self-government it will also be on account of the religion she holds so dear ...
>
> Politicians like Carson and Bonar Law, and poets like Rudyard Kipling, put forward the same arguments of religious oppression and bigotry to stay the march of progress in Ireland. We will see if this appeal to narrow-mindedness will have its effect and the hopes of the majority in Ireland are crushed for another generation. What we may remark is this: Whether Ireland win or lose in this present crisis she will have triumphed over all her ememies and given the world the greatest example of strength and consistency that it has ever seen.[36]

Mark McGowan notes that at the time the *Catholic Register* was founded, the paper 'was obedient to the hierarchy.'[37] Whether this clerical influence extended over the editorial content, or whether the editors chose to tread lightly in a city with such traditions of Orange violence, is hard to determine. But clearly, in the first years of the Home Rule crisis, the *Catholic Register* voiced a moderate form of nationalism.

By contrast, the *New Freeman* of Saint John, New Brunswick, was independent of clerical control and expressed a fervent Irish nationalism. Founded in 1900, the *New Freeman* was owned and published each Saturday by the New Freeman Publishing Company.[38] The paper's first president, Miles E. Agar, was a prominent citizen of Saint John, widely viewed as 'a Canadian through and through.'[39] In 1900, Agar helped found the *New Freeman*, and he remained a board member, as well as the newspaper's president, for the next forty years. In 1903 and again in 1904, he ran unsuccessfully for public office, first as a Conservative candidate for the provincial assembly, later as Surveyor General. In 1909 he was appointed to a seat on the Board of School Trustees, which marked the beginning of a long and prominent public career. After five years on the school board, Agar was appointed to the Board of Commissioners of the Saint John General Hospital, a position he held until he resigned in 1938. In 1912 he was elected a commissioner for the City of Saint John, for which he served as Commissioner of Public Works until 1914.

In 1925, Agar was elected to represent the city in the provincial legislature, a seat he held for more than ten years, until he resigned to accept a position on the New Brunswick Liquor Control Board.[40] Agar was a Canadian who served his country and city with great pride, but he also maintained an intense interest in the affairs of his ancestral homeland.

Under Agar's leadership and the editorial direction of the Reverend D.S. O'Keefe, the *New Freeman* was a fervent exponent of Irish nationalism. While it also covered a multitude of issues relevant to Catholic Canadians, its tenor was assertive when the issue of Ireland arose. The paper repeatedly exposed the glaring inconsistencies in Unionist and British Tory arguments. In an editorial titled 'Ulster's Brag,' the *New Freeman* minced few words:

> There are enough Nationalists in Ulster to beat the Unionists into the sea, and they are not afraid to do it, but one-half of the row Unionist Ulster is raising against Home Rule is simply a scheme to grab more than its share of the spoils when Dublin gets a national parliament. If Ulster had meant to fight it wouldn't have been as tame as a mouse when Winston Churchill held his great meeting in Belfast. Poor Mr. Bonar Law, it is really a pity he ever left the North Shore of New Brunswick, and went over to burn his fingers by meddling with Ulster braggers, who would leave him to do all the fighting himself, if he was foolish enough to lead such boasters ... If Ulster wants a fight they could not look for it in a better way than by opposing a National parliament. Besides a fight they will also have the pleasure of being beaten.[41]

The editorial was somewhat misguided in its diagnosis of Unionist aspirations to grab the spoils of a Dublin parliament; but it was also indicative of the awakened nationalist spirit in Saint John, which early on was more palpable than in Toronto.

It is possible that the *New Freeman*'s assertive editorials reflected the strong Irish-Catholic presence in the city. In the mid-nineteenth century, most of the Irish in the Saint John River Valley were Protestants, but most of the Irish in Saint John were Catholics.[42] By 1921, 28.3 per cent of the citizens of Saint John declared themselves to be of Irish heritage.[43] In percentage terms, that made Saint John the most Irish city in Canada. Equivalent figures: for Montreal, 5.6 per cent; for Toronto, 18.7 per cent; for Winnipeg, 13.0 per cent. It is possible that this created a greater sense of security for the Saint John Irish. For whatever reason, the tenor of the articles and editorials in the *New Freeman* was highly critical of the Ulster Orangemen.

As events in Ireland unfolded throughout 1912, and Ulster unionists' protests against Home Rule escalated in ferocity and outright distortion, the *New Freeman* excerpted articles and editorials from the leading nationalist newspapers in Ireland. In October 1912, after the Ulster unionists signed their Covenant, the *Catholic Register* in Toronto made no comment, while the *New Freeman* issued a blistering editorial:

> One lesson stands out prominently in the present political situation in Ireland and it is this, that the loyalty of the Orangemen of Ulster is in proportion to their certainty of running the country to suit themselves.
> They have called themselves before the people of the Empire as sturdy defenders of the throne, and yet even when the King and His government announce the passage of a law in accordance with the wishes of the majority of the people, they declare that they are ready to fight against the King and his troops rather than let their selfishness go unsatisfied. It is but striking illustration of the meaning of the motto of the Orange Order 'equal rights for all and special privileges to none' – except Orangemen.[44]

Much like the *Catholic Register*, in the first years of the Home Rule crisis, the St Patrick's Society of Montreal rarely if at all made any direct reference to Home Rule. The St Patrick's Society was a charitable, social, and educational Irish fraternal organization founded on 17 March 1834. Two of the founding principles of the Society were 'to care for Irish immigrants and to defend national interests,' which presumably meant Irish national interests.[45] The society was originally non-sectarian, being comprised of Protestant and Catholic members. In 1856, possibly as a result of the 1853 Gavazzi riots in Montreal, during which Protestants and Catholics clashed, a split occurred when the Protestant members left to form the Irish Protestant Benevolent Society. The St Patrick's Society remained an exclusively Irish-Catholic fraternal organization until 1914. In February of that year the issue of a 'Protestant Irishman becoming a member of the St Patrick's Society' was raised. On 2 March 1914 the minute books indicated that a 'Protestant Irishman could not become a member of the St Patrick's Society.'[46]

From 1912 to 1914 very few direct references to Home Rule appear in the minute books of the St Patrick's Society. Instead one finds only indirect references to Ireland, usually in the context of someone passing away and it being mentioned that his life was dedicated to the cause of Ireland. For example, the minutes from 5 February 1912 note: 'Resolutions of sympathy were adopted ... with the family of Frank Langan, a fellow Irishman who had given freely of his means, influence and affection for the cause of Ireland.'[47]

Conversely, although the AOH primarily concerned itself with the immediate success and longevity of their fraternal organization, Irish Home Rule occupied a prominent place in its discussions and resolutions. For example, when the AOH expressed support for the nationalist cause in Ireland, it did so unambiguously. One good example concerns the 1912 Biennial Convention of the Ancient Order of Hibernians of Ontario, held in Hamilton. Ontario Hibernians reported on the progress of their institution and on the financial stability and standing of their insurance benefits, with reports from the Provincial Secretary and Provincial Treasurer. But this same convention expressed an astuteness and earnestness over events in Ireland that the AOH had not shown previously. This occurred for two reasons: months earlier, a Home Rule Bill for Ireland had been introduced in the British Parliament; and this convention was being presided over by a young, energetic, and truly devoted Irish nationalist named Charles J. Foy.

Charles James Foy was born on 7 August 1867, to Michael and Ann (Walsh) in Drummond Township, Lanark County, Ontario. He attended Perth Separate School and then went on to Perth Collegiate Institute. He then studied law at Osgoode Hall in Toronto. After completing his studies there, Foy returned to Perth and eventually acquired his own law practice. Foy proved highly active in local politics, serving in numerous positions, such as the Perth Board of School Trustees and the St John's Separate School Board. He was also elected to the Perth Town Council, a position he held for twenty-five years. He served as mayor of Perth in 1905–6. He was also an active member of the AOH: an officer by 1904 and Provincial President by 1910.[48]

In his 1912 Presidential Address, Charles J. Foy spoke of the issues of deepest concern to Ontario Hibernians. He spoke of the close relationship between the Catholic Church and the AOH, noting that 'of all the Catholic societies in existence, none have proved in a greater degree their loyalty, devotion and fidelity to the Catholic Church, than the Ancient Order of Hibernians.'[49] With obvious passion, Foy also spoke at length about the importance of Irish history:

> National pride is the most powerful incentive to patriotic interest, and

national pride is founded upon and sustained by knowledge of the history of our forefathers. We live in the past by history; in the future by hope and aspirations ... This being the case, we should use every endeavor to have Irish history taught in the Separate Schools throughout the Province. Study it in our homes, and particularly in our Division meetings. I would like very much to see such a step, if possible, made compulsory, and I would recommend action looking towards that end, relative to the study of Irish history.[50]

In his conclusion, Foy again spoke with tremendous passion about Ireland, naming past Irish nationalist leaders as a means of inspiring his Hibernian brothers to dedicate themselves to the cause of Irish independence:

See to it, brothers, that the spirit, the aim, the hopes and aspirations of Wolfe Tone, Grattan, Flood, O'Connell and Emmet, are never allowed to wane until 'Heaven's sun shines radiantly over a free and fetterless Ireland.' We have seen her past; what will her future be? How glorious will that future be, when all Irishmen are united as one and can live for one common purpose. I see Erin arising emancipated. I see her in peace, in concord, in harmony with all the nations around her; and grandest of all, with all of her own children within her. I see her with the light of faith shining upon her. I see her honored, loved, and cherished by other nations.[51]

Charles J. Foy embodied the sincere ethnic identification that these Irish-Catholic Canadians maintained for their ancestral homeland. Through their president, Ontario's Hibernians displayed a passionate commitment to see Ireland emerge from British rule as an independent nation. To that end, the members moved to enshrine these sentiments as resolutions.

The following day, the Committee on Resolutions proposed nineteen resolutions for adoption by the convention. Most of these dealt with the usual Hibernian business, or extended thanks to the mayor and clergy of Hamilton. Resolutions eight, nine, and eighteen confirmed that President Foy's passionate sentiments on Ireland and Irish history were shared by the Ontario members of the AOH. Resolution eight expressed the convention's 'desire to have a Gaelic chair established in one of our universities, and that a special assessment be levied for this purpose.' Resolution nine urged the various AOH County Boards to continue the fight to get Irish history in the separate schools and 'to have Irish histories and Irish literature placed in the public libraries.' Resolution eighteen read:

> That we congratulate the Irish people on the successful culmination of their struggle for liberty and the perpetuation of their national existence, in the fight that has been continued for the past seven centuries. We assure the Irish people of our undying devotion and fealty, and promise them our moral and material support, if the democracy of Great Britain is thwarted in their efforts to bring peace and justice to Ireland.[52]

These resolutions again indicate that many Irish-Catholic Canadian men were not only committed to the cause of Irish freedom, but also committed to preserving their ethno-cultural identity for their progeny, through the teaching of Gaelic at university and Irish history in Ontario's separate schools. Again, as in 1904, this body of Irish-Catholic Canadians favoured maintaining separate schools in Ontario and desired to expand the curriculum to include Irish history. These resolutions and Foy's speech emphasize how passionately these Irish-Catholic Canadians felt about supporting Irish national aspirations and preserving their cultural identity.

By early 1913, Irish-Canadian nationalists, including those in Toronto, were beginning to display a more fiery rhetoric and a more strident nationalism. The reintroduction of the Home Rule Bill, a nationalist electoral victory in Derry, and the British government's reluctance to curtail the actions of the Ulster unionists generated harsh criticisms of British administration in Ireland. In February 1913, David Hogg, an Irish nationalist candidate, won election to the British House of Commons in Londonderry (or Derry, as it was/is referred to by nationalists), winning a seat long held by the Unionists. For a number of reasons, this was a major victory for the nationalist cause. First, it shifted the number of seats held in Ulster to a nationalist majority of one. It also seemed to nullify one of the bitterest and most often trumpeted arguments made by the Unionists: that Catholics were intolerant of Protestants. David Hogg was a prominent Protestant shop owner – a fact that nationalist champions were not going to let pass without comment. The *New Freeman* analysed the election results as follows:

> One of the chief arguments of the opponents of Home Rule has been their repeated declaration that the Protestant minority would suffer from

Catholic intolerance. Such assertions, however, are without the slightest foundation in light of the present day facts. The generosity and toleration of Catholics toward their Protestant brethren will compare very favorably with that exercised towards them by their non-Catholic friends either in the old land or in our own Canada.[53]

With its nationalist colours flying prominently, the *Catholic Register* then described how the Unionists were able to electorally control Derry even though a majority of the populace was Catholic and nationalist. This editorial exemplified how intimately knowledgeable Irish Canadians remained with respect to Irish politics and demographics. The *Register* stated:

> The election just over in the city of Londonderry has caused a good deal of interest in political circles in the Old land and the New. Many people wondered that there should be any doubt at all of 'Orange Derry' maintaining its Unionist principles, but the fact of the matter is that Derry is a preponderantly Nationalist city. It is only the chicanery of unjust registration laws that has ever put in a Unionist in the City of the Prentice Boys.[54]

These editorials indicate a level of interest in and knowledge of events in Ireland that could hardly have been maintained by a community disinterested in Irish affairs. Irish-Canadian nationalists constantly scrutinized events in Ireland, partly in the hope that Ireland would soon be receiving Home Rule, but also as a means of assessing the place of Catholics in the larger context of the British Empire.

When the Ulster Volunteer Force (UVF) was established and never outlawed by the British government, it brought into focus many difficult questions for Catholics within the empire. The *Catholic Register* raised many questions in a scathing editorial that pondered the place of Catholics in British society:

> We read in the daily papers that Sir George Reilly Richardson, an English army veteran, after reviewing 1,500 armed men, was unanimously elected chief of the army of 'Ulster' ... Is not this Ulster farce played out? What would be thought and done if ten thousand Tipperary men were out drilling and had elected, say Blake, of Boer war fame, for their general. What a howl would arise all over the Empire, even from Protestant Ontario, to have the Irish rebels suppressed or hanged. Why are the Ulster men allowed to go so far? Does it make a difference in a rebel whether he is

a Protestant or a Catholic? It evidently does, and a huge difference. At least it does in the British Empire. Why are not the Catholic peasants of the South who are to be the food of the bullets of the Orange battalions – why are they not encouraged to drill and train so as to be able to save themselves in the hour of peril? Is it always to be one law for the Protestants and another for the 'Papists.' Are not the poor 'Papists' subjects and citizens too? Why does the whole Empire look on complacently while the northern men are preparing to slaughter their inoffensive neighbor to the south? ... The world is watching the conduct of the British Government these days, and the world is merciless in its verdict.[55]

To Irish nationalists in Canada, it was obvious that Irish Protestants, especially members of the upper class, were allowed to foment whatever rebellious activities they chose. Irish Catholics, on the other hand, were routinely locked up for the slightest utterance of disapproval of British rule in Ireland.

The continuing perception of British injustice in Ireland, coupled with a sense of exclusion from positions of authority throughout the province and the Dominion, led Irish Catholics in New Brunswick to reassess their place not only in Canadian society but in the British Empire as well. In the early nineteenth century, Catholics in Nova Scotia and New Brunswick had been prohibited from voting or holding elected office, as was customary in Britain.[56] By the early twentieth century, all Canadian Catholics had the right to vote and were no longer prohibited from holding elected office, but many Catholics in New Brunswick believed they were underrepresented as public officeholders, considering their numbers. In June 1913 the *New Freeman* called for Catholic action as a means to secure the political rights and representation they deserved. It called on Catholics of all ethnic groups to form a single voting block. It asked New Brunswick Catholics to consider 'what influence do you exert on its [the Province's] political destiny considering your number[s]?' Because Catholics were politically underrepresented in leadership positions, they exerted little if any influence on the political destiny of the province. The *New Freeman* asked several probing questions: 'Yes, oh French and Irish and Scotch and other Catholic races of New Brunswick, take note of current events and ask your selves the questions: (1) Have we political equality as Catholic or have we not? (2) And if we have not political equality, how long shall we delay to take such action as shall lead to its attainment?'[57]

The *New Freeman* then suggested that a provincial convention be held to promote electoral unity among Catholics. In this way the Catholics of New Brunswick would be sending a clear message that their grievances with regard to political underrepresentation would have to be reconciled or the elected officials would pay a heavy price at the next election. Organizing a 'Catholic Federation' would be a momentous undertaking, and questions remained concerning the organizational acumen of Irish Catholics in Canada and whether they were capable of such a feat. The *New Freeman* invoked the name of the great Irish liberator of the past, Daniel O'Connell, undoubtedly in the hope that Catholics in New Brunswick would be inspired to act:

> But are our Irish Catholic people of Canada losing their sense of organization? Do they forget that less than eighty years ago the great O'Connell, well called the Constantine of Ireland, was [sic] to convene millions of Irish Catholics near Tara's Hill, or on famed Clontarf, to enforce the claims of Catholic Ireland on a bigoted Imperial parliament? Can not the Irish in Canada, in union with Catholics of other nationalities, do something when they remember that their ancestors, unaided, could do so much? Let Catholic Unity be the battle-word of the day, and nothing can more certainly secure such unity and its consequent advantages than a large Catholic convention held here in the principal city of the Province.[58]

Catholics in various American cities held annual conventions with great effect; so, 'why not also in Eastern Canada?' A convention would enable Catholics of various political hues, Liberal or Conservative, to come together on a single platform to build consensus; it would 'make them conscious of their common Catholicity.' In this respect, a unified Catholic voting block would certainly 'teach our parliamentary representatives that we shall have our political rights recognized or 150,000 New Brunswick Catholics will know the reason why.'[59]

The *New Freeman's* campaign for Catholic political equality continued through the summer of 1913. Acadians were asked to join the campaign, but it is not known whether they supported this movement. There were, though, Catholics in New Brunswick who believed that conducting such a campaign was unwise, fearing it would engender hostility and resentment from Protestants in the province. The *New Freeman* commented that since 'we opened the columns of the *New Freeman* for the discussion of the political status of the Catholic people of these Maritime Provinces with regard to their representation in the public offices of the people, we have received various views from our own people, some blaming and other praising us for what so far has appeared.'⁶⁰ Some argued it was unwise for a Catholic newspaper to engage in politics, commenting that Protestants would 'look with suspicion on our attitude and resent the idea of the priest and the church interfering in politics.' The *New Freeman* responded that it was an argument as old as the Church, 1,913 years of age, 'and as new as the Ne Temiere decree or the Belfast 12th of July orations.' The *New Freeman* stated that when it could be proven that priests and bishops were engaged in politics for their own personal gain, *then*, and not until then, would they silence their campaign. The most pertinent question was whether ordinary Catholics would be politically represented by people of the same faith. Furthermore, it was pointed out that no Catholic had ever been premier of any of the Maritime provinces, that Saint John had never had a Catholic mayor, and that there was not 'a single Catholic holding an important civic position.'⁶¹

The campaign continued, with issues of justice and fair play being raised, as were images of injustice in Ireland. Inferences were made that the same injustices associated with the Protestant ascendancy in Ireland had crossed the Atlantic and were being perpetuated in New Brunswick. In an insightful editorial, the *New Freeman* commented:

> Objection was made some time ago by those who could not see eye to eye with those favoring the idea of Catholics coming more to the front in political questions, that it was a mistake to harp on the need of recognizing Catholic claims, as it engendered bad feelings between Protestants and Catholics, and particularly, no doubt, made certain of our separated [Orange] brethren feel bad that we are not satisfied with the small loaves and extremely small fishes. At the time we took the matter up and tried to explain that we did not believe any honest man, Protestant or otherwise, ever felt bad when he noticed that his neighbor was simply asking for recognition when he felt he sincerely deserved it. Catholics are subjects of the Empire, Catholics pay taxes, Catholics live, [sic] and have their being, much the same as Protestants, Hebrews, and Pagans. Why then, in the name of justice, should not Catholics object when they know they are not getting equal treatment with other citizen of the Empire?⁶²

That Irish-Catholic Canadians questioned their place in Canada, and the empire, should not have been surprising, considering the torrent of anti-Catholic bigotry emanating from the Orange Order in both Canada and Britain. Irish-Catholic Canadian exasperation with that effluence was evident in an untitled editorial published by the *New Freeman* on 16 August 1913 in response to a recent Orange diatribe. The *New Freeman* commented that a few days earlier, the Reverend Dean Sandre of Montreal had 'delivered an old-time Orange harangue to the brethren of Montreal.' In it, Rev. Sandre proclaimed that the true duties of the Canadian Orangeman were as follows: 'First, they should oppose Home Rule. Second, work to establish one language in the Dominion. Third, seek to have one school system and one uniform law.' The *New Freeman* responded variously with resentment, bitterness, and even smugness, stating that those like Sande 'would strive to perpetuate Orange ascendency in Ireland and would endeavor to deprive us of that priceless boon of liberty of conscious in this the land of the free.'[63] Seemingly, Irish-Catholic Canadians viewed the Orange Order as the enemy of a truly free Canada – of a nation where all could speak freely and practise their faith as they chose. During this time of crisis in Ireland, the spirits of Irish-Catholic Canadians were buoyed by the announcement that the Irish nationalists had formed their own volunteer force.

In November 1913, news reached Canada that Irish nationalists were forming the Irish Volunteers, largely as a response to the formation of the UVF, which had been established in January of that year to resist the implementation of Home Rule. The Irish Volunteers had been launched not by John Redmond and the IPP, but rather by Eoin MacNeill, the founder of the Gaelic League, and by other cultural enthusiasts such as Michael Joseph Rahilly (The O'Reilly) and Bulmer Hobson.[64] The news that the Irish Volunteers had been formed was received with unalloyed enthusiasm by Irish-Canadian nationalists, including those in Toronto. Recalling the 1798 rebellion in Ireland led by the Theobolde Wolfe Tone's United Irishmen, which had aimed to break down religious distinctions in Ireland in the name of liberty, the *Catholic Register* declared:

> By their foolish clemency to Carson and his gang, the Government of England have put themselves in for strange doings. If the peasantry of Tipperary, Kilkenny and Wexford, for instance, the greatest fighting people in the world, want to arm and organize, what can their masters do about it? In 1798 it took all the available forces England had under her best generals, to put down one of these counties, and then the people were undrilled and unarmed. The movement is evidently to demonstrate that there is more real peril to the Empire in refusing the demands of five-sixths of the Irish people, than in ignoring the threats of the bellicose minority in the North. If Nationalist drilling has this effect, it will be a very good idea.[65]

Irish-Canadian nationalists seemed to take pleasure in pointing out that Ulster Unionist leaders could hardly protest the formation of the Irish Volunteers, given that they themselves had been the first down this path. The *Register* chimed in that the 'present Irish National Volunteer movement has put the Ulster rebel leaders in a quandary. Naturally, they cannot all denounce it since they themselves initiated the game, but they are much disgusted to think that two can play at it.'[66]

Membership in the fledgling organization was low at first, attracting only 1,850 members by the beginning of 1914. But by July 1914, membership had increased dramatically to 160,000.[67] At first, most of the Irish Volunteers were Gaelic Leaguers or IPP supporters. By mid-June, Redmond had 'moved to establish official party control of the Volunteers.'[68] As the Irish Volunteers membership expanded during 1914, the organization found itself infiltrated by members of another organization, the Irish Republican Brotherhood (IRB), which advocated the complete separation of Ireland from Britain and which was prepared to achieve that end by force.

The IRB was the more recent incarnation of the Fenians, some of whom had invaded Canada in the 1860s. The IRB was a secret oath-bound society, headed in Ireland by James Stephens, and dedicated to the forceful end to British rule in Ireland. In the years between the failed Fenian Rising in 1867 and the group's resurrection in 1906, the IRB was sustained largely by its brethren in the United States, headed by John Devoy, editor of the New York–based *Gaelic American*.[69] Men, money, and organizational support were forthcoming from America at a time when the IRB was virtually defunct in Ireland. Irish republicans in the United States sustained the organization in Ireland; however, there does not seem to have been active republican element in Canada prior to 1916.[70] As the Irish Volunteers expanded rapidly in the first half of 1914, the IRB infiltrated the Volunteers as it had the Gaelic Athletic Association and the Gaelic League. Now it effectively infiltrated the Irish Volunteers.

On 26 July 1914, following the precedent set by the Ulster unionists, the Irish Volunteers landed a shipment of guns at Howth. The nationalists acquired and landed 1,500 obsolete Mauser rifles and 35,000 rounds of ammunition. Roy Foster noted that 'the contrast with the Ulster operation [at Larne] could not have been more marked,' for it was not the huge cache of weapons landed by the Ulster unionists in April that brought out British troops, but the nationalists' minuscule landing at Howth.[71] When the troops returned to Dublin, having failed to seize the nationalists' arms cache, they were taunted by an unarmed civilian crowd at Bachelors Walk, upon which they fired, killing four and wounding thirty-eight. George Dangerfield commented that 'comparisons between Larne and Howth could not help being odious.'[72] At Larne and Bangor, the Ulster Unionists had landed 35,000 rifles and 3,000,000 rounds of ammunition with no government interference whatsoever; at Howth, where the Irish nationalists landed 1,500 rifles, British troops and police were out in force and four people were killed.[73] There could not have been a sharper contrast had the British government itself landed the guns at Larne.

Before the Howth landing – and even afterwards – the Irish Volunteers had been desperate to acquire arms. This, of course, was not easy. The British government had done nothing to prevent the Ulster Unionists from landing arms at Larne; yet shortly after the Irish Volunteers publicly declared their existence, the British government conveniently outlawed the importation of arms to Ireland (the official justification for sending troops out to Howth).

In an effort to acquire arms and recruit men for the Irish Volunteers, Roger Casement – a British diplomat turned Irish nationalist – visited to the United States in 1914. While there, Casement, spoke at the Ancient Order of Hibernians biennial national convention in Norfolk, Virginia.[74] By the time he did so, Canadian Hibernians were more closely linked than they had ever been to the American parent organization. McGowan has asserted that it was 'clear that the AOH in Canada had evolved in a very different fashion from the American parent organization.' Actually, as early as 1910 the Canadian Hibernians had requested that they be granted, within the AOH of America, a permanent national vice-presidency. McGowan has written that when 'war erupted in 1914, Canadian Hibernians quickly expressed their loyalty to the British Empire's cause … The near schism between American and Canadian Hibernians underscored how the nature of Irish-Catholic ethnic associations had evolved differently in much of Canada.' In fact, however, by 1912, Canadian Hibernians were already fully integrated into the American organization.[75] In his opening address at the 1912 national convention in Chicago, AOH President James Regan had recommended that the convention 'add to the to the present official roster another Vice-Presidency, the incumbent of which must be a member of the Ancient Order of Hibernians in the Dominion of Canada.'[76] With Regan's endorsement, the Canadian vice-presidency was enthusiastically established. Following this bestowment, the Reverend Dr J. Sherry of

Ontario nominated Provincial President Charles J. Foy to be the first Canadian Vice-President of the AOH. Foy was unanimously elected. In nominating Charles Foy, Rev. Sherry commented that 'while there may be an imaginary line drawn east to west between the north and the south of this continent, yet, when it comes to a question which affects an Irishman's heart there is no distinction ... The Irishman in Canada is not one jot or tittle less patriotic or enthusiastic in his love toward the old home land than you are in the United States.'[77] Rev. Sherry's expression of patriotic love for the 'old home land' exemplified sentiments expressed in editorial pages of the Irish-Catholic weekly press. Clearly, many Irish-Catholic Canadians viewed themselves as Irishmen of the greater Ireland beyond the seas.

In his opening address, National President James Regan discussed, among other things, what he referred to as 'conditions at home.' Regan expounded on Irish Home Rule:

While it is far from being as broad and comprehensive as we would wish, yet it is an important step in the right direction, and the people of Ireland are to be congratulated upon forcing an English Parliament to thus recognize the principle of HOME RULE. A few intolerant spirits in Ulster and elsewhere have been raging a bitter campaign against the measure, arousing, where possible, racial prejudice and religious bigotry. This opposition has not been an unmixed evil, inasmuch as it has united all our people in support of a Nation's rights. The Irish volunteers, organized to look after the interests of our Motherland in this crisis, deserve, and should receive, the support of every lover of liberty, every child of the Gael.[78]

James Regan insisted that 'half a loaf is better than no bread,' intimating that limited self-government was better than no government at all. Nevertheless, Regan added, 'when we take the half a loaf, it shall not prevent us from working tooth and nail for the other half. The whole loaf is ours by every human and divine right – a right written by the Creative Hand when His free waters laved the shores of Innisfall at every point – the whole loaf of Irish Nationality is an independent Republic on Irish soil.'[79] These were the expressed beliefs of the president of all North American Hibernians: 4,737 in Canada and 115,921 in the United States.[80] As a consequence of British failures to bestow Home Rule upon Ireland, the AOH was evolving into a republican organization – a fact underscored on the morning of the fourth day of the convention, 24 July, when Roger Casement addressed the convention.

Casement commented that 'if a certain section of Irishmen [Ulster unionists] have a right to get arms and threaten the British Government, then the majority of the Irish have the right to arm themselves, if the rifle is to be the predominant arbitrator.' Then, after discussing the many sacrifices made by the Irish Volunteers, he declared to the North American Hibernians:

> We do not lack for manhood and we do not lack for courage but we do require rifles and ammunition and the help to train our men. The Ulster Volunteers have had practically the entire resources of the whole British Tory Party at their back. They have had some of the most efficient and capable men in the British Army to help them ... We [the Irish Volunteers] do need the help of officers and if it should be possible, I do not know, for any Irish-American with military experience to come to Ireland on a vacation and take a hand in the drilling of the Volunteers it would be doing us a service indeed.[81]

Casement's comment about the need for arms from overseas was prophetic: two days later, Irish nationalists landed at Howth with 1,500 rifles acquired from Germany. Casement concluded his speech by extending a hand of conciliation, clothed in a glove of grim determination: while 'we are not seeking strife with our Irish Protestant neighbors, we are determined to maintain the rights and principles of the Irish Nationalists until successful.'[82]

Offers of rifles, and of officers for training, were forthcoming from the Massachusetts delegation; from the Virginia delegation came offers of uniforms and rifles. This was the first indication that the AOH was turning toward a more militant republicanism. It still supported John Redmond and the IPP, but now it also supported the Irish Volunteers. Although many revolutionary nationalists, such those in the Clan-na-Gael, criticized the AOH for not being nationalistic enough, there can be no question that the AOH was a nationalist group.[83]

Even while the UVF and the Irish Volunteers were acquiring arms, and over the protests of the Ulster Unionists and the British Conservatives, the Home Rule Bill continued to meander down its legislative path toward final passage and enactment. By the spring of 1914 it had cleared almost all legislative hurdles and was nearing enactment. When the bill passed its third reading on 25 May 1914, it effectively became law.

Irish-Canadian nationalists were full of optimism. The headlines in their press read: 'HOME RULE GOES INTO LAW' – 'Ireland Again A

Nation' – HOME RULE BILL Passes Third Reading, Automatically Becomes Law.'[84] The *New Freeman* declared that 'the news of the passage of the Home Rule Bill by the British House of Commons on Monday was heard with great delight by Irishmen the world over.'[85] This was a triumphant moment for Irish-Canadian nationalists: Ireland had technically been granted Home Rule; after years of struggle, Irish national aspirations were close to being realized.

When the Home Rule Bill received Royal Assent, Irish-Canadian nationalists announced that 'the political struggle of 114 years is closed; all is over now, except the celebrating of this glorious victory throughout the world and the official opening of the new parliament in Dublin.' The *New Freeman* continued: 'This is essentially a victory for Catholicity, in as much as it is a victory, a great constitutional victory for Catholics of the Irish race all over the world.'[86] Yet despite these grand proclamations, Irish Canadians offered only subdued celebrations. In Toronto and Montreal there were no large-scale celebrations, no parades or marches. Even in Saint John there were no rallies or parades celebrating the passage of Irish Home Rule; instead, there was a simple gathering at the AOH Hall to commemorate the event.

On 26 September 1914 the *New Freeman* reported that on the night of 21 September, 'a large, enthusiastic and intelligent audience' gathered at the AOH Hall on Union Street in Saint John, to celebrate the achievement of Home Rule in song, speech, and music. That the people of Ireland had achieved Home Rule was described as the '"event of the day," the brilliancy of which cannot be quite overshadowed even by the lowering clouds of international strife.'[87] AOH County President Thomas Kickham, who presided over the celebration, stated that 'for many a long year Irishmen and their descendants the world over have been anxiously looking forward to this event.'[88] Although no total attendance figure was given, Kickham expressed his pleasure that so many people had turned out even though the call to gather had gone out at the last minute.

Kickham then introduced AOH Divisional Chaplain Father Dr O'Brien, who expressed his gratitude and pleasure at being present: 'The Irish people and their sympathizers might well rejoice over the obtaining of Home Rule. It was a sign of the times that augured well for the future to see the Catholic people of this city rejoicing over such a splendid triumph of their countrymen across the sea.'[89]

Dr O'Reilly then spoke in 'eloquent language' as he reviewed the Irish situation over the past 200 years. He concluded with a stirring tribute: 'John E. Redmond ... has been successful in realizing the glorious result for which Emmet, O'Connell, Parnell, Gladstone and numerous others had laboriously struggled.'[90]

During the Home Rule crisis of 1912 to 1914, many Irish Canadians rallied to support Home Rule in Ireland. In this initial period, support for Irish Home Rule in Canada did not manifest itself in large-scale rallies in the country's cities. It is possible that sums of money were sent to Ireland to support the IPP, but evidence of this is scarce. Support for Irish Home Rule in Canada was most evident in the editorials of the Irish-Catholic weekly newspapers and in the resolutions passed by Irish-Catholic fraternal organizations. These editorials, which echoed the Irish nationalists' arguments, displayed an intimate knowledge of events in Ireland commensurate with those whose nationalism resonated from a profound ethno-religious identification with their ancestral homeland. Irish-Canadian nationalists were overwhelmingly Catholic; they were thoroughly Canadian but Irish at heart. They repeatedly referred to Ireland as the homeland, or the Old Land. They referred to the Irish as their fellow countrymen and as their brethren. They also referred to themselves as part of the greater Ireland beyond the seas. Irish-Canadian nationalists viewed British rule in Ireland as unjust, and they viewed the Orange Order, be it in Canada or Ireland, as an impediment to progress. Unfortunately, Home Rule in Ireland was suspended as Europe found itself engulfed in a war that would require complete dedication from the empire's citizens. This delay only hardened the Irish nationalists' resolve and would ultimately push Irish nationalists in Canada further toward republicanism.

*Chapter Three*

# The War Years: Unity and Disintegration, 1914–1918

As war's darkening clouds began to gather over Europe, the Buckingham Palace negotiations to resolve the Ulster Crisis collapsed in stalemate. On 24 July 1914, after the Irish conferees left Buckingham Palace, while British cabinet ministers discussed the various arguments presented during the conference, Foreign Minister Sir Edward Grey entered and read aloud a message stating Austria's final demands with regard to Serbia. Winston Churchill, initially only half-listening to Sir Edward's words, slowly began to comprehend the implications of the Foreign Office memo. Later, he would write of the Irish question: 'The parishes of Tyrone and Fermanagh faded back into the mists and squalls of Ireland, and a strange light began to immediately, but by perceptible gradations, to fall and grow upon the map of Europe.'[1] The Irish question, which had plagued British statesmen for so many years, quickly faded as a result of the more pressing concerns of the widening European conflagration. As it turned out, the Great War actually served to avert the crisis over Irish Home Rule by delaying its implementation until after the war. Indeed, for a time it would unite the vast majority of Irishmen in supporting Britain's war effort.

When Britain declared war on Germany, Irish nationalists quickly pledged their unity with and support for Britain's war aims. In his speech to the House of Commons on 3 August, John Redmond of the Irish Parliamentary Party declared unity with Britain, stating that all troops in Ireland could be withdrawn and that the Irish Volunteers would stand ready to defend Ireland.[2] Redmond fully believed that Ireland needed to stand united with Britain in its time of need in order to prove itself worthy of Home Rule. As Joseph Lee notes: 'An Ireland that stood by England in her hour of peril could surely then reckon to have laid the bogey of British fears ... Scant sympathy might, however, be expected from a British electorate for a nationalist Ireland that had remained sullenly neutral while Ulster unionists flocked to the flag.'[3] With Redmond's encouragement, nationalist Ireland, at least initially, fully committed itself to supporting Britain in its time of need.

Irishmen from a multitude of socio-economic and religious backgrounds, hailing from every county, willingly enlisted for service in the British Army. The total enlistment from Ireland during the war was roughly 210,000, with about 31,500 coming directly from the Irish Volunteers.[4] Although just over half of the Irish enlistment came from Ulster, 'only about 43 per cent of all Irish recruits were Protestants.'[5] This indicates that Catholics contributed to Britain's war effort in greater numbers than their Protestant detractors would lead one to believe.[6] In sheer numbers, the greatest enlistment came from Belfast and Dublin; recruits were least likely to hail from the western counties of Kerry, Mayo, and Donegal.[7] Not surprisingly, enlistment was strongest in the first two years of the war and declined precipitously after 1916. This decline occurred equally among nationalists and unionists, which indicates that at least early on, Irish support for Britain's war effort transcended political and religious differences.

The British declaration of war had tremendous consequences for Canada as well. Indeed, the First World War was a seminal event in Canada's national development. Most Canadians enthusiastically embraced Britain's declaration of war against Germany, which was fortuitous, given that when Britain declared war, Canada as a subordinate dominion was automatically at war as well. Canadian patriotism swelled, mainly among English Canadians, as Canada offered Britain whatever resources it needed. Canada's most significant contribution to the war effort took the form of men for the British Army. Although some Canadians served in the Royal Navy, and many served with distinction in the Royal Flying Corps, the vast majority of 'Canadian assistance to the common cause was centered on the army.'[8] Many believed that the war would end quickly, with limited casualties, and that volunteers would account for enough men for the cause of liberty. R. Matthew Bray writes that over 'the course of the next two years all of the major premises underlying the English-Canadian patriotic outlook – the brevity of the war, the ancillary nature of the Canadian role, the efficacy of the voluntary system – were to be challenged.'[9]

By the end of September 1914, the First Division of the Canadian Expeditionary Force had enrolled 31,200 volunteers; patriotism and severe unemployment both accounted for this enthusiasm.[10] Yet by the time the First Division reached England, the British government was already petitioning for more recruits.[11] Eventually, well over 600,000 men served in the Canadian Expeditionary Force. Bray succinctly summarized Canada's role as a dominion: 'So long as it was believed that the rationale for Canada's participation was the colonial tie to Great Britain, it was assumed that her role in the conflict would be a subordinate, subsidiary one. The Canadian government, for example, was not expected to play any significant part in the organization and direction of the Allied war effort, not even with respect to the mobilization of the Canadian Expeditionary Force; that was left entirely in British hands.'[12]

As the war progressed, Canadian soldiers received recognition and eventually their own command, having distinguished themselves at Vimy Ridge, which resulted in more than 10,000 Canadian casualties, and in monumentally futile battles such as Passchendaele, which claimed 15,654 Canadian lives. Unfortunately, this belated recognition was extended only after 60,000 Canadian soldiers gave their lives. Arthur Lower asserted: 'She [Canada] began with one division, under the command of a British general, and ended with a corps of four divisions, plus supporting troops and reinforcements, under the command of one of her own sons, Sir Arthur Currie ... Canada had entered the war a colony, a mere piece of Britain overseas, [in the end] she was forging visibly ahead to nationhood.'[13]

Irish-Canadian nationalists agreed with Redmond that they needed to do their part in ensuring that this most recent, and most egregious, example of German aggression was defeated. The *Catholic Register* asserted in September 1914 that Irish and British, Catholic and Protestant, nationalist and unionist, should unite behind Britain in the war: 'Let this war, therefore, be proceeded with, and finished unitedly.'[14] In Saint John, the *New Freeman* reported enthusiastically on the recruitment of an Irish regiment in Montreal, emphasizing the unified nature of the regiment: 'Active recruiting for the new Montreal regiment of Irish Fusiliers has now ceased, with over six hundred volunteers, including Irish-Canadians of all ranks, and from all parts of Ireland, north and south. While naturally the majority of the volunteers are Irish-Catholic, it is stated that there will be a good sprinkling of Irishmen of other religions in the ranks, so that there will be a thoroughly representative Irish battalion.'[15] With the active support of the Catholic leadership, Irish-Catholic Canadians volunteered for service in the Canadian Expeditionary Force, in what they anticipated would be their own regiments.

Archbishop Neil McNeil of Toronto publicly encouraged Ontario Catholics to do their patriotic duty in defending Canada and the empire. In a circular letter published in the *Catholic Register* on 20 August 1914, McNeil declared that Ontario Catholics 'do not need to be reminded of the duty of patriotism. You are as ready as any to defend your country and to share in the burdens of Empire.'[16] Irish-Catholic Canadians responded by enlisting in numbers proportionate to any other denomination in Canada. After extensive research, historian Mark McGowan has determined that 'English-speaking Catholic recruitment has been vastly underrated by historians and by Catholics themselves'; indeed, 'English-speaking Catholic participation in the war effort was substantial.'[17]

By June 1917 more than 51,000 Roman Catholics had volunteered for service in the Canadian Expeditionary Force, representing 14.2 per cent of the total. In terms of denominational enlistment, Catholics ranked third behind Anglicans and Presbyterians but ahead of Methodists and Baptists.[18] As McGowan has observed, however, these figures are quite misleading. Recruits who were uncertain about or uncommitted to a particular 'confession' were most often assigned to the Church of England, and this dramatically inflated the number of Anglicans in the Canadian Expeditionary Force. At the same time, the percentage of Catholic recruits in proportion to the size of the entire Canadian Catholic population seems rather minuscule at 1.8 per cent. Yet if one considers that French Canadians accounted for a majority of Canada's Catholics and for less than 30 per cent of Catholic volunteers, it becomes apparent that Irish-Catholic Canadians volunteered in proportion to their numbers, if not more heavily than that. McGowan asserts that 'an estimated 36,512 English-speaking and 'ethnic' Catholics enlisted, constituting roughly 4.87 per cent of the total of the entire non-francophone Catholic population and roughly 10.29 per cent of all recruits, regardless of denomination.'[19] In Nova Scotia, for example, a province with a limited francophone population, by 1916 Catholics accounted for 47 per cent of recruits, while accounting for only 28 per cent of the province's population.[20] McGowan's impressive work demonstrates that contrary to some established beliefs, Irish-Catholic Canadians voluntarily enlisted for service in the Canadian Expeditionary Force in similar numbers and fashion as every other ethnicity and denomination in Canada.[21]

Irish-Canadian nationalist commitment to a unified war effort emanated even from the Ancient Order of Hibernians, the most intensely nationalist Irish fraternal society in Canada. During the months following Redmond's endorsement of Britain's war aims, the American President of the AOH, Joseph McLaughlin, openly criticized Redmond's decision. These statements and numerous anti-British editorials were published in the official organ of the AOH, the *National Hibernian*. Canadian Hibernians, from Nova Scotia to British Columbia, were incensed by these remarks and editorials. Some Canadian Hibernians were so outraged that they proposed secession from their American brethren and the creation of an independent Canadian organization. Letters and resolutions protesting these inflammatory statements flowed south from county and provincial AOH boards in Canada to the American Hibernian leadership.

Canadian Hibernians, indignant that their beliefs, opinions, and sentiments were being so blatantly ignored by the American leadership, responded with resolutions and letters denouncing the AOH's American leadership as anti-British and pro-German. The AOH County Board of Carleton, Ontario, unanimously passed a resolution condemning McLaughlin's statements and forwarded it to the Canadian National Board:

> AND WHEREAS we feel, as Irishmen and descendants of Irishmen domiciled in this Dominion of Canada, an integral part of that great Empire, fully conscious that the participation of all British subjects in this very unfortunate European war is in the best interest of civilization;
>
> THEREFORE be it resolved that we, the County Board of the A.O.H., in America, of Carleton, Ont., do protest most vigorously against the policy pursued by our official organ, as well as the sentiments expressed in its columns by the National President, Jos. E. McLaughlin, in condemning the actions of John E. Redmond and his loyal and devoted followers, men who have, year after year, occupied the trenches in the British House of Commons battling for the political liberty of that country which we, as Irishmen and descendants of Irishmen, love with a devotion and loyalty not surpassed, we doubt if equaled, by any other race in the world.[22]

This resolution expressed the commitment of this body of Irish-Catholic Canadians to the British war effort, but also indicated the extent to which many Irish-Catholic Canadians retained an affinity for the country of their ancestors. Obviously, Irish-Catholic Canadians demonstrated their devotion to Redmond and the IPP as well. For them, Redmond represented Ireland, and Irishmen the world over, in the Old World and in the New.

Additionally, Canadian Hibernians experienced the war first-hand, three years before American involvement. And Canadian Hibernians were encountering the daily realities of a country at war; their brothers, relatives, and friends were fighting overseas. Canadian Hibernians faced extremely difficult choices, such as whether to fight and die in the name of the British Crown. Most Irish-American nationalists, whose country was not yet engaged in the war, wished to see Britain defeated in the war, hoping that result would further the cause of Irish freedom.[23]

In October, John Hart, AOH Provincial President of British Columbia, sent a succinct letter to McLaughlin indicating that he was resigning his membership, supposedly along with the entire provincial membership:

> The National Hibernian dated October 15th, 1914, has been received by me and I notice with much regret, the stand you take in your letter under the heading 'Irish Volunteers.' After perusing same I am of the opinion that your criticism of Mr. Redmond's action is unjustified and pro-German. I certainly think as president of a society whose membership is composed of many who live under and are loyal to the British flag, that you should have remained neutral.
>
> As Provincial president for British Columbia, and as a keen Home-ruler and an Imperialist, I must strongly protest against your remarks, and consequently have tendered my resignation, and I may further add that in consequence British Columbia Hibernians will sever their connection from the American order.[24]

In November, Hart also wrote to Canadian Vice-President Charles J. Foy. He thought 'the time has arrived to form a Canadian Order,' and he wished to know where Foy stood on that issue.[25] Foy's reply to Hart is not known, but Irish-Canadian nationalist support for the war, as well as for the secessionist movement, continued well into 1915.

Late in the autumn of 1915 a circular letter addressed 'To the Officers and Members of the Ancient Order of Hibernians of the Provinces New Brunswick and Nova Scotia' from the York County Board of New Brunswick called for 'the Secession of the Order in Canada.' The circular noted that such a move would 'be in the best interest of the Order, and will tend to a greater growth and development of the A.O.H. in Canada.'[26] The letter also described conditions in Canada and the activities of Irish-Catholic Canadians:

> In startling contrast to this policy [the editorial policy of the *National Hi-*

*bernian*], we have the facts and conditions obtaining throughout Canada at the present time. The Authorities of the Catholic Church are a unit in their support of the Allies, and are giving all possible assistance to the recruiting movement. Priests are enlisting as Chaplains, many of them now being at the Front, sharing the danger with our brave Canadian lads ... Members of our Order are enlisting for Overseas Service, and some have fallen in battle, giving up their lives in defense of this same Flag so loudly denounced by the 'National Hibernian' ... Throughout all of Canada our Divisions are engaged in raising funds for Patriotic purposes and leading Hibernians are giving their means and lending their influence to this noble work.

If any further example were required to show us what our attitude on this question of the war should be, we have but to point to the great Irish leader in the old land, John Redmond, who is striving by every means in his power to assure the success of the British cause.[27]

The actions of Redmond, 'the great Irish leader in the old land,' were identified by Canadian Hibernians as an example for Irishmen the world over. Many Canadian Hibernians felt that those of Irish descent in North America should follow his lead.

It is not clear how Charles Foy responded to these letters, but it *is* known that the Canadian AOH secessionist movement of 1914–16 did not succeed. Canadian Hibernians never left the American organization; indeed, after the war the past disputes were so well healed that the 1923 AOH biennial national convention was held in Montreal. Even so, these letters indicate the strong commitment of Irish-Catholic Canadians to Britain's war effort.

As these letters indicate, the Catholic Church actively supported recruitment efforts and contributed to the Patriotic Fund. Toronto Archbishop McNeil openly encouraged his parishioners in Toronto to contribute to the Patriotic Fund, which supported the families of fallen or disabled soldiers, regardless of denomination. The Archbishop even contributed $5,000 of his own savings, and asked his priests to donate up to $40 every six months in order that 'all the people of Toronto' could see that 'our professions of patriotism are genuine.'[28] In addition, with McNeil's approval, the basements and meeting halls of Catholic parishes were opened to local battalions, which were in desperate need of space for billets and mess facilities.[29] By war's end, tens of thousands of lay Irish-Catholic Canadians had volunteered for service in the Canadian Expeditionary Force. They gave everything they could in support of Britain, including – many – their lives.

Although early on, Irish support for Britain's war effort seemed earnest and united, not so subtle fissures were quite evident even before the events of 1916. Irish unity with Britain was greatly strained by the British Army's practice of treating Protestant and Catholic recruits differently. With the appointment of Lord Kitchener as Secretary of War, the army's formation of divisions took a decidedly religious and political turn. Lord Kitchener, who was of Irish unionist background, dismissed out of hand Redmond's request that the army create an Irish division. Yet, as James Loughlin notes, Kitchener enthusiastically 'incorporated the UVF as a distinctive Ulster division of the British Army.'[30] This unjust practice turned many Irish nationalists away from Britain at a time when they had been initially prepared to support Britain.[31] Michael Laffan describes the impact of these recruitment practices on some portions of Irish nationalist opinion: 'The army's unionist sympathies were reflected in the prompt formation of an Ulster division comprising former members of the Ulster Volunteers; its long-standing dislike of Irish nationalists was revealed in a policy of dispersing Irish recruits throughout British regiments rather than forming them into an Irish brigade as urged by Redmond. The Ulster division was not sent to the front until 1915 and sceptical nationalists believed it was being protected and kept out of danger.'[32]

Laffan's assessment of nationalist sentiment seems justified if the *Derry Weekly News* was an accurate indicator. In July 1915, the paper sternly protested the fact that the Ulster Division had yet to be sent to the front: 'To announce now that the Ulster Division will not go to the front until its numbers are practically doubled, and Catholic Irishmen being excluded from the ranks, means that the force is not intended to be used in the present war. The conclusion to be arrived at is self-evident. Twelve thousand Protestants enrolled as Ulster Covenanters cannot be procured.'[33]

By mid-1915, cracks in the facade of Irish unity were becoming more evident. The old ethnic divisions that had plagued Ireland for centuries resurfaced, with each side accusing the other of shirking its responsibility for enlistment. Although John Redmond repeatedly asserted that nationalist Ireland was united with Britain, many nationalists became disinterested and disgusted. After running a story of a Derry man who had been refused military enlistment by a recruiting sergeant in Belfast merely because he was Catholic, Dublin's organ of mainstream Irish nationalism, the *Freeman's Journal,* declared: 'There remains here in Ireland a very noisy and bigoted gang ... raised in the foetid atmosphere of the Orange lodges.'[34] Accusations of nationalist disloyalty, and unionist misinformation, were now flying unrelentingly.

Ulster Unionists claimed that nationalists were ducking their responsibility to the empire by not enlisting. In March 1915 the unionist *Weekly Northern Whig* asserted that 'Irish Protestants are barely one third of the population, but they have supplied three fourths of the new recruits who have joined in Ireland since the beginning of August.'[35] These figures were completely erroneous; even so, northern Unionists believed they were essentially the only ones enlisting in the British Army in defence of the empire. As Paul Bew and others have noted, by October 1915, recruits from all over Ireland were enlisting for service in the British Army: 50 per cent coming from Ulster (only 43 per cent of whom were Protestant), and 50 per cent coming from the other three provinces.[36] Nevertheless, these ethno-religious accusations of disloyalty and shirked duty persisted, and even emanated from Canada as well.

At the 1915 annual convention of the Grand Orange Lodge of Ontario West, the Orangemen of Ontario openly criticized the Asquith government for allowing the Home Rule Bill to pass while so many unionists served at the front defending the empire. Noting that Prime Minister Asquith promised Sir Edward Carson that the bill would not be voted on until after the war, the Orangemen of Ontario West unanimously passed a resolution condemning the Asquith government for bowing to nationalist pressure – for having endangered the lives, liberty, and property of one million Irish Protestants by agreeing to pass and then suspend the Home Rule Bill. The same resolution pledged the continued moral, financial, and physical assistance of all Ontario Orangemen.[37] Copies of the resolution were sent to Prime Minister Asquith, Sir Edward Carson, and the Most Worshipful Grand Orange Lodge of Ireland. In addition, the treasurer's report noted that the Orangemen of Ontario West made a $500 donation to the Ulster Defence Fund.[38] As before, this sum may not have seemed too substantial, but it was by far the largest donation listed that year. Other institutions receiving donations in 1915, such as the Toronto Protestant Orphanage Home, and the Presbyterian French Mission Board, and the Methodist French Mission Board, only received $100 or $200.

Orange-Canadian unionists also implied that Irish nationalists were being disloyal because they were not enlisting in sufficient numbers. When conscription was introduced in England but not Ireland in early 1916, the *Orange Sentinel* stated that 'it constitutes an official revelation of the state of affairs in Nationalist Ireland.' The *Sentinel* also proclaimed:

> This recalcitrant attitude upon the part of the Nationalist ought to have the effect of opening the eyes of the English and Scottish people to the probable developments in Ireland after a Home Rule Parliament gets control of affairs. If it convinces the English electors of the full meaning of Home Rule it will serve a good purpose. One can hardly conceive of the Imperial Government refusing to concede the reasonable demands of Ulster for exclusion from the Home Rule Bill after this experience.[39]

Irish-Canadian nationalists refuted these assertions, insisting that in fact it was the Ulster unionists who were not enlisting in sufficient numbers. In July 1915 in Saint John, the *New Freeman* reported in bold type: '**WHERE ULSTER FALLS DOWN** – Where are Carson's Braves? – Not at the Front.'[40] The article was responding to a London article which stated that the Ulster Division required 12,000 more reserves before it could be ready to serve. The *New Freeman* reported that the 'Ulster Division is stranded for want of reserves, and it is not very complimentary to the loyalty and patriotism of the province when the Orangemen and Unionists have to be threatened before they will respond to "the call of King and country" in sufficient numbers to make up even one solitary Division.'[41] The *New Freeman* also reported that the former New Brunswick Grand Master, Mr Hipwell, asserted in a recent speech in Fredericton: 'In New Brunswick fewer than four per cent. of the 6,000 Orangemen have enlisted for service in the present war. It is a shame, a shame, my brethren.' The editorial denounced Canadian Orangemen for professing loyalty to the Crown while failing to enlist in defence of the empire:

> Patriotic Canadians from Sydney to Vancouver will bow their head in shame to think that there is to be found in our fair Dominion an association of men enjoying all of the privileges of Canadian citizenship who, in times of peace, boasted of their loyalty to King and country, and who in time of war, have shamefully shirked their duty ... Today, in the hour of the nation's peril, Orangeism and Orange loyalty have been tried and found wanting.[42]

On both sides of the Atlantic, the relationship between Irish nationalists and unionists continued to deteriorate through 1915 and into

1916. Any remnant of Irish unity with Britain's war effort was shattered when zealous members of the Irish Volunteers planned and executed an insurrection in Dublin, commonly known as the Easter Rising. In the spring of that year, the overwhelming majority of nationalist Irish still supported John Redmond and the IPP. The Irish parliamentarians were the political heirs of Ireland, as the Home Rule Bill was in fact on the statute books awaiting the war's end. Yet the IPP would soon be an historical footnote, swept aside by a nationalist Irish electorate who distrusted the party's close connection with Britain's political establishment and who had come to believe the IPP was incapable of delivering self-government to Ireland.

The leaders of the Easter Rising were an amalgam of old Fenian revolutionaries, poets, Gaelic enthusiasts, educators, and labour organizers. Most important, though, they were all Catholics. Previous Irish revolutionary leaders – such as Theabold Wolf Tone, Robert Emmet, Thomas Davis, and James Stephens – had all been Protestants. This was the first truly Irish Catholic rebellion, and in some limited ways it succeeded. Most of the leaders of the Easter Rising were members of the Gaelic League and had been poets, writers, or educators before developing revolutionary tendencies. Patrick Pearse, the Rising's acknowledged leader, was a poet and an active Gaelic Leaguer who edited the official organ, *An Claidheamh Soluis*, from 1903 to 1909.[43] He then founded St Enda's School for Boys in Rathfarnham outside Dublin, where Thomas MacDonagh taught comparative literature. It has been noted that 'Pearse's educational ideas were in advance of their time. The school's language and games were Irish, and most subjects were taught bilingually.'[44] F.X. Martin asserts that although the Gaelic League's influence was in theory indirect, as the league was professedly non-political, 'it would be hard to exaggerate the influence of the Gaelic League in the Easter Rising ... It was the revival of the Irish language through the League which gave Nationalists a tangible basis for the claim to be a nationality separate from the English.'[45] In 1915, Pearse asserted that Ireland must be 'not free only, but Gaelic as well, not only Gaelic, but free.'[46] As deep as these ideals ran in them, the rebellion's leaders naively overlooked the fact that a significant portion of the population in the northeast, in no way wished to live in a Gaelic-Catholic Ireland and would fight to prevent any such prospect.

The original plan for the Easter Rising called for Pearse, as Director of Organization of the Irish Volunteers, to publicly issue orders for a general mobilization and exercise to take place on 23 April, Easter

Sunday, just as the Volunteers had done the previous Easter. As the Volunteers assembled for the drills and exercise, they would move to strategic points throughout Dublin, seize them, and expel the British from the city. In tandem with the commencement of the Rising, a consignment of weapons from Germany would land in the southwest of Ireland, at which point the arms would be distributed throughout the countryside, enabling the entire country to rise up in support of those brave enough to have started the process in Dublin. Unfortunately for the leaders, most of these plans fell apart before the Rising commenced.

At 12:00 noon on Monday, 24 April 1916, the day after Easter, approximately 1,600 Irish Volunteers, accompanied by 300 members of the Irish Citizen Army, a labour organization, marched to predetermined strategic points in Dublin, seized them, and held these locations for five days, outlasting by four days every Irish rebellion of the previous 118 years. These strategic points included the Four Courts (home of the Irish Judiciary), City Hall, Boland's Mills, South Dublin Union, and St Stephen's Green, as well as the General Post Office (GPO), which served as the headquarters of the Rising and was occupied by Thomas Clarke, Sean MacDermott, Joseph Plunkett, James Connolly, Patrick Pearse, and their contingent. After the GPO was secured, Pearse, Connolly, and a few others stepped outside the Post Office and read the Proclamation of the Irish Republic:

> POBLACHT NA H EIREANN
> The Provisional Government
> of the
> IRISH REPUBLIC
> To the People of Ireland.
>
> IRISHMEN AND IRISHWOMEN: In the name of God and of the dead generations from which she receives her old tradition of nationhood, Ireland, through us, summons her children to her flag and strikes for her freedom.
>
> Having organized and trained her manhood through her secret revolutionary organization, the Irish Republican Brotherhood, and through her open military organizations, the Irish Volunteers and the Irish Citizens Army, having patiently perfected her discipline, she now seizes that moment, and, supported by her exiled children in America and by gallant allies in Europe, but relying in the first on her own strength, she strikes in full confidence of victory.

We declare the right of the people of Ireland to the ownership of Ireland, and to the unfettered control of Irish destinies, to be sovereign and indefeasible. The long usurpation of that right by a foreign people and government has not extinguished the right, nor can it ever be extinguished except by the destruction of the Irish people. In every generation the Irish people have asserted their right to national freedom and sovereignty; six times during the past three hundred years they have asserted it in arms. Standing on that fundamental right and again asserting it in arms in the face of the world, we hereby proclaim the Irish Republic as a Sovereign Independent State, and we pledge our lives and the lives of our comrades-in-arms to the cause of freedom, of its welfare, and of its exaltation among nations.

The Irish Republic is entitled to, and hereby claims, the allegiance of every Irishman and Irishwoman. The Republic guarantees religious and civil liberty, equal rights and equal opportunities to all its citizens, and declares its resolve to pursue the happiness and prosperity of the whole nation and of all of its parts, cherishing all the children of the nation equally, and oblivious of the differences carefully fostered by an alien government, which have divided a minority from the majority in the past.

Until our arms have brought the opportune moment for the establishment of a permanent National Government, representative of the whole people of Ireland and elected by the suffrages of all her men and women, the Provisional Government, hereby constituted, will administer the civil and military affairs of the Republic in trust for the people.

We place the cause of the Irish Republic under the protection of the Most High God, Whose blessing we invoke upon our arms, and we pray that no one who serves that cause will dishonour it by cowardice, inhumanity, or rapine. In this supreme hour the Irish nation must, by its valour and discipline and by the readiness of her children to sacrifice themselves for the common good, prove itself worthy of the august destiny to which it is called.

Signed on Behalf of the Provisional Government,
> THOMAS J. CLARK,
> SEAN Mac DIARMADA,
> THOMAS MacDONAGH,
> P.H. PEARSE,
> EAMONN CEANNT,
> JAMES CONNOLLY,
> JOSEPH PLUNKETT.

Pearse's reading of the proclamation evoked little reaction from the small crowd that had gathered. Although James Connolly was extremely excited, 'there were no wild hurrahs ... The Irish simply listened and shrugged their shoulders, or sniggered a little, and then glanced round to see if the police were coming.'[47]

During the rebellion, the insurgents acted with tremendous restraint and with the greatest respect for the rules of war. Easter Rising historian Max Caulfield cites numerous occasions when the rebels were afforded opportunities to imbibe, which they politely refused each time.[48] This restrained image of an insurgent group of rebels stands in stark contrast to the actions of at least one British officer.

On the second day of the Rising, at roughly 6:00 p.m., having spent the day haranguing mobs of looters on Sackville Street, the pacifist journalist and woman suffrage supporter, Francis Sheehy-Skeffington (whose wife Hanna Sheehy was the daughter of a Nationalist MP) walked to a meeting he had arranged to discuss an idea for a civilian policing unit to thwart looters taking advantage of the Rising. As Skeffington crossed Portobello Bridge he was confronted by a detachment of the Royal Irish Rifles and arrested. After being taken to Portobello Barracks, Skeffington was questioned by Lieutenant Samuel Morgan. When asked by Morgan if he was in sympathy with the Sinn Féiners, Skeffington replied, 'Yes, but I am not in favor of militarism.'[49] Stunned and somewhat at a loss as to what should be done with Sheehy-Skeffington, Lieutenant Morgan ordered him locked up while he inquired to Irish Command HQ for instructions.

At midnight, Captain J.C. Bowen-Colthurst, who was from a landowning family in the south of Ireland, entered and demanded to be given responsibility for the prisoner. At 10:00 the next morning, after a night of prayer, Bowen-Colthurst ordered Sheehy-Skeffington and two other journalists to the backyard behind the guardroom. The three journalists were ordered to walk to the far end of the yard, and as they walked, Bowen-Colthurst shouted, 'Fire!' Even after readily admitting to his superior that he had shot the prisoners, Bowen-Colthurst was allowed to serve through the remainder of the Rising. Only after the Rising, when public outrage reached a fever pitch, was Bowen-Colthurst tried for his crimes. At a military tribunal, he was acquitted for reasons of insanity, and 'Colthurst was sent to Broadmoor Prison for the criminally insane, released after twenty months, and settled in Canada on a military pension.'[50]

Only after British troops surrounded each position, and massively bombed Dublin for two days from the British warship *Helga*, did the rebels surrender. Dublin lay devastated. Around 400 people had died, more than 1,000 had been seriously injured, and seemingly half the city had been destroyed.[51] After the surrender of the General Post Office, while the prisoners were being marched toward Richmond Barracks, crowds lined the streets, shouting 'Shoot the traitors!' and 'Bayonet the bastards!' In one of the poorer sections of Dublin, 'the shawlies [old ladies] pelted them with rotten vegetables,' and some even tossed the contents of their chamber pots.[52] Many of these angry protesters were pensioners, or they were wives whose husbands were serving in the British Army and as such received separation payments from the British Treasury. Fearing that their payments would be cut off as a result of the Rising, these dependent residents of Dublin reacted with derision to the rebels' actions. Whatever their motives, this initially harsh treatment indicated the scant public sympathy afforded the rebels. The Irish public did not understand how these men could so recklessly set out to bring down the full weight of the British military on their city.

Irish-Catholic Canadians worked vigorously to distance themselves from the Easter Rising. The Irish-Catholic weekly press denounced the Rising as an inexcusable act of madness. The *Catholic Register* declared: 'Let it be said with the strongest possible emphasis that it would be difficult to conceive of an act of revolt more utterly unjustified or unjustifiable ... From every conceivable standpoint, then, the rebellion last week, now happily ended, was an unspeakable outrage and a colossal act of folly.'[53] In contrast, the *New Freeman* made few direct denunciations of the rebellion. Instead it focused on the impact the rebellion might have on the image of the Irish populace and the IPP. Although the paper did comment that 'the whole affair would be subject to contempt because of its inherent hare-brained absurdity,' the editorial commentary focused on the hope that the Irish people would not be judged by these events. The *New Freeman* stated:

> It is not an Irish insurrection in any sense except the accident of locality. All the Irish Nationalists have condemned it. The Irish people regard it as insanity. The Irish Bishops and clergy are against it; Irish Nationalist troops have opposed it ... It would be most unjust and deplorable if this episode should be regarded as reflecting injuriously on the good sense and good feelings of the Irish people as a whole.[54]

The St Patrick's Society of Montreal also distanced themselves from the events in Dublin, though it was careful not to criticize Irishmen too harshly. At the society meeting on Monday, 1 May, a debate arose over whether to send a cable endorsing John Redmond. W.J. Hayes and T.P. Tansey favoured sending the cable immediately; Mr Hayes emphasized that if necessary, the cable should be redrafted 'so that it will place us definitely and clearly before John Redmond and Canada in the light we should be placed. We should make it clear we are absolutely loyal and that the mistake made in Ireland has absolutely no sympathy in this country.'[55] Alternatively, E. Curry suggested that the sending of a cable be deferred because it was too soon to pass judgment, noting, 'We have only heard one side of the affair.' Most society members disagreed with this assessment. M.J. McLaughlin argued that they should not delay one more day: 'Let no one imagine we take any particular side in the matter except to endorse John Redmond's policy.'[56] The recording secretary then noted: 'T.P. Tansey said: – Let us voice our feelings now, tonight – but in a way in which no Irishman shall suffer for what we shall say. John Redmond wants us to send a message now, not next week.'[57] It seems as if John Redmond solicited a resolution of support from the St Patrick's Society, which a majority of members favoured. But they were also being careful not to portray themselves, or Irishman generally, in a disloyal light.

Not surprisingly, Orange Canadians responded to the Easter Rising with outrage, disgust, and disdain. They indignantly proclaimed that the rebellion had been a fair representation of what awaited Ulstermen if they were forced to live in a Home Rule Ireland. Could there have been, they asked, any better example of the disloyalty of the Irish? Canadian Orangemen asserted that even John Redmond's guarantees of Nationalist commitment to Ulster's well-being, now carried no weight. The only blessing of this rebellion, Orangemen argued, was that it would suitably serve as a 'warning to the Government and to the people of England and Scotland against the inclusion of Ulster within the sphere of authority of a Dublin Parliament.'[58]

A few weeks later, Canadian Orangemen demanded harsh punishment for the Irish rebels: 'Do the Irish expect that they can make an alliance with Germany, import arms and ammunition, destroy a city ... and suffer no penalty for such atrocious crimes.'[59] Yet when confronted with press reports that similar actions on the part of Ulster's leaders had directly contributed to the rebellion, Canadian Orangemen objected to the comparison, maintaining that for Ulstermen to arm themselves in

1913 and 1914 with German weapons, and to threaten the Imperial Parliament with rebellion was a completely different matter: In that case, Ulstermen had merely been defending themselves. The *Orange Sentinel* railed: 'Sir Edward Carson and the men of Ulster are not the agitators and aggressors. They are defending the peace and security of their own homes. And yet the *Globe* would present them as a group of fanatics who should be thrown into the arms of rebels.'[60]

Nevertheless, even as denunciations of the rebels rose in volume, sympathies began to shift. British reprisals against the rebels were providing the rebel leaders with a degree of honour in Irish public opinion. Within a week, British retaliation converted the rebels from traitors to martyrs. After the surrender, the rebel leaders were imprisoned at Kilmainham Jail on the outskirts of Dublin. In secret trials held at the jail, all were sentenced to death. At dawn on the morning of 3 May, Patrick Pearse, Thomas MacDonagh, and Thomas Clarke were shot by firing squad in the jail's yard. The next day at dawn, Joseph Plunkett (who was dying of tuberculosis), Edward Daly, Michael O'Hanrahan, and Pearse's younger brother Willie all met the same fate, followed on 12 May by Sean MacDermott and James Connolly. Connolly, whose ankle had been shattered by a stray bullet during the Rising and who was in agony from gangrene, was driven by an ambulance from the hospital to Kilmainham, where he had to be propped on a chair to be shot.[61] The British executed fourteen men over the course of ten days. When the news spread of these executions, and the nature in which they transpired, Irish public opinion turned to outrage.

Irish Canadians were not greatly surprised by the harsh penalties meted out to the Dublin rebels. Irish-Catholic Canadians realized that 'men who engage in such enterprises take their lives in their hands, and, intrinsically, it is not easy to complain of severity.'[62] Yet, as in Ireland, Irish-Canadian nationalist opinion began to turn as British authorities dragged out the executions. After another week passed and the full extent of the executions was learned, the *Catholic Register* commented: 'Fourteen men shot after condemnation by courts-martial sitting in secret in the height of excitement and passion, is, in the year 1916, something to startle and appall. It is safe to say that it could not have happened in any other part of the British Empire.'[63]

Irish-Canadian nationalists quickly noted, with unflinching certitude, that the Irish rebels had received a great deal of inspiration from their northern neighbours and that the past actions of the Ulster Unionist leaders should not be forgotten:

As we pointed out last week, the wretched uprising was directly caused by the criminally treasonable conduct of Sir Edward Carson and his associates in preparing and arming for forcible resistance to the law. The punishment meted out that arch-traitor was the appointment to a seat on the King's Privy Council. By that act a premium was put upon treason and armed resistance to lawful authority. But for Carsonist treason there would not have been one unlawfully armed man in Ireland.[64]

The *New Freeman* expressed similar sentiments, assigning Edward Carson the greatest responsibility for the Rising:

Upon the head of the Ulster leader must rest most of the blame for the terrible tragedy in Ireland. It was he who armed Irishmen to fight amongst their own countrymen ...

Sir Edward Carson today assumes the lofty attitude of a patriot but his past actions and past speeches are as before said, of too recent date to be obliterated. He laid down the principle of rebellion against the King in Ireland.[65]

Many Irish-Catholic Canadians again questioned why it mattered whether a rebel in Ireland was Protestant or Catholic.

Even Wilfrid Laurier, Canada's former prime minister, commented with stunned disbelief on how foul he believed the executions to be. Writing to a London friend on 13 May 1916, a surprised and bewildered Laurier 'perceived at once the folly of the executions which followed [the rebellion].'[66] He immediately grasped the inherent duplicity involved with respect to the actions of the British government, which offered leniency toward Sir Edward Carson and the Ulster leadership even while executing the Irish rebel leaders in Dublin for somewhat similar activities:

What a blunder these terrible executions have been, following the foolish attempt at rebellion in Dublin. I could not put into words the feeling of horror these executions inspire, and I cannot conceive a more serious political error. That the Asquith government should display so much severity at Dublin, while it leaves Carson in Belfast free to preach and organize rebellion with impunity, seems to me an act of the utmost feebleness. I know that I am judging from a distance and that there may be circumstances which justify these barbarities, but with the light that we have here, I do not hesitate to repeat what was said about the execution of the Duc d'Enghien by Napoleon, 'It is worse than a crime, it is a blunder.'[67]

In the months following the executions of the Irish rebels, Irish-Canadian nationalists grappled with many issues relating to ethnic identity, equality, and loyalty. Irish-Canadian nationalists still supported the war and the IPP and held out hope that a Home Rule settlement could be arranged. Increasingly, however, they believed that British politicians could no longer be relied upon to broker a fair deal for Ireland. British duplicity, with respect to the treatment of Carson and his cohorts, and the punishment of the Dublin rebels, had all too clearly shown that British politicians governed by notions of allegiance based on religion and ethnic identity, not fairness and justice. For Irish-Catholic Canadians, this dichotomy of British responses raised serious questions about the place of Catholics in the British Empire. Past references to the notion of British fair play, and to British statesmen doing right by Ireland in conferring Home Rule, now turned to references of the stain of British administration in Ireland. For example, the *New Freeman* exclaimed that the 'administration of Irish affairs in the past is a blot on British statesmanship. The violation of Irish trust by the present-day government but adds to the mess. Small wonder the Irish party has severed its connection with the coalition government. Tory intrigue and Tory deceit again seem to have carried the day.'[68]

In September 1916 the *New Freeman* pointedly asked questions that had undoubtedly had been resonating among Irish-Catholic Canadians for some time: 'Is Ireland denied Home Rule primarily and principally because it is a Catholic country?'[69] The paper commented on Ulster Protestant claims that they would not be 'safe from oppression under a Catholic parliament in Dublin.' The *New Freeman* explained that no one really believed this, but it also acknowledged that the 'Ulster Protestants are being used as contemptible instruments by sectarian politicians on the English side of the water.' The paper then asked, 'Does not everything show that Protestants are prepared to imperil the whole Empire rather than do right to Catholic Ireland?'[70] For many Irish-Catholic Canadians, British duplicity fostered Ulster Protestant bigotry and hatred of Catholics, and worse yet, was denying Ireland's right of self-government.

In a similar fashion, the upsurge in Canadian patriotism at the beginning of the war had exposed and exacerbated the ethnic prejudice and chauvinism prevailing in Canadian society; however, nothing as grievous as the 1916 executions occurred. During the first two years of the war, ethnic minorities had been turned away when they volunteered to serve in the Canadian Expeditionary Force. East Indian, Chinese, and Japanese Canadians had all been excluded from joining the Canadian armed forces. When fifty blacks from Sydney, Nova Scotia, arrived to enlist, they were told: 'This is not for you fellows, this is a white man's war.'[71] Repeated offers from minority leaders to form ethnically distinct and separate battalions were rejected by Militia Headquarters.[72] But as the war dragged on and Canadian volunteers dwindled in number, '[by] the summer of 1916 Canadian blacks, Indians, and Japanese were all being recruited into the services.'[73] For the most part, these recruits were formed into work and service units.

As a result of swirling rumours that German Americans were drilling in Milwaukee in preparation for an invasion of Canada, these sentiments of ethnic prejudice were also extended to German Canadians. At the time, there were 100,000 native-born Germans or Austro-Hungarians 'and another 400,000 were of alien enemy extraction.'[74] Censorship of the foreign-language press found great support among Canadians of the 'proper' ethnic extractions. Colonel Sam Hughes, an Orangeman and the Minister of Militia and Defence in Robert Borden's Conservative government, suggested that Canadians of German descent could pose a problem and a 'menace'; in cabinet meetings he recommended that 'they be encouraged to go to the United States.'[75] An Anti-German League was founded in Toronto in 1916. The city of Berlin, Ontario, changed its name to Kitchener after the British Secretary of War. Colonel Sam Hughes notwithstanding, despite government policies designed to encourage tolerance, 'harassment of aliens, collectively and individually, increased during the war.'[76] Ethnic alienation was a logical consequence of such treatment.

As 1917 unfolded, mainstream Irish nationalist political opinion realigned itself dramatically. The great mass of the Irish electorate slowly but surely transferred their allegiance from the traditional constitutional Home Rulers, the IPP, to the republican separatist Sinn Féin party. The name Sinn Féin, Gaelic for 'ourselves alone,' was assigned to a loose amalgam of Irish political clubs in 1905 by Maire Butler, an ardent Gaelic Leaguer.[77] The informal head of this loosely confederated political organization was Arthur Griffith, a Dublin printer and publisher, who in 1899 launched a nationalist newspaper, *United Irishmen,* adopting the name of the 1798 revolutionary movement led by Theobold Wolfe Tone. In 1906 the paper changed its name to *Sinn Féin*. David

Fitzpatrick notes: 'Sinn Féin displaced the Irish Parliamentary Party as the mouthpiece of Irish Nationalist aspirations.'[78] This transformation in Irish nationalist politics was a direct result of the harsh British reprisals against the leaders of the Easter Rising and the IPP's close association with the British government. Most of the Irish populace felt that 'Irishmen must cease to trust the British government because it had returned in wartime to the old mode of coercion and exploitation; [and must cease to trust] the Irish Party because it had become the government's spaniel.'[79] Sinn Féin was tainted neither by the stain of a British connection, nor by the cloud of political scandal, for prior to the events of 1916, it had been a relatively obscure political party.[80]

Throughout 1916 and 1917, Sinn Féin was the greatest beneficiary of British reprisals against nationalist Ireland. British policy in Ireland actually bolstered Sinn Féin at the expense of the foundering IPP. When Britain proposed a new Home Rule solution at the end of 1916, it seemed insincere and belated. David Fitzpatrick observed that with 'astonishing obtuseness the government played into the hands of Sinn Fein. By doggedly trying to restore the Irish Party's prestige, it seemed to confirm Sinn Fein's allegations that Redmond and Dillon had sold their souls to the Saxon ... Lloyd George's Home Rule proposal of 1916 was offered to the Irish Party as a lifeline; but the party grabbed too eagerly, caught up its limbs in the slack and drowned.'[81]

One such episode of British efforts to prop up the IPP was a political conference convened in Dublin that became known as the Irish Convention. This was called by David Lloyd George's coalition government in May 1917, and debated from July 1917 to March 1918. It was an effort to bring the various Irish factions together to solve the impasse on their own.[82] The attendees included the IPP, southern Unionists, and northern Unionists; Sinn Féin boycotted.[83] The attending parties adopted a number of platform resolutions related to a proposed Irish settlement, including a six-county Ulster exclusion from Home Rule. Redmond's acceptance of such a proposal reflected his desperation to achieve any form of settlement.[84] Even though most of those attending the convention approved these resolutions, northern Unionists dissented, and Sinn Féin remained outside the process.[85]

The mere fact that such a convention had been summoned brought forth cries of derision from Orange-Canadian unionists, who viewed it as yet another attempt by conniving British politicians to grind their Ulster brethren under the heel of a Romanist parliament in Dublin. Canadian Orangemen openly expressed support for Ulster unionist resistance to such obvious Irish nationalist machinations. In a seemingly well-orchestrated and well-coordinated campaign of support, as soon as the convening of the Irish Convention became public knowledge, between 12 May and 30 June 1917, Orange-Canadian unionists sent no fewer than thirty-two telegrams of support to Sir Edward Carson at Westminster. The telegram campaign may well have been coordinated, for the phrasing of each message was similar when not identical. The first few read: 'Please convey to Premier Lloyd George solicitude and loyalty to Ulster of eighty-five percent of Canadians'; 'The vast majority of canadians are opposed to any coercion of Ulster in irish settlement'; 'A vast majority of canadian people are very anxious that in any Irish settlement there should be no coercion of Ulster'; 'The vast majority of canadians are opposed to any coercion of ulster in Irish settlement.'[86]

There can be little doubt that the vast majority of Canadian Orangemen supported Sir Edward Carson, but it is unlikely that the vast majority of *all Canadians* felt the same way. Yet there is no doubt that Orange-Canadian unionists supported Ulster unionists' obstructionist tactics well into 1918. Lengthy resolutions of support from Orange lodges in Toronto and London, Ontario, conveying expressions of sincere approval of the Ulster leaders' tactics arrived during the spring and summer of 1918. One resolution, from the Hackett Orange Lodge of London, Ontario, read:

The Right Hon. Sir Edward Carson, M.P.
   Parliament Buildings,
      London, Eng.
Dear Sir & Rt. Hon. Bro: –
   I have been directed to forward you a copy of the following Resolution, passed at the last meeting of Hackett L.O.B.L. No. 805, of the City of London, held on 22nd, May, 1918.
Moved by Wor, Bro. Jos. Murray, Treas.
Seconded by Bro. A. Niven, Rec. Sec.

That the Officers and Members of Hackett L.O.B.L., are most desirous of conveying to the RT. HON. SIR EDWARD CARSON, their unanimous appreciation and approval, in recognition of your unceasing efforts to preserve the Civil and Religious liberties of the loyal Protestants of Ireland, and preventing the dismemberment of the Empire, by the disloyal elements in Ireland and their assistants elsewhere, as manifested by protesting against the Government's Home Rule proposal, as violation of solemn

pledges, and demanding the Conscription be enforced upon those who defy law and order. (Unanimously carried)
By virtue of the true Allegiance expressed in your noble acts, let me further assure you that the Brethren of this Lodge, declare a vote of confidence in your endeavor to frustrate all Papal intrigue and deception, and in the name of the Brotherhood wish you Godspeed and success.

                Your's Fraternally,
                A. Niven, Rec. Sec.
                Joseph W. Carson, Wor. Mas.
                John Morrison, Dep. Mas.
                Wor. Jos. Murray, Treas.
                WM. Johnson, Chap.
                W.J. Hodgins, Fin. Sec.[87]

Not surprisingly, Orange-Canadian unionists viewed any efforts on the part of Irish nationalists to gain any form of independence as part of a Papal plot. These sentiments only intensified in the ensuing years as twenty-six of the thirty-two Irish counties gained dominion status with far more powers than had been offered under Home Rule. Yet Orange-Canadian unionists were far from the only Canadians frustrated by British policy in Ireland.

Irish-Canadian nationalists also felt exasperated by the actions of the British government. In a series of articles for the *Catholic Register*, Robert Lindsay Crawford articulated the frustration that many Irish Canadians felt toward the British government. Crawford was a Protestant Ulsterman and was 'stoutly Orange and Protestant in his outlook until his mid-thirties,' when he became an ardent Home Ruler.[88] In 1910 he moved to Canada and found employment with the Toronto newspaper *The Globe*, on whose editorial board he remained until 1918. In his 1917 series for the *Catholic Register*, Crawford expressed the frustration that most Irish Canadians felt at Britain's unwillingness to confer Home Rule in earlier years, and at the government's sudden enthusiasm to do so after the withholding of Home Rule had caused so much death and destruction. Crawford wrote:

> England's opportunity to make just reparation for the wrongs done to Ireland has passed forever. A year ago – six months, three months ago – and the settlement of Ireland on statesmanlike lines would have redounded to the credit of the Minister and the Government responsible. To-day none [is] so poor in Nationalist Ireland as to profess to believe that any conces-

sion now made to the century-old demands of the people will be granted because of a desire to do justice. England will grant Home Rule to Ireland, not because she loves Irish Nationalism and hates the bureaucratic rule of Dublin Castle, but because of the pressure of public opinion throughout the Allied nations, and to satisfy English and Imperial necessities in time of war.[89]

During 1917, British authorities continued to alienate the Irish populace. It arrested, imprisoned, and generally harassed anyone suspected of connections to Sinn Féin. Families who had traditionally supported the IPP migrated to Sinn Féin as a result of British obstinance. Thus, British authorities were making 'heroes out of nobodies and provok[ing] savage indignation among families which had previously supported the new movement, if at all, only out of herd instinct.'[90] David Fitzpatrick asserts that 'the mistakes of 1916 were repeated again and again.'[91]

Irish indignation translated into electoral success for Sinn Féin, which tapped into Irish hostility toward Britain and gained electoral victories in four by-elections across Ireland. Sinn Féin won seats in North Roscommon, South Longford, North Cavan, and most spectacularly in East Clare, where Eamon de Valera won in a landslide to assume the seat vacated by Major Willie Redmond, John Redmond's younger brother, who had been killed in the war. All of the victorious Sinn Féin candidates refused to take their seats at Westminster. These by-election defeats foreshadowed the fate of the IPP.

Although Irish-Canadian nationalists had been completely dissuaded of the idea that British politicians would ever deliver Home Rule to Ireland, they never advocated complete Irish separation from the empire. In March 1917 the *Catholic Register* warned that British continuance of the same haphazard policies would 'throw Ireland into the arms of the advocates of physical force.' It then asserted: 'There is no hope for Ireland in physical force or in agitation for total separation from the Empire.'[92] After the Sinn Féin by-election victory in South Longford, Crawford asked in his last article for the *Catholic Register:* 'Is Ireland Republican?' He dismissed the South Longford election victory as an aberration, noting Longford's history of agitation and the 'cruel marks of landlord oppression and British misrule.'[93] He concluded that Ireland was far too conservative to truly embrace the republican separatist mantle.

Irish-Canadian nationalists continued to view Redmond's leadership as the only hope for Ireland to achieve some semblance of self-government. That Ireland could completely separate itself from Britain and the empire seemed inconceivable to many of them. The *New Freeman* stoutly proclaimed that 'Ireland's hope lies in loyally following the leadership of John Redmond, the greatest living Irishmen and one of the greatest living statesmen and Parliamentarians in any country.'[94] Even after the initial Sinn Féin success, most Irish-Canadian nationalists continued to support Redmond and the IPP.

In April 1918, tensions in Ireland rose yet again when Prime Minister David Lloyd George intimated that Home Rule would be granted to Ireland, contingent on the introduction of military conscription. Most Irish were stunned. Why was it now possible to grant Home Rule? The vast majority of Irish opposed conscription, and those who might have supported it, by 1918 were so disillusioned with British policy in Ireland they were too sceptical now to support conscription.[95] Additionally, the Irish clergy fervently opposed conscription, further distancing the Irish populace from the British administration. Irish-Canadian nationalists, too, opposed conscription and could not believe that the British government had the audacity to now propose such a plan. The *New Freeman* asked:

> Premier Lloyd George... leads one to believe that the government will immediately grant long-deferred justice to Ireland but, coupled with it, must go enforced military service. The blunders of the administration in Ireland chilled the spontaneous war effort of the Irish people; its subsequent actions have not been the kind to impel either sacrifice or service ... It may well be asked, if the British government of today can do what the press dispatches indicate may be done – give Ireland Home Rule – for the sake of getting much needed reenforcements, why could not the government of 1914 have granted the right of self-determination to the Irish people for the sake of common justice?[96]

The *New Freeman* invoked an idea made popular during the final stages of the war by American President Woodrow Wilson: the right to self-determination. Irish nationalists now argued to great effect, that if the Great War was being fought for the right of small nations to determine their own form of government – which is what the Allied countries claimed the war was about – why should Ireland not be included among those small nations?

Only a year earlier, Canada also experienced a conscription crisis that served to exacerbate ethnic tensions between English and French

Canadians. As a result of mismanagement by Militia Minister Colonel Sam Hughes and a sharp decline in voluntary enlistment after 1915, the Canadian Expeditionary Force faced a severe manpower shortage. Kenneth McNaught writes that this shortfall 'resulted [from] the government's commitment to maintain four full divisions on the Western Front and from the fact that recruiting declined sharply throughout 1916. Borden moved reluctantly toward compulsion in the face of bitter opposition from organized labor, farmers and most French Canadians.'[97] French Canadians opposed conscription for many reasons. To begin with, most French Canadians who volunteered had been dispersed throughout the CEF instead of being formed into French-speaking units. Moreover, French Canadians felt deliberately provoked by educational policies that Manitoba and Ontario had adopted during the war, in 1916: Manitoba had eliminated bilingual schools; and Ontario enacted the highly controversial Regulation 17, which sharply restricted the use of French in public schools. French Canadians asked 'why they should fight for an empire whose supporters denied them equal rights within their own country.'[98]

The next national election, in December 1917, was essentially a referendum on conscription. At this juncture, writes Arthur Lower, 'one of the Prime Minister's young lieutenants, Mr. Arthur Meighen, came forward with two bills designed to influence the [election] result, *The Military Voters Act* and the *War Times Election Act*. These denied the franchise to conscientious objectors, to those of enemy alien birth or those of European birth speaking an enemy alien language and naturalized since 1902.'[99] The 'fierce and violent' election campaign[100] resulted in a clear victory for Borden and conscription: Borden's Union government won 153 seats; Wilfrid Laurier's Liberals only 82. Yet in Quebec, Borden took only 3 seats to Laurier's 62. Quebec had been politically isolated, and the 'conscription crisis of 1917–1918 left on the public life of Canada a deep mark.'[101] The bitterness and resentment generated by this lasted for decades. Not surprisingly, the conscription crisis in Ireland bore a striking resemblance to the one in Canada.

In Ireland, as in Canada, the British government also exacerbated ethnic tensions by making one policy bungle after another. In May 1918 the British government crushed any hope of gaining Irish public support when it arrested and imprisoned hundreds of Sinn Féiners, claiming that a pro-German plot was being hatched. In doing so, it only reinforced the belief held by Irish nationalists that the British government acted out of racial prejudice against Irish Catholics, while allowing Ulster Protestants a free hand to do as they chose. As well, Irish Canadians did not overlook this disparity in treatment. Irish-Canadian nationalists condemned the arrests of apparently innocent Irish nationalists, with the *New Freeman* wondering aloud whether British justice was even possible in Ireland. The paper offered little sympathy for Sinn Féin; it, however, noted that the repeated actions of the British government directly contributed to the party's growth:

> There will be little sympathy for any of the Sinn Feiners, arrested last week, providing the charges made against them are proven ... Unfortunately, past actions of the British Government in Ireland do not inspire that trust which a Government, or Government action, is supposed to inspire. Too much reason has been given the Irish people to suspect every move made by the Government in Irish affairs ... Is it any wonder that Irishmen the world over, knowing these things, regard the arrest of the Sinn Feiners and the little proof offered by the Government of their guilt, as but another step in the perfidious history of British rule in Ireland?[102]

Though most Irish-Canadian nationalists still supported John Redmond's IPP, support for Sinn Féin was by now already developing in Canada. It was becoming more and more apparent that Redmond would not be able to deliver Home Rule to Ireland. The question was, who to support instead? How could Irish-Canadian nationalists best express their desire for Irish self-government?

Debates developed within Irish fraternal societies in Canada regarding how best to support Irish independence. On 4 March 1917, at a meeting of the St Patrick's Society at Congress Hall in Montreal, it was duly noted that several communications had been received from Miss Katherine Hughes suggesting 'lines of action to be taken on the Irish question.'[103] Her key suggestion was that the society, on or before St Patrick's Day, should cable Prime Minister Borden in Ottawa asking him to 'take the necessary action at the [upcoming] Peace Conference that Justice at last shall be done to Ireland, the Little Nation that is the Motherland of our race.'[104] The members of St Patrick's took up this suggestion, believing that it accorded with the Allies' repeated allied declarations that the war was being fought for the principle of self-determination. It was also suggested that this appeal be framed as a request directly to Borden, the Canadian leader, rather than as a general expression of support for Redmond of the IPP. The fact that Katherine Hughes, a prominent Irish-Canadian activist, had contacted the St

Patrick's Society regarding 'lines of action to be taken' suggests that a national movement was emerging among Irish-Canadian nationalists to coordinate and intensify their expressions of support for Ireland.

Further communications with the St Patrick's Society demonstrated that this process was indeed under way among Irish-Canadian nationalists. On 7 May 1917 the society's meeting book referenced a communication from the Montreal branch of the Irish National Union requesting that the society select two delegates annually 'to form an advisory council – within their union.'[105] The St Patrick's Society unanimously appointed President M.A. Phelan and W.J. Hayes as delegates, even though the function of this proposed advisory council was never mentioned. Then a year later, on 13 May 1918, the Ancient Order of Hibernians asked the St Patrick's Society to send delegates to a gathering of 'the proposed Irish Union.'[106] After considerable unrecorded discussion, the society responded that it would defer action on sending delegates pending a response informing them more clearly on the aims and objectives of the proposed Union. Given the conservative nature of the St Patrick's Society, this should not have been surprising. Nevertheless, these correspondences do indicate that some of the more strident Irish-Canadian fraternal organizations were attempting to develop a national infrastructure to coordinate a campaign in support of Ireland's freedom. They also indicate that as a result of wartime events in Ireland, Irish-Canadian nationalist sentiments were shifting.

Indications of nascent Sinn Féin support in Canada seeped out as a result in a speech delivered in the Canadian House of Commons. On 19 March 1918, Charles Murphy, MP for Russell, Ontario, spoke in the House in response to anti-Catholic remarks made by N.W. Rowell, MP, during the recently contested Canadian national election. Mr Murphy's speech inspired a letter of congratulations, and complaint, from the Reverend D.A. Casey, editor of the Catholic weekly *Canadian Freeman*, published in Kingston, Ontario. D.A. Casey thanked Mr Murphy for his 'magnificent vindication of our holy Faith,' adding that Rowell should 'hide his dishonored head in shame.' But then Casey criticized Murphy for additional offhanded remarks:

> Why did you make that unfortunate comparison between the Wesleys and the Sinn Feiners? It is a thousand pities that you did so, as some of our people who make no allowance for what is said in the heat of debate will resent it very deeply. I am sure that it is not necessary for me to tell you that the censored reports of affairs in Ireland cannot be accepted as gospel.

> The Sinn Fein constitute the purest political party in the world to-day, and as one of your ardent admirers I regret more than I can say the indeliberate aspersions upon their motives.[107]

Rev. Casey's comments indicate that he believed Sinn Féin to be an unparalleled political movement and that he knew many people who shared his opinion. Casey's reference to 'our people' was undoubtedly a reference to those of Irish-Catholic descent, among whom – so he believed – support for Sinn Féin was slowly developing. Although Mr Casey's reference indicates that support for Sinn Féin by then existed, in Canada it still lagged well behind support for the IPP. The vast majority of Irish-Canadian nationalists remained supportive of the constitutional nationalists, and in no way supported a political party that advocated complete separation from the empire. At least, that was the case until the end of 1918. After the Irish electorate threw its weight behind Sinn Féin in the 1918 British general election, Irish-Canadian nationalists began to do the same.

In the British general election of 14 December 1918, the IPP was swept off the political map by a Sinn Féin landslide. Sinn Féin won 73 of the 105 Irish seats in the House of Commons. The election rendered the IPP irrelevant, it winning only 6 seats, with the Unionists claiming the remaining 26. Twenty-five races were complete routs, with Sinn Féin candidates actually running unopposed in the western counties of Clare, Kerry, and Cork. After this clear demonstration of the sentiments of the Irish populace, Irish-Canadian nationalist support turned away from the IPP. Thereafter, many Irish-Canadian nationalists cautiously endorsed Sinn Féin, asserting that small nations, including Ireland, possessed the right to self-determination by virtue of the Allied victory in the First World War.

*Chapter Four*

# From Home Rulers to Sinn Féiners: The Rise of the Self-Determination for Ireland League of Canada, 1919–1921

Sinn Féin's landslide victory in the 1918 British general election swept the constitutionalist Irish Parliamentary Party from the political map; it also, at least for a few years, recast Ireland's political contours in a republican separatist mould. Even though most Sinn Féin candidates were sitting in British jails on trumped-up charges of aiding a 'German plot,' Sinn Féin won 73 of the 105 Irish seats in the British Parliament; in the twenty-six counties that later became the Irish Free State, the party garnered 65 per cent of the votes cast by the recently expanded Irish electorate.[1] After the election, those Sinn Féin representatives available to do so – all twenty-seven of them – refused to take their seats at Westminster. Instead, on 21 January 1919, they assembled at Mansion House in Dublin, where they constituted themselves as Dáil Éireann (Assembly of Ireland).[2] The Dáil declared Ireland an independent republic and published the Democratic Program, which asserted that the Irish Republic would care for the Irish people and develop its own resources as the Irish people saw fit.[3] The vast majority of the Irish populace, in voting for Sinn Féin, had resolved to determine their own political destiny by choosing their own form of governance, as they believed was their right. Needless to say, the British government viewed these actions as entirely illegal and moved rapidly to curtail this egregious example of Irish obstinance.

The reaction of Irish-Canadian nationalists to Sinn Féin's landslide victory in many ways resembled that of the Irish in other dominions. As with their Australian counterparts, the impulses of Irish-Canadian nationalists to publicly express support for Irish independence had always been sharply restrained by virtue of the continued imperial connection, not to mention by the intimidation of the potentially violent Orange Order. Richard Davis and Malcolm Campbell both have noted that the responses of Irish Canadians and Irish Australians to events in Ireland were subdued compared to those of Irish Americans. Davis writes that 'harmless Irish rhetoric in the U.S.A. sounded like high treason in British Canada' and therefore 'inhibited Irish-Canadian militancy.'[4]

Unlike their Orange-Canadian unionist counterparts, who vigorously demonstrated against Home Rule for Ireland, Irish-Canadian nationalists prior to 1919 had rarely held public rallies in support of Irish independence.[5] Rather, it was through newspaper editorials and fraternal society resolutions that Irish-Canadian nationalists had proclaimed their support for the IPP and had expressed their justifiable pride at the prospect of their ancestral homeland becoming 'a nation once again.'[6] Nonetheless, Irish-Canadian nationalists grew frustrated with British political orthodoxies, especially when the British government failed to implement the Irish Home Rule legislation residing on the statute books, seemingly because the Ulster Unionist minority held a veto and were relentless in its use. As in Ireland, Irish-Canadian frustrations turned to disgust when it was revealed that the leaders of the 1916 Easter Rising had been executed after secret trials held in Kilmainham Jail. But this frustration translated into only a few measurable expressions of Canadian support for Sinn Féin after its electoral success in the 1917–18 by-elections. Most Irish-Canadian nationalists remained steadfast in their support of the IPP.[7] Only after the Irish populace threw their overwhelming support to Sinn Féin in December 1918 did Irish Canadians begin to support an independent Ireland more overtly. This would lead to the formation of a nationwide Irish-Canadian nationalist institution.

At this time of growing support in Canada for Irish independence, the dominion's Irish-Catholic newspapers unflinchingly attributed Sinn Féin's election victory to the injustice of British administration in Ireland. In Saint John, the *New Freeman* all but predicted a shift in Irish-Canadian allegiances with respect to Irish politics:

> The outcome of the election simply shows that, in the opinion of the great majority of the people of Ireland the Nationalist party has outlived its usefulness, that conditions made a change necessary if Ireland is to enjoy that right for which the great war was fought – the right of self-determination and of development along national lines ... If men like John Redmond and John Dillon built too much on the pledges of British politicians; if despite their pledges British politicians regarded the treaty [legislation],

which bears the royal signature, to give Ireland Home Rule, with cynical indifference; if a rebellious faction in northeast Ulster could be favored and even applauded by these self-same politicians who had nothing but force and suppression for the majority of the Irish people then, indeed, it is very hard to say that the Irish people have done wrong in repudiating the old constitutional movement and set out on another track.[8]

On 9 January 1919, while Sinn Féiners refused to take their seats at Westminster and prepared to convene in Dublin, a large gathering of Irish Canadians assembled in Montreal at National Monument Hall in one of the first rallies in Canada to express support for Irish national aspirations. In his introductory remarks, the event's chair, Dr J.K. Foran, insisted that they had all gathered not to 'enter the field of Irish politics, or advocate any particular policy. That was for the Irish people themselves to decide upon.'[9] Along with the principal speakers that evening – who besides Foran included Charles J. Foy as well as E.B. Devlin, MP for Wright – prominent Canadians of Irish descent appeared on stage to demonstrate their support for Ireland. Among them were Captain Charles 'Chubby' Powers, MP for Quebec West; Martin Malden, MLA; Montreal alderman Mr O'Connell; L.A. David, MLA; and the Reverend Cannon O'Meara.[10]

Dr J.K. Foran prefaced his address by acknowledging the receipt of many letters of apology sent by those who were unable to attend the rally. These included ex-Mayor Scott of Ottawa; the Honourable Charles Murphy, MP; the Honourable John Hall Kelly; Senator Dandurand; Armand Lavergne; Henri Bourassa; and Quebec premier Sir Lomer Gouin, who expressed 'best wishes for your cause.' Wilfrid Laurier himself, though no longer prime minister, acknowledged by letter that 'you may be certain that what is satisfactory to you and your friends in Montreal, will be eminently satisfactory to me.'[11]

Following the remarks of Foran and Devlin, Charles Foy spoke, and he did so with an assertiveness never before heard in Irish-Canadian circles. Foy minced few words as he discussed at length the events in Ireland during the Home Rule Crisis of 1912 to 1914. He reminded the crowd that Sir Edward Carson had made every effort to thwart Irish Home Rule, including importing weapons from Germany: 'He had imported arms into Ireland to resist the law, he made cause with the enemy. Why deny it? Even those in charge of the military district when asked to suppress it turned turtle.'[12] Foy noted that from these events inspired by the Carsonites sprang the Irish Volunteers, who were simply availing themselves of the same methods as those used by the Unionists. Then he commented at length on the rise of Sinn Féin:

> One act followed another until we had the rising of the Easter week that will always remain as a blot on the escutcheon of English rule in Ireland. From that there sprang the only reasonable, logical aggregation or body, or organization that Ireland has ever had, the Sinn Fein. (Prolonged applause.) The genuine Sinn Fein movement is the most misunderstood movement. Everything that could be said against it is being said, and I want to warn you that if you take your Irish news from the censored news, and the subsidized press, you will be far from the truth. You will not get the truth of the Irish situation from the ordinary newspapers. Why is this movement getting such support? Because it is a logical movement and the best movement, and just because it is good it will receive attention from those who would like to see us condemned. True, there may be some irreconcilables in the movement. Does that condemn it? ... You see, this is the medicine that the English aristocracy is not used to. (Laughter and cheers.) It is the medicine that English statesmen are not used to, but they will have to get used to it. Call it what you will, Nationalism, Sinn Fein, there is not a man or woman here who is not a moral Sinn Feiner. There is not a man or woman here who loves liberty who is not a Sinn Feiner. What does it stand for? It is the doctrine of self-reliance and self-confidence.[13]

Foy then asked, 'was it right that the British Premier should advocate the autonomy of Palestine, of Armenia or any of the other small nations, and completely ignore Ireland?' He concluded with a 'brilliant oratory in which was extolled the glories of the Irish race,' and with the parting jab, 'Though foes may jeer, we're Irish yet.'[14]

This gathering of Irish nationalists in Canada, and Foy's extraordinary comments, did not go unnoticed by the Orange-Canadian unionists or their official organ. With respect to the meeting itself, the *Orange Sentinel* declared the 'spectacle of the Irish in Canada cheering for the cutthroats who murdered inoffensive citizens in the name of patriotism is one that shocks the senses. It gives color to the charges that these same Irish malcontents in Canada were as pro-German as certain classes among the French-Canadians.'[15] With respect to Foy's statements, the *Sentinel* alerted readers:

> At the Montreal meeting Mr. Foy said that Sinn Feinism was 'THE BEST, THE MOST LOGICAL, AND THE STRONGEST MOVEMENT IRELAND

EVER HAD.' One must conclude from such a statement that if Mr. Foy had been living in Ireland he would be of the Sinn Fein. His openly declared sympathy with treason, murder, arson, and rebellion marks him as a man unfit for decent society. How can loyal citizens fraternize with a man of that type?[16]

In asking whether loyal citizens could legitimately associate themselves with supporters of Sinn Féin, the *Orange Sentinel* brought into question whether citizens of Canada could support independence movements in their countries of ancestral origin and remain loyal Canadians, particularly if the country in question was breaking away from Britain. But was this question still legitimate? Had not Canada's relationship with Britain changed during the First World War? At the April 1917 Imperial War Cabinet Conference in London, the dominion nations asserted that they deserved a greater degree of autonomy and a greater say in imperial policy as a result of their contributions to the empire's war effort. Although formal alteration to the imperial arrangement was postponed until after the war, certain fundamental principles were firmly stated: 'the status of the Dominions as autonomous nations [was] proclaimed, as [were] their right to a voice in foreign policy and the desirability of a common imperial policy based on consultation.'[17] During and especially after the First World War, the political contours of the empire had altered considerably, so why was Ireland's demand for self-government disloyal?

Charles Foy's hometown newspaper also raised this question of loyalty to Canada. The *Expositor* declared that 'the British sentiment in Perth [Ontario] and Lanark County' regarded Foy's speech as treasonous. In a sharply worded editorial, *The Expositor* left little question as to the treatment Foy would receive from members of that rural community:

> The Sinn Fein speech reflects on the fair and loyal name of Perth. No Canadian, if he is a true Canadian, can characterize Sinn Feinism as 'the best, the most logical and the strongest movement Ireland ever had,' and get away with it, and no Perth man can preach that doctrine and expect the town and district to swallow the stuff, and accept the speaker on the same footing as before.[18]

This typified the response that Irish-Canadian support for Irish independence engendered among Orange-Canadian unionists. Accusations of disloyalty and treason followed those Irish Canadians who freely expressed their support for Irish independence. While Foy's comments made headlines in Orange-Canadian unionist newspapers, the protracted political stalemate and escalating violence in Ireland made news throughout Canada.

Between 1919 and 1921 the news from Ireland was heavily censored by British administrators. Foy had noted as much in his Montreal speech. During those years, Britain and Ireland became ensnared in an armed conflict the complexity of which is best illustrated by the multitude of names ascribed to the conflict.[19] The British government was hardly interested in acknowledging that it was engaged in combating a war of independence in Ireland, with such acknowledgments undoubtedly conferring legitimacy upon the Irish separatists. It was, then, in Britain's best interests to simply suppress freedom of the press in Ireland, which occurred on such a regular basis and to such an extent that numerous Irish nationalist newspapers were closed down.[20]

The commencement of the Anglo-Irish War can be dated to the events of 21 January 1919 at Soloheadbeg, County Tipperary, when a group of Irish volunteers – soon to be known as the Irish Republican Army – absconded with a cartload of quarry explosives, killing the two accompanying police officers in the process.[21] Over the following two-and-a-half years a guerilla war of independence ensued. The British government insisted that law and order would have to be restored in Ireland before it would agree to any negotiated settlement along the lines of Home Rule. Unfortunately, the British Government were engaged in complex postwar affairs: in unrest in Egypt, India, and Mesopotamia that was diverting its attention. The Irish conflict was actually low on its list of priorities, which meant that if not properly managed, the Irish problem could quickly escalate into an Irish crisis.[22] As Keith Jeffery notes: 'It seems clear that the pressures under which the British Government were operating during the immediate postwar years adversely affected the quality of decision-making. Irish security policy was certainly characterized by a tendency to cut corners and discover a "quick fix" of some sort or another.'[23]

To make that quick fix, British authorities established new security forces to augment the Irish police force, the Royal Irish Constabulary (RIC). D.G Boyce notes that during the postwar economic slowdown in Britain, with its accompanying high unemployment – especially among ex-servicemen – 'the government had no difficulty in finding recruits for its gendarmerie in post-war Britain: and from 1 January 1920 to the closing of the rolls at the end of August 1921 over twelve thousand men were enrolled.'[24] Recruits poured into the new force so rapidly that the number of men needing uniforms soon outstripped supply. The recruits were outfitted instead in a mixture of military khaki jackets and RIC dark green trousers, and from this odd uniform developed the nickname 'Black and Tans.'[25] The new recruits 'received only rudimentary police training.'[26] In addition to these green forces, around 2,200 former British army officers had been given the status of temporary cadets in the Auxiliary Division, under the command of Brigadier General Frank Percy Crozier, 'formerly of the Ulster Volunteers and the 36th [Ulster] Division.'[27] This rapid deployment of ill-trained troops to fight an unconventional enemy led to disastrous consequences.

When the Troubles broke out, the type of warfare that emerged was anything but conventional. The Irish volunteers, who were desperately short of arms, ammunition, and men, resorted to fighting one of the first guerrilla wars of modern times. Fergus Campbell has noted that most studies of the social composition of the IRA 'suggest that the IRA drew most of its membership from rural communities.'[28] Operating throughout the countryside in small units of twenty or thirty men known as 'flying columns,' the IRA practised the art of hit and run. Often striking under cover of darkness, these flying columns attacked police stations and soldiers' barracks, and even weapons depots, seized whatever arms they could and then faded back into the countryside. Their main objective was not necessarily to kill as many soldiers as possible – although some soldiers were killed – but rather to merely exist, to not get caught.[29] In this endeavour the Irish republican volunteers received tremendous support and shelter from the Irish people. One historian has acknowledged that the 'I.R.A. could not have operated as effectively as it did without the support, or at least the acquiescence of the majority of the Irish people.'[30]

Frustrated from endlessly chasing an elusive enemy, British forces, especially the Black and Tans, began inflicting reprisals on communities suspected of sympathizing with the IRA. The most notorious of these were the burnings of Cork, Limerick, Ennistymon, and Balbriggan.[31] Charles Townshend points to clear evidence that these reprisals were sanctioned at the highest levels, and that 'the cabinet was prepared to gamble with the Black and Tans' propensity to "see red."'[32] Keith Jeffery acknowledges:

> The 'Tans' gained a fierce reputation for unflinching severity as they sped about the country in armoured cars of one sort or another and their ac-

tivities represented the development, by the end of 1920, of a policy of counter-terror masterminded by [Major General Hugh] Tudor backed up by Lloyd George. The Prime Minister was as anxious as anyone for a quick fix in Ireland ... Tudor's policy of reprisals – attacking people and property with alleged Sinn Féin connections, burning creameries in Republican areas, and so on – flowed directly from the permissive and thoughtless approach to Irish security policy adopted in London.[33]

But the policies did not work, and only served to push more of the Irish populace into the republican camp.

Reports of British troops exacting reprisals and committing barbarous acts in Ireland made their way slowly through the censor's nets and into the pages of Canadian newspapers, especially the Irish-Catholic weeklies. Between 1919 and 1921, Toronto's *Catholic Register* and Saint John's *New Freeman* published many articles chronicling the violence in Ireland. These articles, which appeared irregularly in 1919 but were published more often in 1920, detailed the latest manifestation of British oppression in Ireland.[34] Newspaper reports of the Irish people being brutalized by the hired hands of the Crown only served as a constant reminder that their ancestral homeland remained unfree, ruled by an alien government. In early October 1920, Irish Canadians were informed that British troops sacked defenceless Irish towns. The *Catholic Register* asked why the leading Canadian journals were not publishing such reports. Noting that the Irish clergy denounced violence, and that some English journals were printing these damning stories about government reprisals on Irish towns, the *Register* commented:

> Has there been any like denunciation from the British Government of the crimes committed by their hired servants – the supposed guardians of law and order? Within the space of a few days eight towns were looted by the British soldiery, including Miltown, Malboy, Lahinch, Ennistmoyre, Doonbeg, Bralaha, Cree and Balbriggan ... The murders, the firing of houses and the destruction of creameries, Prussian crimes, have been laid at the door of the Government by responsible organs of opinion at home and abroad ... Misgovernment, which is at bottom the cause of all serious crime in Ireland, is as roundly condemned as the doers of evil.[35]

The following week the *New Freeman* reprinted an article from the *Manchester Guardian* that exposed the carnage exacted in the sacking of Balbriggan:

The police reprisals in Balbriggan this morning are indisputably the worst that have occurred in Ireland. In its brutality, wantonness, and destructiveness, last night's work of the uniformed forces of the crown is comparable only to the story of some Belgian villages in the early days of the war. Two men were dragged from their homes to the police barracks, bayoneted and beaten to compel them to reveal secrets, and then taken out into the street and shot in cold blood, their bodies left to be picked up by any passer-by. When I reached Balbriggan at noon today, smoke was still rising from rows of burned cottages, shops and public houses. People were fleeing the town in conditions as pitiable as any set of refugees ever left Louvian.[36]

Irish Canadians repeatedly confronted these sorts of images with respect to the ongoing conflict in their ancestral homeland.[37] News reports of British reprisals against the Irish populace undoubtedly contributed to growing agitation among supporters of the Irish nationalist cause – agitation that found caustic expression in the editorial pages the Irish-Catholic weeklies.

Expressions of the ever increasing contempt with which most Irish Canadians held the British administration of Irish affairs were found regularly in the editorials of the Irish-Catholic weeklies. These editorials most likely represented the opinions of thousands of Irish Canadians, who possessed virtually no public voice. Irish-Catholic Canadians believed Ireland's claims to nationhood to be as legitimate as any in Europe. Yet not only were British administrators prohibiting self-determination for Ireland, but now, in addition, their hirelings were sacking Irish towns and killing Irish civilians merely suspected of Sinn Féin sympathies. In September 1919 the *Catholic Register* asserted:

We hear a good deal about the prosperity of Ireland under Castle Government. Even the Toronto Globe has opened its columns to propaganda showing how well-governed Ireland is at the present time. There has been, however, an American Commission in Ireland [the Walsh Commission] and it has made a report which makes instructive reading. Castle government does not appear to such advantage in this report. It shows misgovernment and official carelessness of the most appalling kind! ...

From all sides comes testimony of the harshness and brutality of the minions of the Government in dealing with the people of Ireland. Government by aliens is not good for any country and this has been superabundantly proven in Ireland.[38]

Irish-Catholic Canadians clearly favoured a British withdrawal from Ireland. For many years they had supported the IPP and its constitutional methods for achieving Irish Home Rule. But after the 1918 election, Ireland's political contours had been dramatically altered. Partly as a result of the 1918 election, but primarily as a result of British actions since early 1919, many Irish-Catholic Canadians began to shift their support toward Sinn Féin and its demands for an independent republic. In July 1919 the *New Freeman* asserted:

> If the people of Ireland continue in their demand for a republic it may be necessary for their Canadian friends to re-consider their own attitude. Friends of Ireland in Canada are just as disgusted as are the people of Ireland, themselves, over the willful mismanagement of their affairs by an imported administration. If the Dominion of Ireland is not erected, and very soon, a change in the policy of the friends of Ireland in Canada may result for, after all, it is what the people of Ireland really want that counts. If friends of Ireland in Canada find that the British Government absolutely refused to grant a generous measure of Home Rule, then they have but one alternative left and that is an independent Ireland. The choice will have been forced on them.[39]

The *Catholic Register* declared:

> But whilst we condemn the British Government we are told that we champion the Sinn Fein policy of outrage and disruption. In the first place we have never expressed sympathy with outrages, whether committed by Sinn Feiners or the hirelings of the British Government. But whilst the later have been convicted of crimes and calumnies without number, the Sinn Feiners have been proved guilty of neither. Again and again wholesale arrests have been made. It was proclaimed at the time that the most convincing proof would be brought forward of the guilt of those seized upon and deported. After months they were released without an iota of evidence being adduced. In dealing with a Government of that kind it is impossible to say just what are Sinn Fein outrages.[40]

Irish-Canadian nationalists who began shifting their support to Sinn Féin contended that they were doing so specifically because of the actions of the British authorities. With ample evidence to back them, they maintained that the administration of British justice in Ireland was being delivered unevenly. In scathing editorials, Irish-Catholic Canadians openly declared that the apparently racist mismanagement of Irish affairs by British officialdom had compelled them to reconsider their political allegiances not only with respect to Irish political parties, but also as citizens of the empire. These declarations would become even more pronounced – and targeted – with the formation of a national organization whose purpose was to hammer home the point that the Great War had been fought on the principle of self-determination for small nations, including Ireland. The founding of that national organization was well under way by 1920.

By the end of the 1910s, Irish Canadians viewed the continued mismanagement of Irish affairs by British officialdom with ever increasing alarm. The failure of British politicians to exert the political will to implement the Home Rule Bill; the government's unwillingness to put down rebellious elements in Ulster, even while they were ruthlessly executing the leaders of the Easter Rising; their contention that the Great War had been fought for the principle of self-determination for small nations, yet never including Ireland as eligible for self-government; and, finally, the uncontrolled savagery exacted on the Irish people by the forces of the Crown, all led Irish Canadians to re-evaluate what British justice and democracy actually meant. In 1919 and especially in 1920, Irish-Canadian nationalists began to agitate and organize in greater earnestness. As early as March 1918, the Ancient Order of Hibernians envisioned the various Irish societies in Canada united in an 'Irish Union' to strengthen their demands for Irish self-government.[41] As the 1920s began, the vision of an Irish Union seemed a legitimate possibility.

In early 1919, while Canada's Prime Minister Robert Borden attended the Paris Peace Conference, an assemblage of Irish Canadians petitioned him to exert whatever influence he might command on Ireland's behalf. At the peace conference, as the victorious Allied nations redrew the map of Europe, benevolently allocating self-government to newly created nations like Poland, Czechoslovakia, Hungary, and Yugoslavia, Ireland's request to petition for self-government was never even entertained. On 27 February, as the peace conference began, Irish Canadians gathered at a rally at the Russell Theatre in Ottawa to hear John Kelly, MP of Quebec, speak on the Irish question. The rally unanimously adopted a resolution that addressed the greatest concern of Irish Canadians – that Irishmen had fought in the Great War for the rights of small nations, and it now appeared that these same rights were to be denied Ireland.[42] The resolutions stated in part:

Whereas, Thousands of men of Irish birth and blood have taken heroic part in the armies of the British Empire and given their lives for the principles for which this great war was fought, that the principles might endure forever and,

Whereas, The British Government declared that when Britain entered the war, it did so in defense of the rights of small nations ...

Therefore be it resolved, In consideration of the fact that no less than 50000 of our brave Canadian soldiers, many of whom were purely Irish descent have made the supreme sacrifice that Right and Liberty and Justice might not disappear from the earth, we hold that the claim of Ireland to the freedom and common justice obtainable in the modern state should be the immediate concern of every loyal subject of the British Empire, and be it further resolved:

That the Right Honorable Sir Robert Laird Borden, Premier of Canada be asked to use his powerful influence with his colleagues of the Peace Conference to the end that the people of Ireland shall have a voice in determining how they shall be governed, and in framing and fashioning their destiny.[43]

This resolution expressed the utter dismay that Irish Canadians felt at the fact that other small nations were to be bestowed with nationhood even while that opportunity was still to be denied Ireland. This point baffled Irish Canadians when they considered just how many Irishmen had fought in the armies of the British Empire: now the British government was withholding self-government from Ireland. As far as Irish Canadians were concerned, that Britain refused to consider statehood for Ireland contradicted the very democratic principles for which the British Empire stood. It is significant that the resolution identified as loyal subjects those most concerned that Ireland immediately obtain the freedom and common justice of modern statehood.

By early December 1919, news reports of the atrocities in Ireland, and agitation among the Irish diaspora dramatically altered the opinion of many Irish Canadians, including the membership of the St Patrick's Society of Montreal. Only a year earlier, the society had refused to join a proposed Irish Union; now it wholeheartedly advocated holding an Irish Race Convention as a means to unite the various Canadian Irish societies. Influenced by events in Ireland, and by the fact that the Irish in the United States and Australia already held successful conventions supporting Irish self-government, the St Patrick's Society organized a committee to consider a similar convention being held in Canada. On 1

December the committee issued its report, which noted that more than 5,000 delegates had attended an Irish convention in the United States and that a similar convention in Australia had attracted more than 1,000. Presenting the report, T.P. Tansey asked:

> Are we, the Irish portion of the northern half of the American continent to be behind our fellows in the South and our brothers in the Antipodes, in giving that encouragement to our fighting compatriots in the home land, which is their due? Lives there an Irishman today whose heart is not bound up with the fortunes of the old land, and whose eyes are not anxiously gazing thither? And the fighting will not be in vain, for whatever the Peace Conference may have settled or left unsettled, whether it was a success or a failure, one thing is certain, the day when one people, one nation, can domineer over another people, over another nation, is past and gone. The voice of civilization is heard in no uncertain terms ...
>
> Our people at home are fighting for their cause as they never fought before, and are succeeding as they never did before. Let us encourage them by every means in our power, and this race Convention which will, I trust show to all that every Irishman in Canada is with the Irish in Ireland, heart and soul, is one way of advancing the cause both here and abroad.

T.P. Tansey then asked, how could the various Irish societies in Canada not only organize a convention, but also create a national organization to maximize the impact of their demands for Irish freedom. He then suggested that a new 'separate organization, divorced from local concerns, untrammelled by sectional considerations ... regulations and restrictions, be instituted to take up this work, the work of telling the Irish people at home and the world at large, that the Irish people of Canada are one with those in the Green Isle in this momentous hour.'[44] As a result of events in Ireland over the preceding few years, the St Patrick's Society – one of the least nationalistic Irish societies in Canada – now resolutely proclaimed, 'We're Irish still,' and declared its support for those who had taken up arms in the fight for an independent Ireland. Moreover, this came from an Irish society that had never even passed a formal resolution in support of the Home Rule movement six years earlier. It is clear from all this that Irish-Canadian nationalists' ire had been ignited as a result of British policy in Ireland.

On 8 May 1920 the *New Freeman* reported on a new Irish organization in Winnipeg. The previous Sunday evening in the Columbus Hall, the Irish of Winnipeg founded the Canadian Friends of Irish Freedom, which would be 'open to all who sympathize with the cause of Irish Liberty, irrespective of race or creed.'[45] Noting that 'no one can deny that the secular press of the country [Canada] is prejudiced with the prejudice of the bluest kind of imported Toryism,' the Winnipeg Friends of Irish Freedom declared the aim of their organization was simply 'to make a thorough study of the merits of the Irish question themselves, and spread this knowledge amongst their fellow citizens of all shades of opinion.'[46] The *New Freeman* also reported that the Irish-Canadian National League held a rally in Montreal and announced plans to hold a June 'Irish Race Convention in Montreal.'[47] The report further stated that 'Irish-Canadians from Coast to Coast' had already been informed of the objectives of the league and were communicating their enthusiastic support, 'particular of the effort to secure for Ireland the right of self-determination.'[48] In the end, this convention was never held; but by then, more elaborate plans were under way to hold an Irish national convention that would bring together Canada's various Irish societies.

The first known meeting of the Self-Determination for Ireland League of Canada occurred on 30 May 1920, probably in Ottawa or Montreal. The meeting was attended by forty people from Quebec, Ontario, and the Maritimes, although none was identified. This meeting was undoubtedly organizational in nature, intended to lay the groundwork down a framework for a new national organization. The stated aim of this newly formed league was to 'secure organized support for the right of the people of Ireland to choose freely their own Governmental institutions and their relationship with other nations and peoples without coercion or dictation from outside.' The plan noted that all 'sympathizers with Ireland's cause of all races and creeds are eligible for membership.' It was also noted that 'this Canadian League is exactly similar to the League which has been functionary so successfully in Great Britain since March 1919.'[49]

This was indeed the case. The Canadian Self-Determination for Ireland League modelled itself on leagues already established in Britain, Australia, and New Zealand. In fact, Peter Hart suggests that 'in London, some branches of the newly formed Irish Self-Determination League (Sinn Fein's English front) were little more than Labour Party branches under another name.'[50]

The most complete record available for the Self-Determination League's development in Canada appeared in the *New Freeman,* which reported on league progress not just in New Brunswick but throughout Canada. During 1920 and 1921, that weekly newspaper provided a rich overview of the league's activities, although at times its reporting was overly optimistic. In its columns, the *New Freeman* regularly reported on league activities from Halifax to Vancouver.

In the summer of 1920, Katherine Hughes, National Organizing Secretary of the Self-Determination for Ireland League of Canada, toured the Maritimes to rally Irish sympathizers and to help establish local branches. Katherine Hughes was born on Prince Edward Island and was the niece of the Archbishop of Halifax. After receiving her primary education at convent schools, she attended and graduated from Prince of Wales College. Miss Hughes pursued a career in journalism, working for newspapers in Montreal and then Edmonton, where she became the Provincial Archivist of Alberta. Eventually she was appointed the Alberta premier's private secretary. In 1913 she joined the staff of the Agent General of Alberta in London. This posting provided Miss Hughes with the opportunity to tour Ireland and become involved with the Gaelic Revival movement. In 1917 she resigned from her London post to dedicate herself to the cause of Irish freedom. By 1918 she was working for the Irish National Bureau in Washington, D.C. According to Richard Davis, she was handpicked for the position of Canadian National Organizer of the Self-Determination League by Eamon de Valera himself, who was Sinn Féin's president, and she served as his international organizer. Davis writes that her duties 'were of such a sensitive nature that semi-secrecy had to be preserved to avoid deportations from countries like Australia and New Zealand ... Even when speaking in Dáil Éireann, de Valera simply referred to Miss Hughes as "the lady who organized Canada, Australia, and New Zealand."'[51]

This was one of the women whom Mark McGowan hailed as a fine example of Irish-Catholic inculcation into Canadian society. McGowan notes that in 1912, in Edmonton, Katherine Hughes founded the first branch of the Catholic Women's League of Canada (CWL). Of the CWL, McGowan wrote that 'in the early 1920s, the CWL became the vehicle through which Catholic women could promote Catholic values, charitable works, and Canadian patriotism.'[52] In the summer of 1920, Hughes travelled across Canada, helping organize branches of the Self-Determination for Ireland League of Canada. Clearly, Katherine Hughes had expanded her organizational activities since her 1912 involvement with the CWL.

Excepting Fredericton, Hughes spoke and organized in all the significant Maritime centres, including Charlottetown, Sydney, Halifax, Chatham, Moncton, and Saint John.[53] On 11 July more than 1,000 people filled the Majestic Theatre in Halifax to hear Miss Hughes speak on conditions in Ireland.[54] On the evening of 15 July she spoke to a capacity audience at the Opera House in Saint John, at an event chaired by Miles E. Agar. Miss Hughes, in part, spoke of Ireland's commitment during the war, and suggested a course of action for supporters of the Irish cause:

> Little nations – smaller than Ireland – have attained their freedom because of the world war, and Ireland was on their side battling for them. Livonia, Albania, Serbia, are today free nations and Ireland had fought to make them free. Ireland's sons have died for liberty wherever liberty's battles were fought ...
>
> You Canadians who want to show the people of Ireland that you are willing to live for that which you asked the boys of Canada to die – become members of the Self-Determination for Ireland League of Canada. The League is identical with that of England and Australia. The object is to give the Irish people the right to choose their own governmental institutions.[55]

By virtue of their tremendous sacrifices during the war, with over 60,000 casualties, and assuming a three billion dollar national debt, most Canadians now viewed themselves as partners of Britain and as entitled to an opinion on imperial matters such as the Irish Question.[56] The Self-Determination for Ireland League of Canada declared as much in demanding that Ireland be accorded the right of self-determination without interference from Britain.

Katherine Hughes spent the summer of 1920 travelling across western Canada. Just as in the Maritimes, in each city – Winnipeg, Regina, Saskatoon, Calgary, Edmonton, Vancouver – she spoke at rallies and helped found new branches of the league.[57] Hundreds of new members were registered, and the trip was hailed as 'a wonderful success.'[58] In Vancouver Miss Hughes addressed a public gathering of more than 1,000 at the Dominion Hall, at which time she brought prominent business leaders into the Executive Committee of the league's Vancouver branch.[59] By the end of the summer of 1920 she had travelled across all of Canada and had helped to establish league branches in every major city – a fact not lost on those with investigating supposedly 'un-Canadian' activities, the Royal Canadian Mounted Police (RCMP).

Evidence of Self-Determination for Ireland League activity and growth came in reports of the RCMP's Criminal Investigation Branch

(CIB), which by 1920 was conducting surveillance on a host of organizations. With respect to undercover agent surveillance activities, the real formative years for the CIB were 1919 and 1920, a time of severe labour unrest in Canada. In May 1919 the Winnipeg General Strike commenced. It would last six weeks and grind the city to a stand-still. The strike began in the building and metal trades, but within a couple of weeks it included the Winnipeg Trades and Labour Coucil. The leaders of the strike were 'British-born and not, as the government and employers alleged, "alien scum" who wished to subvert British law and order.'[60] At that time, Canada also experienced its first Red Scare, as a result of the successful Russian Revolution and of ongoing labour agitation, which was thought to have arisen from socialist and Bolshevik influence. Gregory Kealey and Reg Whitaker write that undercover RCMP agents were expected 'to become "fully acquainted with all labor and other organizations in their respective districts,"' for the purpose of determining 'any current Bolshevik tendencies, or its Bolshevik nature.'[61] W.H. Routledge, the Assistant RCMP Commissioner who headed the CIB, compiled top secret weekly bulletins summarizing the surveillance of radical leaders and organizations for Prime Minister Robert Borden, and also for Arthur Lewis Sifton, minister in charge of the RCMP.[62] The Self-Determination for Ireland League of Canada was apparently deemed subversive enough to merit intense CIB surveillance.

Most references to the Self-Determination League in the CIB's files (edited and published by Kealey and Whitaker) were rather cursory, and usually made reference to someone joining the league, or to a speech made at a particular locale. Katherine Hughes's appearance in Regina on 29 July was duly noted in the CIB's Bulletin File no. 36, dated 12 August.[63] A similar entry for the week ending 7 October in CIB Bulletin File no. 44 noted that Mrs Rose Henderson of Vancouver was expected to arrive in Winnipeg in early October to deliver an address. The weekly bulletin continued:

> A report from Vancouver says: 'This woman is a regular fire-brand, and whilst here has been interesting herself in O.B.U. [One Big Union] affairs, social and otherwise, and has also addressed meetings held under the auspices of the Federated Labor party.
>
> 'Mrs. Henderson has also actively interested herself in the affairs of the Self Determination for Ireland League at this point, but the best authorities say she is not very conversant with the question.'[64]

As with the passage about Rose Henderson, a number of references connected organized labour to those sympathetic to Irish independence. (However, no records of such connections have been found.) All of this aside, the most comprehensive and interesting CIB weekly bulletin on the Self-Determination League comes not from the pages of Kealey and Whitaker, but rather from the papers of Arthur Lewis Sifton.

The Criminal Investigation Branch Bulletin no. 38, for the week ending 26 August, contained a five-page supplemental memorandum devoted entirely to recent surveillance information regarding the Self-Determination League's leaders and their activities. The memorandum discussed the activities, objectives, and motivations of the league and its leaders, while being interspersed with random bits of surveillance observations. For example, the second and third items presented some highly speculative information contending the league was funded by 'The Roman Catholic Bishop of Chicago,' which supposedly had $14 million at its disposal. This was extremely unlikely. The league's finances were negligible, for it was funded solely by the one-dollar annual membership fees of its members. In the memo's sixth item was another random observation stating that on 30 June 1920, Eamon de Valera, Sinn Féin's president, while travelling and raising funds in the United States, visited Plattsburgh, New York; that a 'considerable number of Irishmen from Montreal motored there and held a conference with him'; and that after this meeting 'the name "Self Determination for Ireland League" used so extensively.'[65]

Much of this memorandum, though, dealt with the status, motivations, and objectives of the league and its leaders. From the opening remarks: 'During this spring and summer a movement in aid of the Sinn Fein agitation has sprung up and made great progress in Canada. It now has an organization covering the greater part of Canada, and is manifesting a good deal of activity.'[66] The memorandum stated in the fourth item that by the spring of 1920, officers began discerning 'the formation in Canada of Sinn Fein societies,' noting four such bodies: Winnipeg – 'Canadian Friends of Irish Freedom'; Toronto – 'Irish-Canadian National League'; Ottawa – 'Irish-Canadian National League'; and Vancouver – 'Irish National Organization.' The memorandum continued: 'While is was stated that both Protestant and Catholic Irishmen would be eligible for membership, none of these were specifically termed "Protestant," and most of those concerned with the movement were Roman Catholics, priests being active.'[67] The bulletin's compiler emphasized the overwhelmingly Catholic composition of the league.

In the seventh item, the compilers again raised Catholicism as an issue of concern, noting that after the Plattsburgh meeting with de Valera, 'Miss Katherine Hughes now came to the front.' In describing Katherine Hughes and her faith, the memorandum asserted:

> For a year or two this woman (who is well known in Alberta as a writer, enthusiastically Roman Catholic in her views) had been in Washington, we are informed as Secretary of the Sinn Fein organization there. She now came to Canada and went across the continent organizing. In addition to work in Montreal and Eastern Canada, she is known to have addressed meetings as follows: – at Winnipeg on 23rd and 26th July, at Regina on 29th July, at Calgary on 1st August, at Vancouver 9th August, at Edmonton 15th August.[68]

According to the memorandum, the league had 'Branches, or separate societies, exist[ing] in:– Charlottetown, St. John, N.B., Quebec, Montreal, Sherbrooke, Ottawa, Kingston, Toronto, Winnipeg, Regina, Calgary, Edmonton, Vancouver.'[69] This accurately described the league's status as far as large cities were concerned, but there were many branches in smaller cities as well. By November 1920, branches of the Self-Determination League also existed in, among other places, Nanaimo, British Columbia; Selkirk, Manitoba; and Humboldt, Saskatchewan; as well as in New Brunswick at St Stephen, Fredericton, Woodstock, Edmundston, Grand Falls, Chatham, and Bath.[70]

The memorandum then described and appraised some of the leading forces behind a number of the provincial movements:

> The organization is described by Miss Hughes as centering in Montreal, and Lindsay Crawford, whose connection with the New York 'Protestant Friends of Irish Freedom' suggest the possession of a certain amount of authority. The organization seems most forward, however, in Winnipeg, where a Provincial body has been formed and a campaign launched by the *Northwest Review*, a Roman Catholic weekly more or less the organ of the local hierarchy, to get 10,000 members in the next month.
>
> In Quebec the moving spirit is M. Monaghan, an insurance man of no great local weight with a taste for writing letters; he recently sent a furiously abusive one to Mr. Lloyd George. In Regina the movement is headed by a rather unimportant hotel-keeper named McCarthy. In Vancouver the moving spirit is one A. Urquart, a Gaelic enthusiast of no local prominence.[71]

The memorandum intoned great concern at the 'rather mysterious combination of organizing ability and lack of ostensible leadership which the movement presents.' The league's leadership was described as 'light-weights,' with one exception: Lindsay Crawford. According to the memorandum, Crawford was 'the most serious figure, and he in the first place is a Protestant in a body overwhelmingly Roman Catholic, and in the second place has shown great levity of purpose.'[72] In referring to league rallies and meetings, the memorandum noted: 'The tone of the meetings is openly and wholly for the separation of Ireland from the British Empire and its settlement as an independent republic. It is intensely anti-British. There are signs of close connection with the anti-British Sinn Fein campaign in the United States.' In its comments about Crawford's involvement, the CIB again intimated that Roman Catholicism was in and of itself a disloyal faith and that for a Protestant to be involved with lay Catholics was highly suspicious.

The fourteenth and final item in the memorandum described the response of Canadian Orangemen to the emergence of the Self-Determination League. With respect to the Orangemen, the tone of the memorandum was near admiration for the Orange restraint:

> So far as the Orange Order is concerned, its attitude apparently is one of waiting ... While the Sinn Fein agitation is provocative to Orangemen, their public utterances (as at 12th July meetings) have included no demonstrations of an unusual nature, and the *Sentinel* has contained nothing beyond its usual standing controversy with the Roman Catholic press and Sinn Fein. It may be surmised that those who control the policy of the Order believe that the Sinn Feiners wish to provoke an 'incident' before November, and are disposed to hold their people in check accordingly.[73]

It is clear from this memorandum that those in charge of security policy for the Canadian government viewed Canadian Orangemen favourably, while Irish-Catholic Canadians were viewed with distrust and suspicion because of their faith and because they freely expressed their opinion regarding Ireland's political status. The memorandum also referred to 'signs of close connection with the anti-British Sinn Fein campaign in the United States.' Earlier in the memorandum, in the second item, reference was made to the fact that 'in the winter of 1919–1920 Crawford was active in the United States,' with 'one of his performances being his attendance at Washington as a member of an Irish delegation which protested to the Senate committee against the ratification of the Treaty of Versailles.'[74] Although the memorandum was slightly incorrect in its assessment of the congressional hearing, there is no question that connections existed between Irish-American and Irish-Canadian nationalists.

On 13 December 1919, indeed, Lindsay Crawford and Katherine Hughes testified in Washington, D.C., before the House Committee on Foreign Affairs in relation to a bill 'To Provide For The Salaries Of A Minister And Councils To The Republic of Ireland.' Crawford and Hughes appeared with 413 prominent Irish Americans, about twenty of whom testified and all of whom presented themselves before the committee to sign their names in support of the bill.[75] Hughes testified as Secretary of the Irish National Bureau of Washington, D.C., and her testimony consisted merely of presenting a number of official documents, such as the Dáil Éireann Declaration of Independence and the Sinn Féin Democratic Program, for the committee to consider at a later date.[76]

Crawford's testimony, in contrast, covered eleven pages and examined why an intransigent Protestant minority in Ireland's northeastern corner was refusing to concede the end of the Union. According to him, the Irish Question was not primarily a religious conflict but rather was a conflict over economics. Protestant businessmen in Belfast wished to keep the status quo 'in order to maintain their hold upon the workers, to prevent anything in the nature of an advance of democracy, they try to raise this religious cry to keep Catholic and Protestant worker apart, so that they will have complete control over the labor situation.'[77] Crawford returned to this theme frequently over the next two years as he travelled across Canada speaking on Irish issues.

Much of the correspondence between Irish-Canadian nationalist leaders and Frank Walsh, head of the American Friends of Irish Freedom, suggests a fair amount of cooperation between Irish-American and Irish-Canadian nationalists. There is no evidence, however, of any American coordination of Irish Canadian activists, as the RCMP implied. Walsh and the Irish-American organizations he represented simply provided printed materials, such as pamphlets of Dáil speeches, for distribution in Canada. In May 1921, Walsh wrote to H.J. Stafford, Quebec Provincial Secretary of the Self-Determination League, thanking him for distributing copies of speeches made in the Dáil Éireann. Walsh confided that he was glad 'to know that you are ready to undertake the distribution of the Dail Eireann Address in the Province of Quebec.'[78] Walsh's comment, 'best wishes for the success of the movement in Canada,' suggests that the relationship between Irish-American and Irish-

Canadian nationalists involved cooperation and assistance rather than coordination and American control.[79] The Irish-American nationalists were far better organized and financed, so it was quite easy for them to lend a helping hand. The issues and parameters relating to Irish agitation in Canada were quite different from those in the United States, as was readily apparent when the Self-Determination League released a public statement outlining its aims and objectives.

Whether it was to counter the impact of Orange denunciations, or primarily to rally the faithful for the upcoming provincial and national conventions, in the late summer of 1920 the leaders of the Self-Determination League published a statement outlining its objectives. In this statement the league stipulated that in calling for the principle of self-determination to be applied to Ireland, it was merely advocating traditional Canadian principles, such as free speech and majority rule. This lengthy statement clearly articulated Irish-Canadian beliefs and the nature of Irish-Canadian identity. It read:

> The League is Canadian first, last and all the time. It knows neither race nor creed; it stands on the broad principle of Canadianism. It is Canadian in its inception and in its operation; it is Canadian in thought and action.
>
> It calls for the application to Ireland of the principles which have worked so well in Canada, i.e., that the people of Ireland, like the people of Canada, be allowed to choose for themselves their own form of government without dictation or coercion from outside.
>
> It does not presume to tell Irishmen what form of government they shall take, any more than it would take from Irishmen any dictation as to what form of government Canada should have. It believes that Irishmen in Ireland, are just as capable of performing functions of government in Ireland as they are in any other part of the world.
>
> The League realizes that armed force will accomplish nothing in the way of a settlement; that a settlement to be enduring must be based on popular consent, as in Canada; that the people of Ireland, as have the people of Canada, have the inalienable right to determine for themselves their own form of government and governmental institutions; that Irishmen have the right to self-determination in Ireland as have Canadians in Canada, Australians in Australia, or Englishmen in England.
>
> The British Empire is a great commonwealth held together by the strongest of ties – that of mutual good will. Discontent in Ireland has been the cause of discontent in England, in Australia, in South Africa, in New Zealand, and Canada, and this discontent becomes daily more manifest as conditions in Ireland are permitted to drift. With the Irish question satis-

factorily settled, settled in accordance with the will of the majority of the people of Ireland (just as we in Canada settle our affairs by a majority of our people), the one big stumbling block to real Empire unity has been removed. There can not be solidarity where there is dissatisfaction. Therefore, it is the very highest brand of patriotism to seek to remove any cause that has the effect of dividing the people of the Empire. That is the aim of the League. That is only the application of Canadianism to Ireland.[80]

The statement linked the league's objectives to true Canadian principles. Irish Canadians saw themselves as patriotic and as working for the benefit of the empire by advocating that a stumbling block to imperial unity be remedied. Through the league, and through the movement to garner support for Irish self-determination, Irish Canadians were expressing true Canadian principles of democracy, free speech, and majority rule. The league saw these as the cornerstones of Canadian democracy and as the guiding principles for which so many young Canadian men had given their lives during the Great War.

Reprinted in the same issue of the *New Freeman* – indeed, on the same page – was a letter that had been sent to the editor of the *Halifax Daily Recorder* by W.P. Burns, Nova Scotia's Provincial Chairman of the Self-Determination for Ireland League. In that letter, Burns addressed similar concerns and issues relating to the question of why Canadians should be interested in seeing Ireland achieve self-determination. The letter read in part:

Why should we Nova Scotians be interested in Ireland? Because (1) As members of the British Empire, whatever touches the honor of the British Empire concerns our honor, too. The present state of affairs in Ireland is not creditable to the Empire; (2) A considerable portion of our population is of Irish descent and in a peculiarly intimate sense concerned in the welfare of Ireland; (3) The Irish crisis is not merely an issue of English and Irish politics. Its basis is a question of principle, a principle for which Nova Scotians sacrificed their lives in the war against the Central Empires. This principle consists in the acknowledgment that civilized peoples do possess the right freely to decide their own system of government – the principle of self-determination. And the Irish are the only white race without responsible government.[81]

These were the ideals for which so many Canadians gave their lives during the war. They were also the guiding principles of the Self-Determination for Ireland League of Canada, which was soon to gather at a national convention intended to bring attention to the vexing Irish Question.

The national convention of the Self-Determination for Ireland League of Canada had been slated for mid-September 1920 in Toronto. Owing to Orange threats and protests and to a Toronto civic edict forbidding the league from holding its convention in the city, it was postponed by a month and moved to Ottawa.[82] A circular letter sent to local branches announced the date, time, and place of the league's national convention; and the same letter provided a good deal of information about the motivations related to holding the convention and the organizational support that underpinned the convention.[83] Those organizations specifically named to send delegates to the convention – the Ancient Order of Hibernians, the St-Jean-Baptiste Society, the Gaelic League, and the Independent Labour Party – represented the spheres of influence in Canadian society from which the league received its greatest ethnic and political support. The letter's salutation declared in Gaelic 'A Chara,' or Dear Friend:

> A Chara,
> The Provisional National Executive of the Self-Determination for Ireland League of Canada hereby calls a Special National Convention of the Irish race in Canada, and of all sympathizers with the Cause of Irish Independence, irrespective of race or creed ...
>
> The Convention will be attended by delegates from every Province in the Dominion and will follow the example set by the Irish in England, Australia and other Dominions, of upholding the just rights of the Irish in Ireland.

The letter then covered typical convention business such as the procedures for distributing temporary credential cards, and it also mentioned that 'special arrangements have been made with the Railways for reduced return [round-trip] fares.'[84] The letter then provided a lengthy discourse on Ireland's right to self-determination, again emphasizing that this was entirely consistent with proclamations made by British statesmen during the war. In stating that it was the duty of every Irish Canadian to attend the convention, the letter was essentially a rallying cry:

> The Irish people assert the right to self-determine their own form of government, in accordance with the principle enunciated by British statesmen

during the War, and as applied by them to other countries with no more valid claim to independence than that presented by Ireland in her seven hundred years to the undeviating attachment to the National idea. In full and free exercise of that right with all the logical consequences it entails, the Irish people themselves must be the sole arbiters of their destiny.

In upholding Ireland's right to full and unrestricted evolution as a separate and distinct nation, the Irish race in Canada emphasizes a principle of good government that has been asserted on her own behalf by England and which is recognized by every patriotic Canadian as the foundation of national progress. We are confident that the response of the Gael in Canada will be such as to encourage the Irish nation in its splendid struggle for freedom.[85]

On 16 October 1920, 500 delegates from across Canada arrived in Ottawa to attend the convention. Although Ottawa Mayor Harold Fisher and the Police Commissioner 'took every precaution to protect the delegates,' hundreds of protesters, hurling not only insults but rotten tomatoes and eggs as well, greeted the league delegates as they entered St Patrick's Hall.[86] Almost the entire police force was needed to surround the hall to protect the delegates from attack. Three thousand Carleton County Orangemen planned to hold a counter-demonstration, but the Ottawa Citizens Committee cancelled the event for fear of setting off a riot.[87] After this initial disturbance, the convention proceeded smoothly. The *Ottawa Citizen* reported that those who wished to see rioting were sorely disappointed, because the convention was a 'most orderly affair, and the "seditious utterances" were conspicuous by their absence.'[88]

Thomas R. Donovan, the Ontario Secretary of the Ancient Order of Hibernians, as well as president of the Ottawa branch of the Self-Determination for Ireland League and chairman of the National Convention Committee, called the convention to order shortly after 11:00 a.m., Saturday, 16 October. By the time the convention resumed for the afternoon session, it had swelled to 700 delegates with the arrival of a contingent from Montreal and Quebec City. Lindsay Crawford then ascended the stage amidst thundering applause and cries of 'Long live the Irish republic!'[89] Crawford read a letter to the convention from Eamon de Valera, the Sinn Féin president, who was touring the United States on a fund-raising mission. That letter concluded:

The people of Ireland are grateful to you, the members of the Self-Determination League, for the interest you are taking in their cause. They send their greetings and are confident that no enlightened Canadian will be able to stand by and see an unoffending people massacred in an attempt to force them under a rule and a sovereignty under which they do not desire to live, a rule which, in fact, is as hateful to them as the rule of the Germans was hateful to the Belgians.[90]

The usual convention business then proceeded, with committee appointments and elections for permanent leadership positions. Ottawa was chosen as the league's national headquarters, and Crawford was elected president. Thomas R. Donovan was elected National Secretary, and the Reverend Father Fay was elected National Treasurer. Katherine Hughes reported that in just three months of existence, the league had attracted 20,000 members, and that by the end of six months, 100,000 members were anticipated.[91] Charles J. Foy was elected president of the Ontario Self-Determination League and was the first of many speakers during the Saturday afternoon session.

Foy stated that he was attending the convention as a delegate of 'one of the oldest and grandest organizations the Irish had ever had, the Ancient Order of Hibernians, which had kept alive the Irish national spirit and made the work of the convention possible.'[92] Foy declared that he was proud to be attending an Irish convention called to assist the land of his forefathers:

How proud I am to see representatives here from every province in this fair land, from the Atlantic to the Pacific, and from Ontario the land of freedom and free speech. (Derisive cheers, hooting and hissing.)

They tell you Ireland is 'Rome-ruled' instead of 'home-ruled.' This cry still passes muster [among the critics], but the presence of men at this convention who are not of the same faith belies it. Lindsay Crawford is a Protestant. (Cheers.)

How about Pitt, Gratton, Wolfe Tone, Parnell, Gladstone? If they had not been sincere in their belief that a Protestant minority in Ireland would not be crushed, would they have espoused the cause of Irish freedom?[93]

Mat Donovan of Glace Bay, Nova Scotia, spoke that evening as a self-declared representative of labour. Donovan hoped, he said, 'to assist in his humble way to secure self-determination for Ireland.' Noting that the question of patriotism sometimes arose with respect to those who were advocating Irish independence, he asserted that no other class had 'shown a truer patriotism than the coal miners of Nova Scotia' whom he represented. Telling his audience that he had lost seven close relatives in the war, he insisted that 'it should not be a crime to be loyal to the land from which one sprang. Time and time again, the 12,000 miners of Nova Scotia had voted solidly in favor of Irish self determination.'[94]

Other speakers included Dr Thomas O'Hagan of Toronto, who was well known in literary circles; and John McDonald, also of Toronto, of the Independent Labor Party. Frank Cahill, MP, introduced Mrs Hector Prenter, also of Toronto, as being of the Presbyterian faith, 'which drew forth cheers.'[95] Mrs Prenter told the crowd that she was a member of the Self-Determination for Ireland League as well as the Independent Labor Party of Ontario and that there was a bond between labour and Ireland. Imperialism and the 'big interests,' she contended, were almost twins, and 'Sinn Fein meant brotherhood.' She asserted that those who perpetuated discord were the enemies of Canada and that 'the ideal of the 20th century is brotherhood.' She noted humorously that she heard a Toronto newsboy remark that the Irish could easily govern themselves if they could only open the English jails.

Major Charles 'Chubby' Powers, MP for Quebec West, also addressed the convention. He passionately expressed his desire to see a union of cooperation between Irish and French Canadians: 'Let us have a union with the French Canadians, and make sacrifices of our personal feelings. Let us get them with us, for it will be a great step in the accomplishment of the freedom of Ireland.' Powers also declared how disgusted he was with those who wore the British uniform. He himself had worn that same uniform for three years during the war, but now, he insisted, 'I am sorry at the way in which it has been disgraced by the unspeakable atrocities in Ireland. The British uniform which stood for justice and freedom, has been made the instrument of atrocity, arson and murder, in Ireland.'[96]

These same sentiments of revulsion at the British atrocities in Ireland, and the hope of uniting Irish and French Canadians in the battle for Irish independence, were reflected in the convention resolutions as well as in the statements of prominent French Canadians in attendance. The first two resolutions were unanimously accepted:

> That this National Convention of the Self-Determination for Ireland League of Canada, views with the most unqualified abhorrence the outrage on the moral sense of humanity perpetrated by the British government, in its ruthless efforts to stamp out Irish National aspirations by methods denounced by Mr. Asquith as 'A hellish policy of reprisals,' that

are 'not acts of self-defence but of blind vengeance' and for which no parallel can be found.[97]

An additional resolution, moved by Charles Foy and seconded by P.J. Henry, the editor of Winnipeg's Irish-Catholic weekly *Northwest Review*, emphasized the strong desire for closer bonds of friendship, support, and respect between Irish and French in Canada. This resolution recognized the special place the French language had in Canadian society and expressed sympathy with all French minorities as they struggled to maintain their cultural identity:

> Whereas the Canadian Constitution was founded on the well recognized principle of equality of religions, races and languages; Whereas by the constitution of this country, the English and French languages are the official languages of the country, and
> Whereas the French language constitutes a most splendid aspect of our country,
> Therefore this convention desires to place itself on record as condemning most emphatically any attempt to curtail the rights of the French language in Canada, and to express its heartfelt sympathy for all French minorities in their fight for the maintenance in their schools and colleges of their beautiful language.[98]

The following day, Sunday, 17 October, additional league business transpired, and not surprisingly, a few more delegates spoke on the present situation in Ireland. These included P.J. Henry of Winnipeg, Peter C. Sharkey of Saint John, and Samuel Jordan of Winnipeg, who suggested that the convention organizers should have placed around the hall the names of the Irish towns that had been sacked by British soldiers, as a reminder to Irish Canadians of the horrific state of affairs in the homeland. Samuel Jordan noted that he hailed from Belfast and had been reared in a narrow sphere of bigotry that was a disgrace to Ireland:

> The only government functioning there [in Ireland] today is Sinn Fein; I know because I have recently come from there and I know my Ireland from Cape Clear to the Giant's Causeway. The question in Ireland is not a religious one, but one of economics. The capitalists who own the industries there and sweat the population at starvation wages are afraid that if an Irish government gets control of the country, these conditions would be changed. And they will. (Cheers.) There are so many industries in Belfast,

not because their proprietors love Ireland, but because they can get cheap labor there. Every member of important families in Belfast, is a Home Ruler, but for obvious reasons he dare not come out in the open.[99]

Samuel Jordan, another Irish-born Canadian, who was now the president and manager of the Manitoba Stock and Food Company, also viewed the Irish Question as one of economics rather than religion.[100]

That evening, after the convention ended, nearly 2,000 ardent supporters of Irish freedom packed the Français Theatre in Ottawa to participate in a rally in support of French Canadians and Irish Canadians. The *Ottawa Citizen* reported that 'husky henchmen of the Irish cause, including ex-Separate School Trustee Mike O'Neill, were stationed at the doors, while outside there was an ample squad of city police who kept the crowd on the move and thus removed any possibility of a disturbance.'[101] The keynote speaker that night was Armand Lavergne, a leading French-Canadian nationalist politician, who received such a tempest of cheers at his introduction that he quipped when arriving on the podium: 'I am pleased and astonished at the greeting which you have given me, and to which I am not accustomed in Ontario. I am afraid you will be sorry when you look in the newspapers tomorrow, for you will see that because you have greeted me so, you must be both traitors and seditious.'[102] Lavergne continued in a more serious tone, recalling that when the Famine Irish arrived in Quebec, they had been received kindly:

> I come to you bringing a message from my own compatriots to those of Irish descent, and would remind you that in 1847, if my memory is faithful, on the shores of the St. Lawrence, we opened our hearts and homes to your people who had been driven from their homes. In our hearts and homes you still have that place. Our whole heart is in sympathy with our sister Ireland.

He then asserted:

> If I were an Irishman, as I am a Canadian, and it was my country that had been treated as Ireland has, I would take my rifle in my hands and fight to the last drop of my blood. (The huge gathering rose en masse and cheered the speaker to the echo, and it was some minutes before order could be restored). Being unafraid of my words, I would say also that I would try a Black and Tan first …

> I want you to think Canada, because the battle for Ireland is one for Canada, because if Britain says Ireland cannot govern herself, it will be our turn one day. It has already been said by the secretary for colonial affairs that the colonies have no moral right to secede from the Empire. We will tell him that the day Canada wants to secede, we'll do so and be an independent nation instead of feeding at the kitchen as we are doing. This country is ours, place it before the Empire. Let the Empire perish if need be, if Canada may be saved.
>
> We, of the old Canadians are with you and Ireland. We have had our struggles with the British Empire and know what you face, but we'll stick by you. For my part I am only a man with breath in my body, but as long as I can help you I will stand by my Irish friends in that fight for freedom.[103]

Lindsay Crawford, the newly elected President of the Self-Determination for Ireland League of Canada, followed Lavergne as the final speaker. He emphasized that Irishmen did not hate England but rather those interests that continually incited hatred and stirred bigotry in order to prevent Ireland from receiving the justice that was so obviously due to her:

> Too long the Irish have been the hewers of wood and the drawers of water for those Imperialist masters. Too long have the Irish here been set at the throats of the French, and tonight we proclaim a lasting peace between the two races, strong in the character of our respective races, we will bind ourselves in indissoluble ties, so that it will be impossible for intriguing politicians to further exploit us. If this convention had done nothing else it has shown us that we are one, neither French nor Irish, but Canadian.[104]

The rally concluded with the singing of 'O Canada,' after which the Irish, French, and other participating Canadians returned to their respective provinces to continue the work of presenting to the Canadian public the true nature of British abuses in Ireland.

Irish-Canadian desire to establish closer ties with French Canadians emanated from the fact that they shared a common religious faith, but also from the likely hope of establishing a political alliance to counter Orange influence. Lindsay Crawford expressed this point when writing to his friend, New York Supreme Court Justice Daniel Cohalan. In reference to the Self-Determination League, he wrote:

Our next move will be to reorganize on Canadian lines and this will, I expect, hold most of our people together for the coming fight against Imperialism in Canada. My strong card with some of our more conservative friends is the drive against Catholic Education by the Orange crowd in Ontario. They feel already that some organization is needed to protect the rights of the French and Irish Catholics in the Dominion and this will be the chief motive that will win them to our side eventually. What form the new organization will take is still in the embryo stage, but I will be guided largely by the needs of the French who are very anxious for an Irish–French alliance that will hold the balance of power. The last election was largely an echo of the war controversies ... The death of La Vergne's [sic] father – a Judge of the Supreme Court – has delayed the conference with French leaders which I have suggested. In a recent speech in Quebec, Bourassa spoke strongly of the necessity of an Irish–French alliance, and the whole audience – at a banquet at the Chateau Frontenac – rose to its feet and cheered. La Vergne [sic] tells me it was the most significant expression of French friendship towards the Irish he has ever seen and attributes it largely to our work in the Statesman and in the S.D.L. [Self-Determination League].[105]

These expressions of cooperation between Irish and French Canadians emanated from elite political leaders in each community, with an obvious nod to the political benefits of such an alliance. Yet this may not have been entirely representative of the feelings of many ordinary citizens from the respective communities, and it certainly contradicts the oft presented image of ecclesiastical conflict between Irish and French over diocesan control. But as events in Ireland progressed, and tragedy struck, many Church leaders and average citizens in both communities came together to mourn the loss of an Irish mayor and Sinn Féin leader.

As Irish Canadians worked to support Irish efforts to achieve independence, news from Ireland again found its way onto the front pages. At a time of continuous arson and other reprisals inflicted upon the Irish people by the forces of the Crown, reports surfaced in November 1920 that the Lord Mayor of Cork, Terrence MacSwiney, had died in a British jail after a seventy-four-day hunger strike. MacSwiney had been arrested by the military the previous July for allowing a Sinn Féin court to sit in the Cork City Hall.[106] Mayor MacSwiney began the hunger strike demanding that he be recognized as a political prisoner. British officials, including the Cabinet, refused him that recognition.

Irish-Canadian nationalist leaders were justifiably outraged at the treatment accorded the Lord Mayor of Cork. Indeed, well over a month before MacSwiney passed away, the New Brunswick provincial convention of the Self-Determination League passed a resolution condemning the treatment of Mayor MacSwiney, and demanded his release: 'Resolved that the Convention of the New Brunswick Self-Determination for Ireland League, (having, we submit, the best interest of the Empire at heart) urge upon the premier and government of Canada co-operation in securing the release of Lord Mayor MacSwiney, as being in keeping with true traditions of British justice.'[107]

After Mayor MacSwiney's death, Solemn High Masses of Requiem were held in many Canadian cities to honour the martyred mayor. On 1 November nearly 1,000 Irish and French Canadians marched to St Patrick's Cathedral in Quebec City to celebrate a mass in his honour. In Montreal, the Reverend Gerald McShane conducted a Solemn Requiem Mass at St Patrick's Church for the repose of his soul.[108] The following day, at the Mount Royal Arena in Montreal, 5,000 people rallied under the auspices of the Self-Determination League to pay tribute to the Lord Mayor. Mayor Médéric Martin of Montreal presided over the gathering, at which Lindsay Crawford and Armand Lavergne spoke. On the same day in Halifax, a procession of 'several thousand men and women formed up at the Common and proceeded to St. Mary's Cathedral where services were held for the late Mayor MacSwiney.'[109]

During this season of sadness, tension, anxiety, and outright anger among Irish Canadians, Lindsay Crawford and Thomas R. Donovan embarked on a speaking tour of the Maritimes in an effort to educate Canadians about the true nature of events transpiring in Ireland. The tour began in Amherst, Nova Scotia, where some brief protests occurred. After that, the tour continued without incident to Halifax, where two very successful meetings were held.[110] It then moved on to Prince Edward Island and St John's, Newfoundland. Crawford and Donovan then returned to Cape Breton, where enthusiastic rallies were held in Sydney and North Sydney.[111] Crawford and Donovan had encountered virtually no opposition to that point in their tour, each event having been received with tremendous enthusiasm.

The first instance of organized opposition to the Crawford–Donovan tour occurred in New Brunswick on 29 November 1920, when hundreds of Orange-Canadian unionists crowded into the Queen Square Theatre in Saint John to protest Crawford's arrival. The Reverend H.A. Goodwin and Canon C.A. Kuhring delivered speeches denouncing

Crawford as disloyal and seditious.[112] A resolution appealing to the civic authorities to prohibit Crawford from speaking in Saint John was passed unanimously.[113] The same resolution asked that the Dominion government suppress the publication of Crawford's Toronto-based newspaper *The Statesman*. It was also resolved that copies of the resolution be sent to the prime minister and to the Honourable R.W. Wigmore, Attorney General of Canada. Mayor Schofield of Saint John, who was attending the meeting, cautioned that the resolution asked the city to do something for which it had no power – namely, prohibit the rights to assembly and to free speech. Chairman Norman McLeod stated that he considered the mayor's comments to be a quibble, and on taking a standing vote on the resolution, 'Mayor Scofield was the only one observed to be seated.'[114] Unfortunately for those most loyal Canadians who wished to prohibit Crawford and Donovan from speaking, the meeting and resolutions had little effect.

On 30 November, Lindsay Crawford and Thomas Donovan addressed a capacity crowd at St Vincent's Theatre in Saint John, with as many people being turned away as were admitted to the theatre. Indeed, so great was the interest in these speakers and in the Irish Question that a week later, two Saint John newspapers, the *New Freeman* and *The Globe*, ran full transcripts of the night's proceedings as recorded by a court stenographer. Crawford's speech mirrored most others he had given on the tour. After a lengthy discussion of Irish history, he argued that the controversy in Ireland was one of economics, not religion, and that to separate industrial Ulster from the agrarian south would be not only foolish but also criminal.[115]

The one variant in the remarks that evening came from the chairman of the proceedings, Miles E. Agar. As a result of the attempts to forbid the public rally, the hypocrisy of British statesmen was no longer the sole target of the speakers' remarks. Agar now addressed the right of Canadians to speak freely at a public assembly. Irish-Canadian nationalist leaders now began identifying themselves as Canadians first, with all of the rights and privileges that citizenship entailed. In introducing the night's speakers, Miles Agar sternly proclaimed:

> We only claim the right that the British subject has maintained all through the ages, i.e., that what he had to say he would insist on saying. We are only asking that here tonight ...
>
> I do not want to refer to what is going on in Ireland; it is too painful to read the despatches from time to time without referring to them here. But

everyone knows that the condition of four and a half millions of people in Ireland today is most deplorable. It is the duty of the statesmen to remedy these conditions ... Are the statesmen of Great Britain today doing that so far as Ireland is concerned? I do not think so. We do not think so. We are making a protest and it is no mark of disloyalty on our part to criticizes a British ministry. It is no mark of disloyalty to the King that this meeting is held today. The people create a ministry by public opinion. We hope to mold the public opinion of this part of the British Dominions so that it will have a pressure and an effect on the British statesmen, so that they will hold their hands and moderate their course and meet the people of Ireland in a spirit of equality.[116]

Three days later, at St Dunstan's Hall in Fredericton, yet another crowd gathered to hear Crawford speak on the Irish Question. That evening, the Honourable P.J. Veniot, New Brunswick Minister of Public Works, chaired the night's proceedings. After stating that he was pleased to be on the platform with two gentlemen (Crawford and Donovan) who had become so well known in the Maritimes recently, Veniot declared himself to be loyal to the British Crown. He then declared: 'I am a Frenchman from head to foot. Why am I here? I want the same treatment for Ireland as was given my forefathers. If I knew Lindsay Crawford had uttered one word of treason I would ask that he be dethroned from the place which he occupies.'[117] Minister Veniot then told his audience that Crawford would be speaking next and that anyone who wished to ask Crawford questions could do so after his address. At that point, G.R. Hawkins rose from his chair and announced that he had been 'appointed to ask Mr. Crawford to reply "Yes or No" to three questions before he began his address.' Hawkins then demanded the right to ask questions whenever he wanted and generally disrupted the proceedings, as others in the audience began to sing and shout. Quite quickly the event flew out of control. As the chairman struggled to regain control of the meeting, Crawford shouted: 'If this is British fair play, no wonder there is an Irish question.'[118]

Four days later, on 7 December, the Crawford–Donovan tour stopped in Moncton, having two days earlier stopped in Bathurst.[119] The Moncton meeting transpired much as the Fredericton meeting had, with a well-orchestrated effort to prevent Lindsay Crawford from speaking. When he ascended the podium, a member of the audience named Mr Doig began screaming that Crawford needed to answer his questions. Doig, apparently intoxicated, actually went up on stage insisting that

Crawford answer the questions.[120] The meeting quickly collapsed into chaos, and Police Chief Doherty ordered it adjourned.[121]

According to Lindsay Crawford, when he left Moncton City Hall, he 'fell into the hands of a hostile mob of about five hundred and was pelted with ice, and struck on the head with fists and kicked about the legs and back.'[122] He was shepherded in and out of a number of shops in an effort to escape the angry mob. Eventually, the police chief arrived and escorted Crawford to his hotel room. Lindsay Crawford blamed the riot on Orangemen and claimed that the disturbance and similar ones had been engineered from Toronto.[123] The 'attack upon freedom of speech in this country by a small minority of unthinking intolerants is not confined to the Irish question,' he asserted. 'It would be a serious day for Canada if free discussion of questions that vitally affect the people of this country is denied by organized terrorism.'[124]

The *Orange Sentinel*, the official organ of the Canadian Orangemen, reported that Mr Crawford was never struck. Rather, he had been confronted by a crowd of returned soldiers, who demanded that he declare his loyalty to the British Crown, and he had been forced to kiss the Union Jack.[125]

A few days later, at a public meeting at the Ship Laborers Hall in Quebec City, under the auspices of the Sarsfield Branch of the Self-Determination for Ireland League, Lindsay Crawford strenuously denied having been made to kiss the Union Jack.[126] Discussing the recent Maritime tour, he assured the audience that 'in the course of their journey, they had fortified their friends and gained many recruits to the cause of Irish freedom, and now they had a membership in Canada of 300,000, and what was especially significant was the fact that for the first time in Canadian history, there was a close union between French and Irish.'[127] Crawford asserted that the self-determination movement was now regarded as one of the most serious movements launched in Canada in recent years. It was 'a movement that stood for Canada, first, last and all the time, and also to prevent the rise of Imperialism on the northern continent of America.' One of the questions put to him in Moncton had been, 'Are you a true British Subject?' Crawford raised the question again in Quebec, and answered, 'I am a Canadian Citizen, and everything Canadian citizenship implies. Is it seditious for a man to love his country, and is it seditious for him to call himself a Canadian?'[128] Continuing, he acknowledged the tremendous level of immigration in Canada over the preceding decades, and he stated that these Europeans brought the traditions of their old countries to Canada, which added to the distinctiveness of Canada. But there were others, 'such as the Orangemen of the North of Ireland, who brought with them their racial and religious prejudices,' which Lindsay Crawford viewed as detrimental to Canada.[129] This Quebec rally, which ended the eastern tour, would be Crawford's last public appearance for several months. Nonetheless, the league's work continued.

On 17 January 1921 the National Council of the Self-Determination for Ireland League of Canada met at its National Headquarters in Ottawa to consider the league's finances and organizational status. The council apparently met and acted in cabinet fashion, somewhat independent of the Executive Council, which included all nine provincial presidents of the league. Lindsay Crawford, along with Frank Cahill, MP, Thomas Donovan, Armand Lavergne, Charles Foy, and the Reverend Thomas P. Fay, were all listed as members of the council, and it was acknowledged that the 'following were also present: National Publicity Secretary, J.J. Larkin, Ontario Organizer, Miss K. Greany, Assistant to the National Secretary, F.J. Leahy, and Rev. Father O'Toole.'[130]

The most pressing issue facing the league in January 1921 – one that was 'recognized by all present' – was the need to raise funds, 'as no part of our work could be carried on without money.'[131] After a great deal of discussion, it was decided that a letter would be sent to each branch of the league expressing the urgency of the situation and requesting that each branch raise whatever amount it deemed advisable. It was further decided that letters would be sent to each Provincial Executive and distributed to the branches by them, to secure their help in raising funds. The Provincial Executives would be permitted to retain 25 per cent of the funds raised in their own provinces.

The Reverend Thomas P. Fay's report of receipts and expenditures from 1 November 1920 to 17 January 1921 detailed the dire financial straits in which the league found itself as of January 1921. The balance on hand as of that day was $72.90. Crawford's eastern tour had gathered only $355.47 in contributions, and the travel and organizational expenses for it amounted to $305.10. The contributions from Quebec were just over $100; the contributions from Ontario were far higher, at $1,398.32. The total receipts for the time period mentioned amounted to $2,746.87, but establishing a National Headquarters in Ottawa cost money. Total disbursements – office furniture ($235.45), an office ($225.00), office supplies and stationary, and telephone and telegraph charges ($342.47) – amounted to $2,673.95. But the single greatest expenditure by far was for literature and printing ($785.95).[132] That activity was of paramount importance to the league, for it was among the best means available to educate Canadians about Ireland's plight.

One of the league's primary goals was to publish and distribute as much literature relating to Ireland's troubles as finances would permit. One example was the Irish Information Series, published by the New Brunswick Executive of the Self-Determination League. Pamphlet no. 6 in the series was titled 'Lord Mayor MacSwiney's Speech and Some Other Speeches: The One Led to Imprisonment and Death: The Others to Honors and High Office.' This pamphlet emphasized the duplicity and hypocrisy of British rule in Ireland, as well as the blatantly favourable treatment received by the leading Unionist politicians even while nationalist leaders were sent to prison for uttering far less offensive statements than the Unionists. In a parenthetical introduction preceding the reprint of Mayor MacSwiney's inaugural address, the pamphlet stated:

> The following is the text of the address delivered by the late Lord Mayor of Cork on the occasion of his inauguration into office. It was fully reported in all the leading papers of England and Ireland at the time. Five months later one of the charges on which he was sentenced to two years imprisonment by a [British] military court was because notes of this speech were found in his desk. It mattered little that the full text of the speech was to be found on the files of every leading newspaper in England and Ireland. It was a 'crime' for MacSwiney to have notes of his speech but apparently any other person or persons could have the full text of the speech with impunity. Such is 'law' in Ireland.[133]

After the reprint of Mayor MacSwiney's inaugural address, the pamphlet presented segments of a number of inflammatory and rebellious speeches from Unionist leaders, including Sir Edward Carson, Andrew Bonar Law, Walter Long, F.E. Smith (Lord Birkenhead), and Sir James Craig. The parenthetical introduction to these speeches, under the subheading 'Throwing the Torch of Rebellion into Irish Politics,' emphasized that Ulster Unionists were rewarded with high office after inciting working-class unionists to rebel:

> A few years ago when Terence MacSwiney and the vast majority of the people of Ireland were anxious to have the Home Rule Act come into effect the Unionist party, led by Bonar Law, Sir Edward Carson, Sir F.E. Smith, etc., were encouraging and abetting armed opposition to enforcement of

the act in northeast Ulster. Bonar Law is, today, leader of the Government in the House; Sir F.E. Smith is Lord High Chancellor of England, and Sir Edward Carson became Attorney General of England and First Lord of the Admiralty. None of them were ever placed on trial, and today they are the main props of a Government which condemns 'treason' in Ireland.[134]

As had many prior editorials and speeches, this pamphlet highlighted the fact that under the present British administration in Ireland, Irish nationalists were jailed for committing the same offences as those for which Ulster Unionists received official appointment.

Similarly, the Nova Scotia Branch of the Self-Determination League published a weekly bulletin as a means to disseminate local branch information as well as news from Ireland. Bulletin no. 4, for example, under the headline 'The Latest Method of Coercion,' stated that British forces in Ireland were now engaging in forced labour; with the 'constabulary and military in many parts of the country have recently formed prominent residents of towns and villages into slave-gangs, and have given them tasks to perform, and have stood by them as overseers until it was finished.'[135] Bulletin no. 5 engaged in an historical discussion of events in Ireland, and bitterly condemned British Prime Minister David Lloyd George for his lack of knowledge of Irish history:

> He knows very little of the way in which Irish industries were killed by Castelreagh – Cutthroat Castelreagh – as they call him – nor of the frightful famines which decimated the country because of that policy, nor of the tragic evictions under English or Anglo-Irish landlords which made thousands of families foodless and homeless, nor of the penal laws which made martyrs of their priests and tried to kill a people's faith, nor of the executions and jailings of Irish patriots through many centuries of resistance to English rule.
>
> He does not realize that anything England does for Ireland, or has done or will do, is not received with gratitude as a favour, or as a generous act, but is regarded as a long delayed concession forced from us, and as dust in the balance compared with half a thousand years of tyranny, robbery and brutality.[136]

Pamphlets such as these served as educational and propaganda devices; but they also exemplified how knowledgeable some Irish Canadians were about Irish history. Yet Lloyd George forged ahead with new proposals for a political solutions in Ireland. Some of his proposals actually created new troubles.

By mid-1921, the political stalemate in Ireland had been broken. In 1920, Lloyd George introduced a new Home Rule bill – the Government of Ireland Act 1920, which established two home rule parliaments in Ireland: one in Belfast for six northeastern counties in Ulster, the other in Dublin for the remainder of the island. By June 1921 the Belfast parliament in the Northern Ireland statelet was functioning. This enabled Lloyd George, 'the Welsh wizard,' to negotiate a settlement with the Sinn Féin leaders without the intrusion of the vexing Ulster issue. At noon on 11 July 1921, Lloyd George's government and Irish republicans agreed to a truce, thereby ending hostilities in Ireland. Eamon de Valera crossed to London and met Lloyd George, initiating a correspondence that sought ultimately to resolve the difference of opinion between Irish republicans and the British government. A settlement conference was set for 11 October 'to discuss a settlement which would bestow upon the Irish people the fullest freedom of national development within the Empire.'[137] De Valera returned to Ireland and sent other delegates, including Arthur Griffith and Michael Collins, to the negotiations, which lasted until 6 December 1921. They produced a settlement treaty that recognized the founding of the Irish Free State.

This treaty conferred dominion status upon Ireland and granted far more autonomy than mere Home Rule, but it fell short of the desired independent republic. Its first article deemed that Ireland would have political status similar to that of Canada, and it even used phrasing taken directly from the British North America Act.[138] With the completion of this settlement, the *raison d'être* of the Self-Determination for Ireland League of Canada vanished. The league remained intact for the following year and continued to function, albeit largely in an advocacy capacity.

During the Irish Crisis of 1919–21, the Self-Determination League provided many Irish Canadians with a public voice for expressing their belief that Ireland was a distinct nation that had been fighting British oppression for 700 years. These Irish-Canadian nationalists, most of whom were Catholic, maintained a sense of ethnic identification with Ireland as their ancestral homeland and believed that Ireland's time for even limited independence had come by virtue of the Allied victory in the First World War. Many Irish-Canadian nationalists shifted their political allegiance after 1918, as did the Irish populace, from the constitutional nationalism of the John Redmond's IPP to the republican separatism of Sinn Féin. Yet this begs the question, to what extent were Irish Canadians republican? There had been a multitude of declarations of support for Sinn Féin in Canada, but Sinn Féin was solely a political party advocating complete independence from Britain. There was *another* element to Irish republicanism: the Irish Republican Army (IRA).

Did Irish Canadians support the revolutionary republicanism of the IRA? Although the league's August 1920 statement of aims and objectives declared that 'the League realizes that armed force will accomplish nothing in the way of a settlement,' that statement was in all likelihood intended for public consumption. Other statements, public and private, indicated that on a visceral level most Irish Canadians believed that Irish republicans were justified in taking up arms to throw off the yoke of British oppression, especially after news reports of British atrocities began flooding out of Ireland after January 1919. No documentary evidence of fund-raising efforts to support arms procurement for Irish republicans has been unearthed. Yet editorial comments, statements at rallies, and T.P. Tansey's comments to the St Patrick's Society – 'Our people at home are fighting for their cause as they never fought before, and are succeeding as they never did before. Let us encourage them by every means in our power, and [we] will, I trust show to all that every Irishman in Canada is with the Irish in Ireland, heart and soul' – all suggested tacit support for revolutionary republicanism, even if there was no evidence of financial support.

John Loye of Montreal, an active Irish-Canadian nationalist, took this support for Irish republicanism one step further. Loye wrote to Frank Walsh in New York, and indicated he wished to convey to the proper Irish republican authorities suggestions that might strengthen the military effectiveness of the Irish republican volunteers. John Loye also asked for financial assistance to travel to the United States to present his ideas. He noted that it had been brought to his attention that Harry Boland would be unavailable for up to a month. For that reason Loye was contacting Walsh in the hope that his organization and contacts might help finance the trip to New York:

> There is nothing of the extraordinary in the nature of the suggestions I have to make. They are not theories awaiting the proof of efficacy. They are simply the employment of the same forces now at our disposal in a manner as yet untried. They were inspired by the necessities of our present circumstances and need but our common ingenuity to give them salient effect.
>
> I see no prospect of a settlement of our cause on just lines by any conference like the one now proposed. Not until we impose our right by our own military power shall our cause be achieved: and I submit that the ob-

taining of any idea conducive to that end would warrant an expenditure covering my expenses in visiting the United States.[139]

Loye clearly believed that Irish republicans were fully justified in taking up arms as a legitimate means of achieving independence. Loye also offered a reference for his Irish republican credentials: 'As for my integrity, I can only recommend you to Diarmid Lynch.'[140] Lynch had been Director of Communications for the Irish Republican Brotherhood after the Easter Rising; after that, he had served in New York as the National Secretary of the American Friends of Irish Freedom during Eamon de Valera's fund-raising tour of the United States in 1919–20.[141] There can be little question that Lindsay Crawford and Katherine Hughes were at least well acquainted with Irish republicans in America, and probably even knew Eamon de Valera personally. That John Loye knew Diarmid Lynch reveals a level of republican involvement that was probably little known among Irish Canadians. It is possible that Loye's relationship with Lynch developed only after Lynch came to work in New York; but it is equally possible that Loye had connections to Irish republicans in Ireland.

For its part, the *Catholic Register* put forward an assertively republican editorial following the truce declaration in July. The editorial gleefully announced that Ireland had brought mighty Britain to the bargaining table, and it hailed Irish republican leaders by name:

De Valera, Commander-in-Chief Michael Collins, John McNeil, Arthur Griffith, and Commandant [Richard] Mulcahy are men of sterner stuff than Redmond or Parnell or O'Connell. They have played dice with death for a long time, and their souls are steeled to endure to the bitter end. When Lloyd George comes out of the fight with these Irish leaders, he will know he has been in a fight, and up against men!

And Ireland, – poor, brave, undaunted Ireland, has done all this with her own two hands! She has brought to terms the strongest nation in the world and forced her to talk of justice and right. In the struggle Ireland suffered sorely. Her towns were burned, her sons shot, and hanged, and imprisoned, but all this did not break her spirit. Vast armies occupied her towns, and her highways reechoed the rattle of the tank and the armoured car! But Ireland's men were brave and bold, and her women were, if possible, braver! They stood behind their men and urged them on to the battle and fed and clothed and bound up the wounds of the fierce battalions of the I.R.A. marching forward to the 'forlorn hope' and the 'gap of danger!'

Ireland fought a lonely and desperate battle, but as events have shown, it was not a losing fight.[142]

As historian Mark McGowan has noted, editorial comment in the ethnic weekly newspapers reflected the sentiments of the parochial communities they represented; had they not, they would have folded. From this editorial, one must conclude that there was a fair degree of Irish-Canadian support for revolutionary republicanism.

Support for revolutionary republicanism undoubtedly found expression in the Self-Determination League, however subtle it may have been. The league's real significance lay not in the extent to which it supported the IRA, or its total number of members, or in the amount of money it raised; rather, it was in the mere fact of its existence. The league was an organized representation of the fact that a significant number of Irish Canadians believed that the dispensation of British justice in Ireland was severely flawed. League members also fervently believed that British politicians were duplicitous in proclaiming that the Great War had been fought for the right of small nations to determine their own form of governance, and then withholding that right from Ireland following the Allied victory. The league voiced these criticisms of the imperial government publicly, and emphasized that freely expressing their support for Irish efforts to achieve independence was an act of Canadian patriotism. Freedom of expression was a fundamental Canadian right, and exercising that right in criticizing the imperial government was patriotic. That the league encountered fierce opposition and attempts to prevent its members from speaking through physical intimidation and civic edicts only bolstered its arguments that its advocacy of Irish freedom was truly democratic.

Unfortunately for Irish-Canadian nationalists, the political upheavals in Ireland did not end with the treaty signing on 6 December 1921. In some respects those upheavals had only just begun. Throughout 1922 and 1923, Irish Canadians sorrowfully watched as Irishmen descended into a bloody civil war. Questions also remained regarding the final settlement of the border with the newly created Northern Ireland, which suggested that Irish Canadians would maintain an intense interest in Irish political affairs for at least the foreseeable future.

*Chapter Five*

# 'No Surrender': Orange-Canadian Unionists and Northern Ireland, 1919–1925

After the First World War ended, and after the euphoria over the British and Allied victory, Orange-Canadian unionists' jubilation quickly turned to concern over the political fate of Ulster. In 1914 the third Irish Home Rule Bill had passed the House of Commons and received Royal Assent, which meant that it still resided on the statute books. Although the Asquith government attached an amending bill that prohibited the implementation of Home Rule until Ulster's frantic misgivings had been addressed, Ulster's political future continued along decidedly ambiguous lines. Orange-Canadian unionists feared that their Protestant brethren might yet be placed under the heel of a Romanist Dublin parliament. Orange-Canadian unionists considered this to be an unpardonable offence, particularly when one considered that thousands of Ulstermen volunteered to fight for the British during the war. Only in June 1921 were unionist fears briefly assuaged, when the rump Ulster statelet, dubbed Northern Ireland, was given its own home rule parliament as well as constitutional guarantees that it would remain in the United Kingdom. Unionist dread persisted, however, with the perceived threat of Irish republicans doing away with the Northern Ireland boundary through the powers invested in the legislated Boundary Commission.[1] Just as they had in 1912–14, Ulster unionists turned to their Orange-Canadian unionist brethren for support in their time of crisis. With unquestioning devotion, Orange-Canadian unionists provided both moral and financial assistance, in whatever amounts they could, in this most recent incarnation of the Battle of the Boyne.

In early 1919, leading Canadian Orangemen publicly expressed their concern over Ulster's uncertain fate. At the annual meeting of the national Grand Orange Lodge of British America, the most exalted Grand

Lodge in Canada, the Grand Master and former Mayor of Toronto, Horatio C. Hocken, referred to Ulster's political limbo in the most dire terms. Hocken's vows of continued Canadian support and sympathy in whatever battles lay ahead were utterly consistent with his previous statements, and they mirrored the stance taken generally by Canadian Orangemen.[2] In his opening address to the Orange brethren assembled at Ottawa in annual session, Grand Master Hocken declared:

> Whatever the future may hold for Ireland, the people of Ulster may depend upon the Orangemen of Canada giving them all the support within their power. Sinn Fein rebels shall not rule Ulster. The war has torn the mask from the face of Nationalism and revealed Nationalists as the implacable foes of the British Empire ... To place a million loyal citizens under the heel of Sinn Fein would be the blackest crime ever committed by any Parliament. Home Rule is a dead issue, made so by the treason and rebellion of its advocates.[3]

Five months earlier, at the annual meeting of the Provincial Grand Orange Lodge of Ontario West, the Committee on Correspondence offered its report and pledged the support of Ontario Orangemen to Protestant Ulster. This report referred to the 'British connection' as the founding principle of Orangeism and asserted that Orangemen routinely proclaimed their 'imperialism aloud to the world.' Although immigration into Canada slowed considerably from its peak in the early 1910s, the report also noted how urgent it now was to bar from naturalization 'all enemy and neutral aliens' and insisted on halting 'the further immigration of these undesirables.'[4] Canadian Orangemen consistently expressed these sorts of xenophobic sentiments, just as they had in previous years.[5] Specifically with respect to the plight of Protestant Ulster in 1919, the Committee on Correspondence declared:

> Dear to the heart of every [Canadian] Orangeman is the happiness and prosperity of Ireland. Though not all of Irish birth or parentage, yet all have reverence for the Irish forebears who fought and suffered and died for the glorious heritage of religious liberty ... But we Orangemen with warmest hearts again pledge our fidelity to British Ulster, and to all our faithful brethren there who through storm and calm – but mostly storm – have remained loyal to the flag and 'British connection.'[6]

Emphasizing the intrinsic British identity of Ulster Protestants, and by extension their own British identity, these Ontario Orangemen left little doubt where their sympathies lay. In the months and years that followed, Orange-Canadian unionists demonstrated their fidelity to Protestant Ulster by financially contributing to its defence, just as they had done during the Home Rule Crisis of 1912–14.[7] However, Grand Master Hocken was incorrect in his prediction that Home Rule was a dead issue, for it was anything but dead.

As events in Ireland progressed through 1919, news reports intoned that the political status of Ulster might soon change. Beginning in February 1919 the *Orange Sentinel* ran a special column titled 'The Week's News From Ireland.' By late 1921, another column titled 'Ulster Scot – To His Friends at Home And Abroad (From *The Belfast Weekly News*)' – had also begun appearing regularly in the *Sentinel*. These columns provided readers with the latest information from Ireland, with a focus on its implications for Ulster. By the end of 1919, reports had begun to appear regarding a new Irish Home Rule proposal put forward by a British Cabinet committee. This one favoured the establishing of two parliaments in Ireland: one in the north, one in the south.[8] This seemed to hold out hope of protecting Ulster's Protestants from the supposed threat of religious persecution at the hands of their traditional Catholic enemies. Surprisingly, though, the issue of an Ulster Parliament was never discussed when a delegation of Ulster ministers arrived in Toronto in early 1920.

On 14 February 1920 a delegation of nine Protestant ministers from Ulster arrived in Toronto to a heroes' welcome. Before coming to Canada, the Ulster delegation had travelled extensively in the United States, stopping at New York, Pittsburgh, Philadelphia, Columbus, Dayton, Detroit, New Orleans, Los Angeles, and Seattle, but it received its warmest welcome when it crossed the border into Canada. Led by Fred Danc, a Belfast native and former Canadian Trade Representative in Glasgow, a large assemblage of Toronto's citizens awaited on the Union Station platform to greet the ministers' train from Niagara Falls. The Ulster delegation was presented with the keys to the city, at which point the leader of the Ulster delegation, William Coote, Unionist MP for South Tyrone, replied: 'We knew we would meet with a royal welcome in Toronto, the Belfast of Canada.'[9]

Rev. Coote then described the objectives of the tour across the United States and Canada: 'It is not a financial nor a political visit, but an educational one, largely to offset the pernicious Sinn Fein propaganda of De Valera and his companions who are selling bonds for the Irish Republic in the United States. We are here in the interests of law and order, of truth, honesty and fair play.'[10] Rev. Coote then emphatically denied that the British were persecuting the Irish. On the contrary, he asserted, the Irish were better off than the majority of the English, Scots, and Welsh; and the Irish were simply the spoiled children of the empire. In referring to Sir Edward Carson and the Ulster Covenant, Rev. Coote 'declared with great vehemence that the loyalists of Ulster would never submit to being placed under the yoke of a Sinn Fein Parliament in Dublin.' Noting that he himself was a commander of an Ulster Volunteer Force regiment, Rev. Coote explained 'that the day the Sinn Feiners attempted to invade Ulster it would be a bad day for the Sinn Feiners.'[11]

The Ulster delegates were then taken to a local County Orange Hall to attend Loyal Orange Lodge no. 387 in monthly session. Whether or not the Ulster delegation would be able to enter was a matter of concern, for not only had the 300 members of the lodge arrived to attend the meeting, but an additional 400 Orangemen had shown up to welcome and support the delegation. The Reverend Wylie Blue expressed the delegation's heartfelt appreciation for their reception in Toronto: 'Our delegation came to Canada not as a mission. We came to the United States in the guise of missionaries. But as regard the Canadians, one does not send missionaries to the enlightened. It was really not our intention to cross the border at all. But now that we have come, we feel that without any explanations of pleading on our part you understand our cause. You are of us.'[12]

Rev. Coote then spoke – in far more strident terms – about the need for those who supported Ulster to stand up and be counted and to align themselves with the only institution willing to confront Sinn Féin:

> The time has come when all who wish Ireland well must line up with the Orange Order. The only force that stands firmly arrayed against Fenianism, Bolshevism, terrorism, and Sinn Feinism in Ireland to-day is, as regards Ulster, the institution of Orangeism. Let not the people of Canada think, when the day comes that Ulster is driven to the wall, and is fighting for its rights that Canada will go unharmed. For, if the pivotal point of the Empire's sovereignty, the British Isles, are destroyed, the whole Empire will soon be a thing of the past.[13]

Over the next two days the Ulster delegation participated in numerous fraternal, civic, and religious events in Toronto. These included a service at Cooke's Presbyterian Church, during which the Reverend

Edward Hazelton extolled true Christian principles when he unrepentantly assured his flock: 'We would rather die than live under Sinn Fein rule. Our freedom, civil and religious, has been bought with blood. If need be we will draw the sword again for it, and we will not sheathe it in leather or steel, but in human flesh.'[14]

The Ulster delegation also spoke on the conditions prevailing in Ireland at a luncheon sponsored by the Empire Club of Toronto, which packed the huge banquet hall of the King Edward Hotel so tightly that tables had to be set up in the corridors to accommodate the crush. The oldest members of the club described it as the largest and most enthusiastic meeting to date.[15]

On the final morning of their Toronto visit, as the Ulster delegation boarded a train bound for Ottawa, the editor of the *Orange Sentinel* asked Rev. Coote: 'What is your last word to Toronto?' Without hesitation or ambiguity, Rev. Coote's reply shot back, 'No Surrender!'[16]

Shortly after the Ulster ministerial delegation left Toronto, the David Lloyd George coalition government introduced legislation aimed at definitively settling the Irish Question. The new Home Rule bill, styled as the Government of Ireland Act 1920, supplanted the old legislation and proposed the establishment of two Home Rule parliaments in Ireland: one in Belfast, and one in Dublin. As on previous occasions, powers relating to national security and foreign affairs, coinage, post offices, and the ability to tax would be retained by Westminster. Only powers relating to purely local interests – including education, local government, land policy, agriculture, roads and bridges, transportation, old age pensions, insurance, housing, and hospitals – would be handed over to the separate Irish parliaments.[17] Surprisingly, by the time the bill was introduced on 25 February 1920, some of its provisions had yet to be finalized. The most pressing of these unfinished provisions related to the territory over which the Northern Ireland parliament would govern.

Because of the altered political terrain in the British House of Commons following the parliamentary elections of 1916 and 1918, Lloyd George's coalition government included a near majority of Conservatives and Unionists. This shifted the balance of power with regard to Irish affairs from southern nationalists to northern Unionists.[18] For example, the cabinet committee charged with reviewing Irish policy and with drafting the new Home Rule legislation included Sir James Craig and was chaired by Walter Long. This was the same Walter Long who, as head of the Union Defence League, had solicited funds from Canadian Orangemen to assist the UVF's arms procurement.[19]

At the time the Government of Ireland Act 1920 was being drafted, Walter Long favoured a unified nine-county Ulster for the area of control for the northern parliament. However, Ulster leaders were so vehemently opposed to this, the matter was left unresolved at the time the bill was introduced.[20] The Ulster Unionists demanded a six-county administrative region, one that would exclude Ulster's most heavily Catholic counties: Cavan, Donegal, and Monaghan.[21] Ulster Unionist leaders wanted 'an Ulster they could hold on to, one in which Protestants would have a clear-cut majority, and this had to be a six-county Ulster whose boundaries would be inviolate.'[22] A six-county Northern Ireland consisting of the easternmost counties with the highest percentages of Protestants guaranteed a 66 per cent majority; a united-nine county Ulster would have provided a Protestant majority of just over 50 per cent.[23]

Ulster Unionists lobbied intensely for a six-county parliament, for 'they feared that in the future their control of all nine counties would be too precarious.'[24] During the second reading of the bill, Charles Craig, Sir James Craig's brother, told the House of Commons: 'No sane man would undertake to carry on a Parliament with [so slender a majority] ... A couple of Members sick, or two or three Members absent for some accidental reason, might in one evening hand over the entire Ulster Parliament and the entire Ulster position [to the South] ... A dreadful thing to contemplate.'[25]

When it became apparent to Walter Long that the bill might not pass – in no small part owing to Unionist intransigence – Long initiated secret negotiations with Carson and Craig to win their support for the measure. Only after Carson and Craig were guaranteed a permanent six-county Ulster, with a significant Protestant majority, did they agreed to support the bill. Walter Long acknowledged:

> The Ulster people stood coldly aloof, they did not want the Bill and they were not inclined to provide the only support the Bill was likely to get. I then had conversations with Carson and Craig and I came to the conclusion that it would be possible to arrange some plan with the Ulster Members [of Parliament] on one condition and one alone, and that was they should receive a definite pledge from me on behalf of the Cabinet to the effect that if they agreed to accept the Bill and to try to work it when it passed, it would be on the clear understanding that the Six Counties, as settled after the negotiations, should be theirs for good and all and there should be no interference with the boundaries or anything else, excepting

such slight adjustments as might be necessary to get rid of projecting bits, etc.²⁶

The Ulster Unionists, who had opposed Home Rule to such an extent that they were prepared to fight a civil war over the issue in 1914 and to bring the empire to its knees, now willingly accepted Home Rule, having secured the conditions to ensure their electoral – and therefore political – control over the area to be governed. In the ensuing decades, these tactics imbued with opportunism and double standards proved to be the hallmark of the Ulster Unionists' political strategy.

Similarly, having strenuously protested the passage of the 1912 Irish Home Rule bill, Orange-Canadian unionists now came out in favour of the 1920 act. They believed it provided the best means of protecting Protestant Ulster's interests and ascendancy, while also maintaining the empire's integrity. The *Orange Sentinel* hailed the legislation, with its six-county provision, as 'an improvement on any previous proposal.'²⁷ The following week the *Sentinel* editorialized that a parliament dominated and controlled by Protestants would serve as an example for the southern Celtic Irish, who would undoubtedly be outclassed by their northern neighbours. In encouraging the southern Irish to try their best to succeed, the *Sentinel* quipped:

> What influence a well ordered government in Ulster would have in the other provinces is something that only experience can determine. There is ground for hope, however, that the example which Ulster will surely set for the south will produce unexpectedly good results. If there is any pride of race in the Celtic Irish – and their bards have put it lavishly into their songs – they will not be content to see themselves outclassed before the eyes of the world by the people of Ulster. Under the proposed division of the country comparisons will be inevitable. If the south fails under identical conditions that bring prosperity to the north, how will it be explained.²⁸

Orange-Canadian unionists hailed Lloyd George's government for codifying what they believed previous governments had ignored – namely, that Ireland had for years been divided by race, religion, and politics. The *Orange Sentinel* unflinchingly stated, 'That Ireland is, and always was, divided, is a fact that cannot honestly be disregarded.'²⁹ With a northern parliament, Protestant Ulster's interests and the empire's integrity would be secured. This was a primary concern to Orange-Canadian unionists, who believed the enemies of Britain to be gaining strength and working in concert to bring down the British Empire, which had recently increased in size. Following the war and the Paris Peace Conference, the empire had grown even larger, and now included not only the dominions – Canada, South Africa, Australia, and New Zealand – but also India, Burma, Malaysia, Singapore, the African territories of Nigeria, Gold Coast, Sierra Leone, Egypt, Sudan, Uganda, Kenya, and Rhodesia, and also the latest Middle Eastern mandates: Cyprus, Palestine, Iraq, and Transjordan. By the early twentieth century the sun indeed never set on the British Empire.

In their continuous outpouring of speeches, resolutions, articles, and editorials, Orange-Canadian unionists made clear their belief that they, along with Ulster unionists, served on the front lines of an insidious war designed and propagated by Irish nationalists to undermine Protestantism generally, and in particular the British Empire itself. One crucial component of this war was the battle over propaganda: Whose message would best resonate with the public? Unionists worked feverishly to discredit the empire's enemies; as a consequence, Irish nationalist agitation for independence – in particular, Sinn Féin republicanism – was cast as intimately linked with any number of other isms, including Bolshevism, German militarism, and Roman Catholicism (i.e., the Papacy). Orange-Canadian unionists lumped together seemingly disparate groups as cohorts in a worldwide conspiracy whose ultimate aim was the destruction of the cornerstone of Protestantism – the British Empire. These sentiments were apparent at the 1919 annual meeting of the Grand Orange Lodge of New Brunswick, when W.E. Williams reported that the 'football of politics in the old country' had yet to be resolved:

> Desperate cases require desperate remedies and Sinn Feinism has reached its last ditch in its efforts to dismember the British empire. As Bolshevism is to Russia so is the Irish body to England, and it has little hopes of accomplishing its object. That a solving of this question is possible, but it certainly must be one fully satisfactory to Ulster. Such a solution is highly desirable, but is seems impossible to form any method that would satisfy the Sinn Feiners and the Irish clergy that leads and controls them.[30]

New Brunswick Orangemen favoured a solution to the Irish Question that would preserve the Protestant ascendancy and that would continue to ensure that the Catholics would be controlled. Clearly, Canadian Orangemen did not invent these conspiracy theories on their own. Sir Edward Carson and Sir Hamar Greenwood, the Secretary of State for Ireland, asserted that Sinn Féin was part of a worldwide conspiracy, and in doing so they provided much of the impetus for similar Orange-Canadian accusations.[31]

Throughout the early 1920s, Canadian Orangemen insisted that direct links between Sinn Féin and Bolshevism were threatening the empire's very existence. An *Orange Sentinel* editorial titled 'An Unholy Alliance' contended 'that Sinn Feinism is only one phase of an international movement to destroy the British Empire.'[32] In their efforts to bring down the empire, Irish republicans had supposedly linked up with rebel movements in India, Egypt, and South Africa. According to Canadian Orangemen, Frank P. Walsh, Edward Dunne, and other 'American Sinn Feiners' were all associated with these rebel movements. The same editorial claimed that 'the financial headquarters for the international rebellion is in the United States.'[33] The editorial also claimed:

> The whole movement is backed up by the papal system, and millions of dollars are being supplied by the Germans, the Russian Bolsheviks, or the Roman hierarchy, or all three combined. The Jesuit, the Hun and the Bolsheviks have joined forces, forming an unholy trinity, for the purpose of accomplishing that which they failed to achieve during the war. They have resorted to an insidious propaganda of class and race hatred, sedition and rebellion in the hope of bringing Britain to the dust.[34]

Also according to the editorial, the Papal plan was designed to break the will of the 'Imperial British race' and could only be defeated 'by a closer unity of all loyal Protestants and friends of British institutions, who realize the seriousness of the situation.'[35]

The Orange theory of racial and religious conspiracy against the empire was further refined by Grand Master William David McPherson in his opening address to the 1923 annual session of the national Grand Orange Lodge of British America. McPherson, a member of the Ontario legislature, asserted that there is 'unquestionably a gathering of the forces of Mohammedanism, Bolshevism, Mormonism, Russelism and Roman Catholicism for the destruction of Protestantism and of the British Empire as the two great Forces that make for Civil and Religious Liberty.'[36] These remarks demonstrated the extent to which Canadian Orangemen truly believed they served on the front lines in a worldwide battle to preserve the integrity of the Empire from destruction by Papists and republicans. As active soldiers in this socio-religious battle, Orange-Canadian unionists found it particularly galling to learn that not only did Irish nationalists find support in Canada, but so did Sinn Féin.

With similar disgust, the British Empire Alliance (BEA) protested vigorously the fact that Irish Canadians – or any Canadians, for that matter – were willingly lending support to a movement whose intention was to weaken the empire. The Halifax Branch of the British Empire Alliance held a rally in March 1921, attended by 1,200 people, to protest what they believed to be disloyal expressions of political allegiance to Sinn Féin. After acknowledging that Canadians were blessed with the freedoms of speech and of the press, the BEA rally adopted a resolution declaring that those in attendance soundly

> deplore the abuse that has been made of that privilege in the utterance of seditious sentiments, calculated to subvert good government, to foster a spirit of disloyalty to our institutions, and to injure the British Empire upon whose strength our welfare depends, and for whose maintenance so many brave men shed their blood, and we respectfully urge the Government to deal firmly with these seditious publications in the interest of the common good.[37]

In the letter accompanying the resolution sent to Canadian Prime Minister Arthur Meighen, the Reverend J.M. Ratcliff, Secretary of the Halifax Branch of the British Empire Alliance, was so incensed by the possibility of Irish republican support in Canada that he needed to ensure that the federal government was aware of government officials who 'associated with disloyal organizations.' He asserted that a certain Mr. Foran 'has been associated with the Sinn Fein movement and on Feb. 9, 1919 presided at a Sinn Fein meeting held in Montreal. It was at this meeting C.J. Foy, of Perth [Ontario], said that Sinn Fein was the grandest movement that had ever been started.'[38] In his reply, Prime Minister Meighen assured Rev. Ratcliff that the 'Federal Government follows with care the matters referred to in this resolution and keeps itself apprized of what is going on throughout the Dominion.'[39] On this point – that the federal government was following affairs throughout the dominion – Arthur Meighen was not mistaken.

As noted earlier, by the summer of 1920, while reports of British reprisals in Ireland slipped through the censors' nets and reached Canada, Irish-Canadian nationalists began to publicly express their support for an independent Ireland. At that time the federal government was in fact well abreast of these activities, for the RCMP's Criminal Investigation Branch was by then conducting extensive surveillance of Irish nationalist organizations throughout Canada.[40] After Irish-Canadian nationalist leaders met with Sinn Féin president Eamonn de Valera in Plattsburgh, New York, most Irish nationalist groups in the major Canadian cities adopted the name 'Self-Determination for Ireland League,' after the Irish nationalist organization by then successfully operating in England.[41]

Not surprisingly, the subsequent public rallies in Canada in support of Irish national aspirations evoked a less than cordial response from Orange-Canadian unionists.[42] In October 1920, when 600 delegates gathered in Ottawa for a national convention of the Self-Determination for Ireland League of Canada, the *Orange Sentinel* responded with derision:

> The recent gathering at Ottawa proved that there is an understanding between the Sinn Feiners, the Bolshevists and other disloyal elements that refused to participate in the great war. 'Anything to smash the British Empire' is their slogan. The most devout Romanists and the most blatant Atheists have combined for the purpose of disrupting the United Kingdom by establishing an independent Irish Republic. If that could be accomplished then they would continue their agitation for a Canadian Republic.[43]

By December 1920, Orange-Canadian unionists viewed the Irish-Canadian nationalist movement in far more threatening terms. The league seemed to hold sinister capabilities, for 'nothing has happened in Canada during the last century to arouse and consolidate the sentiment of loyalty to the British Empire so markedly as the organization of the Self-Determination for Ireland League.'[44] In starkly militaristic language, the *Sentinel* called on loyal Canadian citizens to join in the empire's defence:

> That is why it is necessary for all the loyal citizens of Canada to put on their armor and join the ranks of those who are fighting against this demon of destruction that would throw the world again into the caldron of war to break up the greatest, freest state that has yet appeared among men. The movement to sap the loyalty of Canada is going on as never

before. It is the most dangerous of all the attempts made to alienate this country from the Crown. The duty of every loyal Canadian is clear. It is to offer the strongest opposition of which he is capable to the propagandists who aim at nothing less than the destruction of the Empire.⁴⁵

That Irish republican Sinn Féin found support in Canada was an egregious affront to the sensibilities of Orange Canadians, who believed it their duty to confront this scourge and to prevent whenever possible the spread of republican propaganda.

In April 1921, when the New Brunswick Grand Orange Lodge met in annual session at the Moncton First Baptist Church, Grand Master L.A. Palmer applauded the actions of those Orangemen who had disrupted Self-Determination League meetings in Fredericton, Moncton, and Saint John the previous December. Referring to Sinn Féin's efforts to 'disrupt and dismember the British Empire,' Grand Master Palmer described those who broke up the rallies, and who had assaulted Lindsay Crawford by hurling chunks of ice at him, as truly loyal Canadians:

> To assist in spreading their [Sinn Féin] propaganda here in Canada the 'Self-Determination League' was organized. Lindsay Crawford undertook to spread its precepts in the Maritime Provinces, but his efforts in the larger centres did not accomplish much. Thanks to loyal Canadian citizens, meetings in Fredericton, St. John and Moncton were pro British and showed the feeling of the majority of our New Brunswickers.⁴⁶

One month later, Canadian unionists' abhorrence that Sinn Féin found sanctuary in Canada under the umbrella of the Self-Determination League was enshrined in the form of six resolutions sent to the Provincial Grand Orange Lodges in preparation for the upcoming 12 July celebrations. Those resolutions had been prepared in advance by the national Grand Orange Lodge of British America.⁴⁷ Most of them dealt with issues of the sort that had been enraging Canadian Orangemen since the late nineteenth century. They variously declared that 'all Separate Schools in the Dominion of Canada should be abolished' and that 'bilingualism in British North America should cease to exist.' The sixth resolution, however, dealt specifically with the Self-Determination for Ireland League:

> Resolved: That we, as loyal subjects of His Majesty King George V, do hereby assert that the Self-Determination League for Ireland should find

no place in this Dominion of Canada, and we call upon all British loyalists from the Atlantic to the Pacific to protest strongly against the seditious and treasonable utterances of this League fostered by the Pope of Rome and his satellites.[48]

As a result of these perceived conspiratorial provocations on the part of Irish nationalists in Canada, Orange-Canadian unionists felt it imperative to provide their Ulster Protestant brethren with unquestioned devotion and support in their efforts to obtain a secure, even dominant, position when Britain imposed a settlement on Ireland. No matter how contradictory Ulster's new stance might be relative to previous ones, and no matter how violent the actions of the Protestant working class might become, Orange-Canadian unionists would support their Irish coreligionists without hesitation. One result of this unexamined loyalty to Protestant Ulster was that, when sectarian violence flared in Londonderry and Belfast in the summer of 1920, Orange-Canadian unionists extended political cover to their brethren, and they did so without any flinching whatsoever.

Throughout the spring of 1920, sectarian tensions in the north of Ireland intensified as republicans in the south continued their war of independence, killing Crown forces in the process. Unionists in the north viewed this as but another example of nationalist deceit and disloyalty. Unionist insecurity and sense of vulnerability in Derry was only heightened as nationalists won an election in early 1920, gaining control of the city for the first time since 1690.[49] Sporadic attacks by both communities occurred throughout the spring. On 23 June 1920, the day that 1,500 British troops arrived in Derry to restore order, eight Catholics and four Protestants were killed during rioting.[50] The powder keg erupted on 21 July, when news spread of the assassination in Cork three days earlier of an Ulster-born police commissioner, Lieutenant Colonel G.B. Smyth, and the subsequent refusal of southern railway workers to transport his remains back to Ulster. These events precipitated intense Unionist outrage, which resulted in Protestant shipyard workers armed with clubs marching on the Harland and Wolff shipyard and expelling Catholic workers, many of whom were thrown into the water and had to swim for their lives. Catholics crowds then attacked Protestants, resulting in thirteen more deaths.[51] These scenes of violence spread across the northern province. In Belfast, Catholic relief organizations estimated that between 8,700 and 11,000 Catholic shipyard workers were expelled from their jobs, that 23,000 were driven from their homes, and that 500

Catholic business were destroyed.[52] While Catholics accounted for only 25 per cent of Belfast's population, between July 1920 and July 1922, they suffered 257 of the 416 civilian fatalities. With figures such as these, most nationalists described these events as the 'Belfast pogrom.'[53]

With unquestioning devotion to their Ulster brethren, Orange-Canadian unionists dismissed these events with one simple explanation: Catholics were to blame. If Catholics had not moved in and taken the jobs of loyal men who had enlisted during the war, these events never would have transpired. For example, the *Orange Sentinel* claimed:

> The explanation of the Londonderry situation is that the Sinn Fein population increased during the war by reason of the fact that large numbers removed from southern counties to take the places of the loyal sons of Derry who enlisted. They secured positions held by loyal Protestants and remain there to-day. This immigration from the South changed the proportionate numbers of Protestants and Romanists, much to the detriment of the former. This makes Londonderry the most favorable city in the North in which to stage civil war. The forces are about evenly divided. We may be sure, however, that the spirit shown by the 'Prentice Boys' in 1690 persists in that city, and there will be 'No surrender' to the assassins who, in the name of liberty, are murdering inoffensive people in many parts of Ireland.[54]

Harkening back to the late seventeenth century, when thirteen young apprentice boys closed Derry's gates after observing the Catholic armies of James II on the horizon, and held out under siege to save Derry from the Catholic invaders, the *Orange Sentinel* reinforced these ethno-religious expressions of Catholic blame.[55] With wild inaccuracy, the *Sentinel* again editorialized:

> The underlying cause of the recent trouble in Londonderry has soon transpired. Indeed it could not be hidden. It was an intentional assault upon the Protestant inhabitants with a view to drive them out of the city and reverse the memorable history round which the most intense feelings still clings. Incidently it showed that the driving force of Sinn Feinism is more religious than political. From positions of vantage at the Nazareth Home and St. Columb's College, both Romish institutions, the Sinn Feiners directed a continuous and deadly fire upon the houses of the Protestants and the streets adjoining them. Numbers of defenceless people were compelled to flee from those houses and the remnant who stood their ground

were reduced to starvation. It goes without saying that this unprovoked attack led to retaliation and that the conflict within the ancient walls has taken on much of its old severity. The cry of 'No surrender' has a meaning and reality now very much like that which it had in the days of James II and William of Orange.[56]

The editorial presented half-truths as evidence to justify loyalist violence against Catholics.[57] This was the kind of blind, obedient loyalty that Orange-Canadian unionists provided the Ulster Unionists. The same devotion would be extended to the Northern Ireland statelet once it came into being in June 1921.

When King George V opened the Northern Ireland Parliament on 7 June 1921, he implored: 'I appeal to all Irishmen to pause, to stretch out the hand of forbearance and conciliation, to forgive and forget, and to join in making for the land which they love a new era of peace, contentment, and good will.'[58] As the casualty figures cited above indicate, few Irishmen – including those 'most loyal' Protestants – heeded his words. Nevertheless, the opening of the Northern parliament was an exciting and festive occasion for Northern Protestants, one that was also enthusiastically celebrated in the Belfast of Canada.

In Toronto, on the evening of 7 June 1921, with three bands leading the revellers from various districts of the city, the friends of Ulster commemorated the opening of the Northern Ireland Parliament with a celebratory rally at Victoria Hall. Fred Dane, an Ulster Canadian and former Grand Master of the Grand Orange Lodge of Ontario West, declared that the festivities had been arranged to provide 'the citizens of Toronto an opportunity of expressing their congratulations to the people of Ulster on the magnificent results that they secured.'[59] In addition, Fred Dane proudly declared that Sir Edward Carson had admirably led Ulster and placed it 'in a position to take care of herself under all circumstances and conditions.' He also congratulated Sir James Craig and the people of Ulster, and assured his listeners that 'the future of Ulster is bright. We congratulate her people, and stand behind them in every way in the future as we have done in the past. Long may they live, under the folds of the Union Jack.' After he spoke, the Honourable Thomas Crawford, an Ulster Canadian as well, wished 'that the Government in Ulster will make such an impression that those in the other provinces may be led to live in peace.'[60]

H.C. Hocken, the former mayor of Toronto and now an MP, thought it 'most appropriate that the "Belfast of Canada" should celebrate the events of to-day' and predicted great success for the Ulster Parliament, noting that wherever Ulstermen travelled they succeeded. He then contrasted 'the hard-working men of the north with the shiftless type found in the south and west of Ireland,' stating categorically that 'if a Parliament was not formed in the south they could not go before the courts of the world, while if they did function they would not bring prosperity to that part of the country, because they did not work, but [instead] talked.'[61]

Unfortunately, the euphoria shared by Orange-Canadian unionists and Ulster unionists at the opening of the new Northern Parliament was short-lived. Even before the parliament opened, the *Orange Sentinel* commented: 'There is something going on in Ireland that has not been fully revealed, but from what has been published it looks [as if] efforts are being made to reach a settlement with the Sinn Fein of a character that is not in the interest of Ulster or the Empire.'[62] Indeed, a negotiated settlement was being discussed and debated between Lloyd George's coalition government and representatives of the self-proclaimed Irish Republic. The two sides deliberated throughout the fall of 1921. On 6 December 1921 the parties signed the Anglo-Irish Treaty, conferring upon the remaining twenty-six Irish counties dominion status much the same as Canada's, under the name Irish Free State. Article twelve of the Treaty called for the establishment of a Boundary Commission to consider alterations to the boundary between north and south.

Obviously, this threat to the Northern Ireland's security found immediate and hostile opposition from an Ulster unionist populace possessing an acute siege mentality. When elevated to peerage, Sir Edward Carson rose to deliver his first speech in the House of Lords, and it surprised no one that the recently signed treaty occupied the primary focus of his rather lengthy address. In concluding, he passed on this warning:

> You have tried wilfully and deliberately to make Ulster's position impossible; and what is more, I believe you have told the Sinn Fein delegates so. You have given these people power to have an army and to pay for it out of the taxes which they collect. You give them their Customs, which enable them to bring in arms and munitions and all the weapons of war they like. What do they want an army for unless to invade Ulster? (Cheers.) Is it to invade America, or the Isle of Man, or the Channel Islands? (Laughter.) ...
> But I warn the Government that throughout the whole Empire Ulster-

men are strong, and powerful. Toronto is an Ulster city. Don't do anything which will turn Ulster against the British connection. God forbid! Don't try us too hard. Do recognize that we have tried to help you, as you have helped us, and don't, when we want to stay with you, do anything to turn us out.[63]

Orange-Canadian unionists also sharply criticized the treaty. They believed wholeheartedly that the British government had surrendered to Sinn Féin. Worse yet, to Orange-Canadian unionists it appeared as if Dublin and London were working in tandem to create the environment for a united Ireland. Regarding the treaty's signing, the *Orange Sentinel* observed: 'Lloyd George has surrendered to the Sinn Fein ... For the moment the North is secure. But it is admittedly the aim of the Sinn Fein and of London to bring about what they call the union of all Ireland.' Ironically, the same editorial bemoaned that Orange Canadians might be accused of bigotry for the stance they were taking: 'We know that in certain quarters *The Sentinel* will be accused of bigotry, and that chiefly by men who are ignorant of the whole question, and of the Celtic character and ambition. But time will tell whether the implacable hatred of the Celt for the English has been removed by giving them the weapons to destroy the United Kingdom.'[64]

After routinely describing the Irish as shiftless and lazy, the *Orange Sentinel* now characterized them as ambitious. It also seems interesting that the mouthpiece of Canadian Orangeism was fretting about accusations of bigotry, though its own bigotry was often quite obvious. For instance, after an IRA border raid in early February 1922, the *Sentinel* aired its impressions of the Irish 'race':

Before the Irish 'treaty' is approved by [the British] Parliament the people of Ulster have had a taste of what is in store for them. Their border was crossed by large detachments of the Irish Republican Army and between forty and sixty prominent Ulstermen killed, wounded or captured ...

What has happened is just what was expected by those who know the character of the Celtic Irish. They are a savage race, and it seems impossible to civilize them as long as they remain among their bogs. When they emigrate they change in a remarkable way, but in the atmosphere of superstition that pervades Southern Ireland they remain savages ... So what the British Government has to deal with is a race of semi-savages, with an intense hatred for England, and equally for Protestants. They intend to have Ireland for the Irish, and they don't count the men of Ulster as Irish.

Expatriation or extermination are the alternatives for the Protestants of the North.[65]

For reasons such as these – a supposed worldwide conspiracy designed to bring down the British Empire, inept British statesmen surrendering to Sinn Féin and providing them with the apparatus to snatch Northern Ireland's territory, and semi-savage Celtic Irish conducting raids into Northern Ireland – Orange-Canadian unionists felt compelled, out of a sense of ethnic allegiance and imperial pride, to financially contribute to Ulster's defence.

In a number of resolutions adopted in 1922, Orange-Canadian unionists expressed their trepidation over the perceived assault on the empire and the need to financially commit to Ulster's defence.[66] A resolution prepared at the national level and then sent to the Provincial Grand Orange Lodges in preparation for the upcoming 12 July celebrations promised to financially support Ulster and that 'we may also extend to our Brethren in Ulster the promise of our moral and financial support in their struggle for freedom and British connection. We are mindful of their sacrifices and shedding of their blood for liberty and we assure them that the Orangemen of British America are proud of their challenge of "No Surrender" to traitors and conspirators against our Empire.'[67] In the aftermath of the founding of the Irish Free State, and repeated IRA border raids, Orange-Canadian unionists willingly extended assistance to their Ulster brethren, as well as to those Protestants suffering distress in the south of Ireland. In June 1922, at the annual meeting of the national Grand Orange Lodge of British America, held in Kingston, Ontario, the Report of the Committee on Finance proposed 'that this Grand Lodge take all necessary steps to provide funds for the Ulster Defence Association in their great efforts to save their hearths and homes.'[68] The vote to adopt the report of the Committee on Finance was defeated, but was replaced with a resolution that recommended 'a grant of not less than $3,000 to the Ulster Defence League.' A supplementary Report of the Committee on Finance was then accepted and adopted, which contained the following: 'Your Committee would recommend that this Grand Lodge grant to the Ulster Defence League from its funds a sum of not less than five thousand dollars.'[69]

These supplemental reports of the Committee on Finance indicated that Canadian Orangemen maintained constant and open communications with the Ulster Defence Association, or League as it was called.

They also indicate that Canadian Orangemen contributed freely in support of the UDA's efforts. Also, just as in 1914, well-known Ulster Unionist politicians solicited Orange-Canadian unionists for funds.

In the second half of 1922 the Reverend William Coote made a return trip to Canada, which lasted five months and included more than 100 public lectures.[70] The following year, at the annual meeting of the Provincial Grand Orange Lodge of Ontario West, Grand Master A.A. Gray enthusiastically referred to Coote's visit. In the course of his opening address, Gray mentioned that 'his addresses explaining the position of Ulster in the Irish crisis were greatly appreciated.' He then acknowledged that Rev. Coote 'visited this country under the auspices of the Orange, Black and Loyalist Defence Association and received much support for the Protestant loyalists who have been persecuted.'[71] Similarly, the Grand Orange Lodge of New Brunswick placed in its records a letter dated February 1923 from the Orange, Black, and Loyalist Defence Association of Ireland thanking the members of the Saint John branch for the cooperation and support extended to William Coote during his tour on their behalf.[72] Formed in May 1921 by the two largest Protestant fraternal societies, the Orange, Black, and Loyalist Defence Association was a Belfast-based paramilitary organization whose nominal military function was 'to meet any attack which may be made at any moment to drive us out by force from our British citizenship.'[73] Recent research, though, indicates that 'the Defence Association's military contribution was apparently restricted to feeding recruits into the Ulster Special Constabulary.'[74] As he had been sponsored by this Loyalist Defence Association, it seems likely that Rev. Coote's trip to Canada was specifically a fund-raising mission for Ulster's fledgling loyalist paramilitaries.

The annual reports of the Canadian Orange Order indicate that it contributed funds to Loyalist groups. In his opening remarks of the 1923 annual session of the Grand Orange Lodge of British America, Grand Master William David McPherson mentioned that 'at the last meeting of [this] Grand Lodge the sum of £1,000 was voted to the Ulster Relief Fund.'[75] This figure is duly noted at the end of the 1923 Treasurers Report, but with the following anomaly:

By draft to Orange, Black and Loyalist Defence Association of Ireland (£1,000.00) ... $4,736.60.
By draft to Orange, Black and Loyalist Defence Association of Ireland (£1,000.00) ... $4,692.25.'[76]

Either the Lodge or the treasurer decided to donate £2,000 ($9,428.85) to the Orange, Black, and Loyalist Defence Association – that is, £1,000 on two separate occasions.

Meanwhile, the national Grand Executive also launched an appeal to the entire membership of the Orange Association in Canada. Less than two months after the Grand Orange Lodge of British America sent $5,000 to the Ulster Defence Association, Grand Master McPherson sent letters to all the Provincial Grand Masters in which he announced the establishment of an Irish Relief Fund 'to enable our brethren in Ireland to afford relief and succour to distressed members of the Orange Association and their dependents arising from depredations from marauding bands throughout various parts of Ireland, but particularly in the south and west, the result of which has been to dispossess many families from their holdings and turn them out penniless on the road.'[77] The same letter suggested that for organizational purposes, each Provincial Grand Master 'be requested to call a joint meeting of his executive committee and the County Masters of his jurisdiction as early this month as possible.'[78] The County Masters were then to convene the District Masters, who would in turn inform the Primary Lodges that the Relief Fund had been inaugurated. In this manner the entire organization could be notified as expeditiously as possible. The stated objective was to raise $50,000, and the suggested slogan to facilitate reaching that goal was 'Give us a dollar for Ireland.' The Grand Executive suggested that each provincial treasurer collect the returns and send all collected 'proceeds to the Grand Treasurer of British America and we should be able to make the most magnificent response to the heartfelt appeal of our brethren in the homeland.'[79]

Despite the declarations that reaching a goal of $50,000 would be easy, money found its way into the national treasurer's coffers slowly. According to the national Grand Treasurer, Joseph E. Thompson, by July 1923 the Irish Relief Fund collected and sent to Ireland only $14,191.23.[80] These Irish Relief funds were sent directly to the Orange, Black and Loyalist Defence Association, leading one to conjecture about how much of this money actually found its way to those in distress in the south and west. Although these figures fall far short of expectations, they were quite substantial when one considers that Canada in the early 1920s experienced a severe postwar recession.[81] The Canadian gross national product, the most accurate measure of a nation's economic vitality – had dropped by over 20 per cent in 1921, and sank even further in 1922. Twice as many businesses failed in 1921 as did the year before, and commercial failures reached record levels in 1922 and 1923. Moreover, largely as a result of the protectionist tariff policies of the Republican-controlled U.S. Congress, Canadian exports – the mainstay of the resource-rich northern economy – were cut almost in half in the two years between 1920 and 1922, with farmers being hit the hardest.[82] Historians John Herd Thompson and Allen Seager note that 'it was not until the autumn of 1924 that Canada's economic health was largely regained.'[83] When one considers these economic figures, it is surprising that any money at all was collected for Ulster. In the final analysis, between 1913 and 1924, hundreds of thousands of dollars were sent from Canada to Ulster. An exact figure will never be known because of the numerous options for contributing directly to Belfast. And, just as Canadian and Ulster unionists feared, the apparatus that most threatened Northern Ireland's security was about to be constituted, after numerous delays.

The formation of the Boundary Commission encountered numerous delays for a variety of reasons. Only after yet another change in British governments, which ushered in the first Labour coalition government, led by Prime Minister Ramsay MacDonald, did serious efforts to establish the Boundary Commission commence on 24 April 1924. Although James Craig, by then Northern Ireland's premier, continued to play the obstructionist card, insisting that the Northern Ireland government would 'not have any Boundary Commission under any circumstances whatever,' the British government pressed forward.[84]

The British government independently moved to establish the commission by first securing a chairman. Here it turned to Robert L. Borden, the former prime minister of Canada.[85] In a letter to Loring Christie, who had served as Borden's assistant and in the Canadian Ministry of External Affairs, Borden confirmed that the British government had asked him to serve as the commission's chairman. Borden informed Christie that he doubted the chances of success of the Boundary Commission so long as Craig's Northern Ireland government refused to nominate a representative. Borden also doubted whether his health would last such an appointment. He enclosed a confidential handwritten copy of the dispatch he had sent to London, which stated: 'I appreciate very deeply and Sincerely the honor of being asked to take Chairmanship of Commission. Although considerations of health make me Extremely reluctant to undertake this duty I have reached the following conclusion. If both Irish Free State and Northern Ireland will appoint representatives on Commission and I am assured that both desire me to act, I will accept Chairmanship.'[86]

Later, Borden wrote to his close friend, Canadian-born Maxwell Aitken, Lord Beaverbrook, again expressing doubt that he would be physically able to perform the duties of chairman. This letter read in part: 'Doubtless you know that I was prepared (although with great reluctance) to accept the Chairmanship of the Irish Boundary Commission if northern Ireland would appoint, and if both the Irish Governments would express their desire that I should undertake the task.' In a handwritten postscript at the end of the letter, he confided to Beaverbrook about conversations he held with Andrew Bonar Law and David Lloyd George: 'P.S. Bonar Law once told me that he would be prepared to let Ireland go. Probably he meant the South + that he saw no objection to their Establishing a republic. Lloyd George thought it wd [would] mean war between North + South. I am sure the banshee will not be silent until there is one Government for North + South – and not even then.'[87]

These lines penned by Robert Borden foreshadowed by forty-three years the terrible troubles that befell Northern Ireland in the late 1960s. The idea that Andrew Bonar Law would have conceded an Irish republic is startling. Had the British government simply allowed this designation, the terrible Irish Civil War might have been averted.

As soon as Ramsay MacDonald became prime minister, Orange-Canadian protests began. Within a day of MacDonald's Labour Party assuming the mantle of government, fearing the immediate formation of the Boundary Commission by a government that might favour the Irish Free State, the *Orange Sentinel* editorialized that the people of Ulster would be left with few options:

> The people of Ulster have reason to fear the advent of a Labor Government in Great Britain. The attitude of the Labor Party toward the Irish question is altogether favorable to the Free State. Even a short term of power might enable Ramsay Macdonald to create such complications in Ireland as would bring on civil war between North and South. If his Government should attempt arbitrarily to settle the boundary question in favor of the contentions of the Free State, there would be nothing left for the people of Ulster but to resist by force the dismemberment of the counties solemnly allocated to the Northern Parliament by British law.[88]

Orange-Canadian unionists protested the formation of the Boundary Commission, contending that it violated laws residing on the statute books. This, from an organization that wholeheartedly endorsed the subversion of the lawful enactment of the third Irish Home Rule Bill in 1913 and 1914 and that funded an armed rebellion to prevent its implementation. Editorials of this sort, bitterly denouncing the possible formation of the Boundary Commission by MacDonald's Labour government, continued on a near weekly basis throughout 1924. One report went so far as to describe Parliament's support for the first ever Labour government as 'the Communist British Parliament.'[89]

Such descriptions were hardly confined to the pages of the *Orange Sentinel*. Seven pages of Grand Master William David McPherson's lengthy opening address to the 1924 annual session of the Grand Orange Lodge of British America were devoted to the situation in Ireland, and in particular the boundary issue. McPherson also equated MacDonald's Labour government with communism, stating he believed that MacDonald was eager 'to aid their fellow Socialists and Bolshevik friends in the [Irish] Free State in breaking up Ulster.'[90] Noting that correspondents 'close to the scene of the troubles declare that Ireland is on the brink of civil war,' McPherson then commented that if these predictions were true, the 'bitterness of the two factions is so great that an outbreak of hostilities would probably result in a sanguinary struggle that would make the world shudder.'[91] He continued, in language even more dire:

> The men of the North would be fighting for their homes and their liberties. They would be defending their own territory. And under such circumstances men fight desperately. Having regard to the determined character of the people of the North, they would be extremely difficult to subdue by forces two or three times as great ... It would be a religious as well as a racial war, that might drench the country in blood, and throw Ireland back into a state of chaos.[92]

This chilling prediction by the Orange Grand Master of Canada conceded that unionists viewed the continuing struggle in Ireland as one of religion and race rather than one of political ideology. McPherson concluded by stating that events in Northern Ireland would 'be watched with anxiety and the heartfelt sympathy of loyal citizens of the Empire in every part of the world, and in no part more deeply than in the Dominion of Canada.'

On 29 October 1924 the MacDonald government independently established the Boundary Commission by appointing J.R. Fisher, the former editor of the Ulster Unionist *Northern Whig*, as the body's

Northern Ireland representative.[93] MacDonald had previously secured South African Supreme Court Justice Richard Feetham to act as chairman, and the Irish Free State in turn appointed Professor Eoin MacNeill as its representative. The commission's investigative work lasted a full year, but unfortunately for those nationalists in Tyrone and Fermanagh, who hoped their counties would be transferred to the Irish Free State, the Boundary Commission's efforts amounted to little. In November 1925 the commission's findings were leaked prematurely to the press, prompting Eoin MacNeill to resign. This led to the commission's dismemberment.[94] The Commission had proposed some minor adjustments and small transfers of population, but not in the proportions hoped for by northern nationalists or envisioned by the Irish Free State. The Free State government quickly moved to limit the damage of these disappointing developments, and in return for accepting the status quo on the Northern Ireland boundary, Britain agreed to relieve the Irish Free State of its portion of the British public debt, as arranged by the Anglo-Irish Treaty. The Irish Free State's critics claimed that this sum was negligible, but Winston Churchill estimated that the debt reduction would save the Free State between £6 and £8 million annually.[95]

Orange-Canadian unionists hailed these developments as a great victory for Ulster, while bemoaning that the Irish Free State had gained a financial windfall at the expense of British taxpayers. The *Orange Sentinel* even proclaimed that North and South now resided in 'closer harmony' than ever, though in the same breath it described the southern Irish as bloodthirsty assassins who since 1916 continuously posed a deadly threat to the inoffensive people of the north:

> Victory for Ulster! At last her virtue and patience have triumphed! Both British Houses, the Dail Eireann, and the Ulster Parliament have now passed the latest Irish agreement, and Erin approaches the New Year with North and South in closer harmony than they have been in during their history. The loyalty and patience of Ulster during the whole controversy throughout the years has been as the world has never seen. Living in constant fear of attack from the South, and in fear of further betrayal by the British Government, Ulster has never assumed the part of aggressor, but has consistently guarded her own borders from the Southern enemy. Day and night since 1916 her borders have been constantly paroled [patrolled] by the courageous members of the Ulster constabulary, who alone have stood between the Ulster people along the border and the Sinn Fein as-

sassins, whose chief amusement has been to take pot shots at inoffensive Northerners.[96]

For Orange-Canadian unionists, the question then became, 'How did Ulster come out of this transaction?' According to Orange-Canadian unionists, Ulster received exactly what it had been promised at the time the Northern Ireland government was established: 'a solemn promise … that her boundary would not be interfered with.'[97] Moreover, the British government also agreed 'to assume the cost of equipping and maintaining the Special Ulster Constabulary [Ulster Special Constabulary] required along the Ulster boundary ever since the Free State was set up, to prevent Sinn Fein rebels and criminals from invading Ulster territory.'[98] In the end, the Boundary Commission failed to alter Northern Ireland's position within the empire. The *Orange Sentinel* even sounded jubilant in expressing that 'all loyal citizens of the Empire will join in hoping that Ireland will, at last, enjoy a long period of peace and prosperity.'[99]

From the late nineteenth century through the 1920s, Orange-Canadian unionists provided their Ulster unionist brethren with devout and obedient support in varying forms. Orange-Canadian unionists acted as a North American sounding board to reiterate unionist arguments against Home Rule; and they had assembled mass rallies and offered resolutions opposing Irish Home Rule and thereby informed British politicians that Ulster did not stand alone. But the most impressive demonstration of Orange-Canadian unionist backing of Ulster's demand to maintain its rightful place in the British Empire was the financial contribution of hundreds of thousands of dollars that guaranteed Ulster's ability to procure arms in defence against British disengagement and perceived Irish republican threats. Orange-Canadian unionists viewed Ulster's stand against displacement from the British Empire, and forced unity with the remainder of Ireland, as a self-sacrificing endeavour to preserve the integrity of the empire itself. Only after the entire political process had exhausted itself, with the dissolution of the Boundary Commission, and only after Ulster's position within the empire had been preserved, did Orange-Canadian unionists feel relief. Over the same period, Irish-Canadian nationalists similarly felt jubilation, apprehension, and ultimately disappointment.

*Chapter Six*

# Irish-Canadian Nationalists: Free Staters and Republicans, 1922–1925

After the Anglo-Irish Treaty was signed on 6 December 1921, its terms and conditions remained static until approved by both the British Parliament and the Irish Dáil Éireann. To describe the ensuing treaty debates in the Dáil as acrimonious would be a wild understatement. So divisive was the issue of whether to accept a treaty that offered less than complete independence – not to mention a partitioned and separate Northern Ireland – that the Irish republican movement split into two factions, which led to the Irish Civil War of 1922–3. As historian Patrick O'Farrell has noted: 'To the extent that Sinn Féin and the Irish Republican Army had forced Britain to make a treaty, the Irish had won the Anglo-Irish war: they can hardly be said to have won the peace. In that, the victory went to Britain and Lloyd George.'[1] The tragic events of the Irish Civil War cast a dark and lasting shadow over Irish political culture; to this day, Ireland's two largest political parties continue, indirectly, to bear the names of those two embattled factions. It was a tragic conclusion to a decade-long – some might even argue centuries long – struggle to achieve some form of Irish independence.

Irish nationalists in Canada pragmatically accepted and welcomed the founding of the Irish Free State, as specified in the treaty. Irish Canadians believed that representatives of the Irish people had debated, voted, and passed the treaty. Accordingly, the democratic process worked effectively, for a majority of the Irish people spoke in favour of accepting the founding of the Irish Free State. Some Irish Canadians even acquired jobs with the fledgling Irish Free State. Others, however, harboured the hope of attaining the republican ideal of a truly independent and united Ireland. These republican idealists were undoubtedly a minority among Irish-Canadian nationalists, but their passionate hopes of witnessing the founding of a lasting Irish republic were diminished neither by the vote in the Dáil nor by the brutal civil war, which persisted well into the 1920s.

The Irish-Catholic Canadian press widely publicized the treaty debates. Toronto's *Catholic Register* and Saint John's *New Freeman*, and presumably every other Irish-Catholic weekly in Canada, followed the debates and eventual passage with due attention and detail. In articles and in editorial commentary, these papers boasted that Ireland was to be a 'nation once again.' In early January 1922 the *New Freeman* declared:

> That the treaty signed between the English and Irish plenipotentiaries will be ratified by the Dail Eireann, and Ireland thereby become a nation once again, now seems assured. Congratulatory messages on the conclusion of the treaty have been received by the respective governments from churchmen and statesmen the world over ...
>
> Ireland may well be proud of her Griffiths and Collins. No politicians were they, crossing to England as in days of yore, with hat in hand begging for a pittance of justice, but schoolmen and statesmen, men of literary and political and military ability, true and tried in the fiery furnace of black and tan prussianism and the crucible of English and Irish dungeons. They knew what they wanted and they wanted what they knew and there can be no greater argument for higher education and a highly educated laity than the triumph in the matching of wits of these two educated and able Irish statesmen against the brightest minds of present-day England.[2]

Actually, the Irish delegation – headed by Arthur Griffith and Michael Collins – that negotiated the settlement with Britain had been repeatedly outmanoeuvred by the savvy and experienced British statesmen.[3] When the actual vote on approving the treaty transpired, the *New Freeman* reported with obvious glee that 'momentous events have transpired in Ireland since Saturday last.'[4] Indeed, on 7 January 1922 the Dáil accepted the Anglo-Irish Treaty by a vote of 64 to 57. When this news reached Canada, the *Catholic Register* noted that 'a thrill of joy too deep for words shot through millions of hearts that absence has made but fonder of the cradle of their race.'[5] Taking up Michael Collins's strenuous arguments favouring treaty acceptance in the Dáil debates, the *Register* editorialized that although Ireland had not yet achieved complete independence, its present political autonomy was a stepping stone toward full independence:

There is a Provisional Government now in the saddle in Ireland and the reins of power are altogether in Irish hands. If Parnell or Redmond got the freedom and concessions achieved by the Sinn Feiners, they would have been hailed as supermen and as the saviours of their country ... Ireland has not achieved her desire of complete independence, but she has come pretty close to it, and if the Irish Free State is ably handled by its own Irish rulers, there is no limit to the freedom to which it may aspire.[6]

Although joy pervaded most Irish-Canadian circles following the treaty ratification, Irish Canadians remained troubled by the wrongs of the past. Irish nationalists in Canada continued to hold Britain responsible for Ireland's painful history. Now, with the infamous Dublin Castle to be handed over to Irishmen, a new era dawned, one that instilled hope of future prosperity and contentment for Ireland. The *New Freeman* affirmed:

Dublin Castle, the seat of iniquity, of persecution, of savagery for past generations, the incarnation of all that was evil in the administration of affairs in Ireland, the last resort of barbarism, (if the Belfast mobs be excepted), – has now been handed over to the provisional government of Ireland, which will function until the machinery of the new Government of the Free State will become formally effective ... If walls could speak – what atrocities would those of Dublin Castle tell? What of the Castlereaghs, what of his successor, what of the later regime of Lord French, what of the organized outrages of the Black and Tan bandatti against the property, the liberty and lives of the Irish people? What of the deliberate burning of the business section of Cork by that armed band of ruffians in the pay of the British government.[7]

As this editorial indicated, past wrongs certainly had not been forgotten, and England, as ever, was responsible. In strident republican language, the *Catholic Register* contributed a particularly harsh critique of English statesmen and statecraft in Ireland. These men, the paper asserted, failed to negotiate in good faith with Irish representatives in 1912–14 and had only agreed to negotiate in the early 1920s as a result of Irish physical force:

Now there is no greater professed admirer of 'constitutional methods' than the average Englishman. He indeed often and often proclaims that they are the only method of political attack that deserve any consideration. But in practice he stultifies himself, for the constitutional efforts of the Irish Nationalist party were mocked at and stamped out with brute force. In the House of Commons the Irish members were shouted down and insulted. Their leader, John Redmond, was betrayed and made a tool of. England promised Home Rule, but never gave it, and thus she discredited the Irish Nationalists with her own people ...

By this treatment of the Irish constitutionalists, the English were themselves the direct instigators of Sinn Fein. They flouted Irish constitutionalism, but they surrendered to Irish physical force! A just judgement came upon them for their treatment of Redmond and Parnell. Sterner leaders arose whose weapons were the rifle and the bomb, and who could not be squelched by closure or by the division bell![8]

Clearly, Irish Canadians continued to view British duplicity in Ireland with utter disdain. With the typically more conservative *Catholic Register* cheering the success of physical force republicanism, it seemed that many Irish-Canadian nationalists shifted from mere Home Rulers to Sinn Féin republicans. Unfortunately, some Irish representatives in the Dáil accused those who signed the treaty of having been duped by British treachery and of settling for something much less than an independent republic.

During the treaty debates, as sides coalesced into pro-treatyites and anti-treatyites, Eamonn de Valera introduced an alternative proposal, known as Document no. 2, which essentially was the same treaty writ large with two notable additions relating to the imperial connection. First, instead of Ireland being a part of the British Commonwealth of Nations, the Document no. 2 offered External Association. In this, de Valera claimed Ireland would be associated with the commonwealth but not *in* the commonwealth. Thus, citizenship would be reciprocal rather than common, and Ireland would pledge neutrality in the case of war. Second, whereas the treaty insisted that Irish representatives must swear an oath of allegiance to the British monarch, Document no. 2 acknowledged the British monarch only 'for purposes of the Association [of Ireland with the states of the British Commonwealth;] Ireland shall recognize his Britannic majesty as head of the Association.'[9] De Valera circulated this proposal among his cabinet colleagues in the Dáil. When it received little support, he refused to allow it to be published.[10]

In Canada, Lindsay Crawford also took a dim view of de Valera's proposal. He wrote to his good friend, the prominent Irish-American activist and New York Supreme Court Justice Daniel Cohalan:

Events in Ireland are as you anticipated. De Valera['s] alternative oath of allegiance or fealty did not seem to be based upon any profound knowledge of constitutional or international law. I am inclined to sympathize with the action of Griffith, having regard to De Valera's only alternative proposal ... There is a strong reaction here against both sides in the Dail, and even some of those who were swept in the beginning have come round to the Republican side again.[11]

A little less than a month later, Crawford again wrote to Judge Cohalan: 'De Valera had better retire to his University work. His usefulness in any public capacity has gone. His alternative oath was very amateur and wholly impracticable.'[12]

A few months later, as elections neared, the *New Freeman* wryly commented: 'Mr. de Valera's attitude on the Treaty is regrettable ... It is difficult to understand why he holds aloof and why he does not wholeheartedly co-operate in the holding of the elections wherein the Irish people, by their own free will, will endorse or reject the treaty.'[13] The *Canadian Freeman* of Kingston similarly commented:

As we see it, the credit for the split belongs with Mr. de Valera and his followers, many of whom we believe to be sincere. If the present condition of Ireland is a heart-break to those of us who love it more than we love any Irishman or any body of Irishmen, it is due to the fact that de Valera's followers refuse to fight out the issue in a constitutional manner.[14]

After the treaty's acceptance, Ireland was not immediately engulfed in civil war. As Helen Litton notes, 'six months of negotiation, argument and frustration were yet to pass.'[15] After acceptance, Eamonn de Valera promptly resigned as president of the previously declared Irish Republic to protest the treaty's passage. 'The Irish people,' he claimed, 'had established a republic and until the Irish people disestablish it the republic must go on.'[16] Those anti-treatyite Dáil deputies who supported de Valera also left. Hardliners in the IRA were even more adamant, viewing the treaty's terms as a clear capitulation to British duplicity. Across Ireland, confusion and bitterness spread. As historian Dermot Keogh explains: 'Ideology, conviction, accident, personality and geography all helped divide much of the country into Treatyites and anti-Treatyites, and into different camps with in the blocs. The Irish political world in 1922 remained a kaleidoscope of shifting emotions and ambivalences. It took the violence of the [eventual] civil war to force many finally to take sides.'[17]

In an effort to keep the country from falling into disruption and violence, Michael Collins arranged an election pact with de Valera to ensure that in the upcoming popular election on the treaty, pro-treatyite candidates and anti-treatyites would be elected on a basis proportional to their present strength in the Dáil. As the election approached, Irish Canadians watched in dismay as Ireland sped headlong into civil war. On the night of 13 April 1922, hardline elements in the IRA, led by Rory O'Connor, Liam Mellows, and Ernie O'Malley, took control of the legal centre of Ireland: the Four Courts in Dublin. The symbolism of 1916 was lost on few in this move of bravado and impatience. These republican hardliners, who became known as the Irregulars, continued to occupy the Four Courts until the election of 16 June 1922. In the weeks before the election, the pact fell apart, resulting in a clear victory for the Free Staters. Plainly, the people of Ireland endorsed the treaty. The pro-treaty candidates won 58 seats, anti-treaty candidates 36, Labourites 17, Farmers 7, and Independents 6.[18] Sixty per cent of the population turned out to vote. When one considers that the Labour, Farmer, and Independent candidates all favoured the treaty, roughly 78 per cent of voters had supported it.[19]

Following the election victory, on 28 June, under tremendous pressure from Britain, Michael Collins, as head of the Free State Army, attacked the Four Courts. The Irish Civil War had begun. After the Four Courts surrendered on 30 June, the fighting spread to the south and west of Ireland. Irish Canadians seem to have supported these measures as the only ones available. One newspaper observed:

> Ireland today has a properly endowed and constructed government which is challenged by an armed minority. It is the issue of properly constituted authority against anarchy, nothing else. As such, conciliatory measures having failed, the Government has resorted to the only course left, that of armed force and, in consequence, severe fighting has taken place in Dublin. There have been many lives lost on both sides and the destruction of property has been heavy.
>
> The guilt does not lie on the heads of the Government. It had no choice in the matter. Its authority challenged, it could make but one answer or else cease to even make a pretence at governing. But it is upon the heads of those who are, today, leading a body of young men in a course diametri-

cally opposed to the interests of the Irish nation and the expressed wishes of the Irish people that the guilt must fall for the tragedy now drawing to a close in Dublin.[20]

The ensuing Irish Civil War was brutal in every sense of the word and left a devastating legacy on Irish political culture. Unspeakable acts of barbarity were committed by both sides, and the resulting bitterness lasted decades. The most obvious and ruthless of the atrocities committed was the execution of republican prisoners following the assassination of Free State TD (Member of Parliament) Seán Hales. To make the point clear that political leaders were not to be targets, the Free State cabinet approved the executions of four prisoners being held at Mount Joy Jail. Rory O'Connor, Liam Mellows, Joe McKelvey, and Dick Barrett were executed the following morning. Not surprisingly, 'the executions horrified public opinion in both England and Ireland, not least because Kevin O'Higgins [Free State Minister for Home Affairs] had been best man at O'Connor's wedding less than a year before.'[21] Tragedies like this were repeated again and again as families, friends, and even brothers aligned on opposing sides in a civil war that ostensibly could have been avoided.[22]

The other great tragedy of the civil war was the untimely death of Arthur Griffith, followed by the death of Michael Collins less than three weeks later. Arthur Griffiths died on 12 August 1922 of a cerebral hemorrhage, his health having been broken by the stress of events. After leading Griffith's funeral procession through the streets of Dublin with full military honours befitting a head of state, Michael Collins returned to his native Cork on an inspection tour of the Free State troops in the region. Disregarding reports that it would be dangerous for him to travel in the more remote areas of the county, Collins and his small escort left Cork city on their way to Bandon, passing through the isolated valley Béal na mBláth, where they were ambushed and Collins was fatally wounded. The *Catholic Register* described how people came out by the thousands from all over Ireland to pay their respects to the fallen hero:

> Sunday's total suspension of civic activities permitted the people to render unrestrictedly the homage they wished to render to the memory of their beloved leader. Not from the metropolis alone, but from the county districts nearby there streamed to the City Hall, where the body lay in state, countless thousands to gaze on the features of the man to whom, more

than anyone else, the people had looked for a peaceful settlement of Ireland's woes.

They came by train, by donkey cart, by jaunting car and on foot; they choked Dublin's streets, yet without disorder formed in line, awaiting their turn to enter the Cathedral and passed before the coffin of their comrade, who had given his life in the cause of the Free State.[23]

Unfortunately, the deaths of such men was the lasting legacy of the utterly avoidable and tragically devastating Irish Civil War. The resulting enmity persisted for decades. Helen Litton poignantly reflected:

> What was the point of the Civil War? Hundreds dead and injured, families split for generations, whole areas disaffected from the native government, increased emigration, economic stagnation, severe infrastructural damage, a legacy of bitterness – and for what? Seventy years or more after the events described in this book, it is hard to see it as any more than an enormous waste of lives, resources and energy that could have been better spent in building a new state out of a battered ex-colony which was finally allowed some responsibility for its own affairs, and was anxious to prove it could cope.[24]

Although the signing of the Anglo-Irish Treaty dramatically curtailed the *raison d'être* for the Self-Determination for Ireland League of Canada (because Ireland had essentially achieved self-government), the league continued in an advocacy capacity. For example, the league strenuously protested British inaction in Northern Ireland as the Belfast 'pogroms' of 1922 escalated.[25] On 8 June 1922, Lindsay Crawford sent a telegram to the Governor General of Canada in which he observed that protests were rampant across Canada and would continue until the Catholic minority in Belfast was provided with some safety by the British government:

> Respectfully request that you convey to the British Government on behalf of the Irish race in Canada the feeling of deep indignation which has been aroused by the failure to afford protection to the Catholic minority in Belfast which for three years has suffered barbarous persecution at the hands of forces maintained and paid by British Government while British troops are employed against Southern Ireland on the Fermanagh border. Protest meetings are being held throughout Canada and will continue until Catholic minority of Belfast are safeguarded in their lives and properties.

Signed on behalf of the Self Determination for Ireland League of Canada and Nfld.[26]

This telegram to the Governor General somehow ended up on the desk of the Canadian prime minister, William Lyon Mackenzie King.[27] It seems that even in 1922, the RCMP or the ministries responsible for state security were still interested in the activities of the Self-Determination League. Regardless, it is not known what influence, if any, this telegram had on the Canadian government's imperial policy. Nor is it known whether the Governor General conveyed these concerns to the British government. Nevertheless, as the National Office of the Self-Determination League continued its advocacy work, some local branches of the league had already begun to disband.

In March 1922 the Saint John branch of the Self-Determination League disbanded, reflecting a sense 'that the League had fulfilled its task, and its objective having been attained [an autonomous Ireland] its existence was not necessary.'[28] The resolution drawn up to officially end branch operations concluded that 'the objects for which we organized have been attained, and we cease to function as an organization from this date.'[29]

An article in the 1923 St Patrick's Day edition of the *New Freeman* chronicled the league's activities in New Brunswick over the previous two years. The Saint John branch – the first in the province – only came into existence in July 1920 when Katherine Hughes visited Saint John and helped form 'the nucleus of ... an organization which spread throughout the whole of Canada and was particularly strong in the eastern provinces.'[30] One of the league's primary objectives had been to unite the two opposing factions of the Irish-Canadian nationalist movement: those constitutional nationalists who supported the late John Redmond, and those Sinn Féin republicans who advocated complete Irish independence:

> At the time, in view of the serious situation in Ireland and the extremes to which those in charge of the administration of [Irish] affairs had gone, and were going, the Black and Tan regime being in full cry, that it was incumbent upon the peoples in self-governing Dominions, such as Canada, irrespective of race and creed, to raise their voice and call upon the British Government to employ in Ireland the same methods which had achieved peace and concord in Canada and which had welded this country into a harmonious whole. The League sought to unite, on a common basis, those who held conflicting views as to the extent of Irish aims in their struggle

for self-government – such as the very large element adhered to the policy of John Redmond in asking for Dominion status and those who believed that absolute independence was the only solution. A common platform was drafted which, based on the Canadian model, simply expressed the idea of the League that, as in Canada, as in England itself, the voice of the people of Ireland should be the determining factor.[31]

One example of the divisions generated by the treaty split in Ireland resonating in Canada appeared in the editorial pages of the *New Freeman* in January 1923. In a letter dated the previous December, a disgruntled – more accurately, disgusted – subscriber wrote the publishers of the *New Freeman* requesting that his subscription be cancelled. As a result of the paper's 'pronounced support of the "Free State" government now misruling Ireland.' The letter argued sharply that the *New Freeman*, as well as all those who supported the Irish Free State, were the stooges of British imperialism:

> I can not understand how you can denounce de Valera and the Irish republicans who are fighting to save Ireland from being forever sold as a vassal state of the British Empire. Your editorial utterances of late show you to be a strong champion of British Imperialism. I cannot lend myself to read such propaganda.
>
> My firm conviction is that Ireland shall yet be FREE, a Nation unto herself as God intended her to be. The sacrifices and trials of seven hundred years shall not, and must not, be buried in treachery. Irishmen owe it to those who paved the way for National resurrection to take up the fight where they left off. On the eve of her glorious victory Ireland was betrayed, as often she was before, by her own sons and the cowardly compromise of Collins and Griffith must be wiped out and the honor of Ireland and her sacred dead avenged.[32]

The editors of the *New Freeman* replied to this letter on 8 January 1923, stating they of course regretted losing a subscriber, but admitting it was his right to hold a contrary opinion on the matter of Irish self-government. The paper noted that his was the only cancelled subscription resulting from their supposed support of the Irish Free State, 'a pretty good indication of the trend of Irish feelings among our constituency.'[33] The reply continued:

> We cannot, of course, admit the right of Mr. de Valera and his followers to dictate to Ireland what she shall do or what she shall not do. We cannot

admit the right of a minority, especially an armed minority, to dictate to the overwhelming majority of the nation. The people have spoken and the rule of the people is supreme ...

We believe the Free State will – already has – vindicated itself. It is supported by an overwhelming mass of the electors, it is supported by the Irish Bishops. The nation is marching onwards ... The New Freeman is not Imperialistic. The constitution of Canada calls for loyalty to the three estates – the King, the Senate and the Commons. The Church enjoins loyalty to properly constituted authority. We believe in Canadian principles and shall continue to support them. We believe in good feelings between all nations ...

As we have already stated, we admit your right to a contrary opinion, but to us the path seems straight and that is to support the Irish people and the Government erected by their freely expressed vote – Mr. de Valera & Co. to the contrary.[34]

Interestingly, in another paragraph the *New Freeman* referred to Northern Ireland in terms that expressed the hope that its government would eventually fail, and then unite with the Irish Free State: 'Ten years, five years from now – who knows? Already partition is wobbling. Economic forces will drive Craig and company into the union: it cannot be otherwise.'[35] The editors – and presumably most subscribers – were ardent supporters of the Irish Free State, but their sentiments toward partition and Northern Ireland were decidedly republican.

Another indication of the split in the Irish-Canadian nationalist movement was visible in the varying paths followed by a number of the Self-Determination League leaders. It is likely that by late 1922 or early 1923, the national Self-Determination for Ireland League had disbanded. As a result, Lindsay Crawford needed new employment. With his weekly liberal newspaper *The Statesman* failing, he found a new position in New York City. By the autumn of 1923, Lindsay Crawford's prolific correspondence with his friend Justice Daniel Cohalan arrived on the letterhead of the Saorstát Éireann (Irish Free State) Irish Trade Commission, with Crawford listed as Irish Trade Agent.[36] It seems that Crawford's position was neither token nor ceremonial; indeed, there is evidence that he had some influence on the Free State government of William Cosgrave. At least twice, Crawford made inquiries to the Cosgrave government regarding the release of republican prisoners in Ireland, at the request of Judge Cohalan, who was acting on behalf of relatives of imprisoned republicans in Ireland. On the first occasion,

Crawford inquired as to the possible release of Peter Jackman of Ballyhale, Kilkenny. The reply to Crawford stated: 'The Minister for Defence after careful consideration of the case regrets that, in view of information in his possession, he cannot see his way to order the release of Mr. Jackman at present.'[37] But a little more than a month later, Crawford received another letter from the Ministry of Defence announcing the release of the prisoner.[38]

Then in June 1924, Crawford made a request on behalf of Thomas Mullins of Kinsale, Cork, with similar results. One month after receiving a letter stating that Mullins 'was sentenced by a Military Tribunal to five years penal servitude, for being unlawfully in possession of a loaded revolver, a Mils bomb, and a quantity of ammunition,' the Office of the President of Ireland notified Crawford that Thomas Mullins had been released.[39] This does not suggest that Crawford was solely responsible for the release of these prisoners; undoubtedly, many inquiries had been made from any number of sources within and outside Ireland. It is clear, though, that the Irish Free State employed Lindsay Crawford as its Irish Trade Agent in New York City, a position for which he was well suited, and he seems to have had access to high levels of the Irish government.

By 1924, Katherine Hughes was also living in New York City. It is not known for which organization she was working, but it is plausible that it was an Irish republican organization. A letter to her from Boston attorney John T. Hughes (no relation) referred to a republican memorial fund, which he claimed to be doing his best to support.[40] Also, found in Katherine Hughes's papers is an undated copy of a letter addressed to William Cosgrave, Dublin:

> Representatives of the American Association for the Recognition of the Irish Republic from forty-five States in National conference assembled in Chicago solemnly protest violation law of war and humanity by officials of the British Free State in Ireland, in brutal torture and execution of prisoners of war, and in the name of all liberty loving Americans demand immediate release of Annie MacSwiney now on hunger strike. You will earn the undying execration of mankind if you do to death the heroic sister of the heroic Irish martyr Terence MacSwiney.[41]

This letter was likely written sometime in 1923. Considering the work she had done in the past, it is quite possible that she helped draft this letter. Also, considering her connections to Eamon de Valera, and to

Irish republican circles in the United States, it seems plausible that she was working for the American Association for the Recognition of the Irish Republic. Katherine Hughes was yet another example of an Irish Canadian who diligently worked her way to prominence in America. But what of those Irish Canadians back in Canada?

Rather than migrate south to the United States, most Irish Canadians remained in Canada. If the editorial commentary of the *New Freeman* was an accurate indicator, most of them supported the founding of the Irish Free State. This would hardly have been surprising: there were of course Irish republicans in Canada. Most notable among these republican dissenters were Charles J. Foy and Thomas R. Donovan, both of whom had been national officers in the Self-Determination League as well as in the Ancient Order of Hibernians. Charles Foy served as the Canadian president of the Ancient Order of Hibernians beginning in 1912, a position he relinquished in 1923 to Patrick J. Keane of Montreal. Although often overlooked as being only moderately nationalistic, the AOH was actually a boisterous exponent of Irish nationalism. Its members, be they in the United States or in Canada, were even active republicans.

Contrary to the assertions of Canadian historian Mark McGowan, there was not an unbridgeable chasm between American and Canadian Hibernians during the First World War. Indeed, the dispute was so well healed that the AOH's 1923 national convention was held in Montreal. Canadian and American Hibernians worked cooperatively to strengthen their order, defend Catholicism, and promote independence for Ireland. Disagreements of course existed, but these were slight.[42] One such dispute arose at the 1923 Montreal convention, which was easily enough mended. Apparently, when the Committee on Resolutions offered its report, it included a resolution praising Canadian Hibernians for their dedication and hard work. When the resolutions were submitted for approval, delegate D.J. Shea, Provincial Secretary of New Brunswick, asked that the resolution be rewritten to incorporate a greater appreciation of the contributions of Canadian Hibernians. A strenuous debate followed, eventually prompting an impassioned comment from Charles Foy:

> I don't blame those on the Resolutions Committee for overlooking this place called Canada, but all through their resolutions, not one mention is made of this place ... If you had to contend with what we have had to contend with in this Dominion of Canada, I want to say a great many of you

would be wiped off the map. You have never yet had to address a meeting in the midst of forty or fifty policemen. I have had to do so; I have done so; and I will continue to do so.

The first mention that was ever made of the Sinn Fein movement, which I said then was the best, the biggest and the most logical movement the Irish people had ever undertaken, was made on the 9th of January, 1919, in the Monument Nationale in this city by myself. The next morning I was branded from one end of the Dominion to the other a traitor, and from that day to this, I have been hunted incessantly, in season and out of season, in my own town and in my own province, by those people whom the Irish race has always been maligned.

Therefore I say you have your problems; you have your Ku Klux Klan; we have them here under another form and a different name. Take the Orange order that is today assembling in Winnipeg – it is aimed directly in all its operations at the Catholic Church. Go to Toronto, the Belfast of Canada, where it was said I dared not repeat my Monument Nationale speech, and they dared me. With my good friends in Toronto we engaged Massey Hall, the largest auditorium in Toronto, and we filled that auditorium from cellar to garret, and in the presence of forty policemen waiting to arrest all who spoke – and I was one of them – we repeated there everything that was said in my Monument Nationale speech.

We are entitled to recognition, not with a lightly phrased addition to the report, but we leave that to the judgement of the committee. We are heart and soul with you in every movement made, and we will be [there] for the future, for the benefit of Ireland.[43]

As a result, a new resolution was adopted praising Canadian Hibernians and all of their efforts to bring a truthful appraisal of Irish affairs to the Canadian public.

Following the creation of the Irish Free State, North American Hibernians remained hopeful that Ireland would eventually reconstitute its republican form of government and achieve unity and complete independence. In his opening address to the 1923 Montreal convention, National President James Deery quickly turned to the situation in Ireland, which at the time was still engulfed in civil war. Referring to a resolution adopted at the previous convention held two years earlier, Deery told the audience:

In the resolution adopted at Detroit we recognized the right of the Irish people to conclude peace with England on terms to them seemed expedient, but at the same time, we stated that we would view with grave disappointment the rise of circumstances that would impel the Irish to abandon, even temporarily, the Republican form of government. It is true that our fondest hopes were not realized, and while we regret that the Irish representatives were obliged to accept the terms they did, nevertheless we are pleased to know that the Irish people accepted the Free State only as a step toward complete independence.[44]

These republican sentiments were espoused by the entire organization. They were embodied clearly in a resolution concerning Ireland that the 1923 Montreal convention adopted: 'We earnestly hope that the strife that has torn apart the national ranks, made bitter enemies of former comrades in arms, and brought sorrow to millions of our kinsmen the world around, has ceased and that a reunited Ireland will soon be able to achieve the full measure of freedom that is still the aim of our race.'[45]

This is decidedly unambiguous language. The declaration that one wishes to see a 'reunited Ireland achieve the full measure of freedom' is quite similar to republican language still heard today in Northern Ireland. Moreover, these proclamations and assertions cannot simply be dismissed as the musings of Irish-American republicans: Canadian Hibernians attended this convention and endorsed this resolution as eagerly as the American delegates. Such declarations in favour of a republican Ireland were readily adopted at Canadian Hibernian conventions as well.

Hibernians in Ontario also declared their desire for Ireland to become a free and independent republic. In his last presidential address to the Ontario Ancient Order of Hibernians, delivered in his hometown of Perth on 17 August 1925, Charles Foy kept his remarks brief. Foy spoke of subjects relating to the Order that had always been raised on these occasions: the need for increased membership; the hope that the Juvenile Division would be strengthened; the great work of the Ladies Auxiliary; and most certainly the state of affairs in Ireland.[46] With respect to Ireland, Foy told his audience, somewhat cautiously:

> In attempting to deal with the Irish Question as it exists to-day, one must be very guarded. This fact is self apparent, viz, that Ireland by accepting the Free State Treaty has to a degree metaphorically speaking at least, tied the hands of her friends throughout the world who are fighting for her ideals – a Republic. If the Irish people are willing to live under the condi-

tions as outlined in the Free State Act 1921, then they and they alone are the judges of their conditions, and once the people have decided that question for themselves, we on the outside must of necessity accept the result; but it should not prevent Irishmen the world over from doing everything in their power to work so that Ireland's ideals may yet be accomplished, namely, A Free and Independent Nation.[47]

Foy and his brethren accepted the political reality that the Free State had been endorsed in a national election. Even so, Foy used unambiguously republican language in describing what he believed to be the hope of Irishmen the world over. He still yearned to see an independent Irish republic emerge from its colonial past, and he encouraged his Hibernian brothers to work toward that goal. And there is evidence that these were not merely the musings of a leader trying to inspire his flock. Margaret Churchill, in her correspondence with Hanna Sheehy Skeffington – the widow of the pacifist journalist Francis Sheehy Skeffington, who had been slain by the British during the 1916 Easter Rising – noted that many republicans attained official positions in the Ontario Hibernians. In referring to the 1925 Hibernian convention, Churchill wrote: 'The A.O.H. of Ontario recently had a very successful three-day Convention here ... Also, we got a good number of real Republicans into office.'[48] It is not known exactly how many of the 989 brothers of the Ontario Hibernians were republican, but there were certainly enough to vote like-minded brothers into positions of prominence. One even finds republican sentiments expressed in the editorials of Toronto's *Catholic Register*, particularly with regard to the disappointment over the findings of the Boundary Commission.

Irish-Canadian nationalists had high hopes for the Boundary Commission. The intent to form the commission had been written into the Anglo-Irish Treaty of 1921 (Article 12), ostensibly to 'determine in accordance with the wishes of the inhabitants, so far as may be compatible with economic and geographic conditions the boundaries between Northern Ireland and the rest of Ireland.' The reality, though, was that this clause had been inserted into the treaty by Lloyd George as a political and tactical expediency, to remove the contentious issue of a partitioned Northern Ireland from the negotiating table. Nevertheless, after the treaty had been accepted, Irish-Canadian nationalists believed that the Boundary Commission would certainly revert to the Irish Free State those areas inhabited by absolute nationalist (i.e., Catholic) majorities. These included Fermanagh and Tyrone as well as parts of south Armagh and south Down. Unfortunately, the Irish Civil War delayed the formation of the Boundary Commission for three years. This delay did not sink the hopes of Irish-Catholic Canadians that large numbers of Irish Catholics would be reunited with their brethren in the Irish Free State. Nor were the long-term implications of returning territory to the Free State far from the minds of Irish-Canadian nationalists. They believed that a smaller Northern Ireland would be economically untenable and would eventually agree to unite with the Irish Free State. In September 1923 the *Catholic Register* opined:

> The territory which will be restored to the Free State, as a result of the Boundary Commission, will be for the most part agricultural and the inhabitants of that territory will at once take their place in the normal stream of political life.
>
> When the boundary question is settled and amicable relations are established between the two governments, a network of ties will spring up, which will soon restore a sense of common interest in the general welfare of Ireland ... Labour and Business Men's parties may be expected to evolve from the present solid block of the old Unionist majority. There will be a party for union with the Free State. The heavy loss in the agriculture representation will bring the Parliament in Belfast more and more under the domination of the industrial element, but there will still be a small section representing rural interests. A tendency toward common action between these various parties and the corresponding parties in the Free State will probably arise with the consequent need for a common legislature.[49]

Indeed, Irish-Canadian nationalists had *very* high hopes for a shift in territory, which they thought to be inevitable once the British government established the Boundary Commission. Although their hopes bordered on the fanciful, they were not unrealistic in expecting significant territorial transfers. Indeed, in June 1923 the Free State cabinet approved a draft of the maximum and minimum amount of territory expected to be ceded from Northern Ireland. Even the minimum expectations were significant; they included all of Fermanagh and Tyrone, much of western Derry, and the southern portions of Armagh and Down. In all, this *minimum* transference would have gained the Free State one-third of Northern Ireland's territory and one-fifth of its population.[50] However, even though the Boundary Commission was eventually constituted, no shifts in territory ever occurred.[51]

The issue was ostensibly settled when the Boundary Commission disbanded in December 1925, having transferred virtually no territory. But this did not diminish the hopes that Irish nationalists in Canada held for a united Ireland. The *Catholic Register* longed for a united and prosperous Ireland:

> However adversely the Boundary Commission may have decided, its decision should not be regarded as irreparable or serious enough to cause any lessening of good will between the neighboring islands. Justice will prevail in the end, and Ulster's manifest destiny is for economic reasons to be united with the Free State for the sake of the common prosperity of Ireland.
> 
> Orangemen and Catholics are part and parcel of one people. They have a common interest in Ireland, and cannot always hold apart. Mutual confidence and union with joint friendship for England is the only way out of their trouble. Such a union of hearts, based on reciprocal understanding and justice, will make for the happiness and strength of all.[52]

Between 1922 and 1925 a fledgling Irish Free State stumbled into being and struggled to maintain its existence. After the ratification of the 1921 Anglo-Irish Treaty in the Irish Dáil and a national election, the country split into pro-treatyites (Free Staters) and anti-treatyites (republican Irregulars) and embarked on a devastating civil war. Irish Canadians divided over whether to support or oppose the treaty – without, however, ever resorting to violence. The vast majority of Irish-Catholic Canadians supported the Free State. William Cosgrave's government of the Irish Free State even encouraged the clerical hierarchy in Toronto – and presumably Canada – not to support any republican Irregulars. There were, of course, some Irish Canadians who supported the republican cause; and even those who tended to express their nationalism in more conservative terms, such as those found in the *Catholic Register*, espoused the republican ideal of a united Ireland. These statements cannot be ignored. The total number of Irish republicans in Canada was not the crucial point; the point, rather, is that republican sentiment existed in Canada.

# Conclusion

On 3 December 1920, at St Dunstan's Hall in Fredericton, Lindsay Crawford, a former editor of *The Globe* (Toronto) and President of the Self-Determination for Ireland League of Canada, was expected to speak at a rally in support of Irish independence. As he ascended the podium, a few disorderly men shouted, sang, and generally prevented Crawford from speaking. The rally plummeted into chaos. Obviously frustrated, Crawford descended the podium and shouted: 'If this is British fair play, no wonder there is an Irish question.'[1] During the 1910s and early 1920s the issue of Irish independence aroused hostility and passions not only in Ireland but in Canada as well. People of Irish-Catholic and Irish-Protestant descent in Canada followed events in Ireland intensely and sometimes participated in those events.

During the earliest stages of the Irish Crisis, from 1912 to 1914, Orange-Canadian unionists and Irish-Canadian nationalists took markedly different approaches to supporting – or opposing – the founding of a Home Rule parliament in Dublin. Irish-Canadian nationalist support for Irish Home Rule mainly took the form of fraternal society resolutions and editorial commentary in Irish-Catholic weeklies such as the *New Freeman* of Saint John and the *Catholic Register* of Toronto. Orange-Canadian unionists were more activist in their opposition to Irish Home Rule. They not only wrote editorials and passed resolutions opposing a Home Rule parliament in Dublin, but also held huge rallies like the one at Toronto's Queen's Park in May 1914. Six thousand people attended that demonstration, where Toronto's mayor, H.C. Hocken, called British Prime Minister Herbert Asquith a traitor for trying to enact the Irish Home Rule legislation, which had already been passed. News of this rally was warmly welcomed among Protestants in Belfast.[2]

In opposing the establishment of a Home Rule parliament, Orange-Canadian unionists advanced the same arguments as the Ulster Unionists. The latter opposed any measure of self-government for Ireland with a fanaticism reminiscent of the Crusaders. Unionists, both Irish and Canadian, contended that the British Empire would be diminished if Ireland received independence. They also argued that if Home Rule were granted, the Protestants of Ireland would be deprived of their religious liberties in a country dominated by Roman Catholic priests. And, they maintained that Catholics were inferior and lacked sufficient business acumen to lead a country. Finally, they feared that a Dublin parliament would heavily tax the long-established Belfast business community.

In their efforts to block Irish Home Rule, Ulster Unionists obstructed the lawful will of the British Parliament. They formed their own paramilitary, the Ulster Volunteer Force (UVF), which imported 35,000 guns and 3 million rounds of ammunition from Germany. The Ulster Unionists remained in close contact with their supporters and coreligionists in Canada, especially around Toronto, and regularly solicited money from their Canadian 'brethren.' Orange-Canadian unionists responded by contributing hundreds of thousands of dollars to the UVF. The Canadian Unionist League even opened an office in Belfast to create a direct financial pipeline from Toronto to Belfast.

During the First World War, Irish Canadians of both traditions served with distinction and remained united with Britain's war aims for at least the first year-and-a-half. But British policies eventually divided Ireland along sectarian lines. The suspension of the enacted Home Rule bill for the duration of the war served as an excuse for nationalists to launch a rebellion in Dublin the day after Easter 1916. After crushing the rebellion by destroying half of Dublin, the British rounded up the rebel leaders and executed one or two of them each morning for ten days. The British government's ruthlessness in executing these Catholic leaders, even while it allowed the Ulster Protestants to heavily arm themselves and conduct manoeuvres with impunity, turned Irish public opinion entirely against British rule in Ireland. After the stunning 1918 British general election, in which the revolutionary Sinn Féin ousted the constitutional Irish Parliamentary Party, Irish-Catholic Canadians slowly shifted their support to Sinn Féin as well.

Irish-Canadian nationalists argued that the British government ought to be held accountable for its wartime promises and that all small nations should be granted self-determination. While Irish-Catholic Canadians demanded that Ireland be included in the list of nations to be granted nationhood at the Paris Peace Conference, Irish-Canadian nationalists formed a nationwide activist society: the Self-Determination for Ireland League of Canada. This league founded branches in every major city across Canada, and even in quite a few smaller cities, recruiting around 50,000 members. It held a National Convention in Ottawa in October 1920, where it openly criticized British policy in Ireland. This is not to suggest that these Irish-Canadian nationalists were revolutionaries – quite the contrary. They were hardware merchants, solicitors, secretaries, editors, railway managers, lumber company owners, timber brokers, funeral directors, insurance salesmen, municipal commissioners, and labourers. In short, they were hard-working Canadians who simply expressed a desire for their ancestral homeland to be granted the same measure of independence under which Canada prospered. Orange-Canadian unionists viewed the free expression of these ideas as a threat to the British Empire.

Public criticism of British policy in Ireland spurred accusations of disloyalty from Canada's Orange supporters. Even though they were also critical of British policy with respect to Home Rule during 1912–14, and funded the armed defiance of British law, Orange-Canadian unionists accused anyone who criticized British policy of being a disloyal Canadian. By the 1920s, Orange-Canadian unionists asserted that only those who publicly proclaimed their loyalty to Britain were the truly loyal Canadians. In contrast, Irish-Canadian nationalists argued *they* were the truly patriotic and loyal Canadians, for they exercised their rights as Canadians to free speech and freedom of assembly.

The issue of Irish independence aroused intense hostility and animosity in Canada for two main reasons: ethnicity and religion. Contrary to the myth that Canada is a uniquely 'peaceable kingdom,' Canadians harboured religious and ethnic bigotry and intolerance as much as – perhaps more than – any other nation in that period. The most divisive issues in Canada during the late nineteenth and early twentieth centuries – Louis Riel's execution, separate schools in Manitoba, Ontario, and New Brunswick, and the Conscription Crisis of the First World War – all had their roots in ethnic and religious differences. With regard to Irish independence, allegiances were primarily ethno-religious. Canadians of Irish-Catholic descent supported the Irish nationalist claim that Ireland deserved independence as much as any other nation. Orange-Canadian unionists, for their part, opposed Irish Home Rule mainly because Protestants in Ireland – who cast themselves as the empire's most loyal citizens – would be deprived of their civil and religious liberties in a Catholic country. Irish Canadians, be they Catholic or Protestant, also felt an intense emotional connection to Ireland as their ancestral homeland. People on both sides of the religious divide often referred to Ireland as the 'old country,' or similar. Repeated references to the 'homeland,' the 'motherland,' and 'our people' back home, coupled with language of loyalty or disloyalty to Britain, leave little doubt that the debates and confrontations over Irish independence reflected an ethno-religious division as broad as the English–French divide. Indeed, these ethno-religious networks associated with their corresponding communities in Ireland continued well beyond the 1920s.

After 1925, as the people of the Irish Free State and Northern Ireland slowly recovered from the tumultuous events of the preceding decade-and-a-half, the political leaders of each portion of the island began to push the boundaries of political autonomy of their respective regions. In 1937, Eamon de Valera introduced a new constitution for the Irish Free State, one that withdrew Ireland from the British Commonwealth and that enshrined the idea that Ireland was a Catholic and Gaelic nation. Meanwhile, the Protestant Unionists in Northern Ireland solidified their political control over their region through extensive gerrymandering and by tilting the local voting regulations.

When the somewhat dampened ethno-religious tensions in Northern Ireland re-emerged in 1968 and were exposed to the world, the Protestant loyalist community once again found support among those of Irish-Protestant descent in Canada. Just as in the 1910s and 1920s, an Orange-Canadian loyalist organization known as the Canadian Ulster Loyalist Association (CULA) sprang to life to provide the 'besieged' Protestants of Northern Ireland with the resources to arm themselves. In the Toronto/Hamilton area there also existed the Ulster Benevolent Group, the Independent Loyalist Group, the Ulster Committee of Hamilton, and the Niagara Committee.[3] These support networks raised money for the most recent incarnations of the UVF and the Ulster Defence Association (UDA). The CULA even held dances to raise money to enhance the UVF's arms procurement power. Between May and August 1974 these networks raised more than $4,000, with donations coming from as far away as the Northern Ireland Association of California.[4]

Sociologist Steven Bruce describes the support networks in Canada as 'the main source of support for loyalism outside the United Kingdom ... Ontario is to Ulster Protestants what Boston is to Irish Catholics.'[5] Bruce notes that in 1972, five Toronto businessmen shipped arms in grain container ships out of Halifax, bound for ports in Scotland, Wales, and Northern Ireland.[6] These illegal activities continued through the 1980s, when the RCMP discovered and suppressed them.[7] In this way, Orange-Canadian traditions of the 1910s and 1920s were carried forward to the latter decades of the twentieth century. Arguably, what inspired these Canadian loyalists was an overwhelming sense of ethnic and religious identification with the Protestants of Northern Ireland.

Ethnicity and religion profoundly influenced Canadian national development in the early twentieth century, and they continue to influence Canadian society. During the Irish Home Rule Crisis of the 1910s and 1920s, many Irish Canadians, be they Catholic or Protestant, found events in Ireland too compelling to ignore. Irish Canadians divided themselves primarily along religious lines and allied themselves with the corresponding religious communities in Ireland in order to support, or prevent, Irish independence. This struggle within Canada ignited so much acrimony that accusations of disloyalty and 'un-Canadian' activities abounded. When the Irish Question was settled in 1925, most Irish Canadians turned their attention to political and social themes in Canada. This remained largely true until the next round of Irish Troubles erupted in the 1960s.

# Notes

### Introduction

1 George J. Mitchell, *Making Peace* (Berkeley: University of California Press, 1999), 27, 161. Jean de Chastelain is not merely a Canadian general: he served two separate terms as Chief of Staff of the Canadian Defence Forces, and for a year in between those two terms he served as the Canadian Ambassador to the United States.
2 Ibid., 161.
3 'All, Except Paisley, Welcome Decommissioning,' *Irish Voice*, 28 September–4 October 2005, 3.
4 'Bloody Sunday's Legacy,' *Irish America*, June–July 2000, 26–7.
5 'Probe Hears Last Witness,' *Sacramento Bee*, 14 February 2004, A21.
6 'Finucane's Seek Ahern's Help,' *Irish Voice*, 3–9 September, 2003, 4.
7 D.C. Lyne, 'Irish-Canadian Financial Contributions to the Home Rule Movement in the 1890s,' *Studia Hibernica* 7 (1967), 189, 206; Margaret Banks, 'Edward Blake and Irish Nationalism, 1892–1907' (PhD diss., University of Toronto, 1953), 575, 579.
8 Ibid., 577.
9 Patrick Buckland, *James Craig: Lord Craigavon* (Dublin: Gill and Macmillan, 1980), 22.
10 D.G. Boyce, *Englishmen and Irish Troubles: British Public Opinion and the Making of Irish Policy, 1918–1922* (Cambridge, MA: MIT, 1972), 47.
11 Keith Middlemas, ed., *Thomas Jones Whitehall Diary*, vol. III, *Ireland 1918–1925* (London: Oxford University Press, 1971), 230. For health reasons, Robert Borden declined to act as chairman.
12 Cecil J. Houston and William J. Smyth, *Irish Emigration and Canadian Settlement: Patterns, Links, and Letters* (Toronto: University of Toronto Press, 1990), 191.

13 Ibid., 201.
14 Ibid., 188, 226.
15 Ibid., 226.
16 Murray W. Nicolson, 'Peasants in an Urban Society: The Irish Catholics in Victorian Toronto,' in Robert F. Harney, ed., *Gathering Place: People and Neighborhoods of Toronto, 1834–1945* (Toronto: Multicultural History Society of Ontario, 1985), 53. Murray Nicolson is the Canadian scholar most readily identified as defending the argument that Irish Catholics were an urban peasant people. He asserted: 'With the rise of Irish Catholic institutions after 1850, Toronto became the cultural focus for the Irish in Ontario. It was from the areas of Irish Catholic concentration, with their interacting parish networks, that a distinctive culture arose and spread to the hinterland. Urban-rural ratios made little difference, for Irish Catholic culture was urban-born.' Ibid., 49; *Canadian Census, 1921*, 353, Table 22.
17 Bruce S. Elliott, *Irish Migrants in the Canadas: A New Approach* (Montreal and Kingston: McGill-Queen's University Press, 1988), xiii–xiv.
18 Donald Akenson, *The Irish in Ontario: A Study in Rural History* (Montreal and Kingston: McGill-Queen's University Press, 1984), 186.
19 Donald MacKay, *Flight from Famine: the Coming of the Irish to Canada* (Toronto: McClelland and Stewart, 1990), 15.
20 Tony Gray, *The Orange Order* (London: The Bodley Head, 1972), 55–68; Chris Ryder and Vincent Kearney, *Drumcree: The Orange Order's Last Stand* (London: Methuen, 2002), 5.
21 Ibid.
22 Scott W. See, 'The Fortunes of the Orange Order in 19th Century New Brunswick,' in P.M. Toner, ed., *New Ireland Remembered: Historical Essays on the Irish in New Brunswick* (Fredericton: New Ireland, 1988), 91.
23 Ibid., 91–2.
24 Hereward Senior, *Orangeism: The Canadian Phase* (Toronto: McGraw-Hill Ryerson, 1972), 12; See, 'The Fortunes of the Orange Order,' 92; Cecil J. Houston and William J. Smyth, *The Sash Canada Wore: A Historical Geography of the Orange Order in Canada* (Toronto: University of Toronto Press, 1980), 84. Houston and Smyth note that some German Protestants and Dutch also joined the Order, but the overwhelming majority of members were of British and Irish Protestant heritage.
25 *Laws and Ordinances of the Orange Association of British North America* (Toronto: Rogers and Thompson, 1840), 9, in Scott W. See, *Riots in New Brunswick: Orange Nativism and Social Violence in the 1840s* (Toronto: University of Toronto Press, 1993), 77.
26 Ibid.

27 Houston and Smyth, *The Sash Canada Wore*, 95.
28 See, 'The Fortunes of the Orange Order,' 93.
29 Senior, *Orangeism*, 8.
30 Ibid., 93.
31 Houston and Smyth, *The Sash Canada Wore*, 6.
32 Ibid., 5.
33 Ibid., 6.
34 Ibid., 3.
35 Ibid.
36 David A. Wilson, ed., *The Orange Order in Canada* (Dublin: Four Courts, 2007).
37 Donald M. MacRaild, 'The Associationalism of the Orange Diaspora,' in Wilson, *The Orange Order in Canada*, 25–6.
38 Ibid., 28.
39 One of Kaufmann's impressive works is his recent monograph on the Orange Order in Northern Ireland; Eric P. Kaufmann, *The Orange Order: A Contemporary Northern Irish History* (Oxford: Oxford University Press, 2007).
40 Idem, 'The Orange Order in Ontario, Newfoundland, Scotland, and Northern Ireland: A Macro-Social Analysis,' in Wilson, *The Orange Order in Canada*, 57.
41 Ibid., 55.
42 See, *Riots in New Brunswick*, 115–82.
43 Michael S. Cross, 'The Shiner's War: Social Violence in the Ottawa Valley in the 1830s,' *Canadian Historical Review* 54 (March 1973), 1–26.
44 Gregory S. Kealey, 'The Orange Order in Toronto: Religious Riot and the Working Class,' in Gregory S. Kealey and P. Warrian, eds., *Essays in Canadian Working Class History* (Toronto: McClelland and Stewart, 1976), 26. Hereward Senior portrays these Orange-Catholic riots as opportunities for Orangemen to develop new traditions as memories of old ones faded: 'Yet more important, perhaps was the fact that while the War of 1812 and the American revolution were over, the issues involved in the Battle of the Boyne were still alive. Clashes on July 12 provided new and local traditions which added to Orange folklore, and every celebration of the twelfth offered the prospect of a fresh encounter.' Writing at a time when ethnic and religious violence was rife throughout the world, Senior's advocacy of local violence as a means to develop traditions and folklore seems surreal and incomprehensible. Senior, *Orangeism*, 92.
45 Brian Clarke, 'Religious Riot as Pastime: Orange Young Britons, Parades, and Public Life in Victorian Toronto,' in Wilson, *The Orange Order in Canada*, 112–13.

46 Ibid., 110.
47 Ibid., 111.
48 Ibid., 125.
49 Robert McLaughlin, 'Orange-Canadian Unionists and the Irish Home Rule Crisis, 1912–1914,' *Ontario History* 98, no. 1 (Spring 2006), 68–101.
50 William Jenkins, 'Views from 'the Hub of the Empire': Loyal Orange Lodges in Early Twentieth-Century Toronto,' in Wilson, *The Orange Order in Canada*, 137.
51 Ibid., 138.
52 Ibid., 141–2.
53 J.R. Miller, 'Anti-Catholicism in Canada: From the British Conquest to the Great War,' in Terrence Murphy and Gerald Stortz, eds., *Creed and Culture: The Place of English-Speaking Catholics in Canadian Society, 1750–1930* (Montreal and Kingston: McGill-Queen's University Press, 1993), 42.
54 *Reports of Provincial Grand Orange Lodge of Ontario West*, vol. 6, *1910–1919*, 13 March 1912, 19.
55 Michael Laffan, *The Partition of Ireland, 1911–1925* (Dundalk: Dundalgan, 1983), 24.
56 Historian Roberto Perin wrote: 'Acknowledging the importance of ethnicity has become a convention in North America. Although the phenomenon has existed at least since the turn of the century, it only attracted serious attention with the eruption in the United States of the civil rights movement and in Canada of an increasingly assertive Quebec nationalism during the Quiet Revolution. Is it mere coincidence that ethnic groups began to be 'discovered' at a time when both states faced serious threats to their integrity? Since that time, writers have marvelled at the persistence of ethnicity even though they were not quite sure what was persisting.' Roberto Perin, 'Clio as an Ethnic: The Third Force in Canadian Historiography,' *Canadian Historical Review* 64, no. 4 (1983), 441.
57 Zofia Shahrodi, 'The Polish Community in Toronto in the Early Twentieth Century,' in Harney, *Gathering Place*, 243–56. Shahrodi writes: 'The united effort for the restoration of independent Poland became a first priority. North American Polonia joined in all activities to gain independence for Poland and to help their countrymen at home. In cities across Canada committees were formed to help hungry people in Poland and support the Polish Army in France. Publicizing the Polish cause in North America contributed to the final outcome [Polish independence] in 1918.'
58 Zoriana Yaworsky Sokolsky, 'The Beginnings of Ukrainian Settlement in Toronto, 1891–1939,' in Harney, ed., *Gathering Place*, 290.
59 For only a few examples, see Margaret E. Fitzgerald and Joseph A. King,

*The Uncounted Irish in Canada and the United States* (Toronto: P.D. Meany, 1990); MacKay, *Flight from Famine;* John J. Mannion, *Irish Settlements in Eastern Canada: A Study of Cultural Transfer and Adaptation* (Toronto: University of Toronto Press, 1974); Catherine Wilson, *A New Lease on Life: Landlords, Tenants, and Immigrants in Ireland and Canada* (Montreal and Kingston: McGill-Queen's University Press, 1994); P.M. Toner, 'Occupation and Ethnicity: The Irish in New Brunswick,' *Canadian Ethnic Studies* 20 (1988), 155–65; Gordon Darroch, 'Half Empty or Half Full? Images and Interpretations in the Historical Analysis of the Catholic Irish in Nineteenth-Century Canada,' *Canadian Ethnic Studies* 25 (1993), 1–8; and Gordon A. Darroch and Michael D. Ornstein, 'Ethnicity and Occupational Structure in Canada in 1871: The Vertical Mosaic in Historical Perspective.'*Canadian Historical Review* 61 (1980), 305–33. One fascinating aspect of Catherine Wilson's study is her discovery that the landlord/tenant relationship evident on the Ards Peninsula, County Down, was transferred to Amherst Island in Lake Ontario, where it was maintained, not by force but by choice. These tenant farmers received favourable terms with low rents, long leases, and options to buy. Furthermore, Wilson found little evidence of any class antagonisms on Amherst Island. Wilson, *A New Lease on Life*, 224–5.

60 Gerald J. Stortz, 'The Catholic Church and Irish Nationalism in Toronto, 1850–1900,' in Robert O'Driscoll and Lorna Reynolds, eds., *The Untold Story: The Irish in Canada* (Toronto: Celtic Arts of Canada, 1988), 871.

61 Akenson, *The Irish in Ontario*, 41–2. Through extensive examination of the 1871 census, Akenson found that 77.5 per cent of those of Irish descent in Ontario lived in rural areas. Taking direct aim at those who argued otherwise, Akenson on page 37 quipped: 'To describe the experience of the Irish migrants and their descendants in Ontario as having been an urban one requires an act of faith sufficient to move mountains.'

62 Murray Nicolson, 'The Growth of Roman Catholic Institutions in the Archdiocese of Toronto, 1841–90,' in Murphy and Stortz, eds., *Creed and Culture*, 167.

63 Terrence Murphy, 'Trusteeism in Atlantic Canada: The Struggle for Leadership among the Irish Catholics of Halifax, St John's, and Saint John, 1780–1850,' in Murphy and Stortz, eds., *Creed and Culture*, 145.

64 Brian Clarke, *Piety and Nationalism: Lay Voluntary Associations and the Creation of an Irish-Catholic Community in Toronto, 1850–1895* (Montreal and Kingston: McGill-Queen's University Press, 1993), 9–11.

65 Stortz, 'The Catholic Church and Irish Nationalism in Toronto,' 871.

66 Ibid., 872.

67 Ibid., 876.

68 Terrence J. Fay, *A History of Canadian Catholics: Gallicism, Romanism, and Canadianism* (Montreal and Kingston: McGill-Queen's University Press, 2002), 175.
69 Mark G. McGowan, 'The De-greening of the Irish: Toronto's Irish-Catholic Press, Imperialism, and the Forging of a New Identity, 1887–1914,' CHA *Historical Papers* (1989), 118–45; 'To Share the Burden of Empire: Toronto's Catholics and the Great War, 1914–1918,' in Mark G. McGowan and Brian Clarke, eds., *Catholics at the Gathering Place: Historical Essays on the Archdiocese of Toronto, 1841–1991* (Toronto: CCHA, 1993), 177–207; 'Rethinking Catholic-Protestant Relations in Canada: The Episcopal Reports of 1900–1901,' *Historical Studies* 59 (1992), 11–32.
70 Mark G. McGowan, *The Waning of the Green: Catholics, the Irish, and Identity in Toronto, 1887–1922* (Montreal and Kingston: McGill-Queen's University Press, 1999), 3.
71 Ibid., 7, 11.
72 Ibid., 12.
73 Ibid., 185
74 Ibid.
75 Ibid., 186.
76 An example of the new Irish Catholic sources such as the St Patrick's Society of Montreal can be seen in language used by T.P. Tansey on 1 December 1919 as he encouraged his St Patrick's Society brethren to become involved in the movement to hold an Irish Race Convention in Canada, as had recently been done in the United States and Australia. Tansey stated: 'Are we, the Irish portion of the northern half of the American continent to be behind our fellows in the South and our brothers in the Antipodes, in giving that encouragement to our fighting compatriots in the home land, which is their due. Lives there an Irishman today whose heart is not bound up with the fortunes of the old land, and whose eyes are not anxiously gazing thither? [...]

'Our people at home are fighting for their cause as they never fought before, and are succeeding as they never did before. Let us encourage them by every means in our power, and this race Convention which will, I trust show to all that every Irishman in Canada is with the Irish in Ireland, heart and soul, is one way of advancing the cause both here and abroad.'St Patrick's Society of Montreal, Society Meeting Minute Book 1919-35, 1 December 1919, Concordia University Archives, Montreal, Quebec.
77 'Self-Determination League Ends Successful Convention,' *Ottawa Citizen*, 19 October 1920, 13.
78 *Census of Canada, 1921*, 353, Table 22. The 1,050,384 Canadians of Irish

heritage represented 14.58 per cent of the population in 1911. Donald Akenson's and Murray Nicholson's research placed those of Irish Catholic descent at slightly above one-third of those who declared themselves to be of Irish Protestant heritage.
79 Colonial historian Philip Greven used a factor of five when estimating populations from head-of-household lists for his work on seventeenth- and eighteenth-century Andover, Massachusetts. Philip J. Greven, Jr, *Four Generations: Population, Land, and Family in Colonial Andover, Massachusetts* (Ithaca: Cornell University Press, 1970), 103–5.
80 Robert Choquette, 'English-French Relations in the Canadian Catholic Community,' in Murphy and Stortz, eds., *Creed and Culture*, 13.
81 Carl Berger, *The Sense of Power: Studies in the Ideas of Canadian Imperialism, 1867–1914* (Toronto: University of Toronto Press, 1970); Mason Wade, *The French Canadians, 1760–1945* (Toronto: Macmillan, 1956).
82 Donald M. MacRaild, 'The Irish and Scots in the English Orange Order in the Later Nineteenth Century,' in R.J. Morris and Liam Kennedy, *Ireland and Scotland: Order and Disorder, 1600–2000* (Edinburgh: John Donald, 2005), 163.
83 Ibid., 163.
84 Akenson, *The Irish in Ontario*, 185.

**Chapter One**

1 *Census of Canada, 1921*, 353, Table 22. The 1,050,384 Canadians of Irish heritage represented 14.58 per cent of the population in 1911. At that time, the Irish were the third-largest ethnic group in Canada, behind the French (28.52 per cent) and the English (25.30 per cent). In Table 22 of the 1921 Canadian Census, the term 'Race' was used to identify the ethnic background of the respondent. Included in these figures were those born in the old country who had immigrated to Canada, as well as those who were born in Canada descended from those who had previously immigrated.
2 Cecil J. Houston and William J. Smyth, *The Sash Canada Wore: A Historical Geography of the Orange Order in Canada* (Toronto: University of Toronto Press, 1980), 6–7.
3 Scott W. See, 'The Fortunes of the Orange Order in 19th Century New Brunswick,' in P.M. Toner, ed., *New Ireland Remembered: Historical Essays on the Irish in New Brunswick* (Fredericton: New Ireland, 1988), 93–4.
4 Houston and Smyth, *The Sash Canada Wore*, 3, 10; See, 'The Fortunes of the Orange Order,' 91, 93.
5 Ibid., 177.

6 Gregory S. Kealey, 'The Orange Order in Toronto: Religious Riot and the Working Class,' in Gregory S. Kealey and P. Warrian, eds., *Essays in Canadian Working Class History* (Toronto: McClelland and Stewart, 1976), 13–34; Scott W. See, "Mickeys and Demons' vs 'Bigots and Boobies': The Woodstock Riot of 1847,' *Acadiensis* 21 (Autumn 1991), 110–31; idem, 'The Orange Order and Social Violence in Mid-Nineteenth Century Saint John,' in P.M. Toner, *New Ireland Remembered*, 72–89.
7 Kealey, 'The Orange Order in Toronto,' 26.
8 The third Irish Home Rule Bill, proposing limited self-government for Ireland, was introduced in the British Parliament on 11 April 1912 and was immediately opposed by Irish Unionists and British Conservatives. The bill was introduced by Hebert Asquith's Liberal government, which achieved a parliamentary majority through the support of John Redmond's Irish Parliamentary Party. Redmond's party, which represented 75 per cent of the constituencies in Ireland, was a moderate nationalist party that had been advocating Irish home rule for nearly four decades. Two previous home rule bills, in 1886 and 1893, had been defeated in Parliament.
9 *Reports and Proceedings of Grand Orange Lodge of British America, 1924.* The name alone denotes the ethnic nature of this organization. The term British North America was dropped in 1867 when the Dominion of Canada was formed.
10 See, 'The Fortunes of the Orange Order,' 93–5. The five degrees of the Orange hierarchy were Orange, Purple, Blue, Royal Arch Purple, and Royal Scarlet.
11 *Orange Sentinel*, 20 July 1920, 2. During the 1920 parade, 9,000 Orange Order members marched from Queen's Park to the Exhibition Grounds, while 25,000 people lined the streets of Toronto to watch and cheer.
12 'The 'Belfast of Canada' Running True to Form,' *New Freeman* (Saint John), 31 July 1920, 1; Houston and Smyth, *The Sash Canada Wore*, 157.
13 James Loughlin, *Ulster Unionism and British National Identity Since 1885* (London: Pinter, 1995), viii.
14 Houston and Smyth, *The Sash Canada Wore*, 179.
15 *Reports of the Provincial Grand Orange Lodge of Ontario West*, vol. 6, *1910–19, 1914*, 32. Ontario, with its heavy concentration of lodges, was divided into two administrative units, Ontario East and Ontario West. Toronto was included in the latter.
16 Loughlin, *Ulster Unionism*, 12.
17 See, 'Fortunes of the Orange Order,' 92.
18 Ibid., 92–3.

19 *Reports of Provincial Grand Orange Lodge of Ontario West, 1907–1919, 1912,* 13 March 1912, 19.
20 With the completion of the Canadian Pacific Railway in 1885, and the subsequent opening of the Canadian prairies for settlement, millions of Eastern European settlers flooded into Canada to farm the rich, fertile lands. Between 1901 and 1921, Canada's population increased by 64 per cent, from 5,371,315 to 8,788,949. Canadian Orangemen viewed this influx of non-British immigrants with trepidation and suspicion. The 1914 annual meeting of the Grand Orange Lodge of Ontario West passed a resolution aimed at restricting the voting eligibility of recent immigrants to Canada. Copies of the following resolution were sent to the Borden government but never acted upon:
Resolved – That we, the Members of the Provincial Grand Orange Lodge of Ontario West, assembled at our annual meeting in Guelph, March 11th, 1914, desire to impress upon the Prime Minister and Government of Canada the national importance of: 1st. Withholding the franchise from all foreigners until they have been five years resident in Canada. The large number of foreigners now resident in this country ... are a real danger to our free institutions, and therefore, every possible means should be adopted to mitigate this danger.

2nd. That no man henceforth, native or foreigner, born outside of the Province of Quebec, should be given the franchise until he can read and write the English language. This will help to destroy the happy hunting ground of unscrupulous politicians who have money to spend in corrupting their fellow citizens, and thereby misrepresent the voice of honest men. Good government does not depend on the number, but the quality of the voters. These necessary safeguards we owe to ourselves and our country. They will also raise the standard of citizenship and teach them the value of the franchise.

Canadian Orangemen fully believed in the inferiority of Catholics and non-British peoples, questioning whether they were even deserving of Canadian citizenship. Robert Craig Brown and Ramsay Cook, *Canada 1869–1921: A Nation Transformed* (Toronto: McClelland and Stewart, 1974), 49–82; *Reports of Provincial Grand Orange Lodge of Ontario West, 1914,* 53.
21 Carl Berger, *The Sense of Power: Studies in the Ideas of Canadian Imperialism, 1867–1914* (Toronto: University of Toronto Press, 1970), 3.
22 Ibid., 259.
23 Ibid., 134.
24 Philip Currie, 'Toronto Orangeism and the Irish Question, 1911–1916,' *Ontario History* 87 (December 1995), 398.

25 Ibid., 398.
26 Ibid., 403.
27 Alvin Jackson, 'Irish Unionism, 1870-1922,' in D.G. Boyce and Alan O'Day, eds., *Defenders of the Union: A Survey of British and Irish Unionism Since 1801* (London: Routledge, 2001), 115.
28 Ibid.
29 J.J. Lee, *Ireland, 1912–1985: Politics and Society* (Cambridge: Cambridge University Press, 1989), 1.
30 George Dangerfield, *The Damnable Question: A History of Anglo-Irish Relations* (Little, Brown, 1976), 69.
31 R.F. Foster, *Modern Ireland, 1600–1972* (London: Penguin, 1988), 465; Dangerfield, *The Damnable Question*, 69–70; Lee, *Ireland 1912–1985*, 6; Michael Laffan, *The Partition of Ireland, 1911–1925* (Dundalk: Dundalgan, 1983), 19.
32 Laffan, *The Partition of Ireland*, 22; Lee, *Ireland, 1912–1985*, 6.
33 For more on the Conservative-Unionist alliance, see Thomas C. Kennedy, "The Gravest Situation of Our Lives': Conservatives, Ulster, and the Home Rule Crisis, 1911–1914,' *Éire-Ireland* 36 (Fall–Winter 2001), 67–82.
34 Dangerfield, *The Damnable Question*, 74; Laffan, *The Partition of Ireland*, 19.
35 Ronan Fanning, "'Rats' versus 'Ditchers': The Die-Hard Revolt and the Parliament Bill of 1911,' in A. Cosgrove and J.I. McGuire, eds., *Parliament and Community* (Belfast: Appletree Press, 1983), 191.
36 Lee, *Ireland 1912–1985*, 2–3.
37 Laffan, *The Partition of Ireland*, 21.
38 In 1919, Toronto's *Catholic Register* declared that Ireland's troubles stemmed from Irish Protestant as well as English notions of superiority: 'The root trouble in Ireland is that the minority and their friends in England have for centuries looked upon Catholics as their inferiors and servants, and they cannot yet bring themselves to treat Catholics or others refusing their leadership as equals. It is a defect in their idea of democracy.' 'Ireland's Cause,' *Catholic Register*, 30 January 1919, 4.
39 Kennedy, 'The Gravest Situation of Our Lives,' 73–4.
40 Loughlin, *Ulster Unionism*, 67.
41 Sir Edward Carson to Sir John Marriott, 6 November 1933, in Loughlin, *Ulster Unionism*, 67.
42 L. Perry Curtis, *Apes and Angels: The Irishman in Victorian Caricature*, rev. ed. (Washington: Smithsonian Institution Press, 1997). Chapter 4 – 'Simianizing the Irish Celts' – explores the many ways in which the Irish were depicted as apes.
43 *Belfast Newsletter*, 20 February 1886.

44 At that time, 1912–14, the Harland and Wolff shipyard was the largest in Great Britain, and its drydock was the largest in the world. The York Street Flax Spinning Mill in Belfast was the largest linen mill in the world, producing millions of pounds' worth of exports. John McGarry and Brendan O'Leary, *Explaining Northern Ireland: Broken Images* (Oxford: Blackwell, 1995), 72.
45 Paul Bew, *Ideology and the Irish Question: Ulster Unionism and Irish Nationalism, 1912–1916* (Oxford: Clarendon, 1994), 34–5.
46 *Canadian Annual Review of Public Affairs, 1912*, 141.
47 *Reports of Provincial Grand Orange Lodge of Ontario West*, vol. 6, *1910–1919*, 13 March 1912, 19.
48 *Report of Grand Orange Lodge of New Brunswick 1912*, 19 March 1912, 23.
49 *The Sentinel and Orange and Protestant Advocate (Orange Sentinel)*, 11 April 1912, 2. As events escalated and intensified through 1913 and 1914, editorials constantly ran that espoused the Orange Canadian viewpoint.
50 Dangerfield, *The Damnable Question*, 76.
51 Ibid., 76; Laffan, *The Partition of Ireland*, 28; Lee, *Ireland, 1912–1985*, 6. More women than men actually signed the Covenant – 228,991 women and 218,206 men.
52 Edmund Curtis and R.B. McDowell, *Irish Historical Documents, 1172–1922* (London: Methuen, 1943), 304.
53 *Orange Sentinel*, 3 October 1912, 5.
54 Ibid., 2.
55 Ibid.
56 There are numerous examples of Orangemen occupying positions of considerable importance in Canadian society. The first Canadian prime minister, John A. Macdonald, was an Orangeman. Three other Orangemen served as prime minister, the last being John Diefenbaker (1957–63). At the federal level, prior to the 1930s almost every Conservative government had at least two cabinet ministers who were members of the Orange Order. In the 1911 Conservative government of Robert Borden, Orangemen Colonel Sam Hughes and A.E. Kemp served as cabinet ministers. At the same time, T.S. Sproule resigned as Orange Grand Master to become the Speaker of the House of Commons. At the provincial level, Ontario has had four Orange provincial premiers. In 1920, one-third of Ontario's legislators were Orange Order members. In Toronto, thirty of the city's mayors have been members of the Orange Order. In the late nineteenth and early twentieth centuries, Orange patronage dominated city politics to such an extent that it was almost impossible to land a job as a policeman or fireman or at City Hall without being a member of the Order. Eric Kaufmann, 'The

Orange Order in Ontario, Newfoundland, Scotland, and Northern Ireland: A Macro-Social Analysis,' and Brian Clarke, 'Religious Riot as Pastime: Orange Young Britons, Parades and Public Life in Victorian Toronto,' both in David A. Wilson, ed., *The Orange Order in Canada* (Dublin: Four Courts, 2007), 62, 110.

57 *Reports of Provincial Grand Orange Lodge of Ontario West*, 12 March 1913, 16, 18. The following year, Grand Master Fred Dane was appointed to serve as the Canadian Trade Representative in Glasgow. Fred Dane is another example of the prominent place many Canadian Orangemen held in Canadian society.

58 Ibid., 19.

59 *Reports of Grand Orange Lodge of British America*, 30 July 1913, 17.

60 Ibid., 2 August 1913, 65.

61 'Ulster Will Fight,' *Orange Sentinel*, 12 June 1913, 1.

62 Jim Cusack and Henry McDonald, *UVF: The Endgame* (Dublin: Poolbeg, 2008), 36–7.

63 When writing of the UVF, the *Orange Sentinel* proudly declared: 'The Ulster Volunteers are made up of the best elements of the population – the solid business men, the capitalists, employers of labor, bankers, professional men, and the better class of workingmen – all of whom rub shoulders in the drill halls and meet on equal terms. They are imbued with the same spirit of 'No Surrender,' which characterized their forefathers, and will fight to the death before surrendering to the enemies of the Empire.' *Orange Sentinel*, 16 July 1914, 1.

64 A.C. Hepburn, *Catholic Belfast and Nationalist Ireland in the Era of Joe Devlin, 1871–1934* (Oxford: Oxford University Press, 2008), 157.

65 *Orange Sentinel*, 12 March 1914, 1.

66 Ibid.

67 A.T.Q. Stewart, *The Ulster Crisis* (London: Faber and Faber, 1967), 141.

68 Laffan, *The Partition of Ireland*, 40.

69 Stewart, *The Ulster Crisis*, 109–10; Dangerfield, *The Damnable Question*, 87.

70 Hepburn, *Catholic Belfast*, 151–2.

71 Dangerfield, *The Damnable Question*, 86.

72 *Orange Sentinel*, 26 March 1914, 1.

73 Ibid.

74 *Orange Sentinel*, 30 April 1914, 1.

75 Hepburn, *Catholic Belfast*, 146. Of the six counties, only four had clear Protestant majorities: Antrim, 79.5 per cent; Down, 68.4 per cent; Armagh, 54.7 per cent; and Derry, 54.2 per cent. Two had Catholic majorities: Ferman-

agh, 56.2 per cent, and Tyrone, 55.4 per cent. *Census of Ireland, 1911*, in Lee, *Ireland 1912–1985*, 2.
76 *Orange Sentinel*, 30 April 1914, 5.
77 Most contemporary news accounts of the landing put the number of rifles at 30,000 to 50,000 and the rounds of ammunition at 3 million. Subsequent historical works have settled on a rough figure of 35,000. A.T.Q. Stewart asserts that the figure was lower – 'the total number of rifles landed was thus 24,600' – and that the total number of rifles possessed by the UVF in July 1914 was 37,048; Stewart, *The Ulster Crisis*, 246–8.
78 Paul Bew, *Ireland: The Politics of Enmity, 1789–2006* (Oxford: Oxford University Press, 2007), 370.
79 'Covenant to Indemnify the Ulster Volunteers,' *Orange Sentinel*, 26 March 1914, 5. Any member of the UVF who suffered injury 'in the execution of their duty as such members or in the execution of any order of the Provisional Government' and who made a claim recoverable against this fund was still subject to the 'Provisions of the Fatal Accident Act, 1846, The Employers Liability Act, 1880, or the Workmen's Compensation Act 1906; provided the claim made in respect of such injury is approved of by the Executive of said Provisional Government and provided that the Guarantee Fund shall amount to at least £1,000,000.' Edward Carson, James Craig, Lord Londonderry, Lord Dunleath, Sir John Lonsdale, and Sir George Clark all pledged £10,000. A.T.Q. Stewart asserts that by 1 January 1914 the fund stood at £1,043,816, and 'in this way the business community of Belfast underwrote the U.V.F.' Stewart, *The Ulster Crisis*, 77.
80 Ibid., 136.
81 Ibid., 140, 262. Financial support for the Ulster Unionists cause came from Australia, New Zealand, and South Africa, but the greatest support emanated from Canada. As A.T.Q. Stewart notes, 'an Ulster influence was particularly strong in Canada, where there was a long tradition of immigration from the north of Ireland, going back to the eighteenth century.' Stewart, *The Ulster Crisis*, 138.
82 *Orange Sentinel*, 23 October 1913, 1.
83 *Reports of Grand Orange Lodge of British America, 1914*, 27 May 1914, 19–20.
84 Ibid., 28 May 1914, 42.
85 *Orange Sentinel*, 30 April 1914, 1.
86 *Reports of the Provincial Grand Orange Lodge of Ontario West*, 11 March 1914, 44. The motion was put forward by the Finance Committee's members: J.C. Boylan, F.R. Parnell, B.H. Walsh, E. Cascadden, and W.B. Walker.
87 Stewart, *The Ulster Crisis*, 262.

88 *Orange Sentinel*, 11 June 1914, 7. The contribution was forwarded by, G. Edw. Bradley, Dist. M., L.O.D.L. No. 7, Carleton.
89 Ibid.
90 *Orange Sentinel*, 28 May 1914, 10.
91 Ibid., 6.
92 'Send Ulster Grants to Bro. T.W. Self,' *Orange Sentinel*, 11 June 1914, 7: 'grants should be sent direct to T.W. Self, 78 Howard St., Toronto, Treasurer of the Canadian Unionist League.'
93 *Canadian Annual Review of Public Affairs, 1914*, 128.
94 One Ladies Division advert read: 'Ladies' Branch No. 1 Canadian Unionist League meets every Sunday afternoon at 3 o'clock in the Western District Hall cor. of Euclid Ave and College St. Rev. E.E. Scott of Simpson Ave Methodist Church will address the meeting Jan. 25th. Silver Collection – Everybody Welcome – Come and bring your friends.' *Orange Sentinel*, 22 January 1914, 7.
95 *Reports of Grand Orange Lodge of New Brunswick 1914*, 17 March 1914, 14.
96 *Orange Sentinel*, 14 May 1914, 12.
97 Ibid.
98 *Orange Sentinel*, 14 May 1914, 12. At a previous anti-home rule rally on 11 October 1913, at Victoria Hall, Toronto Mayor Horatio Hocken proclaimed: 'In no part of the British Empire is there more intense sympathy with Ulster's struggle than in Toronto and in Canada. Mr. Asquith introduced the bill only to hold power, and a man, who imperils the safety and integrity of the Empire for personal profit is nothing less than a traitor.' Proclaiming the Prime Minister of Britain to be a traitor seems a fairly provocative statement for a supposedly loyal British subject. *Orange Sentinel*, 23 October 1913, 5.
99 *Orange Sentinel*, 14 May 1914, 12.
100 Ibid.
101 Ibid.
102 Craigavon was the name of the estate of Cpt Sir James Craig, and Lord Craigavon was the name Captain Craig adopted after he was given peerage. With his estate at Craigavon teeming with women clerks and secretaries, James Craig conducted his own North American propaganda campaign through the pages of the *Orange Sentinel*. See A.T.Q. Stewart, *The Ulster Crisis*, 158.
103 *Orange Sentinel*, 21 May 1914, 1.
104 *Orange Sentinel*, 28 May 1914, 2.
105 Ibid.

106 Bew, *Ideology and the Irish Question*, 114; Dangerfield, *The Damnable Question*, 117–18.
107 Ibid., 118–19.
108 *Orange Sentinel*, 24 September 1914, 1.
109 In fact, Carson was so revered in Canada that admirers could purchase statuettes of his likeness from the O.W. Dickens, Co., of Toronto. The *Orange Sentinel* advertised that supporters of Carson should '[s]ecure a Statuette of SIR EDWARD CARSON.' The statuette was pictured with the likeness of the dour-looking Carson fully enshrined, stating: 'If you are a true Orangemen you will show your appreciation of this great man's work by displaying his likeness in your home.' *Orange Sentinel*, 25 June 1914, 7.
110 *Orange Sentinel*, 16 July 1914, 1.

**Chapter Two**

1 A familiar Irish nationalist refrain in reference to the notion developed during the Gaelic Revival of the 1890s that Ireland had been a unified nation during Celtic times and would some day be a nation again. D.G. Boyce, *Nationalism in Ireland*, 2nd ed. (London: Routledge, 1991), 22, 111. This notion was transferred across the Atlantic and openly espoused by at least two Irish-Catholic Canadian newspapers. 'Nation Once More,' *New Freeman*, 6 June 1914, 1; 'Home Rule Goes Into Law – Ireland Again A Nation,' *Catholic Register and Canadian Extension (Catholic Register)*, 28 May 1914, 1.
2 'The Home Rule Bill,' *Catholic Register*, 18 April 1912, 4.
3 'Progress of Home Rule,' *New Freeman*, 20 April 1912, 1, 4.
4 Ibid., 4.
5 It is assumed that Irish-Canadian nationalism was rejuvenating itself rather than arising as a result of an infusion of newly arrived immigrant Irish nationalists. There are two reasons for this assumption: (1) the Irish-Canadian nationalist movement fell dormant from 1893 to 1912; and (2) the number of Canadians who identified themselves as of Irish heritage increased in a seemingly natural manner from 1881 to 1921. Number of Canadians of Irish heritage: in 1881, 957,403; in 1901, 988,721; in 1911, 1,050,384; in 1921, 1,107,817. *Census of Canada, 1881,* IV:11; *Census of Canada, 1921,* 353, Table 22.
6 From 1912 to 1922, events in Ireland swung widely across the political spectrum: from a legislative initiative to gain home rule for Ireland in 1912, to rebellion in 1916, to the landslide electoral victory of the separatist Sinn Féin in the 1918 British general election, to an undeclared war

between Ireland and Britain between 1919 and 1921, to a treaty on 6 December 1921 that established the Irish Free State.
7 David Shanahan, 'The Irish Question in Canada: Ireland, the Irish, and Canadian Politics, 1880–1922' (PhD diss., Carleton University, 1989), 281; Mark G. McGowan, *The Waning of the Green: Catholics, the Irish, and Identity in Toronto, 1887–1922* (Montreal and Kingston: McGill-Queen's University Press, 1999), 151.
8 From 1912 to 1920, Irish-Canadian nationalist sentiment shifted from constitutional nationalism to tacit republicanism. Constitutional nationalists in Ireland supported, and were led by, the Irish Parliamentary Party, which advocated that Ireland be granted a limited form of self-government through constitutional methods – legislative enactment in the British Parliament – while remaining a part of Britain. The vast majority of the Irish populace supported the Irish Parliamentary Party in 1912–14. Irish Republicans advocated that Ireland completely separate from Britain through revolutionary methods.
9 D.C. Lyne, 'Irish-Canadian Financial Contributions to the Home Rule Movement in the 1890s,' *Studia Hibernia* 7 (1967), 183; Stanley W. Horrall, 'Canada and the Irish Question: A Study of the Canadian Response to Irish Home Rule, 1882–1893' (MA thesis, Carleton University, 1966), 10–11.
10 Lyne, 'Irish-Canadian Financial Contributions,' 183.
11 Horrall, 'Canada and the Irish Question,' 59.
12 *Canada: Official Debates of the House of Commons, 1886,* 1097; *Journals of the Legislative Assembly of the Province of Quebec, 1886,* 45; Horrall, 'Canada and the Irish Question,' 75–6.
13 Horrall, 'Canada and the Irish Question,' 9–10, 43–4.
14 Alan J. Ward, *The Easter Rising: Revolution and Irish Nationalism* (Wheeling: Harlan Davidson, 1980), 70. The United Irish League had been formed in Ireland by William O'Brien in 1898. By the time of the third Home Rule bill in 1912, it had grown to become one of the three largest Irish fraternal organizations in the United States, the other two being the Ancient Order of Hibernians and the revolutionary Clan-na-Gael.
15 A.C. Hepburn, *Catholic Belfast and Nationalist Ireland in the Era of Joe Devlin, 1871–1934* (Oxford: Oxford University Press, 2008), 87.
16 Normand Laplante, 'Canadian and British Policy on Ireland, 1882–1914,' *The Archivist* 16, no. 5 (1989), 14. Laplante's article has no footnotes or documentation; so the origin and accuracy of this information is uncertain.
17 Eamon Phoenix, 'Northern Nationalists, Ulster Unionists, and the Development of Partition, 1900–1921,' in Peter Collins, ed., *Nationalism and*

*Unionism: Conflict in Ireland, 1885–1921* (Belfast: Institute of Irish Studies, Queen's University of Belfast, 1996), 110.
18 McGowan, *The Waning of the Green*, 153.
19 *By-Laws of Ancient Order of Hibernians Province of Ontario, 1914*, 14. Charles J. Foy Papers, MU 1062, file 16 – AOH Conventions, Archives of Ontario [hereafter Foy 16].
20 *Reports of Officers, and Proceedings of the Eighth Biennial Convention of the Ancient Order of Hibernians of the Province of Ontario, Canada, 1904*, 6, in Foy 16; *Proceedings of the National Conventions of the Ancient Order of Hibernians of America, 1911–1913*, Balch Institute of Ethnic Studies, Philadelphia.
21 McGowan, *The Waning of the Green*, 153.
22 Ibid., 153–4.
23 Richard Davis, 'Irish Nationalism in Manitoba, 1870–1922,' in Robert O'Driscoll and Lorna Reynolds, eds., *The Untold Story: The Irish in Canada* (Toronto: Celtic Arts of Canada, 1988), 395, 397.
24 Ibid., 397.
25 Ibid., 398–9.
26 *Reports of Officers, and Proceedings of the Eighth Biennial Convention of the Ancient Order of Hibernians of the Province of Ontario, Canada, 1904*, 22–3, in Foy 16.
27 McGowan, *The Waning of the Green*, 154.
28 Michael S. Cross, 'The Shiners' War: Social Violence in the Ottawa Valley in the 1830s,' *Canadian Historical Review* 54 (March 1973), 1–26. Timber king Peter Aylen organized Irish labourers in the Ottawa Valley into a goon squad in order 'to drive the French Canadians off the river and thus guarantee jobs and high wages in the timber camps to the Irish.'
29 Robert Craig Brown and Ramsay Cook, *Canada, 1896–1921: A Nation Transformed* (Toronto: McClelland and Stewart, 1974), 254–6; Léopold Lamontagne, 'Ontario: The Two Races,' in Mason Wade, ed., *Canadian Dualism: Studies in French-English Relations* (Toronto: University of Toronto Press, 1960), 370–1; George F.G. Stanley, 'French and English in Western Canada,' in idem, 344–5.
30 Chad Gaffield, *Language, Schooling, and Cultural Conflict: The Origins of the French-Language Controversy in Ontario* (Kingston and Montreal: McGill-Queen's University Press, 1987), 175–6. A French community in Prescott County and the Irish in Alfred Township resisted ecclesiastical orders to establish separate schools, for they felt that the schools were unwarranted in their communities.
31 Boyce, *Nationalism in Ireland*, 237.
32 Shanahan, 'The Irish Question in Canada,' 281–2.

33 By the early twentieth century, many of the specifically Irish Catholic newspapers had folded. Between 1912 and 1925 a number of papers were still in print: *Northwest Review* in Winnipeg; *Catholic Record* in London; *Catholic Register* in Toronto; *Canadian Freeman* in Kingston; and *New Freeman* in Saint John. For this study the author reviewed *Catholic Register* and *New Freeman*. Through the pages and editorials of weekly ethno-religious newspapers, historians are able to view past eras. In the Irish-Catholic weeklies of 1912 to 1914 one readily finds expressions of community members grappling with their daily lives as Canadian citizens while maintaining an interest in Irish affairs.
34 McGowan, *Waning of the Green*, 191.
35 Ibid.
36 'The Home Rule Bill,' *Catholic Register*, 18 April 1912, 4.
37 McGowan, *Waning of the Green*, 191.
38 *New Freeman*, 16 June 1934.
39 *St John Public Service News*, 21 May 1921, 1.
40 Miles Agar was born in 1858 to English and Irish parents aboard a ship bound for Saint John from England. He attended school in Saint John until 1867, when he moved to Liverpool with his parents, where he continued his studies at the Christian Brothers' school. In 1874 he returned to Saint John; in 1875 he began working for Levin and Allingham, hardware merchants. In 1893, at the age of thirty-five, he began his own hardware firm. Miles Agar was also a member of the Saint John Canadian Club and the Rotary Club, as well as a staunch promoter of the Children's Aid Society. 'A Leading Citizen Passes in Death of Miles E. Agar,' *New Freeman*, 3 June 1944, 1.
41 'Ulster's Brag,' *New Freeman*, 20 April 1912, 4.
42 T.W. Acheson, 'The Irish Community in Saint John, 1815–1850,' in P.M. Toner, ed., *New Ireland Remembered, Historical Essays on the Irish in New Brunswick* (Fredericton: New Ireland, 1988), 43.
43 *Census of Canada, 1921*, 542–3, Table 28.
44 'That Belfast Covenant,' *New Freeman*, 12 October 1912, 4. The editorial concluded: 'They [the Ulster Unionists] were never anything else but a selfish political machine, that used the guise of religion to obtain an influence they never could attain through the exercise of their brains.'
45 St Patrick's Society of Montreal Fonds, 1864–1966, P026. Concordia University Archives, Montreal.
46 St Patrick's Society of Montreal, 2 March 1914, Society Meeting Minute Book, 5 April 1909 to 5 March 1916, 189. Concordia University Archives, Montreal. The St Patrick's Society was extensively involved in local Irish-

Canadian charities and hardly a vociferous exponent of the Irish nationalist cause. The society had been integral in the building and consecration of charitable organizations throughout Montreal, such as St Patrick's Church (1843) and Côte des Neiges Cemetery (1885). It was also instrumental in the formation of St Mary's Hospital, St Patrick's Orphanage, English Catholic Charities, and Father Dowd's Home for the Elderly.

47 Ibid. Similarly, the passing of Charles Devlin provoked a small mention of Home Rule: 'This Society has heard with great regret of the death of the Hon. Charles Ramsay Devlin, a most distinguished Canadian Citizen, a staunch upholder of the Irish cause and a statesman of ability and usefulness in the British and Canadian Parliaments ... His loss will be deeply felt by all who have at heart the welfare of Canada and the success of the Home Rule movement for Ireland.' St Patrick's Society Minute Book, 2 March 1914, 189.

48 In addition, Charles J. Foy was a member and held office in the South Lanark Agricultural Society, Perth Horticultural Society, Canadian Patriotic Society of the Red Cross, Catholic Mutual Benefit Association, Catholic Order of Foresters. His legal practice must have been somewhat successful, for at the time of his death in 1927, Foy was Solicitor for Lanark County, the Bank of Montreal, and the Royal Bank of Canada. Inventory of the Charles James Foy Papers, F1074, Archives of Ontario.

49 *Reports of Officers and Proceedings of the Twelfth Biennial Convention of the A.O.H. of the Province of Ontario, Canada, 1912,* 6. Foy 16.

50 Ibid., 7–8.

51 Ibid., 15.

52 Ibid., 27–8.

53 'The Capitulation of Ulster,' *New Freeman*, 15 February 1913, 4.

54 'The Derry Election,' *Catholic Register*, 6 February 1913, 4. The editorial went on to describe the electoral manipulation that regularly occurred in Ulster: 'Under reasonable registration a Nationalist candidate should have nearly a thousand votes of a majority in the town, but those who control the law there, have so managed things that several hundred votes on the Nationalist side are outlawed every year before an election. The landlords of Derry are all mostly Unionists and Protestants, and utilize their conditions to do a good stroke of work for the Unionist candidate. Any Nationalist workman whose rent falls into arrears, even for a week, by that very circumstance loses his vote. On Monday morning he gets a summons, and next court day there follows an order for his ejectment. As a matter of fact he is never evicted. The idea is to destroy his vote that election, and by this simple process the Nationalist candidate loses a name off his roster of ar-

dent supporters. And so it is that they have been able to talk of Ulster as a Province with a Unionist majority in Parliament!'
55 'The Ulster Embroglio,' *Catholic Register*, 2 October 1913, 4.
56 John Garner, *The Franchise and Politics in British North America 1755–1867* (Toronto: University of Toronto Press, 1969), 131–46.
57 'Catholic Action in New Brunswick,' *New Freeman*, 7 June 1913, 4.
58 Ibid.
59 Ibid.
60 'The Campaign,' *New Freeman*, 9 August 1913, 4.
61 Ibid.
62 'The Campaign,' *New Freeman*, 18 October 1913, 4.
63 *New Freeman*, 16 August 1913, 4. The editorial continued: 'Well, we can inform Mr. Sandre and his Black Knights, that not withstanding their protests and those of their Ulster friends, Ireland will have Home Rule, the Catholics here will have their schools wherein religion is taught and the French-Canadian will continue to speak his language, so Mr. Sandre, gracefully accept the situation and please subside.'
64 Boyce, *Nationalism in Ireland*, 283; J.J. Lee, *Ireland, 1912–1985: Politics and Society* (Cambridge: Cambridge University Press, 1989), 18.
65 'Nationalist Drilling,' *Catholic Register*, 27 November 1913, 4.
66 'The Irish Volunteers,' *Catholic Register*, 15 January 1914, 4.
67 Boyce, *Nationalism in Ireland*, 283.
68 Paul Bew, *Ireland: The Politics of Enmity, 1789–2006* (Oxford: Oxford University Press, 2007), 370.
69 For more on John Devoy and the Irish Republican Brotherhood in America, see John Devoy, *Recollections of an Irish Rebel* (London: 1929).
70 It was not until 1918–25 that evidence suggests an active republican movement in Canada.
71 Roy Foster, *Modern Ireland, 1600–1972* (New York: Penguin, 1988), 471–2.
72 George Dangerfield, *The Damnable Question: A History of Anglo-Irish Relations* (New York: Little, Brown, 1976), 121.
73 Bew, *Ireland*, 371.
74 Roger Casement was an Irishman born in County Dublin, who served in the British consular service until 1911, when he retired. He joined the Irish Volunteers in 1913.
75 McGowan, *The Waning of the Green*, 155.
76 *Proceedings of the 48th National Convention of the Ancient Order of Hibernians in America, Emmet Memorial Hall, Chicago, July 16 to 20, 1912*, 37. Ancient Order of Hibernians National Conventions, 1910–1925, Balch Institute of Ethnic Studies, Philadelphia.

77 Ibid., 137–8.
78 Ibid., 26.
79 Ibid.
80 Ibid.; *A.O.H. Reports for the Year,* appendix.
81 Ibid., 117–19.
82 Ibid., 119–20.
83 For more on the competition between the Ancient Order of Hibernians and the Clan n' Gael, see David M. Emmons, *The Butte Irish: Class and Ethnicity in an American Mining Town, 1875–1925* (Urbana: University of Illinois Press, 1989).
84 *Catholic Register,* 28 May 1914, 1; *New Freeman,* 30 May 1914, 1.
85 'Home Rule at Last,' *New Freeman*, 30 May 1914, 4. The editorial continued: 'While the present Bill does not give to Ireland the fullest self-government, still it is an earnest [sic] of goodwill and desire on the part of the British government to satisfy, in a measure, the laudable aspirations of the Irish people for a government of themselves by an Irish parliament ... We are satisfied that our Catholic brothers of the Old Land will display a generosity to the Protestant minority of Ireland that will dispel any such misgivings ... With the Irish Parliament at Dublin, Home Rule will be a living reality, and Irishmen, both Protestant and Catholic will forget old feuds and will work harmoniously together for the upbuilding of the New Ireland.'
86 'United Catholic Ireland Wins Home Rule,' *New Freeman,* 26 September 1914, 4.
87 'Home Rule Meeting,' *New Freeman,* 26 September 1914, 1.
88 Ibid.
89 Ibid.
90 Ibid.

**Chapter Three**

1 Winston Churchill quoted in George Dangerfield, *The Damnable Question: A History of Anglo-Irish Relations* (New York: Little, Brown, 1976), 119.
2 J.J. Lee, *Ireland 1912–1985: Politics and Society* (Cambridge: Cambridge University Press, 1989), 21; Dangerfield, *The Damnable Question*, 126.
3 Lee, *Ireland 1912–1985*, 21.
4 David Fitzpatrick, 'Militarism in Ireland, 1900–1922,' in Thomas Bartlett and Keith Jeffrey, eds., *A Military History of Ireland* (Cambridge: Cambridge University Press, 1996), 386–7.
5 Ibid., 389.

6 *Weekly Northern Whig*, 20 March 1915, in Paul Bew, *Ideology and the Irish Question: Ulster Unionism and Irish Nationalism, 1912–1916* (Oxford: Clarendon, 1994), 134.
7 Fitzpatrick, 'Militarism in Ireland, 1900–1922,' 389.
8 C.P. Stacey, *Canada and the Age of Conflict: A History of Canadian External Policies*, vol. I, *1867–1921* (Toronto: Macmillan, 1977), 177.
9 R. Matthew Bray, "Fighting as an Ally': The English-Canadian Patriotic Response to the Great War,' *Canadian Historical Review* 61, no. 2 (1980), 146.
10 Robert Craig Brown and Ramsay Cook, *Canada 1896–1921: A Nation Transformed* (Toronto: McClelland and Stewart, 1974), 214.
11 Stacey, *Canada and the Age of Conflict*, 177.
12 Bray, 'Fighting as an Ally,' 143.
13 Arthur R.M. Lower, *Colony to Nation: A History of Canada* (Toronto: Longmans, Green, 1946), 456–7.
14 *Catholic Register*, 24 September 1914, 4.
15 *New Freeman*, 26 September 1914, 1.
16 Mark McGowan, *The Waning of the Green: Catholics, the Irish, and Identity in Toronto, 1887–1922* (Montreal and Kingston: McGill-Queen's University Press, 1999), 251.
17 Ibid., 257.
18

Voluntary Enlistment in Canadian Expeditionary Force by Religious Denomination to 1 June 1917

| Denomination | Volunteers | % of CEF | Total in Canada | % volunteered |
| --- | --- | --- | --- | --- |
| Anglican | 165,145 | 46.8 | 1,043,017 | 15.8 |
| Presbyterian | 70,671 | 19.7 | 1,115,324 | 6.3 |
| Roman Catholic | 51,426 | 14.2 | 2,833,041 | 1.8 |
| Methodist | 35,908 | 10.1 | 1,079,892 | 3.3 |
| Baptist | 18,458 | 5.2 | 382,666 | 4.4 |
| Jewish | 851 | 0.2 | 74,564 | 1.1 |
| Other | 12,409 | 3.8 | – | – |

Source: McGowan, *The Waning of the Green*, 256–7.

19 Ibid., 257.
20 Ibid., 397.
21 *Reports of Grand Orange Lodge of Ontario West*, vol. 6, *1910–1919, 1915*, 39–40.

22 Unsigned and undated resolution, Charles J. Foy Papers, MU 1062, File 14, Ancient Order of Hibernians Papers, 1914–1925, Archives of Ontario [hereafter Foy 14].
23 Francis M. Carroll, *American Opinion and the Irish Question, 1910–1923: A Study in Opinion and Policy* (New York: St Martin's, 1978); Joseph Edward Cuddy, *Irish-America and National Isolationism, 1914–1920* (New York: Arno, 1976); Alan J. Ward, 'America and the Irish Problem, 1899–1921,' *Irish Historical Studies* 16 (1968), 64–90; idem, *Ireland and Anglo-American Relations, 1899–1921* (Toronto: University of Toronto Press, 1969).
24 John Hart to Joseph McLaughlin, 24 October 1914, Foy 14.
25 John Hart to Charles J. Foy, 24 November 1914, Foy 14.
26 Division No. 1, A.O.H., York County, N.B., Signed by President Wm. P. Grannan and Rec. Sec. P. Donnelly, 8 November 1915. Letters emanating from Regina, Saskatchewan, also found their way to Charles Foy; Thomas M. Malloy to Charles Foy, 9 February 1916, Foy 14.
27 Ibid.
28 Quoted in McGowan, *The Waning of the Green*, 251–2.
29 Ibid., 252.
30 James Loughlin, *Ulster Unionism and British National Identity Since 1885* (London: Pinter, 1995), 76.
31 A predominately Irish-Catholic Canadian regiment was also prohibited from fighting as a unified force in the British Army. Unlike the 55th Battalion of the Irish Canadian Division, which was formed to serve in the home militia, the 199th Battalion, Irish-Canadian Rangers, was formed in the spring of 1916 in Montreal expressly to fight overseas. The 199th Irish-Canadian Rangers sailed to England in December 1916 at a time when the British Army was desperate for trained recruits. After arriving in Liverpool, the Rangers learned they 'were to be disbanded and used for reinforcements.' Robin B. Burns, 'The Montreal Irish and the Great War,' *Canadian Catholic Historical Association, Study Sessions* 52 (1985), 75.
32 Michael Laffan, *The Partition of Ireland, 1911–1925* (Dundalk: Dundalgan, 1983), 50.
33 *Derry Weekly News*, 10 July 1915, in *New Freeman*, 17 July 1915, 1.
34 *Freeman's Journal*, 22 August 1914, quoted in Bew, *Ideology and the Irish Question*, 130.
35 *Weekly Northern Whig*, 20 March 1915, quoted in Bew, *Ideology and the Irish Question*, 134.
36 Bew, *Ideology and the Irish Question*, 134.
37 The resolution read:
  Resolved – Whereas the Home Rule bill had passed the British House

of Commons and received the Royal assent, notwithstanding that the House of Lords rejected the bill by a large majority; ...

And whereas this treacherous act of the Asquith Government not only endangers the future of the Empire, and the stability of the throne, but places in danger the lives, the liberties, and the property of over a million loyal Irish Protestants, thousands of whom are now fighting the Empire's battles, and already thousands of whom have laid down their lives for the Empire in the titanic struggle now in progress in Europe, for the very life and liberties of the British people the world over;

And whereas this action of the Asquith Government will, if carried to its ultimate end, place the loyal Protestants of Ireland under the heel of an Irish Parliament, which will be mainly elected and entirely controlled by the Hierarchy of the Church of Rome, and at the behests and mandates of that Church carried out under the direction of the Knights of Columbus, and the Ancient Order of Hibernians, both of which organizations are the most virulent and implacable foes of everything British and Protestant;

Therefore be it resolved that this R.W. [Right Worshipful] Grand Lodge of Ontario West, as loyal citizens of the Empire, not only strongly and in the most emphatic manner possible, deprecates the action of the Asquith Government in passing the dangerous Home Rule bill, but we again place ourselves on record as being in the deepest and most sincere sympathy with our betrayed brethren and fellow-Protestants in Ireland, and we renew to them our pledge of assistance morally, financially, and physically, if necessary, to the resistance they will assuredly offer to their proposed subjugation to the will of an Irish Roman Catholic Parliament.

*Reports of Grand Orange Lodge of Ontario West, vol. 6, 1910–1919, 1915,* 39–40.

38 Ibid., 67.
39 *Orange Sentinel*, 10 February 1916, 1.
40 *New Freeman*, 17 July 1915, 1.
41 Ibid.
42 *New Freeman*, 17 July 1915, 4.
43 David Thornley, 'Patrick Pearse – the Evolution of a Republican,' in F.X. Martin, ed., *Leaders and Men of the Easter Rising: Dublin 1916* (Ithaca: Cornell University Press, 1967), 156.
44 Ibid., 154.
45 F.X. Martin, '1916 – Revolution or Evolution,' in *Leaders and Men of the Easter Rising*, 250.

46 In 1912, Pearse spoke in favour of Home Rule at a rally held on Sackville Street, Dublin, but he added the proviso that Home Rule was merely a stepping stone along the path to complete independence. Thornley, 'Patrick Pearse,' in Martin, *Leaders and Men*, 156.
47 Max Caulfield, *The Easter Rebellion*, 2nd ed. (Boulder: Roberts Rineharts, 1995), 73.
48 Ibid., 157.
49 Caulfield, *The Easter Rebellion*, 153; Dangerfield, *The Damnable Question*, 195.
50 Dangerfield, *The Damnable Question*, 195.
51 Alan J. Ward, *The Easter Rising: Revolution and Irish Nationalism* (Wheeling: Harlan Davidson, 1980), 10.
52 Caulfield, *The Easter Rebellion*, 281.
53 'The Tragedy in Ireland,' *Catholic Register*, 4 May 1916, 4.
54 *New Freeman*, 6 May 1916, 4.
55 St Patrick's Society of Montreal, 1 May 1916, *Society Meeting Minute Book, 4 April 1916 to 27 January 1919*, 7, Concordia University Archives, Montreal.
56 Ibid., 8.
57 Ibid.
58 *Orange Sentinel*, 4 May 1916, 1.
59 'Punishment for Rebels,' *Orange Sentinel*, 25 May 1916, 1.
60 'Unfair to Ulster,' *Orange Sentinel*, 25 May 1916, 1.
61 Caulfield, *The Easter Rebellion*, 288–91.
62 'The Irish Executions,' *Catholic Register*, 11 May 1916, 4.
63 'The Irish Situation,' *Catholic Register*, 18 May 1916, 4.
64 'The Irish Executions,' *Catholic Register*, 11 May 1916, 4.
65 'Sir Edward Carson and the Dublin 'Affair,'' *New Freeman*, 13 May 1916, 4.
66 Oscar Douglas Skelton, *Life and Letters of Sir Wilfrid Laurier*, vol. II (Toronto: Oxford University Press, 1921), 450.
67 Ibid.
68 'The Irish Situation,' *New Freeman*, 5 August 1916, 4.
69 'The Catholic Aspect of the Irish Question,' *New Freeman*, 30 September 1916, 4.
70 Ibid.
71 James W. St G. Walker, 'Race and Recruitment in World War I: Enlistment of Visible Minorities in the Canadian Expeditionary Force,' *Canadian Historical Review* 70, no. 1 (1989), 5.
72 Ibid., 7–11.
73 Ibid., 12.
74 Brown and Cook, *Canada 1896–1921*, 224.

75 Quoted in ibid., 224.
76 Ibid., 225. Historian Gregory Kealey argues that class conflict rather than ethnic divisions motivated most government policies during the war: '[The] largely immigrant composition of the Canadian working class allowed some government actions to be justified in terms of ethnic chauvinism, but the state's willingness to move against Canadian-born and British immigrant workers with equal vigour suggests that class, not ethnicity, motivated its actions.' Kealey acknowledges that a great deal of scholarly attention has been focused on the Canadian government's internment of Japanese during the Second World War, but scant research has focused on the internment of thousands of Ukrainians during the First World War. By the time the internment camps closed for good in June 1920, well over 8,000 people had been interned (8,579 men, 81 women, and 156 children, including 5,954 'Austrians' [Ukrainians], 2,009 Germans, 205 Turks, 99 Bulgarians, and 312 miscellaneous). Gregory S. Kealey, 'State Repression of Labour and the Left in Canada, 1914–20: The Impact of the First World War,' *Canadian Historical Review* 73, no. 3 (1992), 282–93.
77 D.G. Boyce, *Nationalism in Ireland*, 2nd ed. (New York and London: Routledge, 1991), 296.
78 David Fitzpatrick, *Politics and Irish Life, 1913–1921: Provincial Experience of War and Revolution* (Cork: Cork University Press, 1998), 192.
79 Ibid., 107.
80 Arthur Griffith's political philosophy embodied political and economic components designed to enhance, strengthen, and solidify Irish independence. In 1906, Griffith produced a pamphlet and a series of articles titled *The Resurrection of Hungary*, which cited the nineteenth-century Hungarian abstentionist policy as an example of methods that might be applied to attain Ireland's political independence. In 1861 the Hungarian deputies refused to take their seats in the Austrian parliament in protest over their political subservience to Austria; the result was the *Ausgleich* of 1867, whereby Austria and Hungary became two separate political entities linked by the Austrian emperor. Griffith saw a great deal of similarity between the Hungarian model and the 1782 Irish parliamentary arrangement with England known as Grattan's parliament. Griffith proposed that Irish electors abstain from taking their seats at Westminster until Ireland was bestowed with its rightful independence. After independence was conferred, the link with the Crown would be maintained to allay the fears of the Unionist section of Ireland. For Griffith, this seemed a far more substantive solution than Home Rule, regarding which Griffith once noted: 'If this is liberty the lexicographers have deceived us.'

Griffith's economic philosophy cited the economic achievements of Britain and the United States, which had developed indigenous resources and industries through protectionism. Britain and the United States had developed their resources and industrialized by using tariffs to protect fledgling industries. For Griffith, it stood to reason that 'Irish industries must be protected and secured if the nation were to be saved ... Tariff barriers and protection and encouragement for home industries were as much a part of the nation's needs as art and literature.' Seán Ó Lúing, 'Arthur Griffith and Sinn Féin,' in Martin, *Leaders and Men*, 58–61; Boyce, *Nationalism in Ireland*, 296.
81 Fitzpatrick, *Politics and Irish Life*, 123.
82 Ibid., 123.
83 Seamus Dunn and Thomas W. Hennessey, 'Ireland,' in Seamus Dunn and T.G. Fraser, eds., *Europe and Ethnicity: The First World War and Contemporary Ethnic Conflict* (London: Routledge, 1996), 185.
84 Roy Foster, *Modern Ireland, 1600–1972* (London: Penguin, 1989), 486.
85 Dunn and Hennessey, 'Ireland,' 185.
86 E. Morrison to Sir Edward Carson, 15 May 1917; D. Dobson to Sir Edward Carson, 19 May 1917; S.C. Bird to Sir Edward Carson, 23 May 1917; J. Phillip to Sir Edward Carson, 23 May 1917, Carson Irish Papers, MIC/665/5/D1507/A/23/19, 20, 22, 23, Public Records Office of Northern Ireland, Belfast.
87 Sir Edward Carson Irish Papers, MIC/665/5/D1507/A/27/16, Public Records Office of Northern Ireland, Belfast.
88 John W. Boyle, 'Robert Lindsay Crawford, 1910–1922: A Fenian Protestant in Canada,' in Robert O'Driscoll and Lorna Reynolds, eds., *The Untold Story: The Irish in Canada*, vol. II (Toronto: Celtic Arts of Canada, 1988), 635. In Ireland, Crawford was originally a member of the Orange Order and a journalist, serving as editor of the *Ulster Guardian*. At some point around 1903 he came to realize that Ireland's best hope for salvation lay in Home Rule. That same year he helped found the Independent Orange Order, which was dedicated to building closer ties between Protestants and Catholics. In 1906, Crawford wrote the Magheramorne Manifesto calling for Irish Catholics and Protestants to unite for the common good of Ireland. In 1908 his liberal leanings became too much for the *Ulster Guardian*; he lost his editorship and was expelled from the Independent Orange Order. With few employment prospects, Crawford moved to Canada in 1910.
89 'Mr. Lloyd George's Lost Opportunity,' *Catholic Register*, 3 May 1917, 1.
90 Fitzpatrick, *Politics and Irish Life*, 124. These sentiments were not lost on Irish-Canadian nationalists. An editorial in *New Freeman* on 25 August

1917 commented: 'The policy of the government, particularly since the outbreak of the war; the extreme measures employed after the Easter Week trouble, and the general distrust inculcated by the placing in high office of men who, as leaders of the Orange section had set up the standard of revolt in Ulster ... has had the effect of driving to the Sinn Fein standard many men of moderate views who had hither to been supporters of the Nationalist party.'

91 Ibid.
92 'The Irish Situation,' *Catholic Register*, 15 March 1917, 4.
93 'Is Ireland Republican?' *Catholic Register*, 17 May 1917, 1.
94 'The Belfast Fist is Wobbling,' *New Freeman*, 15 September 1917, 4.
95 Dunn and Hennessey, 'Ireland,' 186.
96 'Home Rule for Conscription,' *New Freeman*, 13 April 1918, 4.
97 Kenneth McNaught, *The Penguin History of Canada* (Toronto: Penguin, 1988), 215.
98 Ibid., 216–17.
99 Lower, *Colony to Nation*, 465.
100 Stacey, *Canada and the Age of Conflict*, 218.
101 Ibid.
102 'Ireland,' *New Freeman*, 1 June 1918, 4.
103 St Patrick's Society of Montreal, 4 March 1917, *Society Meeting Minute Book, 4 April 1916 to 27 January 1919*, 23, Concordia University Archives, Montreal.
104 Ibid. The St Patrick's Society meeting book notes on 7 May 1917: 'An acknowledgment of the receipt of the cablegram of the Society to the Premier Sir Robert Borden, London March 16/17 on the settlement of the Home Rule question,' 44. Apparently, a cable was sent to Borden, though exactly what the cable said is not certain.
105 Ibid., 43.
106 Ibid., 107.
107 D.A. Casey to Charles Murphy, 27 March 1918, Charles Murphy Papers, MG 27 III B8, vols. 5–8, 1752–3, LAC.

## Chapter Four

1 B.M. Walker, ed., *Parliamentary Election Results in Ireland, 1801–1922* (Dublin: Royal Irish Academy, 1978), xiii. However, as late as 1910 the Irish electorate was an elite propertied electorate consisting of only 700,00 electors. However, with the passage of the Representation of the People Act of 1918, more than 2 million Irish voters were eligible for the 1918 general election.

2 Diarmaid Ferriter, *The Transformation of Ireland* (Woodstock: Overlook, 2004), 196–7; J.J. Lee, *Ireland 1912–1985: Politics and Society* (Cambridge: Cambridge University Press, 1989), 40–1.
3 Edmund Curtis and R.B. McDowell, eds., *Irish Historical Documents, 1172–1922* (London: Methuen, 1943), 319–20. The Democratic Program stated in part:

> The Irish Republic fully realizes the necessity of abolishing the present odious, degrading and foreign poor law system, substituting therefore a sympathetic native scheme for the nation's aged and infirm, who shall no longer be regarded as a burden, but rather entitled to the nation's gratitude and consideration. Likewise it shall be the duty of the Republic to take measures that will safeguard the health of the people and ensure the physical as well as moral well-being of the nation.
>
> It shall be our duty to promote the nation's resources, to increase the productivity of the soil, to exploit the mineral deposits, peat bogs and fisheries, its water ways and harbours, in the interest and for the benefit of the Irish people.

4 Richard Davis, 'The Self-Determination for Ireland Leagues and the Irish Race Convention in Paris, 1921–1922,' *Tasmanian Historical Association Papers* 24 (1977), 89. Malcolm Campbell notes that as a result of the strong imperial connection, 'the Irish-Australian response to developments in Ireland was throughout the period always more constrained and timid than that found among Irish immigrant communities in the United States.' Malcolm Campbell, 'Emigrant Responses to War and Revolution, 1914–1921: Irish Opinion in the United States and Australia,' *Irish Historical Studies* 32, no. 25 (May 2000), 76.
5 An anti–Home Rule rally held under the auspices of the Canadian Unionist League at Queen's Park in Toronto on 8 May 1914 attracted 6,000 adherents. The rally was chaired by Toronto mayor H.C. Hocken, who read a cable from Edward Carson declaring: 'We fight against betrayal and for civil and religious liberty. Will Canada help us?' The crowd responded with 'a wild burst of cheering, shouting: 'We will; we will,' as they waved their hats and countless small flags and banners.' *Orange Sentinel*, 14 May 1914, 12.
6 A familiar Irish nationalist refrain, in reference to the notion developed during the Gaelic Revival of the 1890s that Ireland had been a unified nation during Celtic times and would some day be a nation again. This notion was transferred across the Atlantic and openly espoused in at least two of Canada's Irish-Catholic weeklies. 'Home Rule Goes into Law – Ireland Again a Nation,' *Catholic Register*, 28 May 1914, 1; 'Nation Once More,' *New Freeman*, 6 June 1914, 1.

7 One example of support for Sinn Féin emanated from D.A. Casey, editor of the *Canadian Freeman*, an Irish-Catholic weekly published in Kingston. Casey wrote to Canadian MP Charles Murphy to thank him for defending the Catholic faith in a recent parliamentary debate. D.A. Casey to Charles Murphy, 27 March 1918, Charles Murphy Papers, MG 27 III B8, vols. 5–8, 1752–3, LAC. For more, see previous chapter.
8 'Ireland,' *New Freeman*, 4 January 1919, 4. Similarly, Toronto's *Catholic Register* assessed the election victory as such: 'The Sinn Fein party in Ireland has won an overwhelming victory at the polls, and the Nationalist Party is practically blotted out of existence. Even those who are opposed to the Sinn Fein policy admit the result was inevitable. A whole people cannot be cajoled and disappointed again and again for generations without at last losing patience with their tormenters ... The Irish people were put off with sly political tricks and subterfuge. Conventions were called and their findings disregarded. Home Rule Bills were passed and not put into execution, rebellions were fomented and mercilessly extinguished in blood ... Sinn Fein is the outcome, a republican party demanding full freedom of a nation for Ireland.' 'The Sinn Fein Victory,' *Catholic Register*, 9 January 1919, 4.
9 *The Gazette* (Montreal), reprinted in 'To the Council of Nations,' *New Freeman*, 18 January 1919, 1.
10 Ibid. A resolution unanimously adopted at the rally read:
It is expedient on the occasion of the general readjustment of European affairs by the Peace Conference that the cause of Ireland and her future status be taken into practical consideration, with a view to the immediate securing for her of the same rights, guarantees and liberties as are proposed to be accorded to the smaller nations of Europe;

That such rights, guarantees and liberties take the form of the advantage of self-government according to their respective requirements and ideals, the assurance of which to the smaller nations the statesmen of Great Britain declared to be one of the principal motives actuating the Allies in taking up arms in the recent war.
11 *New Freeman*, 18 January 1919, 6.
12 Ibid.
13 Ibid.
14 Ibid.
15 'K. of C. in Sinn Fein,' *Orange Sentinel* (Toronto), 30 January 1919, 1.
16 Ibid.
17 C.P. Stacey, *Canada and the Age of Conflict: A History of Canadian External Policies*, vol. I, *1867–1921* (Toronto: Macmillan, 1977), 213–14.
18 Ibid.

19 As historian Keith Jeffery notes, this conflict is varyingly referred to as the War of Independence, the Anglo-Irish War, or the Black and Tan War. Jeffery states that the most 'pleasingly neutral term' is simply The Troubles, but this name generates confusion because the conflict in Northern Ireland since 1969 has also euphemistically been called The Troubles. See Keith Jeffery, 'British Security Policy in Ireland, 1919–1921,' in Peter Collins, ed., *Nationalism and Unionism: Conflict in Ireland, 1885–1921* (Belfast: Institute of Irish Studies, Queen's University, 1996), 163–4.
20 Ibid., 164.
21 Ibid., 165.
22 Ferriter, *The Transformation of Ireland*, 231.
23 Jeffery, 'British Security Policy in Ireland,' 165.
24 D.G. Boyce, *Englishmen and Irish Troubles: British Public Opinion and the Making of Irish Policy, 1918–1922* (Cambridge, MA: MIT, 1972), 50.
25 Paul Bew, *Ireland: The Politics of Enmity, 1789–2006* (Oxford: Oxford University Press, 2007), 397.
26 David Fitzpatrick, 'Militarism in Ireland, 1900–1922,' in Thomas Bartlett and Keith Jeffery, eds., *A Military History of Ireland* (Cambridge: Cambridge University Press, 1996), 404.
27 Ibid.
28 Fergus Campbell, *Land and Revolution: Nationalist Politics in the West of Ireland, 1891–1921* (Oxford: Oxford University Press, 2005), 263.
29 Beginning in early 1920, the *Orange Sentinel* (Toronto) reported on these kinds of attacks and activities in a regular column titled 'Week's News From Ireland.' On one occasion it described the Sinn Féin Volunteers as a well-organized force:

> The British troops are beginning to realize that they have not gone to Ireland on a picnic. They are up against a fully organized Sinn Fein army practicing the tactics of guerilla warfare, which were employed with so much success by the Boers in the first part of the South African War ...
>
> A military and police patrol of twelve fully armed men – Cameron Highlanders – was surprised and disarmed on Saturday night, June 5, by a company of 100 armed Sinn Feiners. The incident took place between Carrigtohill and Middleton, about seven miles from Queenstown.
>
> The men of the patrol were riding bicycles at the time. The Highlanders were traveling with fixed bayonets. The attacking party were also on bicycles, and after collecting the rifles and ammunition and the bicycles of the patrol, they rode off. The disarmed patrol made its way to Middleton on foot.

The men were apparently playing bowls and opened on both sides of the road to let the patrol pass. As the soldiers moved through, the men suddenly closed in, and before resistance could be offered, deprived the military of their rifles and ammunition. They also took away the police's revolvers.

See *Orange Sentinel*, 17 June 1920, 3.
30 D.G. Boyce, *Englishmen and Irish Troubles*, 45.
31 Ferriter, *The Transformation of Ireland*, 233.
32 Charles Townshend, 'British Policy in Ireland, 1906–1921,' in D.G. Boyce, ed., *The Revolution in Ireland, 1879–1923* (Dublin: Gill and Macmillan, 1988), 190. See also Karen Stanbridge, 'Nationalism, International Factors, and the 'Irish Question' in the Era of the First World War,' *Nations and Nationalism* 11, no. 1 (2005), 37.
33 Jeffery, 'British Security Policy in Ireland,' 168.
34 Examples include 'The Rule of Force,' *New Freeman*, 26 April 1919, 4; 'Walsh Report,' *Catholic Register*, 26 June 1919, 1; 'What Military Rule in Ireland Means,' *New Freeman*, 5 July 1919, 1; 'Atrocities in Ireland,' *Catholic Register*, 10 July 1919, 1; 'The Military Raid on 'The Freeman's Journal,'' *New Freeman*, 10 January 1920, 2; 'A Parallel to Murder of Cork's Mayor,' *New Freeman*, 24 April 1920, 5; and 'Organized Terrorism in Ireland,' *New Freeman*, 27 November 1920, 1.
35 'Denunciation,' *Catholic Register*, 7 October 1920, 4.
36 *Manchester Guardian*, 24 September 1920, in 'The Wanton Destruction of the Irish Town of Balbriggan,' *New Freeman*, 16 October 1920, 1.
37 The tone of the report presented to the British cabinet regarding the attack on Balbriggan was far different from that presented in the *Manchester Guardian*. Sir Hamar Greenwood, a Canadian, replaced Sir Ian MacPherson as Chief Secretary of Ireland on 12 April 1920. Regarding the sack of Balbriggan, Greenwood reported to Cabinet: 'The Police ... executed summary vengeance for the death of their comrade by killing two reputed Sinn Féin leaders and committing extensive destruction of property in the town. Among the buildings which were totally destroyed was the well-known hosiery factory of Messrs Deedes Templar & Co., which gave employment to a large number of people in the district.' An English civil servant in Dublin Castle named Mark Sturgis wrote of the disaster: 'Worse things can happen than the firing up of a sink like Balbiggan.' D.G. Boyce, *Englishmen and Irish Troubles*, 47, 52.
38 'The Results of Alien Rule,' *Catholic Register*, 4 September 1919, 4.
39 'Things As They Are,' *New Freeman*, 12 July 1919, 4.
40 'The Irish Question,' *Catholic Register*, 22 July 1920, 4.

41 St Patrick's Society of Montreal, *Society Meeting Minute Book,* 13 March 1918, 107. Concordia University Archives, Montreal.
42 Thomas R. Donovan to Robert Borden, 1 March 1919, Robert Borden Papers, MG 26 H1, vol. 158, 85236, LAC.
43 Ibid. This letter and the resolution were sent to Prime Minister Borden by Thomas R. Donovan of Ottawa, the Ontario Provincial Secretary of the Ancient Order of Hibernians, who was acting as the Secretary of the Resolution Committee for the Ottawa rally. *Minutes of the Provincial Board of the Ancient Order of Hibernians – Province of Ontario,* 8 October 1917. Charles J. Foy Papers, MU 1062, file 14, Archives of Ontario [hereafter Foy 14].
44 St Patrick's Society of Montreal, *Society Meeting Minute Book 1919–1935,* 1 December 1919, Concordia University Archives, Montreal.
45 *Northwest Review* (Winnipeg), in *New Freeman,* 8 May 1920, 1.
46 Ibid.
47 'Irish-Canadian Convention,' *New Freeman,* 8 May 1920, 1.
48 Ibid.
49 *Working Plan for Use in Organization of Self-Determination for Ireland League of Canada,* Foy 14. Hereafter the Self-Determination for Ireland League of Canada will be referred to simply as the League.
50 Peter Hart, *Mick: The Real Michael Collins* (New York: Penguin, 2005), 227.
51 Quoted in Davis, 'The Self-Determination for Ireland Leagues,' 91; Frank Walsh to Katherine Hughes, 13 September 1919, Frank Walsh Papers, box 28, file September 1919, New York Public Library.
52 Mark G. McGowan, *The Waning of the Green: Catholics, the Irish, and Identity in Toronto, 1887–1922* (Montreal and Kingston: McGill-Queen's University Press, 1999), 180–1.
53 'The Will of the Irish People Must Rule in Ireland,' *New Freeman,* 24 July 1920, 1.
54 *Halifax Chronicle,* in *New Freeman,* 17 July 1920, 8. A resolution adopted at the Halifax rally read:
   Whereas Nova Scotians are mindful of the struggle waged by their forefathers for responsible government in the Province and, as free men and women, could not tolerate a return to the autocratic institutions of previous years;
   Be it resolved that we citizens of Halifax – the capital city of Nova Scotia, in mass meeting assembled, July 11, 1920, do extend to the people of Ireland our sympathy in the present crisis.
   And be it further resolved that a cablegram be forwarded to the Honorable Lloyd George respectfully protesting against the refusal to

extend to Ireland the principle for which Nova Scotia soldiers sincerely believed they were battling in the Great War.
55 'The Will of the Irish People Must Rule in Ireland,' *New Freeman*, 24 July 1920, 1. At the beginning of this article, under the bolded headline '**On A Sound Canadian Basis**,' the *New Freeman* printed the objectives of the League: 'To secure organized support for the right of the people of Ireland to choose freely their own governmental institutions and their relationship with other nations and peoples without coercion or dictation from outside.'
56 Arthur R.M. Lower, *Colony to Nation: A History of Canada* (Toronto: Longmans, Green, 1946), 467.
57 'The Will of the Irish People Must Rule in Ireland,' *New Freeman*, 24 July 1920, 1. At the Winnipeg rally, Samuel Jordan was elected Provincial Organizing Secretary for Manitoba. Samuel Jordan was a man of some prominence, not only in Winnipeg but in Irish circles as well. Jordan was an Irish Protestant, born in Belfast in 1866, who migrated to New Zealand at the age of eighteen. He returned in 1890 to participate in the Irish Plan of Campaign, 'a system of rural collective bargaining organized by two of Parnell's chief lieutenants.' Jordan remained loyal to Parnell after the split in 1891, and when unity was re-established in 1900 under John Redmond, Jordan became active in the United Irish League. Joseph Devlin, the Irish leader of the Ancient Order of Hibernians and Nationalist MP for West Belfast, picked Jordan to establish a United Irish League branch in Winnipeg. While in Winnipeg, Jordan became president and manager of the Manitoba Stock Food Company and was instrumental in establishing a branch of United Irish League. Richard Davis, 'Irish Nationalism in Manitoba, 1870–1922,' in Robert O'Driscoll and Lorna Reynolds, eds., *The Untold Story: The Irish in Canada* (Toronto: Celtic Arts of Canada, 1988), 399–401.
58 *Northwest Review*, 28 August, in *New Freeman*, 4 September 1920, 1. New membership applications included 182 from Regina, 200 from Saskatoon, 289 from Calgary, 278 from Edmonton, and 490 from Vancouver.
59 *New Freeman*, 4 September 1920, 1, 4. The members of the Executive Committee were Lieutenant C.C. Kernahan, chairman; Andrew Urquart, secretary; H.J. Loughren, Treasurer, CPR Department of Natural Resources; Vivian Doran, Whalen Pulp and Paper Co.; T.J. Kearney, funeral director; J.M. McNeil, McNeil Lumber Co.; F.E. McFeely, broker; P.F. Sheehan, timber broker; W.E. Hennesey, wholesale tobacconist; Dr W.D. Kennedy; F.J. Gillespie, Municipal Commissioner for South Vancouver; W.P. Tierney, railway contractor; and T.J. Byrne, provincial agent for the Underwood Typewriter Co.
60 Kenneth McNaught, *The Penguin History of Canada* (London: Penguin, 1988), 225–6.

61 Gregory S. Kealey and Reg Whitaker, eds., *R.C.M.P. Security Bulletins, The Early Years: 1919–1929* (St John's: Canadian Committee on Labor History, 1994), 14.
62 Ibid.
63 Ibid., 43.
64 Ibid., 192.
65 *Notes of the Work of the C.I.B. Division for the Week Ending 26th August, No. 38 Memorandum*, 1–2, Arthur Lewis Sifton Papers, MG 27, III D 19, vol. 9, LAC [hereafter Sifton 9].
66 Ibid., 1.
67 Ibid., 1–2.
68 Ibid., 2.
69 Ibid., 3.
70 Kealey and Whitaker, *R.C.M.P. Security Bulletins*, 284; *New Freeman*, 28 August 1920, 5.
71 *Notes of the Work*, 3, Sifton 9.
72 Ibid., 4–5.
73 Ibid., 5.
74 Ibid., 1.
75 *To Provide for the Salaries of a Minister and Councils to the Republic of Ireland*, H.R. 3404, Sixty-sixth Congress, First Session, 12 December 1919, 161–72.
76 Ibid., 292.
77 Ibid., 133. Earlier in his testimony, Lindsay Crawford said of his background and his beliefs: 'I belong to a family that has been established in Ireland for three centuries, one that has been for three centuries a Protestant family. It was an Orange family from the time Orangeism started. In due course, I became a member of the Grand Lodge, the Supreme Lodge, and the Imperial Grand Orange Lodge, representing all the Grand Orange Lodges in the world, a member of the Supreme Orange Lodge of the World, and when I stand before you as a man who believes in the Sinn Fein government, the principles underlying it, I represent the new protestant democracy in Ireland. I represent that section of Ireland that has been awakened to the tragedy of Ireland during the last century when brought into contact with actual facts.' Ibid., 126.
78 Frank Walsh to H.J. Stafford, 14 May 1921, Frank Walsh Papers, box 29, file 7–17 May 1921, New York Public Library. Frank Walsh's letter to H.J. Stafford concluded: 'The distribution for the members of the Federal Parliament is being made through the national headquarters of the Self-Determination for Ireland League of Canada and Newfoundland, through the kindness of Mr. Donovan, National Secretary. With best wishes for the success of the movement in Canada.'

79 N.J. Egan to Frank Walsh, 22 June 1921, Frank Walsh Papers, box 26, file 18–30 June 1921, New York Public Library. Some Irish Canadians suspected that their mail was being confiscated and read. Nicholas J. Egan, President of the League for British Columbia, informed Walsh that sending anything of a sensitive or confidential nature through the normal postal routes was ill advised. He concluded his letter to Walsh: 'As this letter is being mailed by a personal friend of mine who is crossing the border I take this opportunity of informing you that should you at any time wish to send me or this office information of a confidential nature if it is sent c/o E. Coen, New York Bldg, Seattle, it will be sent to me through a private source. I may say that most of the correspondence reaching this office from the States is opened by the authorities before being delivered.'

80 'The Self-Determination for Ireland League of Canada – Its Aims and Objects,' *New Freeman*, 21 August 1920, 1. The statement of objectives included this: 'The League aims to be educational. It proposes to acquaint Canadians, by means of printed literature – a heavy item of cost – with certain aspects of the situation in Ireland now withheld from them; to place Ireland's case for self-government before the people of Canada in its true light; to work and strive for an early and speedy settlement, both in the interests of Ireland and the Empire.'

81 Ibid.

82 'Why They 'Must' Meet in Toronto,' *Orange Sentinel*, 3 August 1920, 1; *Ottawa Citizen*, 19 October 1920, 13.

83 The New Brunswick Provincial Convention of the Self-Determination for Ireland League was held in Saint John, 28–30 September 1920. Katherine Greany, the Provincial Secretary, reported that the 110 attendees represented the 35 League branches and roughly 3,000 members in New Brunswick. One of the unanimously adopted resolutions of the convention read:

The New Brunswick Provincial Convention of the Self-Determination for Ireland League of Canada, in regular session convened in the city of St. John, desire to place on record their loyalty to Canada, her laws and institutions, governed by the King and the Parliament of Canada, and their high appreciation of their political affiliations with the several nations within the British Empire.

(1) 'Resolved, that we deplore the unfortunate conditions that now obtain in Ireland, one of our sister nations.

(2) 'That we as loyal Canadians, conscious of our freedom from enthrallment from without our borders, and happy in the enjoyment of prosperity and contentment, look with pain and alarm at the despotic and obsolete system of government administered in Ireland.

(3) 'That the military occupation and harassment of that country is contrary to all sense of justice and sound policy.

(4) 'That as the government of Ireland by the British authorities has never been to the liking of the Irish people, the time has surely arrived when by all the laws of God and man the people of Ireland should be peaceably permitted to determine their own form of government, along lines that in their judgement will conserve best to their happiness and prosperity. Therefore.

(5) 'Resolved, that this Convention pledge its members to do all in their power to enlist the sympathy and cooperation of the people of the province, irrespective of class or creed to the removal of so dangerous a situation, that not only disturbs the Empire, but reflects discredit on it throughout the world.

'The Provincial Convention,' *New Freeman*, 9 October 1920, two-page additional supplement.
84 Self-Determination for Ireland League of Canada, National Convention Committee Letter, n.d., Charles J. Foy Papers, MU 1062, file 16, Archives of Ontario [hereafter Foy 16].
85 Ibid.
86 'Spiked the Guns of the Canadian Sinn Fein,' *Orange Sentinel*, 26 October 1920, 8.
87 'Ottawa Police Force Protects Sinn Fein,' *Orange Sentinel*, 26 October 1920, 8.
88 'Self-Determination League Ends Successful Convention,' *Ottawa Citizen*, 19 October 1920, 13. The article continued: 'There had been much talk of a counter demonstration, and inflammatory news stories written of the prospects of a 'red riot.' They did not materialize. It is true there was a large crowd outside St. Patrick's hall on Saturday night, but it was chiefly composed of youths and men who were looking for what they described as 'fun.''
89 Ibid.
90 Ibid. Crawford's conclusion of the letter was received 'with wild enthusiasm by the entire gathering, which stood cheering and waving hats, canes, and Sinn Fein flags.' The Sinn Féin flags described in the article were the Irish tricolor – green, white, and orange – first unveiled atop the General Post Office in Dublin during the 1916 Easter Rising.
91 Ibid. Miss Hughes also stated that 'she had been told by a Canadian cabinet minister from one of the provinces, after he had visited Ireland, that opinion over there was that England had forever lost the power to govern Ireland.'

92 Ibid.
93 Ibid.
94 Ibid.
95 Ibid.
96 Ibid.
97 Ibid. The second resolution read:
> Whereas the right to freedom is a natural right appertaining to all people; and whereas the principle of sovereignty resides in the people; and whereas the principle of self-determination is a recognition of these inalienable rights ...
>
> Be it therefore resolved: That the National Convention of the Self-Determination for Ireland League of Canada, comprised of delegates from every province in Canada and from the Dominion of Newfoundland, irrespective of race and creed – recalling with grateful remembrance our own Canadian struggle for parliamentary freedom and conscious of the determination of all Canadians to control the destinies of their own country, hereby resolve to uphold the people of Ireland in the exercise of their rights to determine their own form of government.

98 Ibid.
99 Ibid., 19. The Rev. Father Quilty of Douglas, Ontario, who had also recently returned from Ireland, similarly stated: 'The bigotry in Belfast was due to the money of the big interests, just as much as the bigotry of the Canadian press was due to a bunch at the Chateau Laurier who worked the game to fool the people and get their money.'
100 Davis, 'Irish Nationalism in Manitoba,' 399.
101 'French Canada and Irish Are Now Linked Up,' *Ottawa Citizen*, 19 October 1920, 13.
102 Ibid., 18.
103 Ibid.
104 Ibid. Crawford concluded: 'We go tomorrow to meet President de Valera (cheers) [in Ogdensburg], and will give the same message to him as we send to Quebec. Not because we are of Irish blood, but because we are Canadians, [we] love liberty and are ready to fight for it. Out of this persecution will come a better Ireland where there shall be no leading into captivity or mourning in her streets.'
105 Lindsay Crawford to Daniel Cohalan, 11 January 1922, 2, in Daniel Cohlan Papers, box 3, folder 16, American Irish Historical Society, New York City.
106 *The Gazette* (Montreal), 26 October 1920, 2.
107 *New Freeman*, 9 October 1920.

108 *New Freeman*, 6 November 1920, 5. The St Patrick's Society of Montreal cabled the widow of Mayor MacSwiney. The cablegram read: 'St. Patrick's Society of Montreal joining with you in prayer for the eternal repose of the soul of your husband, the late Lord Mayor of Cork, tenders to you and all the members of the family, its deepest sympathy. The sacrifice and the suffering of the late Lord Mayor, calls for the admiration and respect of all thinking peoples, who realize that he gave up his life in order that the principle of the right of a people to govern itself should not die. His death has furnished the world with proof of the grandeur of the soul of men. May Providence sustain and console you in your great trial, and bring peace and justice to Ireland.'
109 Ibid.
110 'Lindsay Crawford's Maritime Tour,' *New Freeman*, 20 November 1920, 1.
111 'Lindsay Crawford's Maritime Tour,' *New Freeman*, 11 December 1920, 1.
112 'Protest Against Crawford Meeting,' *Evening Times and Star* (Saint John), 29 November 1920.
113 Ibid. The resolution read:
Whereas, it is proposed that an individual by the name of Lindsay Crawford is to address a public meeting in the city of St. John, at an early date, and

Whereas, this Lindsay Crawford has by the writing of seditious, disloyal and unpatriotic articles and by speeches, in public, both in Canada and the United States of America of a similar nature, proven himself to be antagonistic to the constitutional authority of the British empire of which our dominion forms one of the most loyal portions and the people of this city some of its most loyal subjects, and

Whereas, the propaganda of the said Lindsay Crawford is carried on with the avowed intention of the disintegration of the empire, for the preservation of which large numbers of the best of our sons went through all the horrors of years of modern warfare and for which more than fifty thousand made the supreme sacrifice, lying buried in far off Flander's fields, therefore

Be it resolved, that this meeting of loyal citizens of this Loyalist city do strongly and unanimously appeal to the civic authorities to forbid this disloyal individual the right of addressing a public meeting in our city; and further

Be it resolved, that this meeting calls upon the government of the dominion to take immediate steps for the suppression of the publication of the journal, known as 'The Statesman,' edited by the said Lindsay Crawford and published in the city of Toronto.

114 Ibid.
115 'Lindsay Crawford's Address on the Irish Situation,' *New Freeman*, 11 December 1920, 10.
116 Ibid., 9.
117 'Lindsay Crawford's Maritime Tour,' *New Freeman*, 11 December 1920, 1.
118 Ibid.
119 Ibid. Joining Crawford and Donovan on the platform in Bathurst were the local MP, the Hon. O. Turgeon; the mayor of Bathurst, T.M. Burns, and the local district judge, E.L. O'Brien, a more disreputable and disloyal trio in the district having not been found. The resolutions adopted at the Bathurst meeting read:
 Whereas, the last war was fought to end all tyrannies and to free the small nations from oppression, and,
 Whereas, Ireland is a small nation; therefore be it;
 Resolved, that this mass meeting of the citizens of Bathurst and surrounding districts view with horror and indignation Lloyd George's 'hellish policy of reprisals in Ireland,' and join hands with the Irish people in the assertion of their inherent right to determine their own form of government free from outside interference.
 This meeting further protests against the organized efforts which are being made in this country to prevent a full and frank discussion of the Irish question and directs the attention of both the provincial and federal governments to the incitements to riot and disorder which are being made against free and lawful assembly on the public platform and through the columns of the press, and urges those responsible for the maintenance of law and order to bring these disturbers of the peace to book and so help in stamping out the sectarian bigotry and organized rowdyism which are disgracing this province and other parts of the Dominion.
120 'Moncton Rowdyism, A Disgrace to New Brunswick,' *New Freeman*, 11 December 1920, 4.
121 Ibid.
122 *Quebec Telegraph*, 8 December 1920, in *New Freeman*, 18 December 1920, 5.
123 Ibid. Lindsay Crawford stated:
 Efforts were made at St. John, N.B., by the same individuals to stir up opposition, but Mayor Schofield, brother of the Bishop of Vancouver, refused to allow the conspirators to interfere with our meeting ...
 Orangemen who have engineered this opposition throughout the maritime provinces are acting under directions from Toronto. It is significant that in most of the towns we visited the mayors were deluged

with telegrams from Toronto and elsewhere calling upon them to prohibit me from speaking. These Orangemen ignorantly assume that criticism of the British government is an attack on the British Empire and must be treated as seditious. They apparently do not understand the most elementary principles of government.

124 Ibid.
125 'Mobbed at Moncton Was Lindsay Crawford,' *Orange Sentinel*, 14 December 1920, 5; *Orange Sentinel*, 25 January 1290, 1.
126 *Quebec Chronicle*, n.d. On the platform with Lindsay Crawford were Major Chas. 'Chubby' Powers, MP; J.J. O'Connor, President of the Sarsfield Branch; and the chair of the rally, M. Monaghan of the Mutual Life Assurance Company of Canada.
127 Ibid. This figure seems a little exaggerated. A more likely total figure was 100,000.
128 Ibid.
129 Ibid.
130 *Minutes of National Council of the Self-Determination for Ireland League of Canada Meeting*, 17 January 1921, 1, Foy 16.
131 Ibid.
132 *Treasurers Report – 1 November 1920 to 17 January 1921*, Foy 16.
133 'Lord Mayor MacSwiney's Speech And Some Other Speeches,' *Irish Information Series No. 6*, New Brunswick Self-Determination for Ireland League, Miles E. Agar file, Archives of the Archdiocese of Saint John.
134 Ibid.
135 *Bulletin of the Nova Scotia Branch No. 4*, Halifax, 5 March 1921, Col. Maurice Moore Papers, Ms 10,582, 1–2, National Library of Ireland, Dublin [hereafter Moore Papers]. On page 2 of the bulletin under the heading 'The Principle of the League,' it stated: 'The business of the Self-Determination League is to tell the truth about Ireland, to teach the history of that unhappy country in order that there may be understanding of the present.'
136 *Bulletin of the Nova Scotia Branch No. 5*, Halifax, 14 March 1921, Moore Papers.
137 D. Lloyd George to Eamon de Valera, 7 September 1921, 'Copies of Communications between President de Valera, Sir James Craig, and Premier Lloyd George,' Frank Walsh Papers, box 26, file 18–30 June 1921, New York Public Library.
138 'The document was officially referred to in Ireland as the treaty, in England as the articles of agreement.' Curtis and McDowell, *Irish Historical Documents*, 322. Article 1 of the Treaty read: 'Ireland shall have the same

constitutional status in the community of nations known as the British Empire as the Dominion of Canada, the Commonwealth of Australia, the Dominion of New Zealand, and the Union of South Africa, with a parliament having powers to make laws for the peace, order and good government of Ireland and an executive responsible to that parliament, and shall be styled and known as the Irish Free State.'

139 John Loye to Frank Walsh, 1 July 1921, Frank Walsh Papers, box 26, file July 1921, New York Public Library.
140 Ibid.
141 Tim Pat Coogan, *Eamon de Valera: The Man Who Was Ireland* (New York: HarperCollins, 1993), 97, 189.
142 'The Victory of Ireland,' *Catholic Register*, 11 August 1921, 4.

**Chapter Five**

1 Article 12 of the Anglo-Irish Treaty, signed on 6 December 1921 by representatives of the British Government and the self-proclaimed Irish Republic, which created the Irish Free State in the southern portion of Ireland, provided for the establishment of a Boundary Commission to address the issue of the contested boundary between Northern Ireland and the Irish Free State.
2 See chapter 2.
3 *Report of Proceedings of the Grand Orange Lodge of British America 1919, Ottawa – July 30, 1919*, 14.
4 *Reports of the Provincial Grand Orange Lodge of Ontario West*, vol. 6, *1910–1919*, 36.
5 See chapter 2.
6 *Reports of the Provincial Grand Orange Lodge of Ontario West 1919, Woodstock – March 6, 1919*, 37. The Correspondence Committee members were E.T. Essery (Chairman), George L. Page, W.T. Magill, William J. Miller, and Rev. Henry A. Fish, D.G.C. (Secretary).
7 Canadian Orangemen vigorously supported the Ulster Unionists and the Ulster Volunteer Force during 1913 and 1914. In fact, a Canadian Unionist League formed in Canada that maintained an office in Belfast, thus creating a direct money pipeline from Toronto to Belfast. One example of this type of support was found in the *Orange Sentinel*, the official organ of Canadian Orangeism, which reported the approval of money being forwarded to Belfast: 'Regina, May 26 – Expressing approval of the course pursued by the Protestants in Ulster, the Grand Black Chapter of British North America, in session here to-day, passed a vote of $2,000, which will

be forwarded to the Canadian Unionist League in Belfast.' *Orange Sentinel*, 28 May 1914, 10.
8 'Ireland to Have Two Parliaments,' *Orange Sentinel*, 6 November 1919, 9; 'The Week's News From Ireland – Two Parliaments,' *Orange Sentinel*, 13 November 1919, 2; 'The Week's News From Ireland – What Ulster Thinks,' *Orange Sentinel*, 20 November 1919, 2; 'Ulster Will Never Submit To a Sinn Fein Parliament,' *Orange Sentinel*, 15 January 1920, 10.
9 'Toronto Royally Welcomes Visiting Ulstermen,' *Orange Sentinel*, 19 February 1920, 1.
10 Ibid.
11 Ibid.
12 Ibid.
13 'Wild Welcome at the Orange Headquarters,' *Orange Sentinel*, 19 February 1920, 1.
14 'Blue and Hazelton At Cooke's Church,' *Orange Sentinel*, 19 February 1920, 3.
15 'Empire Club Luncheon the Greatest Event in Its History,' *Orange Sentinel*, 19 February 1920, 3.
16 'Toronto Royally Welcomes Visiting Ulstermen,' *Orange Sentinel*, 19 February 1920, 1.
17 'Week's News From Ireland – Parliament's Power,' *Orange Sentinel*, 11 March 1920, 3.
18 Michael Laffan, *The Partition of Ireland, 1911–1925* (Dundalk: Dundalgan, 1983), 63.
19 In April 1914, Walter Long wrote to the Canadian Grand Master appealing for funds to help Ulster defend itself. The appeal was printed on the front page of the *Orange Sentinel*, and read: 'I have authority from Grand Master of Ireland to appeal to you as Grand Master of Canada for financial help, which he believes you will be good enough to give to the cause of Ulster. Contributions will be very gladly received by me. WALTER H. LONG, M.P., Union Defence League, 25 Victoria Street, London, S.W.' *Orange Sentinel*, 30 April 1914, 1.
20 John Kendle, *Walter Long, Ireland, and the Union, 1905–1920* (Dun Laoghaire: Glendale, 1992), 185.
21 According to the 1911 census, the Catholic populations of Cavan, Donegal, and Monaghan were 81.5, 78.9, and 74.7 per cent, respectively. J.J. Lee, *Ireland, 1912–1985: Politics and Society* (Cambridge: Cambridge University Press, 1989), 2.
22 Kendle, *Walter Long*, 188.
23 Patrick Buckland, 'Carson, Craig, and the Partition of Ireland, 1912–21,' in

Peter Collins, ed., *Nationalism and Unionism: Conflict in Ireland, 1885–1921* (Belfast: Institute of Irish Studies, Queen's University of Belfast, 1994), 87. The easternmost counties of Ulster contained the highest percentages of Protestants; as one moved west the percentages decreased: Antrim – 79.5 per cent; Down – 68.4 per cent; Armagh – 54.7 per cent; Londonderry – 54.2 per cent; Tyrone – 44.6 per cent; Fermanagh – 43.8 per cent.
24 Laffan, *The Partition of Ireland*, 65.
25 Buckland, 'Carson, Craig, and the Partition of Ireland,' 87.
26 Walter Long in Kendle, *Walter Long*, 191.
27 'Week's News From Ireland,' *Orange Sentinel*, 4 March 1920, 3.
28 'Possibilities in the New Plan for Ireland,' *Orange Sentinel*, 11 March 1920, 1. It must be remembered that in 1972 the Northern Ireland parliament, controlled from its inception by Ulster Unionists, was dissolved by Britain for its failure to govern justly and equitably.
29 'Two Irelands,' *Orange Sentinel*, 26 October 1920, 1.
30 *Loyal Orange Institution, New Brunswick, Reports and Proceedings 1919, Saint John – April 15, 1919*, 66. The Committee on Correspondence comprised W.E. Williams, John Petty, Stephen Scott, and George E. Day.
31 'An Unholy Alliance,' *Orange Sentinel*, 24 August 1920, 1; 'Another Link between Bolshevism & Sinn Fein,' *Orange Sentinel*, 3 January 1921, 3; 'The Great Conspiracy,' *Orange Sentinel*, 8 February 1921, 1.
32 'An Unholy Alliance,' *Orange Sentinel*, 24 August 1920, 1.
33 Ibid. In 1919, Frank P. Walsh, former chairman of the Commission on Industrial Relations and joint president of the National War Labor Board (appointed by President Woodrow Wilson), and Edward F. Dunne, former mayor of Chicago and former governor of Illinois, led an American delegation across Ireland to investigate accusations of British reprisals exacted against the Irish populace in the conduct of the undeclared Anglo-Irish War. The Walsh Report was highly critical of British forces, accusing them of indiscriminate acts of murder and arson. This undoubtedly did not sit well with Orange-Canadian unionists. 'Walsh Report,' *Catholic Register* (Toronto, Ontario), 26 June 1919, 1; Alan J. Ward, 'America and the Irish Problem, 1899–1921,' *Irish Historical Studies* 16 (1968), 83.
34 'An Unholy Alliance,' *Orange Sentinel*, 24 August 1920, 1.
35 Ibid.
36 *Report of Proceedings, Grand Orange Lodge of British America 1923, Winnipeg – July 18, 1923*, 27. Grand Master McPherson expanded his remarks: 'For a long time Moslems have been dissatisfied with the loss of political status, and Pan-Islamism seeks to restore the state as well as convert the world.' He described the Bolshevist revolution as the 'work mainly of German and

Russian Jews,' cautiously warning that 'the atheistic Jew is not confined to Europe. He is to be found in every walk of life on this continent, struggling to reach the top. His influence is sinister.' He described the Catholic Church as an aggressive force, one with 'aims to extend its influence throughout the entire world along religious, social, political and economic lines. To accomplish this the laity have been given a place never before occupied by them, and they are being organized into great bodies with wide programs.' Ibid., 34–5.

37 'Resolutions Passed at Mass Meeting of Halifax Citizens,' Arthur Meighen Papers, MG 26 I, vol. 31, reel C-3227 [hereafter Meighen 3227], 017923, LAC.
38 Rev. J.M. Ratcliff to Arthur Meighen, 31 March 1921, Meighen 3227, 017922.
39 Meighen to Reverend J.M. Ratcliff, 7 April 1921, Meighen 3227, 017924.
40 According to Gregory S. Kealey and Reg Whitaker, no fewer than forty-two surveillance reports on Irish nationalist organizations were filed by the Criminal Investigation Branch of the RCMP. Gregory S. Kealey and Reg Whitaker, *R.C.M.P. Security Bulletins, The Early Years: 1919–1929* (St John's: Canadian Committee on Labor History, 1994).
41 'Notes of the Work of the C.I.B. Division for the Week Ending 26th August, No. 38 Memorandum,' 1–2, Arthur Lewis Sifton Papers, MG 27, III D 19, vol. 9, LAC.
42 See also 'Spiked the Guns of the Canadian Sinn Fein,' *Orange Sentinel*, 26 October 1920, 8; 'Ottawa Police Force Protects Sinn Fein,' *Orange Sentinel*, 26 October 1920, 8.
43 *Orange Sentinel*, 26 October 1920, 1.
44 'Our Point of View,' *Orange Sentinel*, 28 December 1920, 1.
45 Ibid.
46 *Loyal Orange Institution, New Brunswick, Reports and Proceedings, 1919–1927*, 19 April 1921, 18–19.
47 Richard H. McDonald to Stephen B. Bustin, 31 May 1921, Grand Secretary Correspondence – January–June 1921, MC 1051, MS 5, Provincial Archives of New Brunswick.
48 Ibid., *12th Reolutions*.
49 Michael Farrell, *Arming the Protestants: The Formation of the Ulster Special Constabulary and the Royal Ulster Constabulary, 1920–1927* (London: Pluto, 1983), 18.
50 Thomas Hennessey, *A History of Northern Ireland* (New York: St Martin's, 1997), 13.
51 Marianne Elliott, *The Catholics of Ulster: A History* (London: Penguin, 2000), 374; Hennessey, *A History of Northern Ireland*, 13.

52 Elliott, *The Catholics of Ulster*, 374; Hennessey, *A History of Northern Ireland*, 11.
53 A.C. Hepburn, *Catholic Belfast and Nationalist Ireland in the Era of Joe Devlin, 1871–1934* (Oxford: Oxford University Press, 2008), 216; Elliott, *The Catholics of Ulster*, 374, 377; Hennessey, *A History of Northern Ireland*, 14.
54 'Londonderry Explained,' *Orange Sentinel*, 1 July 1920, 1.
55 Tony Gray, *The Orange Order* (London: The Bodley Head, 1972), 38.
56 'Cause of Trouble in Derry,' *Orange Sentinel*, 27 July 1920, 1.
57 Catholics did hunker down at St Columb's College and exchange fire, but only after the unprovoked attack in the shipyard, and after receiving two days of fire from Protestants perched behind the city walls. 'The fighting was bitter and sectarian ... The death toll by 23 June was twelve, eight Catholic and four Protestants.' Farrell, *Arming the Protestants*, 19–20.
58 Keith Middlemans, ed., *Thomas Jones: Whitehall Diary*, vol. 3, *Ireland 1918–1925* (London: Oxford University Press, 1971), 78.
59 'Toronto Friends of Ulster Congratulate New Parliament,' *Orange Sentinel*, 14 June 1921, 1. The report continued: 'Naturally, many of them were Ulstermen, with all the hot blood and high spirit of the men of that race. At the hall there were a large number of women showing the same spirit as the men. Together they formed an audience that displayed the loyal temper that has been the characteristic of Ulster for a century.'
60 Ibid.
61 Ibid. The adopted resolution at the rally read: 'Mass meeting of the friends of Ulster assembled in Victoria Hall, Toronto, desire to express to the Ulster electors hearty congratulations on the magnificent results of the recent election, and the determined expression to remain within the Union. Our best wishes go out to you for the success of the new Parliament, and we shall watch with greater interest than ever the growth and prosperity of Ulster within the Empire.'
62 'Our Point of View,' *Orange Sentinel*, 17 May 1921, 1.
63 *London Morning Post*, 15 December 1921, in 'Lord Carson's Great Speech on the Surrender to Sinn Fein,' *Orange Sentinel*, 10 January 1922, 1.
64 'Our Point of View,' *Orange Sentinel*, 13 December 1921, 1.
65 'Our Point of View,' *Orange Sentinel*, 21 February 1922, 1. Not to diminish the fact that people were killed, for that has always been the greatest tragedy to afflict Ireland's history, but one would think that if truly prominent Ulstermen had been assaulted in any way, news sources would have known whether they were in fact killed, wounded, or captured, and whether there were forty or sixty of them. (Recent scholarship seems to indicate that forty people were kidnaped; David Fitzpatrick, 'The Orange

Order and the Border,' *Irish Historical Studies* (May 2002), 57. Additionally, it seems odd that Ulstermen, and their descendants abroad, would bemoan the fact that they were not included among the Irish, when they themselves habitually proclaimed – as they still do – to be distinct from the Irish.

66 These sentiments were exemplified in a resolution adopted at the 1922 annual session of the Grand Orange Lodge of British America, which read:

'Resolved, – That this M.W. Grand Orange Lodge of B.A., in session assembled in the city of Kingston, representing the entire Orange Association of the Dominion of Canada and Newfoundland, desires to congratulate the people of Ulster on the magnificent and determined fight put up by them to protect the British people against destruction and endangering the integrity of the Empire by the granting of a parliament known as the Irish Free State, which, in our opinion, threatens the weakening if not the breaking of the ties that bind the Empire ...

The betrayal of Ulster, which for the sake of peace accepted the Northern Parliament, under the guarantee that it was a final settlement, is, in our opinion, one of the blackest acts in British history. It appears as though the British bludgeon is being used against Ulster, which is a most disgraceful return for the self-sacrifice and devotion of the most loyal subjects of His Majesty's Dominions.

This Grand Lodge is alarmed at the base and deplorable abandonment of the Irish Loyalists, and pledges itself to do all in its power to assist them in maintaining their position within the Empire.

*Reports of Proceedings of Grand Orange Lodge of British America 1922, Kingston, Ont. – June 22, 1922*, 92–3.

67 Grand Orange Lodge of New Brunswick Resolutions, MC 1051, MS 3, Provincial Archives of New Brunswick.

68 *Reports of Proceedings of Grand Orange Lodge of British America 1922, Kingston, Ont. – June 22, 1922*, 91.

69 Ibid. Another example of the intimate and emotional connection that Orange-Canadian unionists felt toward Ulster was the resolution of sympathy sent to Lady Wilson, wife of Field Marshal Sir Henry Wilson, one of Ulster's most devout allies and advisers in Britain, following his assassination on his London doorstep. The resolution read: 'Whereas this M.W. Grand Lodge has learned with horror of the brutal murder at London, almost at the foot of the Throne, of Field Marshal Sir Henry W. Wilson, M.P., Be it therefore resolved that we express our profound sympathy and sorrow with Lady Wilson and family, as well as with the people of Ulster and the Empire, in the great loss which they have sustained through the

death of this gallant and distinguished soldier and citizen, and record our indignation and utter abhorrence of the cowardly assassins who are guilty of so dastardly and cruel a crime.' Ibid., 92. For more on the assassination of Sir Henry Wilson, see Peter Hart, 'Michael Collins and the Assassination of Sir Henry Wilson,' *Irish Historical Studies* 28 (1992), 150–70.
70 *Report of Proceedings of the Grand Orange Lodge of British America 1923, Winnipeg – July 18, 1923*, 55.
71 *Report of Proceedings of Provincial Grand Orange Lodge of Ontario West 1923, Owen Sound, Ont. – March 14, 1923*, 21.
72 *Loyal Orange Institution, New Brunswick, Reports and Proceedings 1923, Fredericton, NB – April 18, 1923*, 74. In its entirety, the letter read:

12 Donegall Square West, Belfast, February, 1923.

Our Committee have received the Report of Brother William Coote, M.P., on his tour on our behalf and I am desired to convey our sincere thanks to you and all the friends in St. John, for the practical support you have rendered to the cause of distressed Protestants from the South of Ireland.

We are looking forward with confidence having the united support of the Brethren over-seas and at home to the future success of our Association on their behalf.

We are happy to say at the moment we have Peace in Ulster, but the condition of the South is every day becoming worse and our people there are looking to us in greater numbers for succour. It seems only a question of a short time until the Free State Government is set aside by the Republicans.
73 David Fitzpatrick, 'The Orange Order and the Border,' *Irish Historical Studies* 33, no. 129 (May 2002), 55–6.
74 Ibid., 56.
75 *Report of Proceedings of Grand Orange Lodge of British America 1923, Winnipeg – July 18, 1923*, 58.
76 Ibid., 148.
77 W. David McPherson to S.B. Bustin, 4 August 1922, Grand Master's Correspondence, MC 1051, MS 5, July–December 1922, Provincial Archives of New Brunswick.
78 Ibid.
79 Ibid.
80 *Reports of Proceedings, Grand Orange Lodge of British America, 1923, Winnipeg – July 18, 1923*, 147. The donations from the various Provincial Lodges and other sources was as follows:

Grand Orange Lodge of British America ............................$3,000.00

    Grand Black Chapter of British America ................................1,000.00
    Provincial Grand Lodge of Ontario East ................................6,600.00
    Provincial Grand Lodge of Saskatchewan .............................1,368.19
    Cavan Lodge, Sons and Daughters of Ireland ..........................100.00
    Provincial Grand Lodge of Manitoba ........................................841.00
    Provincial Grand Lodge of Nova Scotia ....................................334.94
    Grand Lodge, Sons and Daughters of Ireland ..........................200.00
    Provincial Grand Lodge of Ontario West ..................................133.00
    Provincial Grand Lodge of Prince Edward Island .....................27.75
    Sundry amounts received by Secy.-Treas ..................................345.85
    Collection at meeting of Grand Lodge, Kingston ....................240.50

81 John Herd Thompson with Allen Seager, *Canada 1922–1939: Decades of Discord* (Toronto: McClelland and Stewart, 1985), 76. This might explain Prince Edward Island's poor showing above.
82 Ibid.
83 Ibid., 77.
84 Sir James Craig in Laffan, *The Partition of Ireland*, 94.
85 Middlemans, ed., *Thomas Jones Whitehall Diary*, 230. Thomas Jones, Assistant Secretary to the British Prime Minister, noted: 'drafted a telegram ... from P.M. inviting Sir Robert Borden to be chairman of the Commission.'
86 R.L. Borden to Loring Christie, 8 May 1924, Robert L. Borden Papers, MG 30, E 15, vol. 12, reel C3883, 11293–11298, LAC.
87 R.L. Borden to Lord Beaverbrook, 9 October 1924, Robert L. Borden Papers, MG 27, II G1, file 16 December 1923–30 June 1925, LAC.
88 'Ulster Boundary Question,' *Orange Sentinel*, 22 January 1924, 1.
89 'Ulster to be Sacrificed Is Resolve of Labor Government,' *Orange Sentinel*, 5 August 1924, 1. The entire sentence read: 'Should such a measure pass the House civil war would be inevitable, as it is inconceivable that the Communist British Parliament would appoint to the Commission any representative who was not ready to carry out the desires of the conspirators [Irish Free State and British Government].'
90 *Report of Proceedings of Grand Orange Lodge of British America 1924, Sault Ste. Marie, Ont. – May 18, 1924*, 104.
91 Ibid., 211.
92 Ibid., 212.
93 Hepburn, *Catholic Belfast*, 256.
94 'The Irish Boundary Commission Resigns,' *Orange Sentinel*, 1 December 1925, 2.
95 Laffan, *The Partition of Ireland*, 104.
96 'Week's News From Ireland,' *Orange Sentinel*, 15 December 1925, 3.

97 'Peace in Ireland,' *Orange Sentinel*, 22 December 1925, 1.
98 Ibid.
99 Ibid.

**Chapter Six**

1 Patrick O'Farrell, *Ireland's English Question: Anglo-Irish Relations, 1534–1970* (New York: Schocken, 1971), 293–4. The passage continued: 'Not only was Britain adamant that any settlement with nationalist Ireland must be on the basis of the exclusion of Northern Ireland, and that Ireland must remain in and profess loyalty to the Empire, but Lloyd George resorted to trickery, threats and eventually an ultimatum of renewed and annihilating war in order to extort the Irish signatures.'
2 'Ireland,' *New Freeman*, 7 January 1922, 4.
3 Michael Laffan, *The Partition of Ireland, 1911–1925* (Dundalk: Dundalgan, 1983), 79–86.
4 'Irish Parliament Accepts Peace Treaty,' *New Freeman*, 14 January 1922, 1.
5 'Peace,' *Catholic Register*, 12 January 1922, 4.
6 'The Irish Free State,' *Catholic Register*, 19 January 1922, 4.
7 'The Irish Free State,' *New Freeman*, 21 January 1922, 4.
8 'Offensive Pity,' *Catholic Register*, 2 February 1922, 4.
9 J.J. Lee, *Ireland, 1912–1985: Politics and Society* (Cambridge: Cambridge University Press, 1989), 51.
10 Helen Litton, *The Irish Civil War: An Illustrated History* (Dublin: Wolfhound, 1995), 27.
11 Lindsay Crawford to Daniel Cohalan, 23 December 1921, 2, Daniel Cohalan Papers, box 3, folder 16, American Irish Historical Society, New York City [hereafter Colahan 16]
12 Crawford to Cohalan, 11 January 1922, 2, Cohalan 16.
13 'Ireland,' *New Freeman*, 22 April 1922, 4.
14 'Mr. De Valera's Position in Present Day Ireland,' *New Freeman* (reprinted from *Canadian Freeman*, Kingston), 6 May 1922, 3. It seems somewhat ironic that in the shift from constitutional nationalists to Sinn Féin republicans, Irish Canadians endorsed the use of non-constitutional methods to achieve independence, but in the leadup to the Irish Civil War they would again endorse constitutionalism as the appropriate method of settling disputes.
15 Litton, *The Irish Civil War*, 30.
16 'Irish Parliament Accepts Peace Treaty,' *New Freeman*, 14 January 1922, 1.
17 Dermot Keogh, *Twentieth-Century Ireland: Nation and State* (Dublin: Gill and Macmillan, 1994), 3.

18 'Complete Returns of Irish Election Show Strong Treaty Vote,' *New Freeman*, 1 July 1922, 1.
19 Litton, *Irish Civil War*, 67.
20 'The Irish Government Acts,' *New Freeman*, 8 July 1922, 4.
21 Litton, *The Irish Civil War*, 112.
22 One of the few editorial comments on the Irish Civil War stated: 'There is but one fly in the ointment – the foolish and regrettable rebellion of a few irreconcileables who doubtless mean well and are inspired by what to them seems high principles, but who are inflicting grave injury on their country and, by flouting the will of the people, have set themselves above the law and outside the pale.' 'The Irish Bishops Denounce Rebellion,' *Catholic Register*, 2 November 1923, 4.
23 'Ireland Bows at Bier of Michael Collins,' *Catholic Register*, 31 August 1922, 1. The *Catholic Register* also editorialized: 'All the world loves a brave man who is a lover of his country and his kind. When Michael Collins died for Ireland, the land of his love, the world bowed its head and laid the homage of its grief at the bier of the patriot. Its dirge was a dirge of praise for his chivalry and manhood, of admiration for his sterling qualities of soldier and statesman.' 'Michael Collins,' *Catholic Register*, 31 August 1922, 4.
24 Litton, *The Irish Civil War*, 131.
25 The press reports of loyalist violence against Belfast Catholics filled the Catholic weekly newspapers. In the first half of 1922 alone: 'Orange Mob Again Let Loose in Belfast,' *New Freeman*, 18 February 1922, 1; 'The Belfast Horror,' *New Freeman*, 25 March 1922, 3; 'The Belfast Terror,' *Catholic Register*, 6 April 1922, 1; 'The Orange Lambs,' *Catholic Register*, 6 April 1922, 4; 'Belfast Catholics Demand Protection for Refugees,' *New Freeman*, 27 May 1922, 1; 'Belfast Catholics Tell of Terrible Persecutions, Giving Facts and Figures,' *New Freeman*, 10 June 1922, 1; '"Christianity" in Belfast,' *New Freeman*, 17 June 1922, 4; 'Belfast's Shame,' *Catholic Register*, 13 July 1922, 4.
26 Copy of Telegram to His Excellency the Governor General from the President of the Self Determination for Ireland League of Canada and Newfoundland. William Lyon Mackenzie King Papers, MG 26, vol. 72, C-2243, 61212, LAC.
27 Memorandum for the Prime Minister. King Papers, MG 26, vol. 72, reel C-2243, 61213, LAC.
28 'Sketch of The Self-Determination for Ireland League in Province,' *New Freeman*, 17 March 1923, 12.
29 Ibid.
30 Ibid., 11.

31 Ibid.
32 'Our Attitude Towards the Free State,' *New Freeman*, 13 January 1923, 4. The letter to the publishers was dated 12 December 1922.
33 Ibid.
34 Ibid.
35 Ibid.
36 Crawford to Cohalan, 5 October 1923, Cohalan 16.
37 Ministry of Defence, Dublin, to Crawford, 12 May 1924, Cohlan 16.
38 Ministry of Defence, Dublin, to Crawford, 26 June 1924, Cohalan 16.
39 The President's Office, Dublin, to Crawford, Irish Trade Agent, 7 June 1924 and 7 July 1924, Cohalan 16.
40 John T. Hughes to Miss Katherine Hughes, 12 September 1924, Katherine Hughes Papers, MG 30, D 71, vol. 1, file 5 – Irish Nationalism, LAC.
41 Ibid.
42 *Proceedings of the Fifty-third National Convention of the Ancient Order of Hibernians in America*, held at Montreal, 17–23 July 1923, 93–5.
43 Ibid.
44 Ibid., 30.
45 Ibid., 91.
46 Report of Provincial President, Perth, Ontario, 17 August 1925, 4–5, Charles J. Foy Papers, MU 1062, file 14, Archives of Ontario.
47 Ibid., 3.
48 Margaret Churchill to Hanna Sheehy Skeffington, 14 September 1925, Hanna Sheehy Skeffington Papers, MS 24, 093, 4, National Library of Ireland, Dublin. Margaret Churchill signed her letters to Skeffington in Gaelic, 'Mairéad Ní Cillín,' with the salutation 'mise le meas mór.' This is a formal salutation meaning, 'I am with great respect.'
49 'Ireland after the Elections – A Review and a Forecast,' *Catholic Register*, 13 September 1923, 4.
50 Laffan, *The Partition of Ireland*, 99.
51 On 10 December the *Catholic Register* reported: 'The boundary will remain as it is. Britain will abandon its claims on the Free State for payment of the latter's share of the war debt, pensions, etc. The Free State assumes the responsibility of Britain for compensating the victims of the troubles in Ireland during the period of active fighting, and will increase by 10 per cent. the compensation it is required to pay under the act of 1923. The powers of the abortive Irish Council set up in 1920 are transferred, in so far as they affect Northern Ireland, to the Government of Northern Ireland.' 'Boundary Trouble Settled,' *Catholic Register*, 10 December 1925, 1.
52 'Ulster and the Free State,' *Catholic Register*, 10 December 1925, 4.

## Conclusion

1 'Lindsay Crawford's Maritime Tour,' *New Freeman*, 11 December 1920, 1.
2 *Orange Sentinel*, 14 May 1914, 12.
3 *Canadian Ulsterman* 1, no. 6 (1974), 2. Microfiche 326, Linen Hall Library, Belfast.
4 Ibid.
5 Steve Bruce, *The Red Hand: Protestant Paramilitaries in Northern Ireland* (Oxford: Oxford University Press, 1992), 168.
6 Ibid.
7 Ibid., 168–9.

# Bibliography

**Primary Sources**

*Census of Canada, 1921, Vol. I: Population,* 98-1921F.
*Canadian Annual Review of Public Affairs, 1912–1921*
*To Provide for the Salaries of a Minister and Consuls to the Republic of Ireland* – H.R. 3403, United States House of Representatives, Committee on Foreign Affairs, December, 1919.

*American Irish Historical Society, New York City*
Daniel Cohalan Papers
Friends of Irish Freedom Papers

*Archives of the Archdiocese of Toronto*
Bishop Neil McNeil Papers

*Archives of the Diocese of Saint John, NB*
Historical Files:
Miles Edgar Agar file
New Brunswick Self-Determination for Ireland League of Canada file

*Balch Institute for Ethnic Studies, Philadelphia, PA*
Ancient Order of Hibernians in America – National Convention Proceedings, 1910–1925

*Concordia University Archives, Montreal*
I/ St. Patrick's Society of Montreal – minutes

254  Bibliography

*Linen Hall Library, Belfast*
Canadian Ulster Loyalist Association Newsletter
Irish Freedom Association (Toronto) Newsletter
Irish Prisoners of War Committee (Vancouver) Newsletter

*National Archives of Canada*
Lindsay Crawford File
Katherine Hughes Papers
Charles Murphy Papers
Arthur Lewis Sifton Papers
Robert L. Borden Papers
W.L. Mackenzie King Papers
Arthur Meighen Papers

*National Library of Ireland, Dublin*
Lindsay Crawford Papers
Col. Maurice Moore Papers
Hannah Sheehy-Skeffington Papers

*New York Public Library, New York City*
Frank Walsh Papers
William J. Maloney Papers

*Provincial Archives of New Brunswick, Fredericton*
Annual Reports of Grand Orange Lodges of British America, Ontario West, and New Brunswick
Correspondence of Provincial Grand Secretary of the Grand Orange Lodge of New Brunswick

*Public Archives of Ontario, Toronto*
Charles J. Foy Papers
H.C. Hocken Papers
C.A. Jennings Papers

Newspapers
*Catholic Register and Canadian Extension* (Toronto, ON)
*Montreal Gazette*
*Montreal Star*
*The New Freeman* (Saint John, NB)
*The Northwest Review* (Winnipeg, MB)

*Ottawa Citizen*
*The Quebec Chronicle*
*Saskatoon Standard*
*The Sentinel and Orange and Protestant Advocate* (Toronto, ON)
*The St John Standard* (Saint John, NB)
*The Statesman* (Toronto, ON)
*Toronto Globe*
*Sydney Record* (Sydney, NS)

**Other Works**

Butler, John. 'Select Documents XLV: Lord Oranmore's Journal, 1913–27.' *Irish Historical Studies* 29 (1995): 553–93.
Jones, Thomas. *Whitehall Diary, vol. III, Ireland 1918–1925*. London: Oxford University Press, 1971.
O'Dea, John. *History of the Ancient Order of Hibernians in America and Ladies' Auxiliary*. 1923, ed. reprint. South Bend: University of Notre Dame Press.

**Dissertations and Theses**

Banks, Margaret A. 'Edward Blake and Irish Nationalism, 1892–1907.' PhD diss., University of Toronto, 1953.
Blake, Nelson M. 'The United States and the Irish Revolution, 1914–1922.' PhD diss., Clark University, 1936.
Horrall, Stanley W. 'Canada and the Irish Question: A Study of the Canadian Response to Irish Home Rule, 1882–1893.' MA thesis, Carleton University, 1966.
Jamison, Alden. 'Irish-Americans, the Irish Question, and American Diplomacy, 1895–1921.' PhD diss., Harvard University, 1942.
Ritchie, Donald H. 'Influences on the Imperial Connection in Ireland, 1928 to 1938.' MA thesis, University of Toronto, 1950.
Shanahan, David. 'The Irish Question in Canada: Ireland, the Irish, and Canadian Politics, 1880–1922,' PhD diss., Carleton University, 1989.

**Secondary Sources on Canada and The Irish in North America**

Acheson, T.W. 'The Irish Community in Saint John, 1815–1850.' In *New Ireland Remembered: Historical Essays on the Irish in New Brunswick*. Edited by P.M. Toner. Fredericton: New Ireland, 1988.

- *Saint John, The Making of a Colonial Urban Community*. Toronto: University of Toronto Press, 1985.
Akenson, Donald. *Being Had: Historians, Evidence, and the Irish in North America*. Toronto: P.D. Meany, 1985.
- 'The Historiography of English-Speaking Canada and the Concept of Diaspora: A Special Appreciation.' *Canadian Historical Review* 76 (1995): 377–409.
- *The Irish in Ontario: A Study in Rural History*. Montreal and Kingston: McGill–Queen's University Press, 1984.
- *Small Differences: Irish Catholics and Irish Protestants, 1815–1922: An International Perspective*. Montreal and Kingston: McGill–Queen's University Press, 1988.
Berger, Carl. *The Sense of Power: Studies in the Ideas of Canadian Imperialism, 1867–1914*. Toronto: University of Toronto Press, 1970.
Bodnar, John. *Immigration and Industrialization: Ethnicity in an American Mill Town, 1870–1940*. Pittsburgh: University of Pittsburgh Press, 1977.
Boyle, John W. 'Robert Lindsay Crawford, 1910–1922: A Fenian Protestant in Canada.' In *The Untold Story: The Irish in Canada, vol. II*. Edited by Robert O'Driscoll and Lorna Reynolds. Toronto: Celtic Arts of Canada, 1988.
Bray, Matthew R. '"Fighting as an Ally": The English-Canadian Patriotic Response to the Great War.' *Canadian Historical Review* 61, no. 2 (1980): 141–68.
Brown, Robert Craig, and Ramsay Cook. *Canada 1896–1921: A Nation Transformed*. Toronto: McClelland and Stewart, 1974.
Brown, Thomas N. *Irish-American Nationalism*. Philadelphia: Lippincott, 1966.
Burchell, R.A. *The San Francisco Irish, 1848–1880*. Berkeley: University of California Press, 1980.
Burns, Robin B. 'The Montreal Irish and the Great War.' *Canadian Catholic Historical Association, Study Sessions* 52 (1985): 67–82.
Campbell, Malcolm. 'Emigrant Responses to War and Revolution, 1914–1921: Irish Opinion in the United States and Australia.' *Irish Historical Studies* 32, no. 25 (May 2000): 75–92.
Carroll, Francis M. *American Opinion and the Irish Question, 1910–1923: A Study in Opinion and Policy*. New York: St Martin's, 1978.
Clarke, Brian P. *Piety and Nationalism: Lay Voluntary Associations and the Creation of an Irish-Canadian Community in Toronto, 1850–1905*. Montreal and Kingston: McGill–Queen's University Press, 1993.
Cross, Michael S. 'The Shiner's War: Social Violence in the Ottawa Valley in the 1830s.' *Canadian Historical Review* 54 (March 1973): 1–26.
Cuddy, Joseph Edward. *Irish-America and National Isolationism, 1914–1920*. New York: Arno, 1976.

Currie, Philip. 'Toronto Orangeism and the Irish, 1911–1916.' *Ontario History* 87 (December 1995): 397–409.
Darroch, Gordon. 'Half Empty or Half Full? Images and Interpretations in the Historical Analysis of the Catholic Irish in Nineteenth-Century Canada.' *Canadian Ethnic Studies* 25 (1993): 1–8.
Darroch, Gordon A., and Michael D. Ornstein. 'Ethnicity and Occupational Structure in Canada in 1871: The Vertical Mosaic in Historical Perspective.' *Canadian Historical Review* 61 (1980): 305–33.
Davis, Richard. 'Irish Nationalism in Manitoba, 1870–1922.' In *The Untold Story: The Irish in Canada, vol. II.* Edited by Robert O'Driscoll and Lorna Reynolds. Toronto: Celtic Arts of Canada, 1988.
– 'The Self-Determination for Ireland Leagues and the Irish Race Convention in Paris, 1921–1922.' *Tasmanian Historical Association Papers* 24 (1977): 88–104.
Dahlie, Jorgen, and Tissa Fernando, eds. *Ethnicity, Power, and Politics in Canada.* Toronto: Methuen, 1981.
Elliott, Bruce S. *Irish Migrants in the Canadas: A New Approach.* Montreal and Kingston: McGill–Queen's University Press, 1988.
Emmons, David M. *The Butte Irish: Class and Ethnicity in an American Mining Town, 1875–1925.* Urbana: University of Illinois Press, 1990.
Fay, Terrance J. *A History of Canadian Catholics, Gallicanism, Romanism, and Canadianism.* Montreal and Kingston: McGill–Queen's University Press, 2002.
Fitzgerald, Margaret E., and Joseph A. King. *The Uncounted Irish in Canada and the United States.* Toronto: P.D. Meany, 1990.
Gaffield, Chad. *Language, Schooling, and Cultural Conflict: The Origins of the French-Language Controversy in Ontario.* Montreal and Kingston: McGill–Queen's University Press, 1987.
Garner, John. *The Franchise and Politics in British North America, 1755–1867.* Toronto: University of Toronto Press, 1969.
Gordon, Milton M. *Assimilation in American Life: The Role of Race, Religion, and National Origins.* New York: Oxford University Press, 1964.
Handlin, Oscar. *Boston's Immigrants: A Study in Acculturation.* Cambridge, MA: Harvard University Press, 1959.
Harney, Robert F. *Gathering Places: Peoples and Neighborhoods of Toronto, 1834–1945.* Toronto: Multicultural History Society of Ontario, 1985.
Houston, Cecil J., and William J. Smyth. *Irish Emigration and Canadian Settlement: Patterns, Links, and Letters.* Toronto: University of Toronto Press, 1990.
– *The Sash Canada Wore: A Historical Geography of the Orange Order in Canada.* Toronto: University of Toronto Press, 1980.
Johnson, Daniel F. *The Irish Emigrants and Their Vessels: Port of Saint John New Brunswick, Canada, 1841–1849.* Saint John: DanTech, 1996.

Kealey, Gregory S. 'State Repression of Labour and the Left in Canada, 1914–1920: The Impact of the First World War.' *Canadian Historical Review* 73, no. 3 (1992): 281–314.
Kealey, Gregory S., and Peter Warrian, eds. *Essays in Canadian Working Class History.* Toronto: McClelland and Stewart, 1976.
Kealey, Gregory S., and Reg Whitaker. *R.C.M.P. Security Bulletins, The Early Years: 1919–1929.* St John's: Canadian Committee on Labor History, 1994.
Laplante, Normand. 'Canadian and British Policy on Ireland, 1882–1914.' *The Archivist* 16, no. 5 (1989): 12–14.
Leyburn, James G. *The Scotch-Irish: A Social History.* Chapel Hill: University of North Carolina Press, 1962.
Lower, Arthur R.M. *Colony to Nation: A History of Canada.* Toronto: Longmans, Green, 1946.
Lyne, D.C. 'Irish-Canadian Financial Contributions to the Home Rule Movement in the 1890s.' *Studia Hibernia* 7 (1967): 182–206.
MacDonagh, Oliver, and W.F. Mandle, eds. *Ireland and Irish-Australia: Studies in Cultural and Political History.* London: Croom Helm, 1986.
MacKay, Donald. *Flight from Famine: The Coming of the Irish to Canada.* Toronto: McClelland and Stewart, 1990.
Mannion, John J. *Irish Settlements in Eastern Canada: A Study of Cultural Transfer and Adaptation.* Toronto: University of Toronto Press, 1974.
McCaffrey, Lawrence J. *The Irish Diaspora in America.* Bloomington: Indiana University Press, 1976.
McGowan, Mark G. 'The De-greening of the Irish: Toronto's Irish-Catholic Press, Imperialism, and the Forging of a New Identity, 1887–1914.' *Canadian Historical Association Papers* (1989): 118–45.
– *The Waning of the Green: Catholics, the Irish, and Identity in Toronto, 1887–1922.* Montreal and Kingston: McGill–Queen's University Press, 1999.
McKillen, Elizabeth. *Chicago Labor and the Quest for a Democratic Diplomacy, 1914–1924.* Ithaca: Cornell University Press, 1995.
McLaughlin, Robert. 'Orange-Canadian Unionists and the Irish Home Rule Crisis, 1912–1914.' *Ontario History* 98, no. 1 (Spring 2006): 68–101.
Miller, Kerby A. *Emigrants and Exiles: Ireland and the Irish Exodus to North America.* New York: Oxford University Press, 1985.
Miller, J.M. 'D'Alton McCarthy, Equal Rights, and the Origins of the Manitoba School Question.' *Canadian Historical Review* 54 (December 1973): 369–92.
Murphy, Terrence and Gerald Stortz, eds. *Creed and Culture: The Place of English-Speaking Catholics in Canadian Society.* Montreal and Kingston: McGill-Queen's University Press, 1993.
Nicolson, Murray W. 'The Irish Catholics and Social Action in Toronto 1850–1900.' *Studies in History and Politics* 1 (1980): 30–54.

O'Connor, Thomas H. *The Boston Irish: A Political History.* Boston: Northeastern University Press, 1995.
Power, Thomas P., ed. *The Irish in Atlantic Canada, 1780–1900.* Fredericton: New Ireland, 1991.
Sager, Eric W., and Christopher Morier. 'Immigrants, Ethnicity, and Earnings in 1901: Revisiting Canada's Vertical Mosaic.' *Canadian Historical Review* 83, no. 2 (2002): 196–29.
See, Scott W. 'The Fortunes of the Orange Order in 19th Century New Brunswick.' In *New Ireland Remembered: Historical Essays on the Irish in New Brunswick.* Edited by P.M. Toner. Fredericton: New Ireland, 1988.
– '"Mickeys and Demons" vs "Bigots and Boobies": The Woodstock Riot of 1847.' *Acadiensis* (1991): 110–31.
– 'The Orange Order and Social Violence in Mid-Nineteenth Century Saint John.' In *New Ireland Remembered: Historical Essays on the Irish in New Brunswick.* Edited by P.M. Toner. Fredericton: New Ireland, 1988.
– *Riots in New Brunswick: Orange Nativism and Social Violence in the 1840s.* Toronto: University of Toronto Press, 1993.
Tarpey, Marie Veronica. *The Role of Joseph McGarrity in the Struggle for Irish Independence.* New York: Arno, 1976.
Thompson, John Herd, and Allen Seager. *Canada 1922–1939: Decades of Discord.* Toronto: McClelland and Stewart, 1985.
Toner, P.M., ed. *New Ireland Remembered: Historical Essays on the Irish in New Brunswick.* Fredericton, NB: New Ireland Press, 1988.
Wade, Mason. *The French Canadians, 1760–1945.* Toronto: Macmillan, 1956.
Wade, Mason, ed. *Canadian Dualism: Studies of French-English Relations.* Toronto: University of Toronto Press, 1960.
Walker, James W. St G. 'Race and Recruitment in World War I: Enlistment of Visible Minorities in the Canadian Expeditionary Force.' *Canadian Historical Review* 70, no. 1 (1989): 1–26.
Ward, Alan J. 'America and the Irish Problem, 1899–1921.' *Irish Historical Studies* 16 (1968): 64–90.
– *The Easter Rising: Revolution and Irish Nationalism.* Wheeling: Harlan Davidson, 1980.
– *Ireland and Anglo-American Relations, 1899–1921.* Toronto: University of Toronto Press, 1969.
Wilson, Catherine. 'The Irish in North America: New Perspectives.' *Acadiensis* (1988): 199–215.
– *A New Lease on Life: Landlords, Tenants, and Immigrants in Ireland and Canada.* Montreal and Kingston: McGill–Queen's University Press, 1994.
Wilson, David A., ed. *The Orange Order in Canada.* Dublin: Four Courts, 2007.

## Secondary Sources on Twentieth-Century Ireland and Britain

Akenson, Donald. *Education and Enmity: The Control of Schooling in Northern Ireland, 1920–1950*. New York: Harper and Row, 1973.
Arthur, Paul. *Special Relationships: Britain, Ireland, and the Northern Ireland Problem*. Belfast: Blackstaff Press, 2000.
Bartlett, C.J. *British Foreign Policy in the Twentieth Century*. London: Macmillan, 1989.
Bartlett, Thomas, and Keith Jeffery, eds. *A Military History of Ireland*. Cambridge: Cambridge University Press, 1996.
Bew, Paul. *Ideology and the Irish Question: Ulster Unionism and Irish Nationalism, 1912–1916*. Oxford: Oxford University Press, 1994.
– *Ireland: The Politics of Enmity, 1789–2006*. Oxford: Oxford University Press, 2007.
Bew, Paul, Peter Gibbon, and Henry Patterson. *The State in Northern Ireland, 1921–72*. Manchester: Manchester University Press, 1979.
Boyce, D.G. *Englishmen and Irish Troubles: British Public Opinion and the Making of Irish Policy, 1918–1922*. Cambridge, MA: MIT, 1972.
– *The Irish Question and British Politics, 1868–1996*. 2nd ed. New York: St Martin's, 1996.
– *Nationalism in Ireland*. 2nd ed. New York and London: Routledge, 1991.
Boyce, D.G., and Alan O'Day. *The Making of Modern Ireland: Revisionism and the Revisionist Controversy*. New York and London: Routledge, 1996.
–, eds. *Defenders of the Union: A Survey of British and Irish Unionism Since 1801*. London: Routledge, 2001.
Brown, Terence. *Ireland: A Social and Cultural History, 1922 to the Present*. Ithaca: Cornell University Press, 1985.
Bruce, Steve. *The Edge of Union: the Ulster Loyalist Political Vision*. Oxford: Oxford University Press, 1994.
– *The Red Hand: Protestant Paramilitaries in Northern Ireland*. Oxford: Oxford University Press, 1992.
Buckland, Patrick. *James Craig: Lord Craigavon*. Dublin: Gill and Macmillan, 1980.
Campbell, Fergus. *Land and Revolution: Nationalist Politics in the West of Ireland, 1891–1921*. Oxford: Oxford University Press, 2005.
Chubb, Basil. *The Government and Politics of Ireland*. New York: Longman, 1992.
Coakley, John, and Michael Gallagher, eds. *Politics in the Republic of Ireland*. Galway: PSAI, 1992.
Collins, Peter, ed. *Nationalism and Unionism: Conflict in Ireland, 1885–1921*. Belfast: Institute of Irish Studies, Queen's University of Belfast, 1996.

Coogan, Tim Pat. *Eamon de Velera: The Man Who Was Ireland.* New York: HarperCollins, 1993.
Curtis, Edmund, and R.B. McDowell, eds. *Irish Historical Documents, 1172–1922.* London: Methuen, 1943.
Cusack, Jim, and Henry McDonald. *UVF: The Endgame.* Dublin: Poolbeg, 2008.
Dangerfield, George. *The Damnable Question: A History of Anglo-Irish Relations.* Boston: Little, Brown, 1976.
Doherty, Gabriel, and Dermot Keogh, eds. *Michael Collins and the Making of the Irish State.* Dublin: Mercier, 1998.
Dwyer, T. Ryle. *Michael Collins: 'The Man Who Won the War.'* Dublin: Mercier, 1990.
Elliott, Marianne. *The Catholics of Ulster: A History.* London: Penguin, 2000.
English, Richard. *Armed Struggle: The History of the IRA.* Oxford: Oxford University Press, 2003.
English, Richard and Graham Walker, eds. *Unionism in Modern Ireland: New Perspectives on Politics and Culture.* London: Macmillan, 1996.
Farrell, Michael. *Arming the Protestants: The Formation of the Ulster Special Constabulary and the Royal Ulster Constabulary.* London: Pluto, 1983.
Ferriter, Diarmaid. *The Transformation of Ireland.* Woodstock: Overlook, 2004.
Fitzpatrick, David. 'The Geography of Irish Nationalism.' *Past and Present* 78 (1978): 113–44.
– 'The Irish in Britain, 1871–1921.' In *A New History of Ireland,* vol. VI. *Ireland under the Union, 1870–1921.* Edited by W.E. Vaughan. Oxford: Clarendon, 1996.
– 'The Orange Order and the Border.' *Irish Historical Studies* 33, no. 129 (May 2002): 52–67.
– *Politics and Irish Life, 1913–1921: Provincial Experience of War and Revolution.* Cork: Cork University Press, 1998.
– *The Two Irelands, 1912–1939.* Oxford: Oxford University Press, 1998.
Follis, Brian. *A State under Siege: The Establishment of Northern Ireland, 1920–25.* Oxford: Clarendon, 1995.
Foster, Roy. *Modern Ireland, 1600–1972.* New York: Penguin, 1988.
Garvin, Tom. *1922: The Birth of Irish Democracy.* New York: St Martin's, 1996.
Graham, Brian. *In Search of Ireland: A Cultural Geography.* London: Routledge, 1997.
Gray, Tony. *The Orange Order.* London: The Bodley Head, 1972.
Griffith, Kenneth, and Timothy O'Grady. *Ireland's Unfinished Revolution: An Oral History.* 2nd ed. Boulder: Roberts Rinehart, 1999.
Harkness, David. *Ireland in the Twentieth Century: Divided Island.* New York: St Martin's, 1996.

Hart, Peter. *Mick: The Real Michael Collins*. New York: Penguin, 2005.
– 'Michael Collins and the Assassination of Sir Henry Wilson.' *Irish Historical Studies* 28 (1992): 150–70.
Hennessey, Thomas. *A History of Northern Ireland*. New York: St Martin's, 1997.
Hepburn, A.C. *Catholic Belfast and Nationalist Ireland in the Era of Joe Devlin 1871–1934*. Oxford: Oxford University Press, 2008.
Holt, Edgar. *Protest in Arms: The Irish Troubles, 1916–1923*. New York: Coward-McCann, 1961.
Irvine, Maurice. *Northen Ireland: Faith and Faction*. London: Routledge, 1991.
Kaufmann, Eric P. *The Orange Order: A Contemporary Northern Irish History*. Oxford: Oxford University Press, 2007.
Kearney, Hugh. *The British Isles: A History of Four Nations*. 2nd ed. Cambridge: Cambridge University Press, 2006.
Kendle, John. *Ireland and the Federal Solution: The Debate over the United Kingdom Constitution, 1870–1921*. Montreal and Kingston: McGill–Queen's University Press, 1989.
Kennedy, Michael. *Ireland and the League of Nations, 1919–1946: International Relations, Diplomacy, and Politics*. Dublin: Irish Academic Press, 1996.
Keogh, Dermot. *Ireland and Europe, 1919–1948*. Dublin: Gill and Macmillan, 1988.
– *Twentieth-Century Ireland: Nation and State*. New York: St Martin's, 1995.
Laffan, Michael. *The Partition of Ireland, 1911–1925*. Dundalk: Dundalgan, 1983.
Lee, J.J. *Ireland, 1912–1985: Politics and Society*. Cambridge: Cambridge University Press, 1989.
Lee, Joseph, and Gearóid Ó Tuathaigh. *The Age of de Valera*. Dublin: Ward River, 1982.
Linge, John. 'The Royal Navy and the Irish Civil War.' *Irish Historical Studies* 31 (1998): 60–71.
Litton, Helen. *The Irish Civil War: An Illustrated History*. Dublin: Wolfhound, 1995.
Loughlin, James. *Ulster Unionism and British National Identity Since 1885*. London: Cassell, 1995.
MacDonagh, Oliver. *States of Mind: A Study of Anglo-Irish Conflict 1780–1980*. London: Allen and Unwin, 1983.
MacKay, James. *Michael Collins: A Life*. Edinburgh: Mainstream, 1996.
McLean, Iain, and Alistair McMillan. *State of the Union: Unionism and the Alternatives in the United Kingdom Since 1707*. Oxford: Oxford University Press, 2005.
Middlemas, Keith, ed. *Thomas Jones Whitehall Diary*, vol. III, *Ireland 1918–1925*. London: Oxford University Press, 1971.

Mitchell, George. *Making Peace*. Berkeley: University of California Press, 1999.
Morris, R.J., and Liam Kennedy, eds. *Ireland and Scotland: Order and Disorder, 1600–2000*. Edinburgh: John Donald, 2005.
O'Duffy, Brendan. *British–Irish Relations and Northern Ireland: From Violent Politics to Conflict Regulation*. Dublin: Irish Academic Press, 2007.
O'Farrell, Patrick. *Ireland's English Question: Anglo-Irish Relations, 1534–1970*. New York: Schocken, 1971.
O'Sullivan, Patrick, ed. *The Irish World Wide: History, Heritage, Identity*, vol. V, *Religion and Identity*. London: Leicester University Press, 1996.
Patterson, Henry. *The Politics of Illusion: Republicanism and Socialism in Modern Ireland*. London: Hutchinson Radius, 1989.
Regan, John M. 'The Politics of Reaction: The Dynamics of Treatyite Government and Policy, 1922–33.' *Irish Historical Studies* 30 (November 1997): 542–63.
Ryder, Chris, and Vincent Kearney. *Drumcree: The Orange Order's Last Stand*. London: Methuen, 2002.
Stanbridge, Karen. 'Nationalism, International Factors, and the 'Irish Question' in the Era of the First World War.' *Nations and Nationalism* 11, no. 1 (2005): 21–42.
Stewart, A.T.Q. *The Ulster Crisis*. London: Faber and Faber, 1967.
Williams, Desmond, ed. *The Irish Struggle, 1916–1926*. London: Routledge and Kegan Paul, 1966.
Winder, Robert. *Bloody Foreigners: The Story of Immigration to Britain*. London: Abacus, 2004.

# Index

Agar, Miles E., 63, 64, 141
Aiken, Maxwell, 6
Akenson, Donald, 7–8, 17, 24
Alberta, 123, 127
Allen, A., 49
American Friends of Irish Freedom, 149
Ancient Order of Foresters, 13
Ancient Order of Hibernians, 20, 21, 22, 56, 57, 58, 59, 66, 67, 75, 76, 78, 83, 84, 85, 107, 119, 132, 133, 134, 188, 190, 191; American Hibernians, 75, 76, 84, 188, 189; Canadian Hibernians, 57, 75, 76, 84, 85, 86, 188, 189, 190; Ontario Hibernians, 59, 133, 190, 191
Anglican, 32, 83
Anglo-Irish Treaty, 6, 150, 166, 167, 174, 176, 179, 180, 183, 190, 191, 193
Anglo-Irish War, 114, 176
Armagh, Co., 41
Asquith, Herbert, 39, 41, 42, 50, 135, 194
assimilation, 14, 17, 61
Astor, Waldorf, 44
Australia, 56, 58, 61, 109, 110, 120, 121, 122, 124, 130, 158

Balbriggan, 115, 116, 117
Balfour, Arthur, 5
Bangor, 43, 75
Baptist, 32, 83
Barrett, Dick, 182
Battle of the Boyne, 9, 27, 37, 39
Beaverbrook, Lord, Maxwell Aitken, 6, 172
Belfast, 19, 27, 33, 34, 35, 36, 37, 39, 42, 43, 46, 50, 72, 81, 97, 129, 136, 137, 147, 153, 155, 163, 164, 165, 169, 171, 178, 183, 194, 195; distilleries, 33; linen mills, 33; rope manufacturing, 33; shipyards, 33, 163; tobacco manufacturing, 33
Belfast of Canada, 19, 27, 165, 167, 189, 206
*Belfast Newsletter*, 33
*Belfast Weekly News*, 153
Bew, Paul, 33, 50
bilingual schools, 15
Black and Tans, 115, 137; violence, 116, 117, 118, 134, 136, 139, 146, 160, 178, 184
Blair, Tony, 4
Blake, Edward, 5
Bloody Sunday, 4

266  Index

Blue, Rev. Wylie, 154
Boer War, 29, 31, 69
Boland, Harry, 148
Bolsheviks/Bolshevism, 154, 158, 159, 161, 171
Bonar Law, Andrew, 5, 6, 31, 35, 41, 63, 64, 69, 145, 146, 172
Borden, Robert, 6, 56, 105, 106, 119, 120, 125, 171, 172
Boston, 8, 197
Boundary Commission, 6, 151, 166, 171, 172, 173, 175, 191, 192, 193
Bourassa, Henri, 111, 139
Bowen-Colthurst, J.C., 93
Boyce, D.G., 114
Bray, R. Matthew, 81
British Army, 4, 12, 77, 81, 86, 88, 93, 96, 115, 149
British Columbia, 84, 127
British Commonwealth, 19, 179, 197
British Empire, 9, 18, 20, 21, 24, 26, 28, 34, 35, 37, 38, 39, 41, 42, 48, 53, 61, 96, 98, 103, 120, 129, 130, 131, 138, 140, 147, 151, 154, 158, 159, 160, 161, 162, 166, 168, 173, 175, 185, 195, 196
British Empire Alliance, 160
British Empire League, 28
British Free State, 187
British government, 29, 41, 42, 70, 72, 73, 75, 77, 81, 96, 98, 100, 102, 105, 106, 109, 114, 116, 118, 147, 150, 167, 171, 172, 174, 183, 195
British justice/injustice, 70, 104, 118, 119, 138, 140, 150
British North America, 9, 10, 39, 41, 147, 162
British North America Act, 147
British Parliament, 16, 36, 41, 45, 57, 58, 167, 173, 176, 195

Bruce, Steve, 197
Buckland, Patrick, 5
Burke, Alfred E., 62
Burns, W.P., 131

Cahill, Frank, 135, 144
Calgary, 124
Cameron, John, 55
Campbell, Fergus, 115
Campbell, Malcolm, 110
Canada, 5, 6, 8, 9, 14, 16, 17, 19, 21, 22, 23, 24, 26, 32, 33, 37, 39, 40, 43, 45, 49, 50, 51, 53, 56, 57, 58, 62, 70, 72, 73, 75, 83, 93, 94, 105, 106, 108, 112, 118, 119, 120, 121, 122, 123, 126, 129, 130, 131, 133, 136, 138, 143, 144, 148, 152, 153, 154, 158, 160, 161, 162, 163, 166, 171, 173, 179, 183, 184, 185, 186, 188, 193, 194, 195, 196, 198
Canadian Expeditionary Force, 81, 82, 83, 86, 98, 105
*Canadian Freeman*, 107, 180
Canadian Friends of Irish Freedom, 121, 122, 126
Canadian House of Commons, 55, 107, 186
Canadian Ulster Loyalist Association, 197
Canadian Unionist League, 15, 46, 47, 195
Carson, Sir Edward, 31, 32, 36, 38, 39, 40, 41, 42, 44, 47, 50, 51, 63, 88, 89, 97, 99, 101, 111, 145, 146, 154, 156, 159, 165, 166
Casement, Roger, 75, 76, 77
Casey, D.A., Rev., 107, 108
Catholic Army Huts, 23
*Catholic Register*, 20, 62, 63, 65, 69, 73, 83, 94, 96, 102, 103, 116, 117, 149,

177, 178, 179, 182, 191, 192, 193, 194
*Catholic Weekly Review*, 62
Catholic Women's League of Canada, 123
Catholicism, 17, 27, 63
Catholicism, anti-, 10, 11, 14, 26, 47, 55, 72, 107
Caulfield, Max 93
Cavan, Co., 156
Ceannt, Eamonn, 92
Celtic/Celts, 19, 32, 33, 157, 167, 168
Choquette, Robert, 22
Christie, Loring, 171
Churchill, Lord Randolph, 44
Churchill, Winston, 64, 174
Clarke, Brian, 12, 13, 18
Clarke, F.M., 46
Clarke, Thomas, 91, 92, 96
Cohalan, Daniel, 138, 179, 180, 186
Collins, Michael, 147, 148, 177, 181, 182, 185
Connolly, James, 91, 92, 93, 96
Conservative Party, 31, 33, 71, 77, 155
Coote, Rev. William, 153, 154, 165, 171
Cork, Co., 7, 25, 139, 178, 182
Cory, Peter, 5
Cosgrave, William, 186, 187, 193
Craig, Charles, 156
Craig, Sir James, 31, 36, 40, 49, 50, 145, 155, 156
Crawford, Robert Lindsay, 102, 103, 127, 128, 133, 134, 138, 140, 141, 142, 143, 144, 149, 162, 179, 180, 183, 186, 187, 194
Crawford, Hon. Thomas, 165
Crown, the British, 26, 27, 32, 36, 51, 116, 119, 139, 140, 142, 143, 162, 163, 179
Crozier, Gen. Frank Percy, 115

Curragh Mutiny, 41, 42
Currie, Philip, 13
Cussack, Michael, 60
Cyprus, 158
Czechoslovakia, 119

Dáil Éireann, 109, 123, 129, 174, 176, 177, 179, 180, 181, 193
Daly, Edward, 96
Dane, Fred, 37, 153, 165
Dangerfield, George, 75
Davis, Richard, 58, 123
de Chastelain, John, 3
de Valera, Eamon, 103, 123, 126, 127, 133, 147, 149, 153, 161, 179, 180, 181, 185, 186, 187, 197
Deery, James, 189
democracy, 19, 119, 129, 131, 150
Denison, George Taylor, 37
Derry/Londonderry, 38, 68, 69, 163, 164
*Derry Weekly News*, 87
Devlin, E.B., 111
Devlin, Joseph, 56
Devoy, John, 74
Dillon, John, 56, 100, 110
Doherty, Charles, 56
Dominion of Canada, 15, 44, 70, 73, 75, 84, 89, 132, 139, 141, 160, 162, 173, 188, 189
dominion status, 102, 113, 118, 142, 184, 185
Donegal, Co., 156
Donovan, Mat, 134
Donovan, Thomas R., 133, 134, 140, 141, 144, 188
Dublin, 15, 19, 21, 31, 33, 53, 64, 74, 78, 81, 87, 90, 94, 96, 97, 98, 100, 109, 111, 155, 167, 178, 181, 182, 183, 195

Dublin/Irish Parliament, 15, 31, 33, 36, 38, 39, 64, 89, 95, 98, 100, 151, 155, 194, 195

Easter Rising, 90, 91, 93, 94, 95, 96, 100, 110, 112, 119, 149, 191, 195
Edmonton, 123, 124, 127
Egypt, 114, 158, 159
Elliot, Bruce, 7
Emerald Benevolent Association, 56, 57
Emmet, Robert, 67, 79, 90
England, 52, 80, 82, 88, 95, 102, 103, 124, 130, 132, 133, 138, 145, 146, 158, 161, 167, 177, 178, 179, 185, 189, 193
English, 9, 27, 89, 104, 112, 122, 130, 136, 146, 154, 167, 178
English Canada/Canadians, 11, 19, 23, 28, 29, 54, 81, 83, 197
English Parliament, 53, 76
ethnic allegiance, 6, 24, 49, 163, 165, 168, 196, 197, 198
ethnic identity, 6, 12, 56, 59, 60, 61
ethnic/sectarian bigotry, 11, 167, 195, 196
ethnic/sectarian violence, 8, 11, 12, 13, 14, 25, 26, 38, 63, 65, 143, 150, 160 162, 163, 165, 173
ethnic superiority, 32, 33, 40, 49, 157, 195

Famine, The, 7, 9, 53, 137
Fay, Terrence, 18
Fay, Rev. Thomas P., 144
Feetham, Richard, 174
Fenians, 10, 39
financial support for Ulstermen, 15, 21, 34, 44, 45, 46, 47, 88, 155, 168, 169, 170, 171, 175, 195

First World War, 16, 18, 21, 23, 29, 80, 81, 104, 108, 113, 119, 120, 131, 132, 147, 150, 151, 161, 195, 196
Fisher, Harold, 133
Fisher, J.R., 173
Foster, Roy, 74
Foy, Charles J., 66, 67, 68, 75, 85, 111, 112, 113, 114, 134, 136, 144, 160, 188, 190
Fredericton, 12, 142, 162, 194
*Freeman's Journal*, 21, 87
French Canadians, 22, 23, 25, 27, 28, 40, 55, 58, 59, 60, 83, 105, 112, 135, 136, 137, 138, 139, 142, 143, 197

Gaelic, 76, 90, 127, 132, 197
Gaelic Athletic Association, 60, 74
Gaelic League, 60, 61, 73, 74, 90, 132
Gaelic Revival, 60, 124
Galway, 53
Gavazzi riots Montreal, 65
*Gazette, The*, 62, 96
General Post Office, Dublin, 91, 93
German/Germany, 9, 19, 76, 80, 81, 82, 91, 95, 96, 105, 109, 111, 112, 133, 158, 195
Glasgow, 5
*Globe, The*, 62, 96, 102, 117, 141, 194
Good, Harold, 4
Good Friday Peace Agreement, 4
Gough, Sir Herbert, 42
Gouin, Sir Lomer, 111
Government of Ireland Act, 156
Gowan, Ogle R., 8
Grand Black Chapter of British North America, 46
Grand Orange Lodge of British America, 24, 26, 27, 38, 39, 45, 151, 159, 162, 168, 169, 170, 173

Grand Orange Lodge of Ireland, 88
Grand Orange Lodge of Ontario West, 15, 24, 27, 34, 37, 45, 88, 165, 169
Grattan, Henry, 67, 134
Gray, A.A., 169
Great Britain, 6, 14, 15, 20, 23, 32, 33, 41, 48, 49, 57, 61, 68, 72, 74, 78, 79, 80, 81, 101, 103, 104, 120, 122, 124, 137, 142, 151, 163, 174, 176, 195, 196, 197
Greenwood, Sir Hamar, 6, 158
Grey, Sir Edward, 80
Griffith, Arthur, 99, 147, 149, 177, 180, 182, 185
Grosse Isle, 7

Hales, Sean, 182
Halifax, 9, 18, 123, 124, 160, 198
*Halifax Daily Recorder*, 131
Hamilton, ON, 66, 67, 197
Hart, Peter, 122
Hayes, W.J., 95, 107
*Helga*, 94
Henderson, Rose, 125, 126
Henry, P.J., 136
Hibernian Benevolent Society, 18
Hobson, Bulmer, 73
Hocken, Horatio C., 37, 48, 152, 153, 165, 194
Hogg, David, 68
Holkeri, Harri, 3
homeland, ancestral, 17, 19, 21, 54, 55, 56, 61, 63, 170, 196, 197
Home Rule, 13, 14, 15, 18, 20, 26, 29, 30, 31, 32, 33, 34, 35, 36, 37, 38, 39, 41, 42, 43, 44, 47, 48, 49, 50, 52, 53, 54, 55, 56, 57, 62, 64, 65, 68, 69, 72, 73, 76, 78, 79, 80, 88, 89, 95, 98, 102, 103, 104, 110, 111, 114, 117, 118, 119, 137, 147, 151, 152, 153, 155, 157, 173, 175, 178, 194, 195, 196, 198
House of Commons, 29, 31, 35, 52, 78, 84, 108, 151, 155
House of Lords, 29, 166
Houston, Cecil, 7, 10, 11
Howth, 74, 75
Hoyt, William, 5
Hughes, Katherine, 21, 106, 123, 124, 127, 129, 133, 149, 184, 187, 188
Hughes, Col. Sam, 99, 105
Hungary, 119
Hyde, Douglas, 60

immigration/immigrants, 7, 12, 15, 17, 18, 25, 26, 28, 143, 152, 164
imperial/imperialism, 14, 15, 23, 28, 29, 37, 46, 48, 55, 103, 113, 135, 138, 143, 150, 152, 168, 185, 186
Imperial Federation League, 28
Independent International Commission on decommissioning, 4
Independent Labour Party, 132, 135
Independent Loyalist Group, 197
India, 114, 158, 159
Ireland, 6, 8, 9, 11, 13, 15, 17, 20, 21, 23, 24, 26, 31, 35, 37, 41, 42, 44, 45, 52, 57, 62, 63, 65, 66, 68, 69, 70, 72, 74, 78, 80, 84, 88, 89, 92, 95, 97, 98, 102, 103, 104, 105, 107, 108, 109, 110, 113, 114, 117, 118, 119, 120, 128, 129, 130, 131, 133, 135, 136, 138, 139, 140, 141, 142, 145, 147, 148, 153, 160, 163, 167, 170, 172, 177, 178, 180, 181, 183, 184, 185, 186, 188, 189, 191, 193, 194, 195, 196, 197
Irish American, 77, 129, 130, 179, 190
*Irish Canadian*, 62

Irish Canadians, 6, 20, 53, 61, 106, 110, 113, 116, 117, 119, 120, 122, 130, 131, 136, 139, 140, 147, 148, 149, 150, 160, 176, 178, 181, 188, 193, 195, 197, 198
Irish-Canadian nationalists, 6, 21, 23, 52, 53, 54, 55, 61, 68, 69, 70, 74, 77, 78, 79, 82, 83, 89, 96, 98, 103, 104, 106, 107, 108, 109, 110, 119, 121, 141, 147, 148, 150, 161, 175, 176, 178, 179, 184, 191, 192, 193, 194, 195, 196
Irish Catholic Benevolent Union, 56, 57
Irish-Catholic Canadians, 14, 17, 18, 19, 20, 21, 22, 27, 28, 30, 53, 54, 55, 59, 60, 64, 67, 70, 71, 72, 73, 76, 79, 82, 83, 84, 85 86, 89, 96, 98, 117, 118, 128, 177, 192, 193, 194, 195, 196, 197
Irish Catholics, 6, 7, 9, 12, 32, 33, 40, 52, 57, 70, 81, 85, 97, 105, 126, 129, 130, 163, 164, 165, 183, 192, 193
Irish Citizen Army, 91
Irish Civil War, 171, 172, 173, 176, 177, 180, 181, 182, 183, 192
Irish Free State, 6, 109, 147, 166, 171, 172, 173, 174, 175, 176, 178, 182, 183, 185, 186, 187, 188, 189, 190, 191, 192, 193, 197
Irish Fusiliers, 82
Irish history, 59, 67, 68, 141, 146
Irish independence, 6, 13, 19, 21, 23, 106, 109, 110, 113, 118, 132, 135, 149, 176, 184, 190, 191, 194, 196, 197, 198
Irish language, 59, 60, 67, 90
Irish National Bureau, 129
Irish National League, 55
Irish National Union, 107
Irish nationalists, 6, 18, 20, 21, 22, 30, 52, 56, 57, 58, 77, 79, 80, 84, 87, 89, 90, 95, 99, 100, 106, 117, 121, 140, 146, 158, 161, 163, 174, 196
Irish Parliamentary Party, 5, 29, 31, 32, 34, 53, 54, 56, 59, 73, 74, 77, 79, 80, 84, 90, 94, 98, 99, 100, 103, 108, 109, 110, 117, 147, 195
Irish Protestant Benevolent Society, 65
Irish Republic, 92, 109, 129, 133, 147, 161, 166, 177, 180, 188, 190
Irish Republican Army, 114, 115, 148, 149, 150, 167, 168, 176, 180, 181
Irish Republican Brotherhood, 74, 91, 149
Irish republicanism, 14, 54, 90, 104, 147, 148, 149, 150, 158, 159, 160, 162, 175, 176, 178, 186, 188, 190, 191, 193
Irish volunteers, 73, 74, 75, 77, 111, 114
Iveagh, Lord, 44

Jackman, Peter, 187
Jackson, Alvin, 30
James II, 9, 27, 164, 165
Jeffery, Keith, 114, 115
Jenkins, William, 13, 14
Jesuits, 10, 35, 159
Jordan, Samuel, 136, 137
July 12th, 9, 13, 27, 37, 168

Kaufmann, Eric, 12
Kealey, Gregory, 12, 13, 125, 126
Keane, Patrick, 188
Kelly, John Hall, 111
Kennedy, Thomas, 32
Keogh, Dermot, 180
Kickham, Thomas, 78
Kilmainham Jail, 96, 110

King George V, 36, 50, 162, 165, 186
Kingston, ON, 107, 168, 180
Kipling, Rudyard, 44, 63
Kitchener, Lord, 87

Labour Party/Government, 4, 122, 171, 172, 173
Laffan, Michael, 87
Lagan, Frank, 66
Land League, 18, 55
Land War, 55
Larkin, J.J., 144
Larne, 43, 75
Laurier, Wilfrid, 97, 105, 11
Lavergne, Armand, 111, 137, 138, 139, 140, 144
Leahy, F.J., 144
Lee, Joseph, 32, 80
Liberal Party, 31, 34, 71
Litton, Helen, 180, 183
Lloyd George, David, 100, 101, 104, 116, 127, 146, 147, 149, 155, 166, 172, 176, 191
London, 122, 123, 167, 171
London, Ontario, 7, 15, 19, 101
Long, Walter, 37, 44, 45, 145, 155, 156
Loughall, Co. Armagh, 8, 25
Loughlin, James, 27, 87
Lovelock, Harry 15, 34
Lower, Arthur, 82, 105
loyal/loyalty/disloyalty, 9, 10, 20, 22, 23, 36, 44, 45, 51, 88, 89, 101, 113, 120, 141, 142, 159, 160, 161, 162, 163, 164, 165, 174, 175, 186, 196, 197, 198
Loyal Orange Association. *See* Orange Order
Loyalist Defence Association, 169, 170

loyalists, 9, 10, 27, 154, 163, 168, 169, 197, 198
Loye, John, 148, 149
Lynch, Diarmid, 149

MacDermott, Sean, 91, 92
MacDonagh, Thomas, 90, 92, 96
Mackay, Donald, 8
MacNeill, Eion, 60
MacRaild, Donald, 11, 23, 24
MacSwiney, Annie, 187
MacSwiney, Terrence, 139, 140, 145, 187
Malden, Martin, 111
*Manchester Guardian*, 116
Manitoba, 58, 105, 127, 137, 196
Maritime provinces, 7, 55, 71, 72, 122, 123, 140, 162
Martin, F.X., 90
Masonic influence, 8, 9, 27
Massey Hall, 16, 37, 189
McDonald, John, 135
McGowan, Mark, 19, 20, 21, 57, 58, 63, 75, 83, 123, 188
McKelvey, Joe, 182
McLaughlin, Joseph, 84
McLaughlin, M.J., 95
McNaught, Kenneth, 105
McNeil, Neil, Archbishop, 83, 86
McPherson, William David, 48, 159, 169, 170, 173
McShane, Rev. Gerald, 140
Mellows, Liam, 181, 182
Methodist, 32, 83
Miller, J.R., 14
Mitchell, George, 3
Mohammadism, 159
Monaghan, Co., 156
Monaghan, M., 127
Moncton, NB, 143, 162

Montreal, 9, 21, 55, 56, 61, 73, 78, 82, 106, 111, 114, 122, 123, 126, 127, 133, 140, 148, 160, 188, 190
Morgan, Samuel, 93
Mount Joy Jail, 182
Mulcahy, Richard, 149
Mullins, Thoms, 187
Murphy, Charles, 107, 111
Murphy, Terrence, 17, 18

Napoleonic wars, 7, 25
*National Hibernian*, 84, 86–7
nationalism, 6, 14, 16, 17, 18, 19, 20, 23, 28, 29, 57, 62, 79, 152; Irish, 57, 58, 64, 67, 68, 73, 87, 188
New Brunswick, 5, 7, 9, 12, 25, 28, 70, 71, 85, 140, 141, 142, 145, 162, 184, 188, 196
Newfoundland, 6–7, 38, 39, 45
*New Freeman*, 21, 63, 64, 65, 82, 89, 94, 97, 98, 104, 106, 110, 116, 118, 121, 122, 131, 177, 180, 184, 185, 186, 188, 194
New Freeman Publishing Co., 63
New York, 8, 18, 138, 148, 149, 186, 187
New Zealand, 5, 61, 121, 123, 130
Nicolson, Murray, 7, 17
North America 25, 26, 27, 28, 29, 34, 57, 76, 86, 143, 175
Northern Ireland/The North, 3, 4, 6, 9, 73, 147, 150, 151, 155, 165, 166, 168, 171, 172, 173, 174, 175, 176, 178, 183, 186, 190, 191, 192, 197, 198
Northwest Mounted Police, 49
Northwest Rebellion, 10
*Northwest Review*, 127, 136
Nova Scotia, 7, 45, 83, 84, 85, 131, 134, 135, 140
Nova Scotia legislature, 56

O'Brien, William, 19
O'Connell, Daniel, 67, 71, 79, 149
O'Connor, Rory, 181, 182
O'Connor, T.P., 58
O'Donovan Rosa, Jeremiah, 13
O'Farrell, M.J., 58
O'Farrell, Patrick, 176
O'Flanagan, Michael, 58
O'Hagan, Dr. Thomas, 135
O'Hanranhan, Michael, 96
O'Higgins, Kevin, 182
O'Keefe, D.S., 64
O'Malley, Ernie, 181
O'Neill, Mike, 137
O'Reilly, Michael J., 73
old land/country, 15, 16, 21, 29, 30, 34, 44, 69, 79, 197
Omagh, 41
One Big Union, 125
Ontario, 7, 12, 17, 19, 24, 25, 28, 37, 40, 57, 105, 125, 135, 137, 139, 144, 196
Ontario legislature, 48, 55
Orange-Canadian unionists, 15, 16, 29, 33, 34, 40, 41, 47, 48, 49, 50, 51, 88, 101, 102, 110, 112, 151, 160, 161, 162, 163, 164, 165, 167, 168, 172, 174, 175, 194, 195, 196, 198
Orangemen: Canadian, 12, 14, 15, 26, 29, 33, 34, 35, 36, 37, 38, 39, 40, 41, 43, 44, 45, 73, 88, 89, 95, 100, 128, 133, 143, 151, 152, 153, 154, 155, 157, 158, 159, 162, 167, 168, 169, 172; Ulster, 26, 34, 36, 37, 40, 51, 65, 144, 193
Orange Order, 8, 9, 10, 11, 13, 15, 25, 27, 28, 29, 32, 46, 55, 65, 72, 73, 79, 110, 128, 132, 138, 139, 154, 169, 189
*Orange Sentinel*, 14, 35, 36, 37, 39, 41, 42, 44, 46, 47, 49, 61, 88, 89, 96, 112,

113, 128, 137, 143, 153, 157, 161, 164, 166, 167, 172, 173, 174, 175
Ottawa, 61, 110, 119, 122, 126, 127, 132, 133, 137, 144, 151, 155, 161, 196
*Ottawa Citizen*, 133, 137
Ottawa Citizen Committee, 133
Ottawa Valley, 7, 12

Paget, Sir Arthur, 42
Palestine, 112, 158
Palmer, L.A., 162
Papal/Papacy, 13, 14, 38, 39, 102, 159, 160, 163
Papists, 70
Paris Peace Conference, 16, 106, 119, 120, 158, 196
Parnell, Charles Stewart, 5, 52, 55, 56, 79, 134, 149, 178, 179
Partridge Island, 7
Passchendaele, 82
patriotic Canadians, 20, 89, 98, 131, 133
Patriotic Fund, 86
patriotism, 20, 131, 150
Pearse, Patrick, 90, 91, 92, 93, 96
Pearse, Willie, 96
Peep o' Day Boys, 8
Perth, ON, 66, 113, 160, 190
Phelan, M.A., 107
Plattsburgh, NY, 126, 127, 161
Plunkett, Joseph, 91, 92, 96
Poland/Polish, 16, 17, 119
potato blight, 7
Powers, Charles, 111, 135
Prenter, Mrs Hector, 135
Presbyterian, 5, 30, 31, 32, 83, 135, 154
Prince Edward Island, 123, 140
Proclamation of the Irish Republic, 91

Protestant Friends of Irish Freedom, 127
Protestant Protective Association, 55
Protestantism, 9, 10, 25, 46, 158
Protestants: Canadian, 27, 46, 54, 126, 128, 197, 198; Irish, 6, 7, 8, 9, 10, 12, 15, 16, 23, 24, 25, 30, 33, 42, 43, 44, 49, 51, 70, 76, 77, 81, 88, 90, 97, 194, 195; Ulster, 9, 32, 40, 44, 51, 98, 102, 106, 152, 153, 156, 157, 163, 164, 165, 167, 194, 195, 197
Provincial Orange Lodge of New Brunswick, 24, 35, 46, 162

Quebec, 40, 105, 119, 122, 127, 129, 137, 144
Quebec City, 7, 18, 127, 133, 135, 140, 143, 144
Quebec legislature, 55

Ratcliff, Rev. J.M., 160
Redmond, John, 39, 50, 54, 56, 59, 73, 74, 77, 80, 81, 82, 84, 86, 87, 90, 94, 100, 103, 104, 106, 110, 149, 178, 179, 184
Redmond, Willie, 103
Red Scare, 125
Regan, James, 75, 76
Regina, 46, 125, 127
Regulation, 17, 105
Reid, Alec, 4
Richardson, Sir George, 40, 69
Roman Catholics, 56, 83, 126, 127, 128, 195
Romanists/Roman Catholicism, 18, 27, 35, 56, 86, 158, 159, 161, 164
Rome, 18, 34, 35, 134
Rothschild, Lord, 44
Routledge, W.H., 125
Royal Canadian Mounted Police,

124, 125, 129, 161, 183; Criminal Investigation Branch, 124–5, 126, 128, 161
Royal Flying Corps, 81
Royal Irish Constabulary, 114, 115
Royal Navy, 81
Russia, 158, 159
Russian Revolution, 125
Ryerson, George Sterling, 37

Saint John, NB, 7, 12, 18, 21, 52, 63, 78, 136, 141, 162, 177, 183, 194
Saint John Valley, 7, 12, 63
Sandre, Dean, Rev., 73
Saskatoon, 124
Saville, Mark, 4
Saville Commission, 4
Scotch Canadians, 9, 70
Scotland/Scots, 5, 19, 89, 95, 154, 198
Scott, James H., 38, 45
Scottish Covenanters, 36
Seager, Allen, 171
See, Scott, 9, 10
Seely, J.E.B., 41, 42
self-determination, 104, 106, 108, 119, 124, 130, 131, 132, 135, 143, 195
Self-Determination for Ireland League of Canada, 21, 22, 122, 123, 124, 125, 126, 127, 129, 130, 131, 132, 133, 134, 135, 138, 139, 140, 143, 144, 145, 146, 147, 150, 161, 162, 163, 183, 184, 186, 194, 196
Senior, Hereward, 10
separate schools, 15, 28, 37, 38, 59, 60, 67, 68, 162, 196
Shahrodi, Zofia, 16
Shanahan, David, 61, 62
Sharkey, Peter C., 136
Shea, D.J., 188
Sheehy, Hanna, 93, 191

Sheehy-Skeffington, Francis, 93, 191
Sherry, Dr J. Rev., 75, 76
Sifton, Arthur Lewis, 125, 126
Sinn Féin/Sinn Féiners, 93, 99, 103, 106, 107, 108, 109, 110, 111, 112, 113, 116, 117, 118, 122, 123, 126, 127, 128, 133, 136, 139, 147, 152, 153, 154, 155, 158, 159, 160, 161, 162, 164, 166, 167, 168, 176, 178, 179, 184, 195
six-county Ulster, 43, 156
Smith, F.E., 145, 146
Smyth, Lt. Col. G.B., 163
Smyth, William, 7, 10, 11
Solemn League and Covenant, 36, 37, 65, 87, 154
Somers, Sir Edward, 5
South Africa, 29, 44, 61, 158, 159, 174
Stafford, H.J., 129
Stephens, James, 74
Stewart, A.T.Q., 44
St-Jean-Baptiste Society, 132
St John's, NL, 38
Stortz, Gerald, 17, 18,
St Patrick's Society, 21, 56, 65, 95, 106, 107, 120, 121, 148
St Vincent de Paul Society, 18
Sydney, NS, 123, 140

Tansey, T.P., 95, 148
Taras Shevchenko Society, 16
Thomas, Byron, Rev., 35
Thompson, John Herd, 171
Thompson, Joseph E., 170
Tipperary, Co., 7, 60, 73, 114
Toronto, 12, 13, 14, 15, 16, 17, 18, 19, 26, 27, 29, 35, 37, 46, 49, 52, 55, 64, 73, 78, 101, 132, 135, 143, 153, 154, 155, 165, 167, 177, 189, 191, 194, 195, 197

Toronto Unionist League, 46
Townsend, Charles, 115
Treaty of Versailles, 129
Trinity College, Dublin, 31
Tudor, Maj. Gen. Hugh, 116

Ukraine/Ukrainian, 16, 17
Ulster, 5, 9, 14, 16, 29, 31, 32, 33, 36, 37, 40, 41, 42, 43, 46, 49, 56, 64, 73, 81, 89, 95, 96, 97, 100, 101, 111, 129, 141, 145, 146, 147, 151, 152, 153, 154, 155, 156, 157, 158, 163, 164, 165, 166, 167, 168, 171, 172, 173, 174, 175, 193
Ulster Benevolent Group, 197
Ulster Canadians, 49, 50, 165
Ulster Committee of Hamilton, 197
Ulster Defence Association, 168, 169, 170, 197
Ulster Defence Fund, 88
Ulster economics, 30, 33, 34, 36, 129, 136, 137, 141, 186, 192, 195
Ulster Equipment Fund, 45, 46
Ulster plantation, 38
Ulster Provisional Government, 42
Ulster/Irish Relief Fund, 169, 170
Ulster Special Constabulary, 169, 175
Ulster Unionist Party, 3, 34, 38, 73
Ulster unionists, 5, 15, 20, 29, 31, 33, 35, 38, 40, 42, 43, 48, 50, 51, 64, 65, 68, 75, 77, 81, 88, 96, 144, 145, 155, 156, 157, 158, 163, 165, 166, 171, 173, 192, 195
Ulster Volunteer Force, 40, 41, 43, 49, 50, 51, 69, 73, 76, 77, 87, 115, 155, 195, 197
Union Defence League, 44, 155, 168
unionism, 15, 36
United Irish League, 56

United Kingdom, 27, 36, 46, 48, 151, 161, 167
United States, 32, 34, 56, 57, 120, 121, 128, 130, 133, 148, 149, 153, 154, 188
United States Congress, 129, 171

Vancouver, BC, 123, 124, 125, 126, 127
Veniot, P.J., 142
Victoria Hall, 37
Vimy Ridge, 82

Wales/Welsh, 9, 154, 198
Wall, J.A., 62
Wallace, William B., 47
Walsh, Frank, 117, 129, 148, 159
Walsh, John, Archbishop, 62
Walsh Commission, 117, 129
*Weekly Northern Whig*, 88
Wexford, Co., 73
Whiteboys, 8
Whiteside, T.R., 37
Wilde, Oscar, 31
William of Orange, 9, 27
Williams, W.E., 158
Wilson, David A., 11
Wilson, Henry, 41
Wilson, Woodrow, 104
Winnipeg, 58, 121, 122, 124, 125, 126, 127, 136, 189
Wolfe Tone, Theobald, 67, 134
Woodstock, NB, 12, 57

xenophobia, 28

Yaworsky Sokolsky, Zoriana, 16
Yeats, William Butler, 60
Young Mens Saint Patrick's Association, 18
Yugoslavia, 119

www.ingramcontent.com/pod-product-compliance
Lightning Source LLC
Chambersburg PA
CBHW020358080526
44584CB00014B/1076